hRac

MAY -- 2018

Canned

CALIFORNIA STUDIES IN FOOD AND CULTURE

Darra Goldstein, Editor

Canned

The Rise and Fall of
Consumer Confidence in the
American Food Industry

Anna Zeide

UNIVERSITY OF CALIFORNIA PRESS

University of California Press, one of the most distinguished university presses in the United States, enriches
lives around the world by advancing scholarship in the
humanities, social sciences, and natural sciences. Its
activities are supported by the UC Press Foundation and
by philanthropic contributions from individuals and
institutions. For more information, visit www.ucpress.edu.

University of California Press
Oakland, California

Library of Congress Cataloging-in-Publication Data

Names: Zeide, Anna, 1984– author.
Title: Canned : the rise and fall of consumer confidence
    in the American food industry / Anna Zeide.
Description: Oakland, California : University of
    California Press, [2018] | Includes bibliographical
    references and index. |
Identifiers: LCCN 2017036822 (print) |
    LCCN 2017038677 (ebook) | ISBN 9780520964754
    (Ebook) | ISBN 9780520290686 (cloth : alk. paper)
Subjects: LCSH: Canned foods—United States—20th
    century. | Canned foods industry—United States—
    20th century.
Classification: LCC TX552 (ebook) | LCC TX552 .Z45 2018
    (print) | DDC 363.19/290973—dc23
LC record available at https://lccn.loc.gov/2017036822

Manufactured in the United States of America

26 25 24 23 22 21 20 19 18
10 9 8 7 6 5 4 3 2 1

To my Papa, Boris Zeide,
whose muscadine vines and okra plants,
ability to find rabbit holes in any forest,
and genuine engagement with my intellectual work,
no matter how it befuddled him,
have inspired me from the very beginning.

Contents

List of Illustrations _viii_

Introduction _1_

1. Condensed Milk: The Development of the Early
   Canning Industry _10_
2. Growing a Better Pea: Canners, Farmers, and
   Agricultural Scientists in the 1910s and 1920s _41_
3. Poisoned Olives: Consumer Fear and Expert Collaboration _74_
4. Grade A Tomatoes: Labeling Debates and Consumers
   in the New Deal _103_
5. Fighting for Safe Tuna: Postwar Challenges to Processed
   Food _135_
6. BPA in Campbell's Soup: New Threats to an Entrenched
   Food System _163_

Conclusion _186_

Acknowledgments _195_
Notes _199_
Selected Bibliography _251_
Index _261_

Illustrations

1. Growth of the US canning industry in value of products and expansion across states, 1899–1914 / 21
2. The Giant Pea Grader, 1914 / 25
3. Growth of the pack of canned fruits and vegetables, 1870–1950 / 39
4. Map of Wisconsin, the leader in canning peas, 1923 / 44
5. The Horal pea, resulting from the cross of two varieties, the Horsford and the Alaska, 1926 / 69
6. Cases of botulism in commercially canned, home-canned, and imported goods, 1905–55 / 79
7. Comparison of the grade-labeling and descriptive-labeling models, as depicted by the *Canner* trade journal, 1935 / 117
8. "Visual display fixture" that canners hoped would help consumers overcome the opacity of the can, 1933 / 123
9. Emphasis on branding and labeling within the canning industry, 1935 / 132
10. Influential female publishers and press representatives visiting the National Canners Association laboratory to see its state-of-the-art technology, 1963 / 144
11. "Recycle Wastewater" advertisement in the *Canner* trade journal, 1973 / 160

Introduction

Canned food is not something most of us spend much time dwelling on. It occupies that corner of our pantry shelves, reached for unthinkingly on days when we want a quick meal or a simple ingredient. We may think of cans as a staple of food pantries or as ingredients in favorite childhood dishes—Campbell's tomato soup, green bean casserole, one-pot bean chili. We may imagine tin cans as part of stockpiles ready for the apocalypse. But wherever the can appears, it is typically in the background of our thoughts.

Canned food is also not something historians think much about. Larger, complicated technologies like the automobile or the electrical grid take center stage, while the mundane tin can recedes into the background.[1] It just does not register in considerations of how our country, or our world, came to be as it is. And, even among the many historians who try to understand the ordinary aspects of life and of our diets, canned food has received scant attention.[2]

But this book argues that the tin can and the sometimes mushy food inside deserve our full and rapt attention. Canned food—produced in factories and packed in manufactured metal cans—has played as significant a role in shaping our daily lives as have many more highly touted technologies, both directly and in the ways it laid the groundwork for other processed food. The invisibility of canned food is particular to our moment in time, when factory-produced foods of all forms surround us.[3] It is only relatively recently that we have begun to think of cans as normal, or boring. There was a time, just over a century ago, when canned food seemed magical.

In a time when most Americans' diets changed with the seasons and were limited by their geographic locations, cans opened up a whole new world of foods and flavors. For the first time, for many kinds of food, the offerings on the dinner table were not bound by the natural laws of decay. In the words of early canners: "All the hoarded gifts of summer live in the can." Canned food "put the June garden into the January pantry."[4] As emphasized by the mythology that the canners created, canning made it possible for the juice of a summer peach to run down American chins in winter. Peas were no longer limited to a brief period in spring. Salmon from the Pacific Northwest could grace dinner tables in land-locked Arkansas. The idea that farmwives and fishermen could seal up food in one part of the year, only to eat it months or years later, when it was still edible and healthful, was revolutionary.

Still, when canned food began to appear on general store shelves, customers eyed the metal objects with equal parts awe and suspicion. Growing and buying food had always been a sensory experience, involving picking up food, smelling it, feeling it for ripeness. A savvy farmer or consumer could always identify a good tomato by the smell of its vine, the firmness of its flesh, the hue of its skin. Canned food broke that relationship, offering consumers only hard metal adorned by colorful paper. As historian Ann Vileisis writes, "Before cans, foods were leafy and earthy with attached greens and clinging soil. They were odorous animals with ears, eyes, and tongues. . . . But cans—be they filled with salmon, dandelion greens, oysters, or tomatoes—had no swish or splash."[5] The transition—from growing your own tomatoes to reaching for an opaque can of tomatoes packed in an unknown place by unknown hands—did not come easily, taking more than a century. And even when the unfamiliarity was no longer the central impediment, spoilage and overcooking often made canned food unappetizing or even frightening. Consumers had to develop a relationship of trust to these industrial products. Only then were they convinced to bring canned foods into their homes on a regular basis.

Early canners, the businessmen who used new technologies to convert the fruit of the field into the fruit of the factory, dedicated themselves to fostering trust in consumers. At first, they worked to perfect the technologies of the canning process, breed can-ready crops, and banish the bacteria that led to spoilage. All of this was done in the name of building a better product to gain consumer confidence. Later, as they became more secure in the technical aspects of their products, canners shifted to marketing, advertising, and currying political favor. In doing this, they created a vast network of relationships among farmers, scientists, physicians, universities, governmental bodies, media outlets, and advertising agencies. This network served as the foundation upon which a broader food industry, beyond cans, grew in the twentieth century. In analyzing the overarching systems that built American food, this work makes clear that it wasn't just consumer choice driving the move to processed food: machinations beyond the view of consumers were critical.[6]

The story of canned food offers crucial insight into understanding how and why Americans eat the way that we do. Many of us are familiar with contemporary conversations linking processed foods to obesity, and we see cases of foodborne illness splashed across the headlines, leading to ebbs and flows in the public's confidence. But, thinking historically, where did processed foods originate, what were their precursors, and how was public confidence in industrialized food earned in the first place? How did we come to accept and trust that these packages filled with foods of unknown origin and age would be worth eating?

Following the trail of processed food backward leads to canned food, in the early nineteenth century. It was the first nationally marketed, factory-processed, packaged food. Canning, along with meatpacking and grain processing, was the original technique of processing food, yielding a product that emerged from the factory in a form quite different from what you would find in nature or on the farm. Two characteristics distinguished canned food from meat and grain: one was the opaque metal container in which it was packaged; the other was the unfamiliar process by which it seemed to halt nature's process of decomposition. Both of these factors made canned food a tough sell. The product and the process by which it was created were opaque to the average consumer, both literally and metaphorically. Before the spread of canning in the late nineteenth century, most Americans had just begun the shift away from eating foods that they either grew themselves or obtained locally.[7] The foreign nature of canned goods, along with the industry's early difficulties in making its products safe and appealing, led to a lack of confidence among consumers and an early market that grew slowly.

Today, a commercial can is far more familiar, but it is still an opaque object, in both senses of the word. Its metal body conceals the contents; its industrial origins conceal the story.[8] The fruit or vegetables inside have typically been grown on huge industrial farms in some faraway place, then packed by whirring machines and the hands of strangers. The can is then shipped to our local grocery stores by way of enormous warehouses, anonymous cardboard boxes, diesel trucks, wholesalers, and the hidden labor of many. The men and women who profit most from the production of our industrially canned food are the CEOs of far-flung multinational corporations, along with the bankers and advertisers whose hands never touch the food in question.[9]

To accept industrially canned food today, we must either adopt unquestioning faith in the industrial food system in which we are all enmeshed or embark on a study of a labyrinthine network involving thousands of people. Doing the former might come naturally to a twenty-first-century consumer. After all, the majority of us have come of age in a time when international food companies, processed food, advertising, and complicated food technologies are central players in determining how we eat. But what about a nineteenth-century consumer, when this complicated network was just forming? Would the same leap of faith have come naturally to her? What would it have taken for her to make sense of a tin can of tomatoes that came from a factory? What led her to trust that commercially canned product and decide to feed it to her family? And how did these factors differ for consumers depending on their varying backgrounds?

This book explores the question of trust in processed food.[10] It seeks to understand how the complicated network of production that underlies today's factory-produced food came to be. It is, in many ways, a story of institutions and policies that exerted power to shape the American diet, laying the groundwork for key components of the growing industrial food system: factory production, packaging, national marketing, the deployment of scientific expertise, and involvement in the regulatory process. Understanding these systemic forces is crucial for the modern food movement. Many commentators today criticize the lack of transparency in the American food system. Michael Pollan has written: "Forgetting, or not knowing in the first place, is what the industrial food chain is all about, the principal reason it is so opaque, for if we could see what lies on the far side of the increasingly high walls of our industrial agriculture, we would surely change the way we eat." Even McDonald's has launched a marketing effort to answer consumer questions, with the claim that this project "promotes radical transparency."[11] These metaphors of "transparent" and "opaque" suggest just how difficult it has become for interested consumers to understand food production. The operations of companies that supply the majority of

American food are not open to public scrutiny. The complicated steps of production, processing, distribution, and marketing obscure the source of American food, building a wall between producers and consumers.

While this book is certainly about cans, it is also about much more. When we open up the can, we see it becomes a lens through which we can understand social organization, science and technology, corporations, politics, marketing, labor, and the environment—and the way that all of these come together through the food industry. Further, by studying trust, we can see how the story of cans reflects a larger story of American history, one that tells of a more general move toward opacity. For it is not just the food system that has become larger and less comprehensible to the average American. So many of our twenty-first-century institutions—political, financial, technological—have come to feel impenetrable. They have all become black boxes. Most of us accept the nature of these massive systems that govern our lives, even as critics attempt to highlight the flaws.[12] This story about trust, then, is a story about knowing and not knowing, about first feeling powerless in the face of impersonal structures and then finding ways to push back and exert control.

. . .

Through extensive historical research across archives of the federal government, universities, canning companies, agricultural experiment stations, and trade organizations, this study uncovers how canners—those sometimes-ignored middlemen in the chain of food production—shaped modern American food.[13] It examines the relationships of negotiation and contestation that underlay the creation of a way of eating shaped by scientific research, governmental regulation, consumer trust, and ideas about health and environment. It is also about the complicated behind-the-scenes events that inform the seemingly simple decisions we make each day. Should we pick up this item of food or that one from the grocery store shelf? Such ordinary daily behavior is indirectly influenced by a deep history and a large infrastructure that most of us never see. This project seeks to make visible some of those stories and structures, to open a window on the place of processed food in the United States.

Individual corporations and government agencies tend to get the most attention in examinations of the inner workings of the food system, both present and past. But one of the most powerful, yet overlooked, players is the trade association. These groups of businesses in a specific industry band together under a common agenda, finding power and influence through unification. In her 2006 food industry exposé *Appetite for Profit*, public health attorney Michele Simon points to a few key players in what she calls "Big Food." In addition to the usual culprits—McDonald's, Coca-Cola, and Kraft Foods—Simon focuses on one name that is somewhat less familiar: the Grocery Manufacturers Association (GMA).[14] This is a trade association representing nearly every major food manufacturer in the United States, with almost three hundred members. The GMA, though unknown to the average consumer, exerts inordinate influence on policy, science, and consumer access through its concentration of power and its large pool of money to spend on influencing politics.

The GMA has over 250 member companies. Of those, the ones with the longest histories are nearly all canning companies. This is because the influential GMA began, in part, as the National Canners Association (NCA) over a century ago.[15] The NCA is one of the main characters in this story, making clear how trade organizations have influenced the direction of our industrial food system. Individual entrepreneurs and large firms certainly play a part, but the NCA emerged as the driving force of change. From its beginnings during the debates about the purity of food in the early twentieth century, the NCA brought together canners of fruits and vegetables under a common mantle. It launched research initiatives, funded advertising campaigns, promoted inspection programs, represented the industry before the federal government, and intervened in political processes. The organization also met annually at a national conference and published a regular journal that apprised members of goings-on in the field. These events and documents defined the canning industry, creating a model of unified action that guided other processed-food companies as they developed atop the foundation laid by the canners. By looking at trade associations, we can expand the institutions considered important to histories of capitalism and industrialization, seeing these collaborative groups as central to shaping economic and social outcomes. Because they are positioned in the middle between factories and consumers, they allow us to understand more about both.[16] And, in telling this story, we find a new view on the history of industrial food, which provides tools to better understand and influence the contemporary food system.

The story told here unfolds both chronologically and thematically. Each chapter uses a different food and a different issue to frame the development of the canning industry. The foods chosen—condensed milk, peas, olives, tomatoes, tuna, Campbell's soup—are narrative devices that anchor each chapter but are often only symbolic of the larger central arguments of each section. Similarly, the varying focus—on technology, agriculture, bacteriology, regulation, and consumer activism—is also a way to broadly chart what canners were concerned with in a given moment, rather than suggesting these were their exclusive concerns.

To give a sense of the growth that serves as a backdrop to this story, consider these data: the first commercial canneries opened in New York, Maryland, and Delaware in the 1850s, focusing largely on vegetables, fruits, and oysters. Ohio, Indiana, Illinois, Iowa, and California followed in the next two decades. The 1870s saw new seafoods canned: salmon in Alaska and California, shrimp in New Orleans, sardines in Maine. Wisconsin began canning peas in 1881, and Hawaii took to pineapples in 1891. By 1899, there were 2,570 canning establishments across the country. In 1914, there were 4,220 canneries, with the largest numbers in New York (987), Virginia (441), Maryland (465), and California (289). Indiana, Illinois, Ohio, Wisconsin, and Missouri all had over 100 canneries as well. The country's canneries, by 1914, had spread to forty-two states, producing over 55 million cases of canned vegetables (nearly one-third tomatoes), 9.5 million cases of canned fruits, and 8.8 million cases of canned fish and oysters. By 1939, through consolidation, there were 2,612 canning companies across forty-five states, packing 354 million cases of canned foods, with a distribution across vegetables, fruits, and fish similar to the one twenty-five years earlier. By 1961, the number of cases grew to 722 million, double the 1939 production. Throughout the industry's life span, these companies were in rural areas near farms, and most were small, few with more than one hundred employees on average over the course of a year. While some foods, like citrus, pineapple, apricots, and seafood, were packed in specific parts of the country, many others—green beans, tomatoes, corn, and peas, for example—were packed in many states, with a variety of climates. This information presents a constant upward trajectory of per capita production of canned food, even as consumption remained below that of fresh food.[17]

To understand the texture that fleshes out the above statistics, this study begins with a focus on canners' proactive efforts to gain the trust of their imagined consumers. After the invention of canning in 1795, over a century of technological improvement, increasingly scientific processing techniques, trade organization, and food legislation led to an industry reliant on biological research by 1913. These elements made canned food cheaper, safer, and somewhat more trustworthy, even as they led to the deskilling of craft labor, the ousting of smaller canners who could not conform to regulation and organization, and the rise of standardization within the food sector.

Beginning around 1910, canners began to address two resistant problems: agricultural quality and bacterial contamination. In the improvement of raw crops, canners saw an opportunity to secure consumer confidence. This led to new relationships with farmers and agricultural scientists. Canners worked with state agricultural experiment stations and some farmers to solve a range of agricultural problems— collaboratively battling pests, improving soil composition, and breeding heartier and more manageable plants. In so doing, the canning industry paved the way for the practice of businesses funding university research. Further, in 1919–20, a highly publicized outbreak of botulism in canned olives led California canners and the NCA to form alliances with the California State Department of Health, academic bacteriologists, and federal health inspectors. Research after the botulism outbreak led to a standardized system of processing that was implemented throughout the canning industry, building consumer trust.

By the 1930s, canned food had come to be important to the American diet. But with this increase in consumption, some consumers and government advocates grew concerned that the standardized food system and prominence of brand names obscured the true quality of canned goods. In response, consumer advocates within the New Deal's National Recovery Administration called for grade labeling as a way of empowering consumers. Now armed with the stability to resist, canners pushed back against this intrusion, hoping to protect brand identities and influence consumer shopping habits more directly.

The 1940s and '50s saw a kind of truce among food business, consumers, and the government. By the early 1960s, canned food had become part of—and had helped to produce—a much larger processed-foods industry, rooted in American postwar culture. But this trust was once again called into question in the late 1960s and 1970s as emerging consumer and environmental movements highlighted broader issues of the food system, tied to concerns about chemicals, nutrition, and pollution. Canners rejected the consumer advocates' authority and pushed back against the rising tide of regulation by embracing political involvement and marketing campaigns. The forms of scientific expertise on which the industry primarily relied shifted from the biological to the social and political. Even as canned food itself became familiar to American consumers, the processes that underlay the food system grew more obscure, leading to calls for increased transparency.

In the twenty-first century, fears about the chemical Bisphenol-A, or BPA, an endocrine system disruptor used in can linings, have emerged to threaten the canning industry. While most scientific evidence points toward the conclusion that BPA indeed causes substantial harm, the food industry (along with trade organizations representing the chemical and plastics industries) has funded its own scientific research and has manipulated the regulatory process to raise doubt and limit significant regulation. This move characterizes the increasingly opaque nature of American food—now no longer unfamiliar to consumers in the way that first made canned food questionable in the nineteenth century but characterized by an even more intractable systemic opacity.

Many food activists today fight to lay bare the path from farm to table. They believe that this knowledge can counter the lack of transparency so ingrained in our twenty-first-century industrial food system, leading to needed change at both the farm and the table. But finding transparency has not proven to be as simple as just lifting the lid off the can. A rallying cry of the food movement, which it has inherited from its Progressive Era predecessors, contends that knowledge will lead to social change: if the "public" could simply see the messy truth, there would be a social and political push to for transformation.[18] But the story within these pages shows that transparency has been a complicated and shifting goal since the canning industry's inception and that canners have used it strategically for their own purposes, just as they have any other marketing tool. The modern food system has become so complex that simply uncovering it may not automatically lead to dramatic structural change. But perhaps understanding its history is one place to begin.

Condensed Milk

The Development of the Early Canning Industry

In July 1864, David Coon, a member of the Thirty-Sixth Wisconsin Infantry Regiment, wrote a letter home to his wife and children. Such letters from soldiers were common during the Civil War, but this one was a little different: Coon had written it on the back of a label peeled from a can of Borden's Condensed Milk.[1] Perhaps he was short on paper, or maybe Coon had just reached for the nearest writing surface available, peeling back the label from an empty can of milk to find a clean writing space. Either way, Coon's letter documents the presence of canned milk in the life of Union army camps.

The Civil War (1861–65) brought staggering changes to the United States. With over six hundred thousand casualties, it forced Americans to confront death and loss as never before. There were deep and lasting effects to economies, landscapes, and families—in both the North and the South, among blacks and whites. But amid the abolition of slavery and other colossal upheavals, one seemingly insignificant change resulted from the war: Americans of many stripes had tasted their first canned food. Like David Coon, most soldiers encountered canned foods—whether condensed milk, blueberries, or peaches—during the war, often for the first time in their lives. And when they came home, they brought with them an inclination to trust commercially canned food and to pass that familiarity on to their families. This change in taste and trust among soldiers would have a substantial impact on the ensuing rise of the food industry in the United States.[2] Wartime encounters like Coon's began to pave the path for exposure that became crucial for the building of consumer confidence in formerly unknown processed foods.

Before the Civil War, canned foods had been used mostly in exceptional situations, rather than as part of regular meals. Although canning technology had existed for more than fifty years, canned food fed those who were on expeditions or at war, disconnected from sites of agricultural production. The average American consumer had limited experience with this new packaged product, and many feared the opacity of the unknown. To build an industry, canners had to turn their simple invention into a trustworthy commodity. In the years after the Civil War, canners built trust in their products through the projects of technical improvement, trade organization, federal regulation, and laboratory science. All of these served to increase production and dissemination of commercially canned goods. Although large-scale projects were carried out on the production side, they were explicitly a means toward the end of increased consumption and trust, remaining central to the growth of a processed-food market over the next 150 years.[3]

A much wider world beyond the cannery office shaped the acceptance of processed food and felt the cascading effects of industrialization.[4] Canners were involved in complex relationships with scientists, government officials, consumers, advertisers, and others. And the concerns that drove canners' decisions emerged from the cultural and consumer responses to this technology, as Americans negotiated how canned food affected their relationships with nature, health, and labor.[5]

Along with the growth of the canning industry over the nineteenth century came a broader industrial revolution, of which canning was a part. The American Industrial Revolution saw a dramatic shift in people's relationships to nature and technology. Economic growth depended on abundant natural resources, and the exploitation of those natural resources in turn depended on a powerful technological infrastructure. As self-sufficient rural Americans shifted from using their own land and labor to buying factory-produced goods—from milking a family dairy cow to purchasing Borden's Condensed Milk, for example—their dependencies also shifted. They still relied on forces larger than themselves, but the forces of nature became less important than the forces of technological systems and networks. As historian Ruth Schwartz Cowan has written, Americans exchanged "nature for technology."[6] Of course, the production of canned food was still intimately connected with the natural world, but the tin can's ability to transcend the bounds of geography and season embodied a conquest of nature through advanced technology.[7]

Between 1810 and 1910, commercially canned food went from being totally unknown to being an increasingly familiar product. How did that transition happen? Before the rise of an organized industry, canned food served people who were away from home—at sea, in the wild, or at war. In the Civil War, American soldiers came to know canned food and to bring that knowledge home to their families. Between 1865 and 1905, canners developed numerous technologies that boosted production and lowered prices, making canned food more abundant and recognizable to average consumers. By 1910, the industry began to move away from the fragmentary structure of nineteenth century and to benefit from trade organization, as canning leaders came together to lobby for pure food legislation and to establish a national laboratory. With strength in numbers, canners began to use the language of science to build consumer trust and taste. By the second decade of the twentieth century, canners believed they had overcome the initial problems that held back their industry, laying the groundwork for deepened consumer confidence in the years to come.

FOOD ON THE MOVE: SERVING EXPLORERS AND SOLDIERS (1795–1865)

Before canners even began thinking about building trust among ordinary consumers, they got their start by catering to not-so-ordinary consumers. Commercial canning best served people who could not access fresh food products. The major canning centers of the first half of the nineteenth century—France, England, and the United States—were also countries with a mission of expansion during this same time. Canned food enabled imperial conquest, the exploration and settlement of new lands, and the provisioning of armies fighting for national unity. French and British colonialists, gold seekers in the American West, and Civil War soldiers all ate canned goods for the sustenance that fueled their ventures. For these people, canned food was more of a necessity than it was for average Americans in their homes, making a lack of trust in the unfamiliar canned product less of a barrier.

Seventy years before the Civil War, across the Atlantic Ocean, another military venture gave canned food its start. In 1795, much of Europe was caught up in the French Revolutionary Wars, as French armies took up arms to replace monarchic governments with liberal democracies across the continent. Frustrated by the difficulty of efficiently feeding soldiers on the march, the French government offered a prize of 12,000 francs (roughly $40,000 in the modern United States) to anyone who could devise a better method for provisioning troops. Soon-to-be emperor Napoleon Bonaparte is credited with saying, "An army marches on its stomach," capturing how important to successful military campaigns it was to provide wholesome food to soldiers. Among those who submitted proposals to the prize committee was Frenchman Nicolas Appert, who began as a confectioner and chef and ended up the "father of the canning industry." After experimenting with food preservation methods for years, he struck upon a technique of canning, or, in the words of his 1810 publication title, "The Art of Preserving All Kinds of Animal and Vegetable Substances for Several Years."[8] Believing that heat held the key to food preservation, Appert turned to his stove. He packed a variety of foods in sealed containers and subjected them to different temperatures until he finally struck upon the right combination. He found that when he sealed foods—vegetables or fruit or meat—in airtight containers and cooked them in boiling water, the items would stay edible for long stretches of time afterward, though he did not understand the mechanism.

Appert proved his method by putting some of his preserved-food articles on ships that sailed around the world. When the ships returned to France, the food was still edible. Napoleon granted Appert the 12,000-franc prize in 1809. The modern method of canning, or "Appertizing," was born. One French newspaper commented, "M. Appert has discovered the art of fixing the seasons. With him spring, summer and autumn exist in bottles like delicate plants that are protected by the gardener under a dome of glass against the intemperance of the seasons."[9] This highlighted the most revolutionary aspect of Appert's new method: the ability of humans to use technology in the fight against seasonal limitations and natural decay.

Canning was invented in France, but the canning industry soon flourished in England and later the United States. Several English firms that had given Appert financial assistance began production soon after 1810.[10] One Englishman coined the term *can* to refer to the metal "canister" he preferred over the glass and ceramic crocks that Appert used. Tin-plated canisters largely replaced glass by the mid-nineteenth century, as steel lined with tin was both cheaper and less prone to breakage. The canning process came to the United States through several English immigrants, beginning around 1817, buoyed by the new country's surplus of meat and agricultural products and its rapid urbanization.[11] Still, early American canners largely worked through a haphazard system, producing mostly delicacies like turtle soup that they sent abroad, as there was not yet a domestic consumer base.[12] As one early observer commented, canned food was "a mere vehicle for pandering to the luxurious appetites of the wealthy."[13]

The other major consumers were travelers on military or exploring expeditions. As one contemporary put it, canned food "rob[bed] scurvy of its dread, on the high seas, in the burning desert, or in the frozen polar regions."[14] Typical provisions before the mid-nineteenth century consisted of beef, pork, beer, dried bread, cheese, oatmeal, peas, and flour. Stories of hungry sailors, rotten meat, insect-infested grains, and overall bad food run throughout records from the age of exploration.[15] Cans not only provided variety but also helped preserve the health of sailors. Even after the discovery of vitamin C led sailors to eat limes to prevent scurvy, the wide adoption of canned food markedly improved nutrition.[16] Still, many risks were involved in eating early canned goods—everything from the mild concern of food that tasted bad to the significant fear of lethal food poisoning. Those who encountered canned foods in this early phase may not have understood the bacterial cause of spoilage or the toxicity of leaching metals, but they saw enough swollen or rusted cans with rancid contents to understand that canned food was often limited by the same laws of decay that could spoil any food.

One case that vividly illustrates some of these early risks is that of Sir John Franklin's mid-nineteenth-century Arctic expedition. Franklin was a British explorer who famously mapped great swaths of North America's unexplored Arctic coast but met a premature end around 1845. For his final voyage, Franklin decided to bring along an extra ship loaded with enough canned food—a newly available item—to last three years.[17] Instead, Franklin and his men were last seen in July 1845 in the Arctic, early in their expedition. Years later, the bones of expedition members were analyzed, and autopsies were performed on a few bodies that had been frozen solid and preserved. The investigation showed evidence of scurvy, pneumonia, and tuberculosis in some of the men. But the entire party also had elevated blood lead levels—an average of 228 parts per million (ppm) compared with 22 to 36 ppm in the bones of the Inuit who lived in the same area. One young man had lead levels of 600 ppm in his hair. Although the definitive cause of death is still not clear, forensic analysis offers lead poisoning as a central possibility, with the lead likely coming straight from the soldering of those tin cans on the extra ship.[18]

At the time of Franklin's expedition, the technology for canning meat was less than forty years old, and cans were sealed with a solder of tin with a high lead content. This solder could have seeped into the contents of the can, causing classic lead poisoning symptoms: lack of appetite, fatigue, intestinal discomfort, and paranoia. The canned food, the very product that was intended to prevent the starvation that had ruined earlier expeditions, could have poisoned the men of the Franklin expedition. Here, taking Franklin's British case as a contrast with Napoleon's French one, we see how sustenance affected the success or failure of colonial interventions of the early nineteenth century. Simple imperial ambition was not enough to conquer foreign lands and develop new trade routes. Explorers and soldiers had to find a way to eat, even when they were far away from agricultural lands.

The story of these explorers and their deaths was widely publicized in England in the years after 1847.[19] In the absence of a clear cause, speculation touched on all aspects of the expedition, with some wondering whether the unfamiliar canned food had poisoned the sailors. But this was idle speculation, because the canning industry was just getting started, both in England and in the United States, and had no organized way of responding. Further, no government structures existed for oversight or regulation of food during this time. Finally, even if canned food, when improperly soldered, could lead to death, it was still better than the alternative of starvation for explorers, making the gamble worth it. Even though the canning industry's reach had expanded significantly by the time an 1886 *New York Times* article commented on this gamble, the sentiment also applied to the earlier expeditions: "[This industry] is now a world's necessity. [Any shipmaster] would take the risk of poisoning his men, and they would prefer that he should. Of course, without the universal tins, exploration either of the desert or the poles would come to a full stop."[20] For the average consumer, the risk calculus was understandably different, as the threat of starvation loomed less large at home.

Many settlers moving west in the United States also made use of canned foods. In the mid-nineteenth century, nearly half a million Americans made their way west to find land to settle, mine, farm, or ranch. Traveling by wagon along primitive trails, the travelers had to carry the majority of their food for the four- to six-month trip with them. They relied on foods that did not spoil easily and that were relatively lightweight: flour, cornmeal, bacon, sugar, coffee, dried vegetables and fruit, jerky, sugar. Some herded livestock along with their caravans or brought caged chickens aboard.[21] But as the canning industry developed, some settlers decided to bring along foods canned in the East. Although they were heavier and their risk uncertain, canned foods offered exciting variety and "fresher" flavors. One 1848 advertisement in the *New York Herald,* titled "Good Living on the Way to California," marketed preserved food "such as roasted meats, poultry, soup, vegetables, fish, lobsters, oysters, clams, &c," which were "put up in canisters holding one and two pounds each, and retain perfectly their natural flavor and nutritious qualities for twenty-one years in any climate."[22] Rusted tin cans often littered recently abandoned campsites along western trails.[23] Massive western migration following the Gold Rush fueled the growth of the canning industry, helping to launch many new canning firms between 1850 and 1860. Historian Walter Prescott Webb described how tin cans could tell a story about a traveler's direction: "If he is going west, the camp is surrounded by tin cans and paper sacks, if he is going east it is littered with fieldlark feathers and rabbit-fur."[24] Because canning production was centered in the eastern part of the United States, travelers who had made it to the West Coast and were returning home were unlikely to carry canned goods with them, instead having to rely on hunting and trapping.

Despite the wide use of canned foods among specialized markets, the early American industry was in its infancy. Industry leader Hugh S. Orem wrote in 1914, "Until 1860, it can be well said the industry was in a comatose or dormant state."[25] Canneries were few, produced small quantities, and used methods that were the result of trial and error. The launching of the canning industry into the domestic market after 1860 was prompted by two developments, both related to increased consumer exposure: the start of the Civil War, which increased demand, and the emergence of key technologies, which allowed for expanded production. Many Americans encountered canned foods for the first time during the Civil War, when soldiers were away from home, and the military found itself needing to supply great quantities of food to hungry men on the move.

Soldiers' newly acquired taste for canned foods emerged from the wartime context and transferred into civilian life.[26] The years after the Civil War saw a phenomenal increase in the production of canned foods. Whereas there had been five million cans produced in 1860, there were about thirty million by 1865 and more than ninety million by 1880.[27] The war had made a name for the canning industry by bringing together young men from all parts of the country and all walks of life and exposing this diverse group to a homogeneous food supply, which featured the tin can. Further, a number of canning companies that had just begun operations before the war gained financial stability through wartime contracts and grew to become major food processors.

Among these processors, the one that benefited and grew most in the ensuing years was Borden's Condensed Milk Company.[28] The company's founder, Gail Borden, had begun commercial production in 1857 after several failed attempts. His method for condensing milk involved removing as much water content as possible by cooking milk in a vacuum pan over low heat. His business was propelled forward in 1858 by the "swill milk trade" scandal in New York. Newspaper exposés revealed that much of the city's milk supply came from so-called swill dairies, in which malnourished and sick cows were fed with the spent grain of whiskey distilleries, leading to milk that was thin and adulterated. The articles suggested that this swill milk had led to the deaths of eight thousand infants in New York City in 1857 alone.[29] Borden capitalized on this shocking announcement, marketing his own canned milk as pure and unadulterated. Because the canning technology enabled milk to be collected at a distance from the city, Borden's milk could come from rural cows with plenty of space and green grass to keep them healthy. The swill milk scandal gave a boost to Borden's company, as some consumers began to wonder if the risks of unfamiliar canned goods were actually any worse than the risks of an urban diet.[30] This seemingly opaque industrial food became *more* knowable relative to the urban milk supply.

The start of the Civil War found Borden in an excellent position to benefit from a contract for his condensed milk. In 1861, a Union Army commissary agent entered Borden's New York office to request an initial order of five hundred pounds, and more in the future, to fulfill a large contract.[31] Soon, with high demand for his product, Borden was paying two hundred area dairy farmers for their twenty thousand gallons of milk, which was condensed and preserved through heating and the addition of sugar.[32] The Civil War contract was crucial to Borden's success. As other commentators have noted, condensed milk might have risen to popularity without the war, but it would have taken many years and much promotion to do in peacetime what just a few short years of wartime accomplished.[33]

Union soldiers encountered canned foods through a variety of venues. Their standard rations did not include canned items because of the industry's low supply at the start of the war. Instead, most soldiers subsisted on salted pork, stale biscuits known as hardtack, dried fruit and vegetables, and sometimes beans, rice, and coffee. But the Union Army's commissary department, in charge of providing food, did offer cans periodically when sufficient supply could be obtained.[34] Officers tended to have easier access to canned goods, but troops also received them from the US Sanitary Commission, especially in army hospitals, or from traveling merchants called sutlers.[35] Sutlers sold a wide range of canned goods—canned beef, lobster, blueberries, jams, pickles—that appealed to soldiers who grew tired of their monotonous rations.[36] The Sanitary Commission, a volunteer-run private relief agency that supported sick and wounded Union soldiers, also provided condensed milk in large quantities.[37] Canned condensed milk was considered "the sick soldiers' nectar" and was especially used in hospitals to provide nourishment to ailing men.[38] Confederate soldiers, in contrast, were less likely to be exposed to canned food because it was not usually served by sutlers or the US Sanitary Commission. But they did encounter it sometimes, whether acquiring it from raids of Union supply trains or mess pantries, eating it when imprisoned in Union camps, or importing it from overseas.[39]

Technological development went hand in hand with wartime exposure for increasing production of canned foods. One important innovation, in 1861, was the addition of calcium chloride to the water in which the cans were immersed and boiled. Isaac Solomon, a Baltimore canner, discovered that he could raise the boiling point of the water in which cans were processed by the addition of calcium chloride to the water bath. By raising the boiling point, he was able to use higher temperatures to cook the canned food more quickly, which allowed for an increase in production volume and a resulting decrease in prices. For example, using a temperature of 240°F (rather than water's normal boiling point of 212°F) cut the processing time from six hours to just forty minutes. This, in turn, allowed canners to produce 20,000 cans per day, where they'd previously produced around 2,500.[40] This development, along with the first patents for can openers—a sickle version in 1858, and a rotating-wheel version in 1870—helped the canning industry to grow.[41]

Much of this development of industrially processed canned food took place alongside the introduction of home canning. Although humans had been devising methods for preserving foods for many centuries— such as drying, smoking, fermentation, cold storage, salting, and the use of sugars and vinegars—Appert's 1810 publication introduced, both to the factory and to the home, his new method of preserving through vacuum heating. Women in their homes slowly began experimenting with this new method. But technology limited their progress as well. It wasn't until 1858 that John Landis Mason invented the glass jar and threaded lid with a rubber gasket that made home canning safer and easier. By the 1870s, instructions for using these new jars in hot water baths began appearing in cookbooks, though the practice of home canning didn't take off until the 1910s.[42] American farmwives were the group most likely to be familiar with home canning in the years after the Civil War, as it allowed them to preserve surplus summer and fall crops for the lean winter and spring months. This knowledge likely made some families more willing to try commercial cans, since at least the process of preservation was familiar. But for others, if they were even familiar with home canning, there was a large disconnect between trusting what came from their own kitchens packed in transparent glass and trusting what came from an unknown factory packed in opaque metal.

Soldiers' wartime exposure to commercially canned foods, though intermittent, generated the beginnings of consumer trust. This trust flowed back up the chain of production, providing the first glimmers of wider demand that canners needed in order to innovate and expand. Tastes were often slow to change when ordinary consumers were given a choice between new products and their go-to standards. But because army men in the Civil War had little choice when it came to their food supply, they gave new foods a chance and widened their palates to partially accommodate canned foods.[43] After the war, they brought these new preferences home with them. The nature of trust that these battlefield encounters fostered was not yet rooted in scientific certainty, a better understanding of the risks, or knowledge of where the food had come from. Rather, it sprang from exposure and familiarity that made a new kind of food seem worth sampling and its convenience and accessibility worth appreciating.

Of course, veterans and their families were only a segment of the demographic that canners hoped to reach. Many Civil War soldiers were farmers from rural areas, often from poorer families. Their influence was thus limited. But the contracts the Union Army granted to Borden and other companies gave canners the necessary foothold to imagine expanding beyond veterans to reach other retail customers, who they hoped would be the future of their industry. Once canned foods entered some homes through soldiers' exposure, canners felt equipped to work toward extending their consumer base through technological innovation.[44]

AN INDUSTRY ASCENDANT: TECHNOLOGICAL INNOVATION AND EXPANSION (1865-1905)

In 1870, for the first time, the US Census recorded the canning industry as a distinct business entity. There were fewer than one hundred canneries, centered largely in the Mid-Atlantic region, around Maryland, New York, New Jersey, and Pennsylvania. These small operations usually operated seasonally, with basic technology, employing local farmwomen and children in packing local produce and selling it to local audiences. Small outbuildings or sheds would be used to house the operations and simple equipment: tin cans formed by hand, large open kettles for boiling the cans. By 1900 the number of canning companies had grown from one hundred to nearly eighteen hundred, now spanning a more dispersed geographic region, and including many established institutions (figure 1).[45]

The completion of the transcontinental railroad system in 1869 helped canners deliver their goods to all ends of the country. This growth of the canning industry mirrored the larger process of American industrialization in the post–Civil War years.[46] Two kinds of innovations especially important to the growing industry were machines that increased efficiency (and deskilled labor) and bacteriological research techniques.

Much of the industry's growth centered on the city of Baltimore. While canners may have referred to Nicolas Appert as the "father of the canning industry," they called the city of Baltimore the "mother of the canning industry."[47] One early canner explained that Baltimore "was far better adapted to pursue this infant industry than cold, bleak New England or New York. Situated in the midst of a great area of kindly soil, with an equable climate, it has ever been capable of producing the best yield of every variety of fruits and vegetables the earth could furnish." Along with Baltimore's rich agricultural lands, the fertile oyster beds of the Chesapeake Bay helped the city achieve prominence in canning.[48] Baltimore's natural riches made it the center of the new canning industry until 1900, when the rise of canning in the Midwest and in California balanced the geographical distribution of canning operations, and overharvesting and pollution in the Chesapeake led to a decline of the oyster population.

The canning industry was one of the first to become mechanized on a large scale, relative to other American industries. A stunning array of machinery became available to the largest canners—machines that produced the cans themselves, peeled and chopped and packed the food into the cans, and cooked the filled cans to preserve their contents.[49]

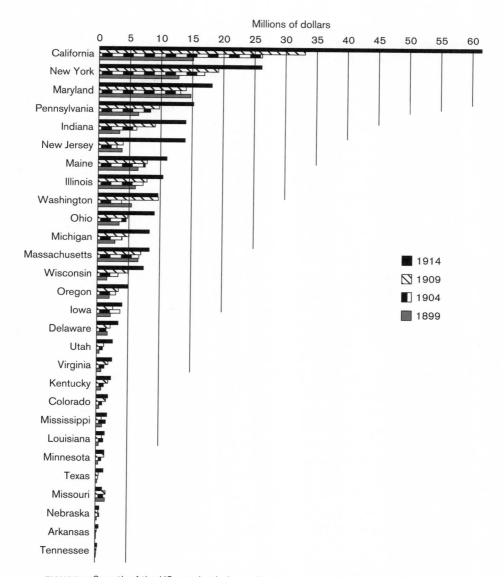

FIGURE 1. Growth of the US canning industry in value of products and expansion across states, 1899–1914. Eastern canneries were more numerous in the late nineteenth century, but California led in value of products throughout the early years of the canning industry. (1914 Census of Manufactures, Industry Series. Washington, DC: US Department of Commerce, Bureau of the Census.)

Even as the adoption of these machines was slow and halting, many canners viewed them as a way to help in the industry's domination of nature and seasonal cycles. In the words of one leader, "Even the unseen, mysterious and heretofore supposed inert forces of nature have been wrought into mechanical servants, harnessed and made subservient to the will of man."[50] Canning leaders sought to use these "mechanical servants" to build their industry and replace some of the human "servants" who had previously labored in the canneries. Despite these goals, canneries throughout the country, and particularly those at a distance from the canning center of Baltimore, continued to rely on manual laborers, especially women, for the next century.

The shift towards mechanization began with the invention of the stream retort, or pressure cooker, in 1874.[51] Although the introduction of calcium chloride at the beginning of the Civil War helped increase production, the chemical had significant drawbacks that made inventors search for a better alternative.[52] By 1874, Andrew Keyser Shriver, a Baltimore canner, had introduced the stream retort, a large, closed-kettle, steam pressure cooker that allowed for higher processing temperatures. The retort was important not only because it dramatically increased output but also because it altered the social relations of the canneries that could afford the expensive machines, laying the groundwork for mechanization to follow. Before the steam retort, the use of calcium chloride had introduced a level of secrecy into the canning process, as each company developed its own methods of processing foods, with different temperatures, cooking times, and amounts of the salt. The secrecy led to guardedness among firms and gave the man who controlled the processing recipes—the processor—ultimate power. A contemporary canning leader described how the processor "stalked abroad in the power of his might. . . . Locked in his room with his kettles and thermometer, none dared approach him in his lair."[53] Under the calcium chloride system, the processor held the knowledge for how to use the substance to boil cans most efficiently. The introduction of the steam retort, however, standardized the procedure, so that there were fewer variables to consider and almost anyone could perform it. This undermined the processor's power, leading to a degree of standardization that spread processing knowledge more widely.

On the heels of the steam pressure cooker came a wave of new machines. Some of the most important were those that mechanized the production of the cans themselves. Tin cans were actually steel cans lined with tin—the steel was used for its strength and low cost and the tin for its resistance to corrosion. Before the middle of the nineteenth century, such cans were made by hand in the form of the "hole-and-cap can."[54] Human can makers cut the tin sheets down to size, wrestled them into shape, and soldered the pieces together. Then they cut a hole in the circular top, inserted food into it, and soldered on a metal cap to seal the hole. This laborious process required significant time and strength, with each can maker able to make at most roughly two dozen cans per day. As a result, there was real demand for machines to mechanize this process. By 1883, the Norton Brothers Company of Chicago had introduced a can maker that exponentially increased production capacity, first to 2,500 cans per hour and then, by 1893, to 6,000 an hour.[55] In addition to making cans more rapidly, new machines made it possible to produce cans of many different sizes. Earlier cans had often been large, in order to feed many people at once on the battlefield or on long voyages. But as the household became a clearer market for canned food, canners began to replace these larger sizes with smaller cans that were more affordable and could feed a family in one sitting.[56]

The invention of such machines over the second half of the nineteenth century not only increased the output of can production but also reshaped labor relations and ideas about disposability. When the can was a hand-crafted container, the cost and value were high enough that some consumers held on to the cans and repurposed them when possible. But when can production became mechanized and cans proliferated, the empty tin became a disposable cast-off, a waste product of modern life. Material production became so much cheaper and more plentiful that ideals of expendability replaced those of thrift.[57]

The rise of industrialized canned food required the creation of a large, efficient system that could reach a growing population after the Civil War. But to achieve this system, the canning industry had to move toward replacing craft labor with machinery, for reasons of both efficiency and control. Mechanization wrought changes in labor relations because it devalued specialized knowledge held by only a few skilled craftsmen. Many cannery jobs required unskilled hand labor, like chopping vegetables, filling cans with fruit, or labeling and boxing the final canned products—the work of a largely replaceable female workforce.[58] But the skilled processes—capping the cans and cooking them for just the right lengths of time—were carried out by specialized metalworkers or processors. Thus the development of machinery that standardized these procedures of capping and processing led to the harshest resistance. Many canning workers vigorously fought against the introduction of machines, which they crudely called "iron slaves." There are numerous colorful stories of standoffs between canners and workers over machinery. In one case in Baltimore in the 1870s, a canner who had installed a can-filling machine had to stand guard over it with a "pistol in one hand, a club in the other," to keep at bay the angry workers who wanted to destroy it.[59]

Economic historians Martin Brown and Peter Philips have made the convincing argument that canners adopted many technologies in the earlier days less because these made labor more efficient than because they transferred power from skilled laborers to cannery owners. Because the craft labor of the processors and cappers put them in a position of control over factory operations, the introduction of machines that made the craft laborers less important gave canners the upper hand.[60] Industries therefore stood to gain much if they could weaken laborers' power through mechanization. This story repeated itself, with the Cox Capper that mechanized the capping of open cans and with "the Little Joker," a mechanical soldering device. Some canners reportedly purchased the latter not even to use but to display as an open threat to any workers who might consider striking.[61] The machines sent the message to the worker: you are replaceable.

By the 1890s, a flood of new inventions had poured forth: machines had been introduced to butcher salmon and grade peas according to size (figure 2), to peel tomatoes and husk corn, to fill cans and glue on labels, and much more. These machines, while deskilling labor in some areas and replacing some workers, also made new jobs available by helping the canning industry to expand. Many canneries, now requiring fewer laborers, could open in areas where existing labor pools had previously been unable to support a factory. The machines required a slightly higher capital investment, but small towns sought to attract and extend credit to cannery operators.[62] One 1895 report estimated that the industry supported "at least 400,000 people in the height of the season."[63] By entering new areas, canning factories also exposed more potential consumers to their novel and promising products. Finally, mechanization greatly reduced the costs of producing canned foods, thus lowering prices, allowing the market to expand to middle- and lower-class families.

Along with new machinery, a key new technology was the so-called sanitary can to replace the "hole-and-cap" can. In 1898, the George W. Cobb Preserving Company developed a can that used a lid whose edges could be folded over and stamped together after filling, requiring no solder. The Cobb Company soon became the Sanitary Can Company,

GIANT PEA GRADER

PERFECT REELS, avoiding buckling of screens.

RINGS of heavy angles and true to circle and face.

HEAVY GAUGE PERFORATED SCREENS add to strength and durability of reels.

STEADY, UNIFORM DRIVE,—Friction Clutch Drive Pulley on cross drive shaft, connected to reel shafts by reduction bevel gears.

DRIVE PULLEY upon cross shaft and always in line.

Prices Until Jan. 15th

20 ft. 4 reels
$650.00

30 ft. 6 reels
$875.00

40 ft. 8 reels
$1100.00

To secure these prices and early delivery, order now

A. T. FERRELL & COMPANY
SAGINAW, W. S., MICHIGAN

FIGURE 2. The Giant Pea Grader, advertised here in 1914, was just one of the many new machines that remade the canning industry in the late nineteenth century. (Courtesy of the Grocery Manufacturers Association.)

and its major product rose to prominence, used universally in Europe and in the largest American canneries by 1914.[64] The publicity director of the Max Ams Machine Company, which had patented the sanitary can, sang its praises this way: "This method has the advantage over the ordinary method of soldering, as vegetables and fruits may be filled into the cans whole. There is positively no danger of acid or solder getting inside of the can, no danger from lead poisoning, no scorching sugar or fruit, and no black spots in the syrup of the Sanitary Can."[65] These improvements helped address some of the issues that kept canned food from being seen as trustworthy.

In addition to machinery, a second kind of technology that promoted the growth of the canning industry between 1865 and 1905 was the practical application of the new science of bacteriology. Many canners and consumers were concerned about the negative health effects of canned foods due to spoilage. Newspaper reports abounded with stories about so-called ptomaine poisoning—the generic name for digestive upset resulting from spoiled food—often attributed to canned food.[66] The discovery of germ theory in the late nineteenth century explained these ptomaines by connecting them to microscopic organisms, or germs, that lurked in human food and in the human body. Canners now had specific organisms to target in fighting spoilage.[67]

Although Appert had known nothing of bacterial action when publishing his foundational work in 1810, he laid the pathway for Louis Pasteur, a fellow Frenchman, the "father of germ theory." Pasteur himself acknowledged that Appert had been his precursor, writing: "When I published the first results of my experiments on the possible preservation of wine by previous heating, it was evident that I was only presenting a new application of Appert's method."[68] Of course, while both men discovered that heat could preserve food, only Pasteur understood the underlying reason: heat killed microscopic organisms, or bacteria, within the food that would otherwise lead to spoilage. Pasteur's work, and that of German Robert Koch, put germ theory on the map throughout the 1870s and 1880s, but many Americans were slow to accept its implications. Canners were among the first in the food industry to recognize the value of bacteriology to their business, using it as a tool to decrease spoilage—a prime cause of consumer skepticism toward canned food.

The earliest recorded instance in which canners drew on this new knowledge was in 1894 in Wisconsin. That state had only begun to develop its canning industry within the last decade, but the state's first-established cannery was experiencing heavy spoilage in its canned peas.

That cannery, led by Albert Landreth, decided to draw on the expertise of its state's college of agriculture for help. The college sent the young bacteriologist Harry Luman Russell, who had trained in Europe with Robert Koch, to diagnose and treat the problem of spoilage. Russell rightly speculated that bacterial growth was responsible and made recommendations for how Landreth could increase his processing time and temperature to reduce the growth. Russell published his report, but because few canners read scientific studies, the knowledge was not widely disseminated. The Landreth Company's practice of making use of scientific expertise remained unique for decades to come.[69]

The Atlantic States Packers' Association, however, did devote some attention to bacteriology at their 1898 annual meeting in Buffalo, New York, marking the first time that a convention of food processors attended to scientific research. There, Boston scientists Samuel C. Prescott and W. Lyman Underwood presented to the canners their contention that microscopic bacteria were responsible for sour canned foods and that higher processing temperatures would keep the problem at bay.[70] In contrast, many canning processors preferred to shorten cooking time in order to prevent vegetables from becoming mushy. Prescott and Underwood asked the canners to shift their trust from the processor to the scientists, thus also shifting where they believed ultimate expertise lay. Though that particular audience of canners gave only halfhearted attention to Prescott and Underwood's scientific claims, within a decade canners as a whole began to follow their advice as they began to invest in scientific research.[71] Canners themselves had to learn to trust in scientific expertise, which paved the way for consumer trust in canned goods through decreased spoilage.

During the second half of the nineteenth century, the canning industry grew into a recognizable entity, producing ever more cans in more factories and serving more consumers. As the cans became more familiar, Americans in their homes began to see canned goods as a potentially stable part of their expanded diets. Especially in the North, mechanization on the farm reduced labor needs in the countryside, and industrialization in the urban factories required more labor in the cities, leading to the movement of millions of people into urban areas. Between 1870 and 1920, over forty million Americans moved into cities. Increasing urbanization brought with it smaller kitchens, no root cellars for winter cold storage, and easier access to urban grocers that sold commercially canned goods. With more men and women working long hours in urban factories, working-class families sought foods that required less preparation.[72]

Canners made use of this changing landscape to increase production and consider ways of increasing consumption alongside. But even as the industry adopted new tools to build taste, they inevitably reshaped human relations as well, deskilling labor, creating opportunities in rural areas, and boosting trust in scientific expertise.

A NATIONAL PRESENCE: FEDERAL REGULATION AND ORGANIZATION (1900–1910)

Before the turn of the twentieth century, canned goods were marginal enough that they merited little focused concern. But around 1900, bad press for the increasingly visible canned foods began to emerge. In 1906, the president of the Western Packers' Canned Goods Association, Dr. A. C. Fraser, presented the situation frankly: "Canners' warehouses [are] filled with products the public [does] not demand because press, pulpit, women's clubs, and state food commissions had joined in branding canned foods as impure."[73] The publicity director of the Sanitary Can Company especially complained about the abusive attitude of the press toward the canning industry: "Authors have devoted miles of type to the channels of electricity, mechanical arts and allied industries. . . . Very little, in comparison to all this, has been the space devoted to one of the greatest industries in the world, and one as far-reaching in its work and mission, and this is the Canning of Food Products. . . . All that the canner asks for is fair play."[74] The Sanitary Can director believed that the press gave positive publicity to the large-scale technologies that shaped early twentieth-century American society while ignoring the everyday stuff of life, which he considered to be at least as important.[75]

The canning leaders denounced the unfair treatment of their industry. But they did not deny that some canned foods were indeed impure or produced with poor methods. The big, well-organized canners believed that standardization and the stamp of approval conveyed by governmental regulation would help foster positive public opinion of canned foods. They also hoped that regulation would force smaller canners out of business, both to reduce competition and to decrease the incidence of bad practices. Even though several large firms were coming to dominate the national stage in the first years of the twentieth century, the majority of canners still operated out of small, rural establishments.[76] Even the much-maligned press acknowledged the canners' predicament in a 1903 *New York Times* article that asserted, "Few great national industries have suffered so much from legislative mistakes as has the canning and food products' trade from the lack of a uniform national pure food law and few have gained such an unenviable reputation from the sins of the few black sheep in their fold."[77] Canners hoped that a national food law would rid the industry of these "few black sheep" and, along with them, the canning industry's "unenviable reputation."

Canners, for the most part, welcomed food safety regulation in the early years of the twentieth century because of its role in building consumer trust. They believed that a law might serve as a proxy for overcoming the opacity of the tin can. The existence of a standard federal law could help build trust because it served as a guarantee of what was in the can, upheld by a federal government that was growing in visibility and power in the early twentieth century.

A single federal law would also be easier to follow than many different state laws. Before a uniform national law came to fruition, numerous conflicting state regulations existed. Previous attempts at federal food regulation had failed; although nearly two hundred food measures had come before Congress between 1879 and 1906, only eight were signed into law.[78] Canners, too, had requested federal food laws, forwarding a petition to Congress as early as 1882. The short-lived National Association of Canned Food Packers, at its 1897 meeting, emphasized its desire for a national law that would "compel every packer to put his name on every can of goods packed by him [, which] would be of advantage to all honest packers, and against the packers of trashy goods, who have done more to injure the canned foods' trade than all other causes combined." This association proposed drawing up a report that would be the basis for a congressional bill.[79] Lawmakers met many of these early actions with a lack of interest, largely because of what they perceived as an absence of demand among their constituents.

The central figure at the federal level who spearheaded food and drug reform was Dr. Harvey W. Wiley, the chief chemist at the US Department of Agriculture from 1883 to 1912. Wiley's strong personality and convictions about the need for a national food law led to public attention and support for reform. As one canner cleverly commented of Wiley's personality, "They say down in Washington that Dr. Wiley is so smooth that he has to put sandpaper in his pajamas to keep from sliding out of bed at night." Wiley also built close relationships with canners, finding them to be ready allies in his fight for regulation. Speaking before a canning convention in 1906, Wiley praised canned goods, saying they were "the most important, economically, of the whole list of unobjectionable methods of preserving goods . . . preserv[ing] natural flavor better than any other methods."[80] Wiley and the leading canners became close allies.

A major opponent of Wiley's proposed legislation was the National Food Manufacturers' Association (NFMA). This group was composed of nearly three hundred processors who made jellies, condiments, pickles, and preserved fish—largely with methods other than canning, like the use of chemical additives. The association had formed in 1904 with the explicit purpose of developing an alternate food law that allowed preservatives like salicylic acid, benzoic acid, and borax.[81] The canners' support of Wiley and his bill stood in stark contrast to the position of the NFMA, largely because most canners eschewed preservatives and so stood to gain more than they would lose through federal food regulation. The NFMA wanted to maintain the status quo that allowed the use of preservatives, while the canners wanted to make change in ways that would benefit their burgeoning industry. The contrast between the National Association of Canned Food Packers (and later, succeeding it, the National Canners Association [NCA]) and the NFMA highlights ways that different discourses—between tradition and modernity, and between purity and artificiality—came into play. Both groups touted the ability of their preferred method of preservation, by vacuum heat versus the addition of chemicals, to rise above the limitations of nature, using the power of modern technologies. But the canners emphasized purity, while the food manufacturers celebrated artificiality. The NFMA maintained that their artificial preservatives posed less of a risk to health than "natural" bacterial contamination.

This conflict over the ability to define the pure and natural was a key theme of the age of adulteration at the turn of the twentieth century. As the majority of the American population shifted from rural to urban spaces around the turn of the twentieth century, the distance between production and consumption expanded, yielding more opportunities for contamination of the food supply. Authenticity was called into question as physical distance made it harder to build personal levels of trust. This problem extended beyond the food supply to larger cultural trends, as rural Americans who had always relied on community ties moved into unfamiliar cities with new codes of conduct. The face-to-face interactions that had previously governed trust in transactions were interrupted by several degrees of separation. Consumers were left without proper information to know what was pure or whom to trust in making that judgment.[82]

In the early twentieth century, many Americans felt that dramatic social reform was necessary to address the ills of industrialization. Women, especially white, middle-class women, were particularly active in the crusade to clean up the cities, factories, governments, and corporations. This movement stimulated the push for purity and trust in the food system, joining in support of a federal food law. Representing groups like the General Federation of Women's Clubs and the National Consumers' League, these women joined Wiley, the canners, and other groups like the National Association of State Dairy and Food Departments and the American Medical Association to push for federal regulation.[83] They took up food safety as a major point of reform, seeing industrialized food as one embodiment of a corrupt society. As a contemporary journalist put it, "Enough of [the women] had lived through the transition from home and village food-industry, to large-scale corporation food-industry, to know the taste, odor, and sight of pure products of nature; and to recognize that in . . . what they could not avoid feeding their children, there were elements new and mysterious, and therefore disquieting."[84] In this way, although canned food itself was still viewed by many as "new and mysterious, and therefore disquieting," its lack of artificial preservatives made it less worrisome than some of the even newer chemically altered products on the market.

In addition to Wiley's work and women's activism, a crucial tipping point that led to legislative change was the muckraking work of Upton Sinclair's 1906 exposé *The Jungle*. This novel, based on Sinclair's investigative work in Chicago's meatpacking districts, aroused public consciousness to the gruesome details of industrial food production.[85] Consumers joined in the call for reform along the lines of Wiley's earlier proposals. Now, given the public impetus it needed to make a move, Congress responded with the passage of the Pure Food and Drug Act of 1906 and the Federal Meat Inspection Act, both passed on June 30, 1906, and enacted on January 1, 1907.[86] The acts made it illegal for food and drug manufacturers to enter into interstate commerce any product that had been misbranded or adulterated, according to established guidelines.

These acts signaled a shift toward increased governmental intervention in protecting consumers and providing them with more information about their food supply. The early twentieth century saw the first consumer responses to a food system that had grown beyond comprehension.[87] For the first time, many foods available to Americans were packed in faraway places by companies with whom consumers did not have a direct relationship of trust. These companies might adulterate their products in various ways to increase weight, improve color, or cover up spoilage—but consumers would have little way of knowing. This is why the public began to call for scientific research and government inspection in the years leading up to the acts of 1906.

The effects of the Pure Food and Drug Act on American canners were numerous. The act required a strict branding scheme, prosecuting many products for misbranding.[88] In the case of American sardine canners, this provision had a negative effect. American canners throughout the nineteenth century had found that consumers preferred French sardines. And so, in the ironic words of one chronicler of the canning industry, American sardine canners before 1906 "cater[ed] to this demonstration of American democracy" by using French names on their can labels. But the Pure Food and Drug Act made this custom illegal, leaving American sardine canners without a market in the several years after 1906.[89] In many sectors of the canning industry, however, the law had little practical effect on cannery practices, as most canners had stayed away from adulterants and preservatives beforehand.[90]

But the major effect the act did have on the canning industry was that it stimulated the formation of the NCA, a national trade organization that would represent and support the country's industry for decades to come. Canners engaged in this broader network because of their desire to build trust in their industry, which was newly mechanized and undergoing a managerial revolution. The canning industry largely followed the mold set out by other realms of professionally managed big business. Like companies selling soap, cigarettes, textiles, and other products, successful canners focused on growth, vertical integration, and hierarchical management. The formation of a national trade organization, then, fit neatly into this model.[91]

Before the formation of the NCA in 1907 there had been numerous attempts at organizing, at both the state and the regional level, but none had the necessary staying power.[92]The first such group had gathered in Indianapolis in February 1889, bringing together canners from the Midwest and East Coast, calling themselves the National Association of Canned Food Packers. This group lasted for nearly ten years, lobbying for a pure food law, sharing information, and establishing general business rules. But by 1899, the group's energy and financial resources had dwindled, and it was dissolved. Trade historian Earl C. May suggested that the average canner of the 1890s was "too individualistic, too secretive, and not clannish enough to become part of a solid front for the growing industry."[93] There was not yet a general appreciation for what cooperation could do.

But in 1905, some prominent canners, spurred on by their dedication to pure food reform, organized the National Association of Packers of Pure Canned Goods, the immediate precursor to the NCA. The canners largely funded their own efforts and had a fairly narrow reach in terms of membership, but the work of this group, and especially of its secretary Frank Gorrell, significantly propelled the pure food law. One canner, reflecting on this organization from the vantage point of 1914, wrote, "If the National Canners Association leaves no other monument, it should be here recorded that its initial accomplishment was the active work it did in helping to create a sentiment which inspired Congress to pass this [pure food] law."[94] Public concern and push for reform drove cooperation at the highest levels of the canning industry. On the heels of the 1906 passage of the Pure Food and Drug Act, the existing canners' association reorganized and gave birth to the larger and more successful NCA in Buffalo, New York, in February 1907.

From the beginning of these attempts at trade organization the largest and most successful canners took the lead. By 1909, just about half of the country's 4,220 canning establishments were associated with the NCA, with the largest numbers concentrated in Maryland (514 member organizations), Virginia (233), Missouri (281), New York (141), Indiana (145), California (114), and Maine (103), packing a wide variety of vegetables (especially tomatoes), fruits, and some fish. By midcentury, NCA member canneries would be responsible for about 90 percent of total US canned-foods production.[95] While it is true that a rising tide often lifts all boats, so that some smaller canners indirectly profited from the formation of the NCA in 1907, it is also true that some benefits of the association required an input of money dependent on the kind of expendable income available only to the more successful canners. For example, in 1910, the NCA voted to gather $100,000 for an advertising fund. Any canners who contributed to the fund then had access to a seal that would guarantee the purity of the enclosed goods. But if a canner could not pay, his goods would likely suffer in comparison. If consumers saw one item with a purity seal and another without, the certified can would likely win out. Yet despite the dominance of larger canners, smaller and niche canners persisted throughout the twentieth century, serving rural or specialized audiences.[96]

This newly reorganized NCA became the leading voice of American canners in directing their mission after 1907. Public concern over food safety ultimately drove their interest in collaboration with federal food authorities, as canners worked to increase consumer trust in canned goods. The consolidation that the NCA embodied would come to define the industry. Two of the biggest projects of the organization in its early years, which both picked up on previous trends and helped set the industry's broader agenda, were the development of scientific research and attendant publicity campaigns, both intended to move canned goods beyond the realm of suspicion.

THE STRENGTH OF SCIENCE: THE NATIONAL CANNERS LABORATORY AND SALTS OF TIN (1910–14)

In our modern world, it is clear that food science and technology are at the heart of commercial food production. This emphasis finds its origins in the early canning industry. By the time the NCA was organized in 1907, some canners had already come to appreciate the value of scientific research. That emphasis only intensified as the NCA made bacteriological and toxicological research a centerpiece of its focus in the second decade of the twentieth century. In the period between 1910 and 1914, the NCA established a laboratory of its own, embarking on an ambitious series of research and publicity ventures to protect the industry against potential attacks. The pharmacological investigations involved in one case—concerns about soluble tin salts leaching from the can into the human body—illustrate the emphasis the canners placed on using the fruits of scientific research to protect their reputation and reassure the public. They began to combat the opacity of the unknown by using scientific knowledge to increase transparency.

Before the 1910s, early efforts at research were unsystematic and partial—taking place in a dispersed manner, with no unified trade support and with limited canner interest.[97] Beginning around 1910, however, a defined industry, united at the national level and with a centralized budget, enabled the formation of a systematic relationship between scientists and canners. Several trade groups began to work with universities to fund research for the benefit of the industry. For example, the NCA endowed a chair of chemical and bacteriological research at Johns Hopkins University in 1911, and the Illinois Canners' Association established a fellowship for bacteriological food research at the University of Illinois in 1912.[98] The canners benefited from the rise of research universities and the institutionalization of science in the early twentieth century, leading the way in bringing business and academia into closer contact and pioneering the practice of businesses funding university research.[99]

By 1913, canners built upon their university programs to establish a National Canners' Laboratory of their own in Washington, D.C. It drew on experts from the US Bureau of Chemistry to build the staff, hiring several of Harvey W. Wiley's close compatriots. The laboratory devoted itself to ascertaining the general research needs of the industry and especially to systematizing processing methods across the industry as a whole. The NCA was innovative in its establishment of a research laboratory, especially among consumer product industries. Electric and telecommunications companies, which pioneered industrial research laboratories in the United States, had opened their own laboratories only within the last decade.[100]

Alongside and connected to its scientific work, the NCA devoted itself to publicity, setting the stage for a modern food industry dependent on self-promotion. The NCA created an official Bureau of Publicity in 1909 and established a $100,000 advertising fund in 1910.[101] This bureau engaged in many forms of publicity, but an important one was the use of scientific investigation to undermine claims of poisoned canned foods as published in the popular press. The bureau investigated stories about alleged food poisoning from canned foods by requesting samples of the product and then subjecting them to laboratory analysis. When the reports turned out to be libelous, the canners pushed newspapers to publish retractions. Sometimes the bureau would hire private detectives to identify the true cause of sickness or death, if not canned food. In at least one case, the detective discovered that the actual cause of death had been, not spoiled food, but homicide! The blame for the murder had been diverted to canned goods, which served as a convenient scapegoat.[102] The Bureau of Publicity drew on the increasing cachet of scientific research, applying the fruits of new knowledge to public reassurance.

Such scientific and investigative work, of course, required significant funds. But although the leadership of the NCA understood the value of the Bureau of Publicity, individual canners across the country apparently did not. The NCA president Walter Sears wrote in September of 1910, "We have appealed to the canners from every standpoint possible, but it seems hard to enlist their financial support." He continued that it was "very humiliating to admit the fact that the allied associations, consisting of Supplies and Machinery men and Brokers, have furnished about as much money for this purpose as the canners."[103] Some canners still resisted the cooperative effort being built by the NCA at the national level, especially when it required them to spend money. Again, small canners were less likely to have additional funds to support the national association or to feel that their local markets were as dependent on nationwide sentiment.

One case study that especially highlights the worries of the NCA around 1910, relative to scientific research and publicity, is the "salts of tin" case. The federal government and some consumers became concerned about compounds like tin chloride—salts of tin—that were formed when tin from cans reacted with elements like chlorine in the can's contents. Canning leaders responded by undertaking extensive efforts at containment and research to clear their products of blame. In fact, NCA secretary Frank Gorrell and director of research W. D. Bigelow pursued rigorous scientific investigation into salts of tin long after public attention to the issue had subsided. The canners' devotion to research as a tool of exoneration underscores the increasing value of laboratory investigation for achieving consumer confidence.

In May 1910, England's leading medical journal the *Lancet* reprinted a report by Dr. Otto Hehner, a prominent British medical figure, warning the public against eating acidic canned foods because of the fear of "salts of tin." These salts of tin were compounds that entered the human body through the consumption of canned food, supposedly causing health problems. When this article came to the attention of the NCA secretary Frank Gorrell, he immediately wrote Hehner a letter denouncing his claims: "These attacks seems so very unnecessary, for the public mind now is anyway aroused to the very highest pitch on food dangers that really exist. . . . [You] prejudice their minds on imaginary ills that will grow out of the use of canned foods on account of the presence of tin, when science and experience are both against your position." Subsequent testing by Hehner revealed that a selection of cans sent by Gorrell had only trace amounts of salts of tin, but Hehner continued to push the industry toward what he considered safer practices.[104]

Hehner's concern was not unique. Harvey W. Wiley's US Bureau of Chemistry had been in an open dialogue with canners for a number of years, encouraging them to improve the quality of their tin plate in order to prevent corrosion. By mid-1910, Wiley sought to put out a bulletin warning the public of the dangers of tin in canned foods after a case of sardines was found to contain unacceptably high levels of salts of tin.[105] But the NCA intervened, convincing Wiley's Board of Food and Drug Inspection to issue not a public statement but instead the trade-focused Food Inspection Decision No. 126, creating a legal limit for quantities of salts of tin to three hundred milligrams per kilogram.[106] This was a strategic move for the canners. Subjecting themselves to further regulation proved that theirs was a compliant industry, and it allowed them both to protect the industry's public image and to benefit from the scientific and regulatory power of the federal government. Around the same time, the canners also launched research ventures to determine what kinds of foods and linings led to the highest rates of leaching.[107]

After this initial attention, however, the issue of salts of tin receded into the background—not a single case was ever prosecuted under Inspection Decision No. 126.[108] W. D. Bigelow wrote that since 1913 the Bureau of Chemistry "has regarded F.I.D. No. 126 [on salts of tin] as dead. It has not annulled it, however, and I think the reason for that is that the Bureau of Chemistry, like other Government Bureaus, hesitates to annul a ruling which was made for the protection of the people for fear it may be charged with . . . acting in the interest of manufacturers of foods."[109] Bigelow suggested that the federal government and the canners both used regulation—even if unenforced—as insurance against public reproach.

Despite this lack of external attention from at least 1913 on, the canners continued to pursue research into the toxicity of tin for more than a decade. They wanted to find whatever scientific evidence was necessary to defend their industry from any future possible attacks, even without the impetus of public attention. Throughout the late teens and twenties, even as canners carried out their own in-house research, they corresponded with colleagues across the country to find a co-researcher from an elite university who had no taint of commercialism.[110] By 1929, the NCA, the federal government, and Columbia University scientists released a joint statement attesting to the safety of tin, which finally relieved the canning leaders of the burden of proving that the ingestion of salts of tin was not injurious to health.[111] This story indicates just how proactive the canning industry was in pursuing scientific research in a time of industry vulnerability, beginning around 1910. Scientific evidence was a powerful part of the canners' tool kit in showing their industry's improvement, a part of the larger arsenal used to build consumer trust.

By 1914, scientific research had come to be a central part of the canning industry, an emphasis that would only deepen in the decades to come. One chronicler wrote in that year of the industry's familiarity and resonance with some of the great scientific minds of the time: "Not that all canners are scientists, but the industry as a whole has adopted the teachings of Tyndall, Lister, and Pasteur, whose discoveries showed that sterilization by heat was the only effective germ destroyer."[112] The opening of the National Canners' Laboratory in 1913 especially signaled the industry's desire to standardize along scientific lines. The laboratory offered fixed guidelines to all American canners, assisting them in producing uniform products that had been processed and packed according to certain quality standards, as established by the national canning scientists. Dr. C. L. Alsberg, Wiley's successor as chief of the US Bureau of Chemistry, saw the opening of the laboratory as a marker of the success of the canning industry, writing, "This association [the NCA] is remarkable above all others in the United States because it has taken the first steps in which must ultimately be a pretty general practice in this country . . . the establishment of a research laboratory to solve the problems with which your members are confronted."[113] Scientific research came together with technological innovation, governmental efficiency, and canning industry organization as key tools in the canners' efforts to appeal to their imagined consumers.

. . .

When Wisconsin infantryman David Coon wrote his family a letter on the back of a Borden's Condensed Milk label in 1864, he may not have known that he was helping to build an industry by introducing his wife and children to a new way of eating. But this and many other varieties of exposure combined in the coming years to build a market for a new processed-food industry in America (figure 3). By 1914, when considering the changes in the industry since 1841, leading canner Hugh S. Orem could exclaim, "What great gulfs of time separate then and now!"[114] He had observed the dramatic shift in the market for canned food from "men on the move" to some consumers in their homes. He had seen the technological improvements in the industry and the incorporation of bacteriological and toxicological research. He had also been part of the federal government's new involvement in industry and the passage of the pure food law. All of these changes made the technology of canning unrecognizable from its origins in Nicolas Appert's workshop in 1795 and paved the way for what would become an organized and powerful industry. However, even with the changes and Orem's optimistic industry perspective, it is important to remember that canners' products were only beginning to enter the consumer marketplace—many cans continued to be expensive, produced by small canneries reliant on hand labor, and unreliable in their taste and purity.

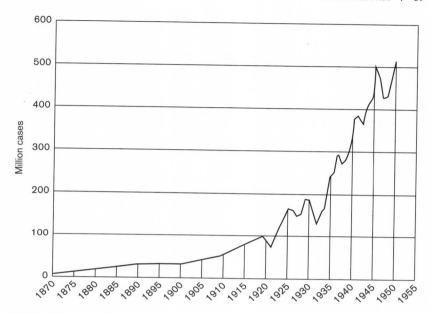

FIGURE 3. Growth of the pack of canned fruits and vegetables (number of cases), 1870–1950. Although the annual pack was increasing between 1870 and 1915, that was just the beginning. The real growth came after 1915, with the most dramatic growth after the 1930s. (Courtesy of the Grocery Manufacturers Association.)

By the early twentieth century, canning technologies, through a cascade effect, came to reshape labor relations, consumer activism, government regulation, and scientific research. As more consumers became exposed to canned goods, however, concerns began to emerge about adulteration, fueled by a press prone to sensationalized reporting. Canners called for regulation, hoping that a pure food law would validate their products in the eyes of consumers. In the wake of the Pure Food and Drug Act of 1906, canners organized at the national level, creating in 1907 the NCA, which supported linked agendas of scientific research and publicity. By 1914, canners endowed chairs of research at prestigious universities, created a National Canners Laboratory, and combated fears around salts of tin with a dedicated political and scientific program that minimized consumer alarm. Canned food was now much more than a mundane consumer good. It was the center point around which new industrial, consumer, and scientific relations pivoted.

By 1914, the canning industry saw itself as putting forth a united front that signaled patriotism and progress throughout the land, based on the power of science and technology. A leading milk canner claimed, "Evaporated and condensed milk will rapidly supplant the use of fresh milk when its purity, uniform quality, food value and ready supply become generally known to the consuming public."[115] This optimistic tone was characteristic of canner rhetoric in this time of expansion, regardless of the reality that canners still faced limited markets. Canned food was pictured as a symbol of progress, epitomized by the ideal cannery, which had a "scientific, hygienic manager in its process room, and a factory filled with iron slaves shining like silver."[116] Comments like these display not only the industry's desire to emphasize canners' business acumen and innovation, but also their ease in capturing progress through an image of enslaved labor, laden with racial connotations in an era of Jim Crow segregation. The industry had distinct racial and class dimensions, with its imagined consumers—typically white, middle-class women—and its real laborers—working-class women and men, from a variety of racial backgrounds.[117] The canners' image of who would benefit from their industry's progress and modernity included some people but not others.

But the confident and celebratory tone of these canners was at least partly a conceit and a defense mechanism, as canners of 1914 were not prepared to rest on their laurels just yet. Even as they celebrated their success with grand claims, canners knew that significant consumer skepticism remained and that they had to work to address remaining problems in the canning industry in order to promote trust and consumption. In the second and third decades of the twentieth century, American canners began to focus their attention on the foundation of the canning industry—the problems of agriculture.

2

Growing a Better Pea

Canners, Farmers, and Agricultural Scientists
in the 1910s and 1920s

In the 1939 film *Pick of the Pod,* a little girl with two pigtail braids and a crisp blue dress examines a bowl of canned peas with suspicion. She asks, "Daddy, did you have peas like this when you were little?" Her father, in a three-piece suit and tie, responds, "Yes, Lynn, we had peas that tasted just like these, only not as often as you do . . . [because] we had to wait until they were in season. I used to go out in the garden and pick them fresh for dinner." This answer doesn't fully satisfy little Lynn's curiosity and she follows up with "Daddy, how do peas grow? . . . I mean, how do they get in the can?"

Lynn's question is soon answered, when the children retire to the living room with their father (while their mother presumably stays in the kitchen to clean up) and he opens a big book to a photograph of a farm, shot from above. As he lights his black pipe, Lynn's father begins to reminisce, connecting his childhood memories to the story of technological wonder he is about to share: "You know, when I was a boy, we had a small vegetable garden, not far from the kitchen door. When peas were in season, Mother . . . and your Aunt Carrie used to shell them by hand. But nowadays think how much easier it is. Why, we can have fresh peas any day of the year, grown especially for canning on great farms like this." The camera then slowly zooms into the photograph they are looking at and the scene transitions to the farm itself. The father's narration gives way to a voice-over that goes on to describe the whole process of canning peas in what amounts to a very compelling advertisement for the California Packing Corporation.[1]

It is significant that the father's explanation of canned peas begins on the farm. When consumers see a tin can of peas with a bright label on a grocery store shelf, they may not immediately think of those peas as agricultural products, but, of course, canned vegetables—like all vegetables—start their stories in the ground. They are fundamentally tied to seed and soil. To understand the canning industry as a whole, we must first understand the agricultural story at its foundation. And to understand how canners built trust in their products, we must look to agricultural science. Conversely, a study of agriculture in the United States in the early twentieth century would be incomplete without an understanding of the food-processing industry. By 1938, nearly 40 percent of American farmers (about 300,000 of some 750,000) grew vegetables for canning, and the total acreage of vegetables grown for the general market was almost equivalent to that of vegetables grown for canning.[2]

Although Lynn's father equated his childhood garden peas with the peas from the can, the canned peas were significantly different biological products. *Pick of the Pod* shows some of the scientific work carried out on the pea fields but only hints at the vast operations that underlay the path of canned peas from farm to consumer. Lynn's family was able to buy these peas at an affordable price, at any time of year, only because of an expansive system of programs and relationships that transformed the pea over the first three decades of the twentieth century. And they likely desired and trusted those peas only because of the foundation of reliability the canners had built through scientific authority in previous decades, even if that scientific research remained invisible beneath the opaque tin can. This chapter explores how canners, farmers, and agricultural scientists worked together in the first decades of the twentieth century to create a pea that both conformed to the needs of the industry and attempted to appeal to consumers as something reminiscent of Mother's garden.

The desire to win the confidence of abstract consumers, consolidated into one single market force, drove many of the canners' agricultural concerns. Canners hoped that by making their food taste better they could overcome consumer fears. One canner, in a 1917 address, described how a housewife's pleasure with one can of food would lead her to tell "her friends how delicious a certain brand of Canned Foods were" but added that if she were displeased she might decide that all canned foods were unsatisfactory. "Multiply this one housewife by thousands and tens of thousands," he concluded, "and you approach the real condition, and certainly appreciate the extreme importance of quality." The secret to quality, he asserted, was this: "The Canners must start with good fruits or vegetables, and here is where the canner and the farmer can cooperate."[3]

This was the key to building a market and getting consumers to trust canned foods: canners needed to cooperate with farmers as they together worked toward quality in growing raw crops. One of the primary ways to improve the raw produce was through agricultural research. This chapter narrows in on how canners addressed these production needs by enlisting farmers and researchers to grow a pea better suited to industrial production—though a similar story could be similarly told about a range of other products, from tomatoes to corn. Peas were one of the more frequently canned vegetables in this era. Before 1950, they were the only vegetable that consumers ate more in their canned form than their fresh form.[4] Their short growing season and delicate flavor meant that they were available fresh for only a limited period of time each year. Canning extended the life of peas. The vegetable's genetic makeup also lent itself to laboratory manipulation. This meant that scientific research enabled American consumers to have a big bowl of peas, butter melting atop, as a side dish not just in the spring but throughout the year. Peas were also used in cream-based sauces to make dishes like chicken pot pie, were blended in green pea soups, and were served with carrots.[5]

The canners' monolithic vision of the consumer remained in the background throughout their work. The almost exclusively male canners kept the "housewife" in mind as they negotiated contracts with farmers, as they built relationships with agricultural research stations, and as they worked with breeders to develop a better canned pea. These processes took place behind the scenes but indirectly seeped into grocery stores and kitchens. All of these players—the farmers, the breeders, the canners, the consumers—were links in a chain of food production. They were intertwined and often interdependent; the actions of one shaped the success of the others.

This discussion also highlights the food processor as an actor in agricultural change, along with the more commonly considered farmer and experiment station scientist. Canners' desires drove agricultural research and helped develop a new market for farmers' crops. Canners strove for agricultural improvement and looked to two different groups to find it: the farmers who grew crops for the cannery and the scientists who could help alleviate entrenched problems. Canners had many aspirations

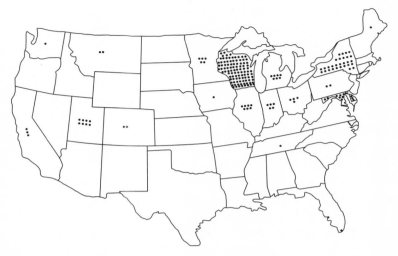

FIGURE 4. Wisconsin was, by far, the leader in canning peas, as shown in this 1923 map. Each dot represents the production of approximately 100,000 cases of peas. (Courtesy of the Grocery Manufacturers Association.)

toward their end of creating products consumers could have faith in: they wanted to make their business more profitable; they wanted to breed a pea that had higher yields and that more easily conformed to the increasingly mechanized factory environment; they wanted to eradicate pests like the pea aphid and diseases like the fungal pea blight; and they wanted to develop contracts with farmers that would leave both partners' needs met. All of these desires reshaped the agricultural landscape of the 1910s and 1920s.

Although many of the changes that shaped canning agriculture played out at the national and even international level, much of this particular story revolves around the state of Wisconsin and its most important canned product, peas (figure 4). Wisconsin was a major player in the canning industry and the leading producer of canned peas, had one of the most successful agricultural experiment stations in the nation, and was a leader in agricultural genetics.[6] Under the leadership of agricultural experiment station scientist Ernest J. Delwiche, Wisconsin became one of the first states to carry out advanced breeding work, as early as 1912. Narrowing in here helps us understand how the story of canning agriculture played out in a specific context.

Studying canning agriculture offers insight into the relationships among science, government, and industry in the early twentieth century.

Many scholars have written about the tendency of agricultural colleges to cater to the needs of agribusiness and the expanding role of industry in the agricultural sector.[7] But these studies have largely focused on how agricultural research tended to help larger, more capitalized farmers at the expense of small-scale family farms. Less attention has been paid to the ways in which land-grant colleges modified their agendas to meet the needs of food-processing businesses, in addition to those of industrializing farmers.[8] This chapter shows that pea canners were among the earliest businesses to provide money to agricultural colleges to sponsor research into the particular needs of their industry, as early as the 1910s. This link between industry and science only strengthened with time.

This work also shows the importance of biological technologies in agriculture, even before the introduction of hybrid corn in 1929.[9] Canners began to focus on insects, diseases, and plant breeding in order to improve their industry, starting as early as 1911. Canners, especially in Wisconsin, turned to plant breeding to create a better pea for their industry. Further, the story of one scientist we'll meet, E. J. Delwiche, attests to the importance of Mendelian genetics in breeding for the canning industry as early as 1908, even before Mendelism became the dominant model used by American plant and animal breeders.[10]

By examining how consumers' desires for high-quality, low-priced canned foods encouraged canners to seek improvement through agricultural research, we also see how consumer needs drove agricultural change, linking production and consumption.[11] Improvement in raw crops made canned food more trustworthy and figuratively transparent, even as the underlying production processes became more complex and rooted in scientific methods that the average consumer did not understand. Canners improved their agricultural foundation to win over consumers between 1900 and 1925, in the process altering farming patterns and agricultural knowledge, forever changing industrial food production in America.

FORGING ALLIANCES, 1900–1914

In 1911, the Wisconsin College of Agriculture received its first industrial fellowship, a category of funds furnished by a company for research into a particular area of agricultural science. After this initial fund, the college would go on to receive fellowship funds from nearly one hundred companies over the next thirty years, including such big names as the Campbell Soup Company, Dow Chemical, General Foods, and Pfizer. But the very first fellowship that started it all was funded by the

Wisconsin Pea Packers Association, a consortium of those who canned peas in the state.[12] The pea packers recognized the value of agricultural research to their canning enterprise and gathered funds from their ranks in order to direct the knowledge and resources of their state's primary research institution. The 1911 pea canners' fellowship followed from developments in both the Wisconsin canning industry and the state's agricultural infrastructure over the previous decades. These developments—the establishment of the college of agriculture, the rise of the pea-canning industry in Wisconsin, the relationships canners built with both farmers and agricultural scientists, and early pea-breeding work—fueled what is known as the Golden Age of Agriculture, a period of general agricultural prosperity that peaked in the 1910s.[13] During this period, state agricultural institutions began to direct their attention toward helping not only state farmers but also industries related to agriculture, like the canning industry.

Before the pea canners started the trend of sponsoring specific lines of research in 1911, the Wisconsin College of Agriculture and its experiment station typically focused on addressing the problems of farmers, who were ostensibly its primary constituents. When the college of agriculture was established in 1889, it expanded upon a series of agricultural initiatives already in place at its home institution, the University of Wisconsin, which had established an agricultural experiment station in 1883 and farmers' short courses in 1885.[14] By promoting agricultural education, the United States could ensure that agriculture, "the foundation of all present and future prosperity," would flourish.[15]

Even as the university was developing its agricultural institutions, economic and political currents among American farmers created resistance to scientific interference. In the years after the Civil War, improved technologies and an expanding land base from western settlement led to surplus production. Because consumer demand did not keep up with production, crop prices sank, leaving farmers struggling financially. To voice their frustration, many farmers banded together, calling for change that would boost their economic and political positions. They formed agrarian protest organizations like the National Grange in the 1870s and the Farmers' Alliance in the 1880s, which helped farmers develop cooperative schemes for purchasing and marketing. These organizations, and the larger Populist movement of which they were a part, had an antielitist bent, encouraging farmers to work together to build their own economic base rather than relying on outsiders or middlemen.[16] Ironically, at the same time that the Hatch Act established agricultural experiment stations throughout the country, the very men whom the stations had been directed to serve were turning toward the strength of their rural peers and away from the professional class that ran the stations. As Harry Luman Russell, director of the Wisconsin College of Agriculture in the early twentieth century, described the scene of the 1880s: "The practical farmer was very skeptical as to what science could do to aid him in his work. The early station leaders had an untried field before them, and a critical public with which to deal."[17]

Agricultural scientists worried about farmers' skepticism. They believed that farmers would benefit from research if they only gave it a chance. What's more, the scientists themselves benefited from collaboration, often using data from the farmers' fields in their own work. They hoped for a mutualistic relationship, in which the scientists' experimental knowledge and the farmers' practical knowledge could come together in the discovery and promotion of best practices.[18] The Wisconsin station, while also struggling to engage farmers, quickly became one of the nation's most productive experiment stations, after its founding in 1883 under the leadership of W. A. Henry.[19] Around 1886, the Wisconsin College of Agriculture began a series of initiatives: an agricultural short course that brought state farmers to Madison to engage with the experiments of the university, and traveling Farmers Institutes, which, long before the federal establishment of extension work in 1914, took the resources of the experiment station to the far corners of the state. One historian wrote of the agricultural short course that it had "the effect of bringing the scientists out of their laboratories to talk to farmers under circumstances that permitted the farmers to talk back. They did. The exchange was beneficial to all concerned."[20]

By 1890, the economic conditions that had led to agrarian protest in earlier decades were beginning to improve. Farm prices began to stabilize, as western settlement and the opening of new lands slowed and as urbanization expanded domestic markets.[21] With the increase in farm prices, the value of farmland dramatically increased, growing between 200 and 300 percent from 1900 to 1910.[22] Many well-established farmers took advantage of this increase in value, leading to some stratification among different classes of farmers. These wealthier farmers, along with other businessmen who benefited from agricultural prosperity, began to more clearly see the value of investing in experiment station research. As historian Charles Rosenberg has written about agricultural science around 1906: "Educated and more highly capitalized farmers, editors of farm and rural papers, country bankers, insurance agents, merchants and implement dealers [made] up the visible agricultural consensus."[23] To Rosenberg's list we might add food processors, like the Wisconsin pea canners, who appealed to their local college in 1911 to secure aid in researching the problems of canning agriculture.

The stations, in turn, sought the cooperation of these powerful men for their own reasons. Agricultural scientists, by the turn of the twentieth century, had become part of a growing profession, which set them apart from the largely self-taught independent farmers. As historian David Danbom has argued, station scientists sought to boost their professional identity by serving the needs of well-connected community members, rather than just being "the servant of hicks and bumpkins."[24] Because the stations were often funded by state legislatures, it was also politically expedient for stations to tend to the needs of powerful business and agricultural men, in order to garner the support of influential backers.[25] Many of the fruits of station research, from the late nineteenth century on, led to economic gain for large producers and industry—from Stephen M. Babcock's butterfat test profiting the Wisconsin dairy industry in the 1880s to Illinois hybrid corn research fostering farmer dependence on seed companies beginning in the 1930s.[26]

In many cases, however, the corporate leanings of experiment stations were not blatant or fully intentional. In the case of Wisconsin, the station's attention to the canning industry began as an attempt to help bolster farmers as the state went through a period of agricultural transition. Around 1900, the major forms of agricultural production in the state were shifting away from wheat and toward dairy and more intensive crops like peas. The Wisconsin agricultural experiment station directed much of its attention toward the problems of these new products. Because the new pea crop soon assumed center stage among Wisconsin's canning industry, the state's agricultural scientists came to have a close relationship with the pea canners and to see them as important constituents. They believed that helping the pea canners wouldn't just help the canning industry but would benefit the health of the state as a whole.[27]

When the pea packers funded their industrial fellowship in 1911, they were part of a burgeoning pea-canning industry that had begun to grow only in the last fifteen years, in part because of the rise of the dairy industry. Before around 1890, Wisconsin was one of the breadbaskets of the country, growing one-sixth of the country's wheat. But as wheat taxed the state's soil fertility, wheat agriculture declined and some prominent farmers urged their peers to turn to dairying. In this shift from wheat to dairy, many farmers were more flexible, as they were already changing their previous practices. They were open to other ventures in this moment of transition. Many turned to the cultivation of vegetables, and peas especially. Peas worked well alongside dairying because they made good forage crops for cows and because peas could be grown during just one season along with dairy production the rest of the year.[28]

Peas grew especially well in the Wisconsin environment because of the state's high latitude, cool nights, moist clay soils, and proximity to lakes. Immigrants to Wisconsin from Germany and the Netherlands had been growing peas in their own gardens for many years, sharing the knowledge that the state's lakeshore farmland lent itself to the cultivation of this vegetable.[29] Peas were grown for a number of uses in the early years: forage, seeds, drying, and canning. Peas grown for drying, often known as soup peas, were a more profitable cash crop than wheat, offering twice the price per bushel.[30] The first pea canner in Wisconsin, Albert Landreth, came to the state in the late 1870s in order to grow seed peas for a Pennsylvania seed company, knowing that pea growing was already well established in Wisconsin for environmental and cultural reasons. In 1883, Landreth began to experiment with canning his fresh seed peas, and by 1887 he had built his first commercial canning plant.[31]

Small Wisconsin towns soon found that canneries offered significant employment opportunities, making them desirable additions to local economies. To give a profile of laborers in the canning industry as a whole in 1914, 51.8 percent of wage earners were female, 4 percent were children under sixteen, and 97 percent of proprietors and officials were male.[32] As canneries slowly began popping up across the state, one small Wisconsin newspaper wrote in 1898, "The canning works have been of real benefit to the town in many ways without question. The amount paid out for help alone is no small sum and the best of it is, it has been paid out to the people who most needed it and has been a help to them more than is generally understood."[33] Many other newspapers echoed this sentiment. The money paid to townspeople also infused the local economy through their purchases, benefiting merchants. Canneries also paid farmers to help grow vegetables for canning or for the use of their land through leasing arrangements. And because there was such hope for the development of the canned-pea market, many city boosters sought to attract canning operations to their towns in order to take advantage of future markets. By 1900, there were twenty plants in operation in the state of Wisconsin, up from just two six years earlier, in 1894.[34]

Growing and canning peas, however, had its risks. From the farm to the cart to the factory, every step in the production of peas was "exceptionally hazardous."[35] Peas in the ground were particularly susceptible to disease and to adverse weather—shriveling up when it was dry or growing moldy when wet. Then, in transporting the peas from the farm to the cannery, it was crucial to work quickly and process the peas immediately upon their arrival. George P. Hambrecht, chairman of the Industrial Commission of Wisconsin, noted peas' exceptional vulnerability to spoilage: "There is a very limited time in which to get [peas into cans] because of the danger of mold after the peas reach the cannery. That condition does not apply to other vegetables."[36] Finally, in processing the peas, precision was crucial to preserve the particular delicate texture and flavor of the canned product. Many canners believed that consumers particularly sought this "fresh" quality of peas and that it therefore had to be protected by careful management.[37]

This vulnerability made pea canners among the first to invest in canning-crop research. Although after World War I it became common practice for canners to value agricultural research, Wisconsin pea canners were ahead of the curve with their prewar investigations. These investigations were carried out primarily between the Wisconsin College of Agriculture and several prominent canning companies. But even before this relationship was formalized with the 1911 industrial fellowship from the Wisconsin Pea Packers Association, both the university and individual canners were engaging in early forms of research. One canning company in Manitowoc, Wisconsin, had opened its own experiment station as early as 1900 to investigate problems related to its business.[38] And the university began its own canning-crop research in the first decade of the twentieth century, with Professor R. A. Moore presenting a paper entitled "Possibility of Improving Choice Varieties of Canning Peas by Breeding" at a 1909 canners' convention.[39] This built on an even earlier instance of collaboration, in 1894, when the college of agriculture sent bacteriologist Harry L. Russell to help pioneer canner Albert Landreth with repeated problems of heavy spoilage in his pea pack, as described in the previous chapter. The 1894 case was the first time that canners anywhere in the United States had made use of this new science of bacteriology, setting the precedent for future laboratory research.[40] A Wisconsin canner, reflecting on the first years of twentieth century, observed that several departments in the college of agriculture "had been going along in their quiet way for years, receiving little or no encouragement from the canning industry as a whole, but doing their best to solve our problems as they saw them and even anticipating our future problems."[41]

In 1911, though, the pea canners decided they had a big enough problem on their hands that they needed to more formally sponsor the college's research. They suffered from pea blight, a form of fungus that impaired the production of peas by severely limiting yield. But when the canners appealed to the college they found that the station's general budget for the year had already been allocated. The pea packers decided to sponsor a separate fund to allow the station to undertake pea blight research.[42] This was the first instance of an industrial group providing funds for targeted research at the University of Wisconsin's College of Agriculture. This money, $1,000 a year, allowed the college to hire a specialist, R. E. Vaughan, to investigate the problem of pea diseases.[43]

These pea blight investigations would continue for decades to come, with attention from the USDA in the later years, but the early findings revealed several root causes of the problem. The primary concern was that any disease that did develop, even marginally, in one year would be transferred and intensified the next year. The practice of feeding vines and cannery refuse to livestock, and then spreading their manure on the fields as fertilizer, furthered the blight problem, as the disease would be spread from field to animal and back. The underlying issue was the basic production method of company-grown crops.[44] Because nearly all early Wisconsin pea canneries—from the industry's establishment in 1887 through about 1912—grew their pea crops on the same land year after year, the blight was reintroduced each year. Canners had only so much land for crop production, which meant they had no way of rotating crops in order to break the cycle of fungal growth.[45]

The identification of these problems led to a number of immediate solutions. First, canners began to treat pea vines and other cannery waste before using them in feeding operations. This process of curing green material in airtight conditions in a storage tower, or silo, helped the vines undergo a process of fermentation and decomposition, thereby killing the blight fungal parasite.[46] But even more importantly, the pea-canning industry underwent a fundamental transition in how it produced crops, transitioning from a company-grown to a contracting arrangement, in which canners outsourced the cultivation of peas to area farmers, who had more land and could therefore rotate their pea crops every year, preventing the annual recurrence of blight. By 1915, on the advice of the experiment station, nearly all canners had abandoned the intensive growth of peas on company land. Even under the new contracting system, canners would send field agents out to the farmers' fields to oversee crop production. At the first sign of pea blight, the field agent would recommend that the farmer abandon pea cultivation on infested fields for a few cycles, eliminating the risk of recurrence. This new practice largely eliminated the problem of pea blight, allowing the canning industry to grow tremendously in the decade that followed.[47] This new system also led to increased interactions between Wisconsin canners and farmers.

A final, longer-term solution to the problem of fungal growth that many canners and agricultural scientists pursued after 1911 was the development of blight-resistant pea varieties. This work was one line of a more general breeding program that began around 1908 under the direction of E. J. Delwiche at the Ashland branch experiment station in northern Wisconsin. In 1903, after a rural upbringing and an early career as a schoolteacher, Delwiche made the 160-mile trek from his home in Door County to Madison, traveling by bicycle, in order to engage in agricultural studies. Upon graduating from the college of agriculture, Delwiche was appointed the superintendent of the northern agricultural experiment substation in 1906.[48] In this capacity, he directed all the scientific work of the stations and carried out extension projects with the farmers of northern Wisconsin. Although his breeding work made him important to the pea-canning industry, it was his extension work that endeared him to the farmers of the state, thereby improving the farmers' esteem for the larger system of agricultural education and research. Because Delwiche was working in the northern part of the state, which was former forest land, farmers were new to the game and were more receptive to the help that the university extension work could offer. As one chronicler of Delwiche's career wrote, "Every farmer consider[ed] E. J. his personal friend. . . . His campus was the entire state. His laboratories were the Branch Experiment Stations, the demonstration plots, and privately owned farms on every soil type and in every county of Northern Wisconsin."[49]

Around 1908, Delwiche began to explore pea plant breeding "as an avocation, so to speak, something quite outside the prescribed line of work."[50] This division between extension and research was quite common within colleges of agriculture, as the former had to meet the practical needs of state farmers, while the latter pursued more theoretical science.[51] When he began his experiments, there were no true canning varieties of peas; canners largely used market-garden types, especially the popular Alaska variety, which had been introduced around 1880. However, because market gardeners and canners desired different characteristics for their different purposes, distinct varieties were needed. So

Delwiche set out to improve old strains and to breed new ones, for the benefit of the pea-canning industry and the larger economy of the state of Wisconsin.

In a 1911 project report to the director of the Wisconsin Experiment Station, Delwiche wrote, "Approximately one hundred crosses of different varieties have been made. Some rather striking results were apparent . . . when taken from the scientific standpoint (Mendel's Law)." By this, he likely meant that by observing the similarity in characteristics between parent and offspring plants he was able to notice Mendelian patterns of inheritance. Later, when reflecting on this early work, Delwiche gushed, "It was a great thrill to see exemplified with peas, results which had been obtained by Gregor Mendel—and to visualize the possibilities for improving one of our leading food crops."[52] Clearly, the Wisconsin breeder felt indebted toward his predecessor, the Austrian breeder Gregor Mendel, who had laid the foundation for the science of genetics through his early experiments with pea plants around 1860. Mendel's work, though first published in 1865, came to the attention of scientists and breeders around 1900. This rediscovery led to what some have called "the marketing of Mendelism," as scientists made grand claims about the promises of Mendelism to reshape plant- and animal-breeding programs.[53] Delwiche's thrill at "visualizing the possibilities" of Mendel's Law was in keeping with these grand claims.

Despite the initial excitement over Mendelism in the United States, several historians of biology have argued that the hype was not justified. Many farmers had been successfully breeding for decades without the need for the theoretical underpinnings provided by Mendel's work. Practical breeders found little of use in the new scientific theory. Historian of biology Paolo Palladino has further argued not only that most farmers were not helped by Mendelian science but that they may have in fact been held back by it, as American academic plant breeders used Mendelism as a tool for professionalization and "greater social prominence and power" relative to farmers. By laying claim to the esoteric knowledge conveyed by Mendelism, scientists created a line between "professionals" who engaged with Mendelian genetics, and the "amateurs"—farmers and practical breeders—who did not.[54]

In Delwiche's case, whether or not he saw Mendelism as a tool for professionalization, his primary engagement with Mendelian theory was certainly based in utility. He attributed his breeding success to the theory, writing in 1926: "Because of a knowledge of Mendel's laws of inheritance, and their proper utilization in the practice of breeding, the possibility of breeding for an ideal was given a definite basis and much time was saved in the subsequent work necessary to the production of a fixed type."[55] This knowledge came from intensive study. His biographer wrote, "E. J. was always a student of genetics. He . . . read every text available on the subject. He was a member of the American Genetic Association, and was a regular reader of its publications. The science of genetics was the basis of all his plant breeding work, so naturally he became an authority on the subject as pertaining to farm crops."[56] Delwiche's education in the methods and theories of Mendelian genetics laid the foundation for his work.

Delwiche's focus on peas in his breeding work was motivated both by his Wisconsin setting where pea farmers and canners were plentiful and by the nature of the pea plant. Peas could be easily manipulated by genetic breeding. Garden peas were not only the subject of Gregor Mendel's historic experiments but also the first crop to be systematically bred for the development of new varieties. There were several reasons for this: many stable forms of the pea were in existence, pea characteristics seemed to separate along individual lines of inheritance, and the pea plant was typically self-fertilized and therefore produced purebred lines.[57] All of these qualities encouraged early canners to seek breeding programs that would remake the pea to fit the vision of the industry.

The development of the canning industry and associated breeding programs led to many fundamental changes in the nature of the pea plant, in response to both production and consumption needs. The early varieties of garden peas matured incrementally, over a long growing season—a quality that suited hand-picking, since human labor could handle only so many peas at any one time. But with the advent of mechanical technologies in the late nineteenth century—viners that removed whole vines all at once, podders that processed vines in order to break open pods and release the fragile peas en masse—the qualities of the primitive garden pea were no longer suitable. Canners desired peas that matured all at once, so that the vines from a whole field could be cut at the same time. Canners also preferred peas with plentiful yields, with straight stems that could be easily cut by viners, with large pods that were easier to handle with machinery, and with pods that would easily crack open between the cannery beaters. Many garden varieties, however, produced small pods on zigzag stems, which suited the smaller-scale production of market gardening but not cannery needs.[58]

Another crucial need that emerged with the development of pea varieties for canning was resistance to both pests and fungal blight.

Researchers began breeding varieties that would be less susceptible to injury from common enemies, like the pea aphid insect and the *Fusarium* wilt fungus. Wisconsin scientists were at the lead of this kind of work, as with Delwiche's work on finding varieties resistant to pea blight after 1911.[59] Of course, producers of peas for the fresh market were also interested in pest resistance, but because their crops were typically farmed on such a smaller scale and were more diversified they were less invested in finding a solution to pest problems.

In addition to meeting production needs, breeders began to develop pea varieties that would meet the needs of consumers, on whose ultimate approval the success of the industry rested. The gold standard in canning peas was the taste and appearance of "freshness." Canners wanted to get as close to that taste of hand-shelled peas from the garden as they could. Of course, consumers weren't easily fooled. One author wrote, "Instead of regretting that canned peas do not taste like those fresh from the garden (incomparable ones!) let us be glad that they taste as good as they do."[60] Even as consumers resisted the suggestion of equivalence, canners still turned to scientific research to produce canned food that tasted good and at least looked more like the fresh version. This was a significant shift in the history of American food. Canners invested in agricultural science and the development of new technologies to meet consumer demand for packaged food that tasted less processed.[61]

Consumers cared about the color of their peas. Within the fresh market for peas, by around the 1910s, consumers began to prefer dark-green pods and seeds, believing that a lighter color indicated that the vegetable was over-ripe or stale. In canned peas, however, perhaps because customers knew that the peas had been cooked, light-green pods and seeds continued to dominate and were therefore selected for in breeding operations.[62] Color was important not only for the canned peas themselves but for the liquid in which they were suspended. Consumers preferred a liquid that was as clear as possible, since they associated any murkiness with contamination. Some pea plants, though, had purple blossoms, which led to a colored seed coat "and the tendency to discolor the liquor in the can." To combat this, breeders worked to eradicate all peas with purple blossoms, selecting for lighter-colored blossoms.[63]

The different consumer markets for which fresh and canned peas were intended also shaped their changing character. Most fresh peas were sold in markets and eaten in homes, while some canned peas, in addition to being eaten primarily by regular consumers in their homes, were sold through brokers and merchandisers and ended up in institutional settings, like restaurants, cafeterias, and even prisons. In both individual homes and institutions, peas were typically reheated and served as a common side dish, perhaps with butter, in a cream sauce, or mixed with diced carrots. The reheating step necessitated that some peas for canning be hardier and tough enough to withstand more handling and temperature change than the fragile garden pea, while still retaining the tender, fresh taste that consumers so desired.[64] Taste was ever the elusive goal, for canners understood that no matter how straight stemmed or large podded or wilt resistant a pea variety might be, if it didn't taste good when put in the can no housewife would buy the final canned product. To this end, the Ashland agricultural experiment station where Delwiche worked even established an experimental canning setup to "determine those varieties having an objectionable taste in the can."[65] In a time before tasters or consumer panels, Delwiche himself tasted the peas to see how different varieties held up in the canning process, calling on the scientist to also play consumer. The need for peas to please consumers and to taste good—not just to grow well—drove agricultural scientists to get into the unlikely practice of canning and taste testing, as opposed to the typical breeders' practice of just growing plant varieties to test for field properties, like heartiness, color, and fungal resistance. Here agricultural science was deeply intertwined with the issue of consumer taste. Throughout, the abstracted consumer remained central in the canners' minds as a behind-the-scenes force encouraging improvement.

A TIME OF TRANSITION, 1914–19

The rise of agricultural prosperity that had begun at the end of the nineteenth century reached its zenith with the First World War. The canning industry found itself adjusting to a fluctuating economy, waning farmer interest in contracting, and a heightened desire for agricultural research collaborations. Although the United States didn't directly enter the conflict until 1917, the increasing needs of European countries beginning in 1914 created a great demand for the export of US agricultural products and the resulting prosperity of American farmers. With the entrance of the United States into the war, President Woodrow Wilson created a number of new federal agencies with the power to redirect the American economy toward the war effort, including the powerful Food Administration, led by Herbert Hoover. "Food Will Win the War" became the motto as the government helped farmers increase production by providing them with easy lines of credit, farm machinery to take the place of labor lost to the military, and free access to seed and fertilizer. Food conservation was promoted alongside food production, with Americans encouraged to forego staple items through Meatless Mondays and Wheatless Wednesdays and to preserve as much produce as they could through home canning. Colorful posters encouraged housewives to engage in the war effort, with slogans exhorting them to "CAN Vegetables, Fruits, AND the Kaiser, too," pasted above drawings of jars labeled "Tomatoes," "Peas," and "Kaiser Brand Unsweetened."[66]

The commercial canning industry, along with the other sectors of agriculture, was also swept up in the war effort. Hoover's Food Administration urged Wisconsin canners to put up more peas than ever before.[67] All across the country, canners came together to provide food for the troops, sending more than five hundred million cans of food overseas.[68] In 1918, Colonel W. R. Grove of the US Army shared these verses with the country's canners, testifying to the importance of their products in keeping American soldiers fed:

We can march without shoes
We can fight without guns
We can fly without wings;
To flap over the Huns.
We can sing without bands,
Parade without banners,
But no modern army
Can eat without canners.
We can eat meat without gravy,
Fried mush without cream
Corn beef without cabbage,
And pie without cheese.
But how can our soldiers
Far over the seas
Make war on the Kaiser
Without their canned peas.[69]

However, the war also caused difficulties for the canning industry. For one, the war claimed much of the country's rural male labor supply for the military. Some farmers who would have otherwise grown canning crops turned to less labor-intensive forage crops, leaving canners with a production shortage in some regions.[70] E. J. Delwiche's breeding research at the Ashland Experiment Station, too, was suspended, both because of insufficient funds for such work and because he was directed by the state to increase "peas for food supplies for home needs and abroad," rather than devoting himself to research.[71] Further, because the war increased demand for food products and made observers more sensitive to high prices, the canning industry came under increased scrutiny for its system of distribution. Canners typically relied on brokers, wholesalers, and "jobbers" to get the canned product into retail markets and ultimately into the hands of consumers. But as an Illinois district court report on the food trade wrote in 1917, especially in times of war it became clear that "these middlemen exert the power that inheres in this system to extort unconscionable profits from consumers, with no proportionate benefit to those who furnish the principal service."[72] This kind of criticism, part of a broader movement against middlemen during the years of inflation around World War I, put pressure on the industry to reform its practices.[73]

Wartime saw changes not only in how farmers and canners each operated but also in the relations between the two groups, especially with regard to the contracting situation. In the early days of the pea-canning industry in the late nineteenth century, canners largely grew their own crops, which required that they maintain their own horses and equipment and grow on land either owned by the company or leased from neighboring farms. Though this was largely out of necessity—few farmers were familiar with growing peas and were not willing to take on the risky business—this company-grown system also offered canners full control and limited transportation costs. Over the course of the 1910s, however, canners began to shift most of their production to farmers, both because farmers began to see the potential profit as canners became more successful and because of the pea blight problem described above.[74] Canners developed a contract system in which farmers grew the pea crops from seed supplied by the canner and with oversight by a cannery field agent before delivering the pea vines to the cannery for processing. The price for a specific quality and set amount was established in advance of the growing season. This new contracting system had the potential to significantly increase the farmers' income. During just one 1913 season in one Wisconsin county, the local cannery paid out more than $73,000 to area farmers for green peas.[75]

Though the war demand for canned food made it possible for canners to pay farmers higher prices, many canners found it increasingly difficult to find growers willing to contract during the war years. In explaining why his company was having "troubles in getting the usual acreage," William C. Leitsch of the Columbus Canning Company wrote, "It has not been so much a concerted action on the part of the growers, as the falling off here and there of farmers who have grown regularly for some years and are tempted by the high price of other products to drop peas for something else that will give their land a rest and pay them equally well."[76] The war bolstered the confidence of farmers as well as canners, giving both groups a sense of their economic importance.

These years saw the beginning of a move toward industrial agriculture, in which larger, more businesslike farms came to dominate the scene. The same government aid that had led to increased production in order to have "food win the war" also led to farms that were more reliant on bank loans, machinery, fertilizers, and other external inputs. In Wisconsin in particular, the rise of the dairy industry brought with it the rise of marketing cooperatives and other elements of farm management. One commentator wrote in 1922 that dairying had brought "business principles, so painfully lacking under the old agriculture," to the farm, making "the average farmer something of a scientist, and a good deal of a business man."[77] These new principles also had ties to the increasing role that extension agents and other land-grant-college representatives came to play in the life of the farmer in the years during and after the First World War. Continuing the trend that had begun earlier in the century, the more businesslike farmers tended to get more aid from agricultural experiment station scientists.

Like more industrialized farmers, larger canners tended to find more points of connection with state agricultural institutions. In Wisconsin, the company that had both the state's largest canning plant by 1910 and the closest relationship with the university was the Columbus Canning Company. This company was involved in nearly all the canning-crop-related research carried out by the Wisconsin Agricultural Experiment Station, including both the pea blight and breeding work discussed above. As early as 1912, Columbus was collaborating with the station on pea-breeding efforts. Then-superintendent of the company Fred A. Stare explained the relationship this way: "We have doubtless come in contact with them more closely than some of the other concerns in the state, as we are located closer to them and are growing seed quite largely ourselves, and have therefore been in position to render them assistance in their work."[78] Besides the proximity of the Columbus cannery to the college of agriculture in Madison, the fact that the company was organized and successful enough to produce its own seed put it in a position to work closely with the professional agronomists.

The Columbus Company sought help from the college of agriculture in order to improve their business on all fronts—improved crops would earn the company more profit, thereby allowing them to contract with the best farmers; and improved crops would also help the company please more consumers through a better canned product. When the Columbus canners had difficulty finding farmers with whom to contract in 1917, they were able to voluntarily raise prices and pay growers more, "which helped very much."[79] Of course, the situation would have been more difficult for companies who did not have the means to pay farmers more out of pocket. One of the reasons that Columbus had this extra expendable income was its relationship with a perhaps-unexpected department within the Wisconsin College of Agriculture—the department of animal husbandry.

Columbus turned to the animal husbandry scientists for help with its sheep-raising operations, which provided the company with a profit that could serve as financial leverage in recruiting farmers for contracts. Keeping sheep on company land served two purposes. First, the sheep ate the pea vines that remained after processing so that the company would not have to dispose of these as waste. Second, the sheep provided the manure that was valuable fertilizer for the company's pea-growing operations. This closed-loop system was among the main factors that enabled the company's growth and success. Columbus's correspondence reveals that one of the reasons that a venture into establishing company outposts in Arkansas failed was the prohibitively high costs of acquiring chemical fertilizers in the absence of animal manure. F. A. Stare, of the Columbus Company, referred to this fertilizer from sheep fed on fermented pea vines as "a very valuable asset, [which] would be a profit in itself, if we did not realize a financial profit on the feeding operations themselves."[80]

Columbus was not the only Wisconsin cannery to have sheep, but it was likely the one that relied the most heavily on college scientists to optimize these operations.[81] The company sought data from the animal husbandry department on various matters: the cost of putting weight on lambs fed on fermented pea vines, the relative benefits of feeding heifers or steers instead of sheep, and the relative quality of three different feed preparations. The university initiated all of these projects in response to the company's requests. In return, the canners offered the university their own valuable data, cementing the collaboration.[82] The Columbus

Canning Company also invited representatives of the animal husbandry department to come out to the company grounds in person to see the sheep-feeding operations so they could be recorded "for the benefit of others throughout the state."[83]

Throughout these war years, even as farmers and canners alike were strengthening their business through heightened production, more rigorous organization, and closer connections to state agricultural institutions, consumer markets continued to exert pressure. Canners, especially, were attentive to the crucial element of consumer interest, which guided much of canners' interaction with farmers. At a meeting of the Maryland Agricultural Society in 1917, one canner encouraged his colleagues to offer feedback about crop quality directly to the farmers, for the sake of the consumer: "The consumer or the housewife, who knows good food when she sees it, prompts [the canner to communicate with the farmer]. . . . There is no appeal from her decision. The canner is compelled to go to the producer and persuade him to correct, as far as possible, the conditions which are pointed out to him."[84]

Just as the canners' success with consumers relied on cooperation with farmers, so did the canners' success with farmers rely on a positive relationship with consumers. Walter J. Sears, president of the National Canners Association (NCA) in 1920, said, "Only as the canning industry shall have won for its products the confidence of the consumer, and thus established for it a degree of stability which it lacks today, can it ever be in a position to meet the competition offered by the staple foods produced by the farmer, and thus secure for the industry the farmer's willing and satisfied support."[85] Sears understood that farmers would be willing to grow canning crops only when they were offered a higher price for them than for other crops. But canners could afford these high prices only if consumers bought larger quantities of canned foods.

One problem Wisconsin pea canners faced in securing this consumer support, however, was that their product was not a staple item. One commentator noted, "There are so many kinds of food that we have a wide choice. We could live quite comfortably, for instance, if we never ate another spoonful of peas, so why pay fancy prices for peas with potatoes at forty cents?"[86] High prices for canned peas in the marketplace, then, were a real threat to the industry's ability to convince consumers to buy more. As we will see, canners struggled to build relationships with farmers and agricultural scientists that would enable them to lower prices while improving quality, giving consumers a reason to look past the forty-cent potatoes and instead reach for the fancy peas.

Still, as Wisconsin canners reflected on their position in 1919, they noted that they had packed over one hundred million cans of peas that year, "almost one can for every man, woman and child in the United States."[87] This pack was valued at $12 million and had made use of almost fifty-seven thousand acres of Wisconsin land, more than any other intensive crop for human consumption (not including the staple crops of corn, oats, potatoes, and barley).[88] Canning peas had risen to occupy one of the most important positions in Wisconsin's economy, but the end of the First World War in 1918 signaled a shift in agricultural production that would again alter the interactions among canners, farmers, and the agricultural colleges of the country.

INVESTING IN COLLABORATION, 1919–25

The end of the war brought an agricultural depression that lasted throughout the 1920s and 1930s. But even as individual farmers suffered financially, the agricultural landscape continued to grow and change. These years saw the rise of farmer cooperative organizations, the renegotiation of farmer-canner contracts, a strengthened relationship between canners and professional agricultural scientists, and technological innovation. Many of the programs that canners had initiated in the first two decades of the twentieth century, like striving for cooperation with farmers and engaging with agricultural research, found their fullest realization during this period, leading to an entrenchment of canners' position within the agricultural arena.

When the Allies and Germany signed the Armistice that ended World War I on November 11, 1918, their actions led to a dramatic retooling of the structures that had been put in place to support the war effort. During the war, American farmers had increased production to meet the needs abroad. But with the war's end, Europeans resumed their own agricultural production, leaving American farmers with a large supply that far exceeded demand. This situation led to a nosedive in prices, dramatically reducing farmer income. And because many farmers had acquired more and more land on credit during the war, they now had no income with which to make their payments. Many farmers went bankrupt, leaving the wealthier, more commercialized farms to gobble up the land of the small subsistence farms, with the former growing even bigger in the process. Even as small farmers struggled, however, scientific and technological innovation raced ahead, leading to plant varieties more suited to industrial production, more machinery, and improved fertilizers and pesticides. But all of these so-called improvements led to still higher rates of production, which only furthered the problem of oversupply.[89]

Canners, too, were left with a problem of overproduction and lowered profit after the war. Pea canners were particularly hurt by this production problem because the peas' short season meant canners had only one or two chances in a given year to recoup their investments, when they made a sale of their canned product to the brokers who then stored the canned goods for sale to retailers. Producers of canned foods that had more consistent production lines and thus more frequent turnovers carried less risk. Also, the fact that pea-canning plants operated only during the four to eight weeks of the season made them even more vulnerable.[90] Canners had hoped that European consumers would create a new market for the surplus products, having been exposed to canned food through its popularity among American soldiers during the war, but these hopes were dashed when they found that Europeans had little interest in canned goods, partly because of foodways that did not value convenience and an underdeveloped local canning infrastructure. As one commentator put it, "The use of canned vegetables by the people of France is about as limited as the use of horse meat in America."[91]

The industry turned to the domestic market, hoping to increase consumption among Americans. One campaign involved educating consumers on production costs so that they would understand the price they saw on the grocery shelf. For example, if a housewife knew that canners paid farmers 3 cents for a can of peas, she would expect to pay something similar at the store and would balk at a 12-cent price tag. However, canners knew that the final cost of a canned food reflected the cost not only of the raw produce but of the metal cans, shipping boxes, labels, advertising, and other factory costs. Canners believed that if they could educate consumers on these true costs, advertising that the final product cost canners not 3 cents but 10.21 cents to manufacture, consumers would feel more justified in spending 12 cents for a can of peas. As agricultural economist Theodore Macklin wrote, "This knowledge leads to greater demand."[92] Beyond this sort of public relations campaign, canners further hoped to increase demand by bolstering cooperation with farmers and investing more deeply in scientific research.

Many agricultural leaders believed that a better situation for both farmer and canner could come through the collaboration of the two groups and the recognition of their mutual interests. Because canners were so dependent on farmland within a small radius around their factories, and because many of these nearby farmers benefited from the canneries in their local areas, one canning leader commented, "Tenant-less canning houses bespeak the near presence of tenantless, unyielding farmlands."[93] Walter J. Sears, president of the NCA in 1920, offered grand reflections on the relationship between the farmer and the canner: "I call upon both . . . [to] enter with joy and thanksgiving, proud of the privilege of working together in conserving during seasons of plenty, the perishable products of nature, and to carry them over into the time of need."[94]

If the pure desire for "joy and thanksgiving" wasn't enough reason for farmers and canners to collaborate, canners hoped that perhaps the fact that they faced many of the same problems and wanted the same solutions would be. Around 1920, both groups—united under the banner of "crop-producing interests"—were interested in better seed supply, more fertile soil, and reduced diseases and pests; both could benefit from a more efficient labor system; and both wanted the market for their products to stabilize.[95] Fundamentally, advocates for cooperation wanted farmers and canners to realize their interconnectedness, such that an "injury to one link in the chain inevitably is felt all along the line."[96] Consumers were ultimately seen as the final link in the chain. If consumers were unhappy, wholesalers and canners and farmers would all feel the effect of this displeasure, through lower income as a result of lower rates of consumption. And indeed, it appeared that the same states that had the largest and fastest-growing canning industries—New York, Ohio, Indiana, Illinois, Michigan, and Wisconsin—were also the states that actively moved toward institutionalized farmer-canner collaboration.[97]

Regardless of this call for cooperation and the poor financial condition of farmers, some canners continued to have trouble finding farmers with whom to contract, even into the early 1920s. Although the contract-farming system that dominated the Wisconsin canning industry by 1915 seemed mutually beneficial to both parties involved, many points of conflict emerged when the interests of canners and farmers seemed to be at odds. True, there were significant benefits, as outlined by one industry source: "Supply and demand of the raw product are kept in close balance; the grower has an assured market for his crop at a satisfactory profit, and the canner has an assured supply at a price which he estimates will make his product one of value in the eyes of the consumer."[98]

But many problems rocked this happy picture, leading both groups to feel that they were being short-changed, for different reasons.[99] Canners believed that farmers, who were often producing a number of different crops at a given time, didn't give canning crops the attention they deserved. There was also often conflict about when farmers would bring crops into the cannery—when the crops were most ripe or when the cannery was equipped to handle the sudden influx. But in cases where canning companies were large and powerful, they were able to choose among many small sellers until they found enough who would agree to the terms of the canners' preferences. The central problem, however, always hinged on the question of price. Most farmers, comparing the prices canners offered them and the prices of cans once on the grocery store shelves, concluded that the canners were not offering a fair price on the production end.[100]

Canners, for the most part, considered this conclusion unsupported and sought to show farmers that the price offered was a fair one. They pointed to their own "modest and inadequate" profits, and the high rates of failure in their industry, to show that canners were not fleecing the farmers.[101] Leaders within the canning industry urged their colleagues to have open dialogue with farmers by showing them statistics on canning expenditures, much like the campaign of consumer education.[102] Canners hoped that they could set contracts that would appease farmers, both to further their own production and because they saw farmers as bedrocks of democracy. In a 1920 article in an industry journal, Walter J. Sears wrote of the farmer, "At times we may think him unreasonable, but his just demands must be met. He is today the one conserving and conservative force holding steadily against the violence of developing storms which threaten the landmarks of civilization, standing unequivocally for the economic solvency which rests upon toil, thrift, initiative and cooperation."[103]

It is important to note that most of these calls for cooperation came from leaders in canning, rather than from those in farming. Farmers were just beginning to organize at a national level in the postwar years. Although the National Grange and the Farmers' Alliance organized in the 1870s and 1880s, those groups became largely political in nature, and their influence waned by the end of the nineteenth century. The years around 1920 saw a resurgence of the educational and cooperative aspects of early farmer movements, along with a rise in information sharing among growers in order to determine appropriate costs and prices.[104] The war played a central role in spurring this type of organization—both because postwar financial struggles encouraged farmers to find a system to stabilize their output and income and because the importance of food production to the war effort gave farmers the conviction that their occupation was deeply valuable and worth promoting in a cooperative fashion. The American Farm Bureau officially formed in 1919, growing out of the county bureaus that had existed for most of the past decade and allowing farmers to benefit from cooperative engagement.[105] Politicians and legislatures began to attend to this issue, with the establishment of agricultural cooperatives by most state legislatures by the end of the 1920s.[106]

Within the larger class of farmers, those particular farmers who grew canning crops also wanted a forum specific to their needs. In 1919, New York growers began to lobby for a statewide association as an attempt to level the playing field with the well-organized canners.[107] When officially organized in February 1920, the New York association hoped that its existence would mean that "the day of canning crop production in New York State at a loss to the growers is definitely ended. . . . [The association] will hereafter act for the growers in their contracts with the factories."[108] Although not all canners welcomed these grower organizations, in several states committees to address farmers' needs were actually established in direct partnership with canners. In 1917, the Maryland Agricultural Society held a "Joint Meeting of Growers and Canners" to establish how the two groups could work together. In 1920, the Wisconsin Canning Crop Growers' Association was established not only by farmers but by a mixed committee of canners, growers, state marketing specialists, and representatives from the college of agriculture.[109] Also in 1920, a group of growers, canners, and investigators gathered together in Harrisburg, Pennsylvania, to "to take up the matter of an equitable cost system" for the crop-producing interests of that state.[110] On the whole, the early 1920s saw the farmers who produced canning crops beginning to organize, often with the support of their canning partners.

As canning-crop growers were organizing, the NCA was brewing its own initiative, one that would both help meet the farmers' demands and, more generally, improve the agricultural foundation of canning. In August 1920, the NCA officially formed the Bureau of Raw Products Research to direct the attention of the state agricultural institutions to the problems of canning crops. If the university scientists could help develop better crops—more disease resistant, easier to process, and with sweeter flavor and more vibrant color—then consumers would buy more canned food, giving canners more profit, which they could then pass on to farmers in the form of higher prices. Canners believed that agricultural research was one of the keys to the canners being able to meet the farmers' needs.[111] This improved relationship between canners and farmers would then further increase consumer confidence in canned goods. Charles G. Woodbury, the director of the new bureau, referred to the consumer as the "third partner . . . by whose necessities they both [canners and farmers] exist, but by whose good will and understanding and generous support only can they both prosper."[112] Canners believed that, although any individual consumer might not have known anything about canner-grower contracts or seed breeding, she certainly benefited from the higher-quality products that could be achieved when canners and growers sought collaboration with each other and with the agricultural colleges.

The Bureau of Raw Products Research formalized and systematized, at a national level, the relationship between canners and agricultural scientists that had already been in place in Wisconsin for nearly a decade. Although the bureau did no independent research of its own, it helped direct the work of existing agencies toward canning-crop problems, maintaining for the canners "an organized, nation-wide contact with the agricultural colleges and experiment stations and with the agricultural research activities of the United States Department of Agriculture."[113] The bureau was one of the earliest trade committees to be devoted to promoting research and collaboration among scientific, business, and governmental interests, and it became so successful that a national report on US research activities prepared for President Roosevelt in 1941 used it as an "excellent example" of trade-association research activity.[114]

During the 1920s, the canners increased their emphasis on the importance of high-quality raw products to the creation of high-quality canned goods. One canner, in a January 1920 speech, said that focusing on problems of distribution rather than on agricultural production "would be like building a skyscraper upon a foundation of sinking sands." He argued that farmers preferred growing for regular agriculture rather than canning agriculture because the former had grown more profitable through agricultural research.[115] As mentioned earlier, the period after the First World War saw a dramatic increase in scientific investigations into breeding, cultivation, and pest management. The canners, through the Bureau of Raw Products Research, now wanted to get in on the action. Other notable partnerships among industry and agricultural science emerged later, in the 1920s and 1930s. Food historian Harvey Levenstein describes how private organizations like General Foods and the Grocery Manufacturers Association began to subsidize agricultural experiment station research—particularly in New York State and with Cornell University—in the early 1930s in response to the Depression-era state budgets. And the industrial fellowship file of the Wisconsin College of Agriculture, besides describing the 1911 Pea Packers' Fellowship, covers the period 1923 to 1942, when other industries began to sponsor university research.[116] So although this kind of partnership became more common later years, the Wisconsin pea-canning industry was significantly ahead of the game with its work sponsoring research beginning in 1911.

Now, in the 1920s, Wisconsin canners sought to deepen and expand their projects with and connections to their state college of agriculture. Building on the early work in pea blight, breeding efforts, and animal husbandry, canners now launched a number of other initiatives with their experiment station partners. Besides two significant projects initiated in 1923—research on the pea aphid pest cosponsored by the USDA and the development of a Canners Short Course—the most important area of research that brought the agricultural scientists and canners together was Wisconsin's expanded seed-breeding program of the 1920s.[117] With some breeding projects going back as far as Delwiche's work in 1912, Wisconsin distinguished itself as one of the first states to carry out advanced breeding work using plant genetics. Historian Deborah Fitzgerald writes of this era, "Wisconsin and Cornell were without question two of the three most sophisticated schools applying Mendelian methods to agriculture."[118] And the Columbus Canning Company, working in conjunction with the Wisconsin breeding program, was one of the early companies to have its own laboratory for seed testing and to employ an agronomist.[119] This work responded to the desires of state canners, who in a 1919 survey rated improved seed stocks as one of the greatest needs in the industry.[120]

The major breeder of canning peas, as described above, was Ernest J. Delwiche. He was one of the most prominent pea breeders in the country, bringing a scientific approach that distinguished his work from previous sporadic efforts.[121] By the early 1920s, much of the previous effort to breed a pea to blossom, produce, and ripen uniformly had been achieved. Now most of the breeding efforts were directed at finding a strain of pea that was high quality and was resistant to *Fusarium* wilt, the major fungus that beleaguered pea growers. Around 1921, Delwiche created the Horal pea, which was a cross between two varieties, the Horsford and Alaska (figure 5). He first noticed Horal's exceptional resistance to wilt when visiting the pea disease plots set up by University

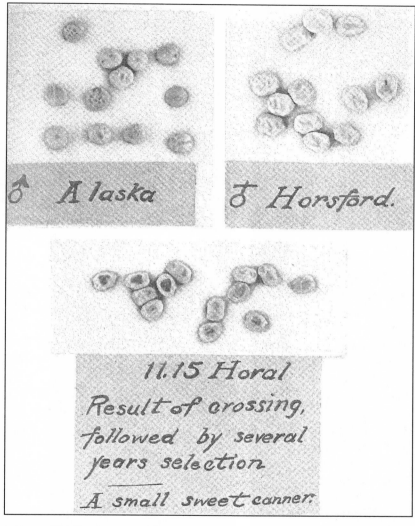

FIGURE 5. The Horal pea, a small sweet canner, resulting from the cross of two varieties, the Horsford and the Alaska, 1926. (Courtesy of the University of Wisconsin-Madison College of Agriculture.)

of Wisconsin plant pathologist M. B. Linford at the Columbus Canning Company. This new variety had many positive qualities, inheriting its "hardiness and small seed size . . . from the Alaska parent while true wrinkledness, double podding habit, vine type, and maturity period were inherited from Horsford."[122] It also matured early and uniformly and had a high yield.

The Wisconsin pea canners quickly realized the potential of the Horal pea and sought a way to keep it largely within the control of the state's canning industry. At that time, any new varieties that the experiment station developed had to be sent to seed companies for expansion and production, since the state-funded station couldn't itself enter the field of commerce.[123] But by the 1920s, most pea seed companies had moved westward, setting up shop in Montana, Idaho, Washington, and Oregon. As a result, Wisconsin canners had to pay Western seedsmen for any pea seed that they purchased, even if that seed was of a variety created at the Wisconsin experiment station. Because of this, state agronomists hoped to find a way to keep this money in state, believing "that the state can produce seed peas just as well as the western states" and could perhaps produce seed peas that were better suited to the Wisconsin climate.[124] Another organization, the Wisconsin Experiment Growers Association, was already doing this work for regular farm seeds—it had been multiplying the stock of corn and small grain seeds from the Experiment Station since 1901.[125]

In 1923, a group of the state's leading canners from the Wisconsin Pea Canners Association established the Canners Seed Corporation (CSC) with the explicit mission of "taking over where the Experiment Station had to leave off, or to take the small volume of seed stock thought to be desirable for canners use, and multiply it, and it's [sic] progeny, under the careful supervision of a trained agronomist, for the direct benefit of the pea canners of Wisconsin." The CSC intended not to profit directly from seed production, but to pass this benefit on to the state canners.[126] By December 1925, the CSC had hired an expert agronomist (and Delwiche's nephew), Earl J. Renard, to supervise trial groundwork.[127] Although the corporation paid his salary, Renard was housed in the university's agronomy department, again bridging the gap between canners and the college of agriculture. By the early 1930s, Renard had introduced wilt-resistant varieties of Perfection, Alaska, and Early Perfection peas, all of which were adapted to Wisconsin conditions and were well reviewed by state canners.[128] Perhaps even more importantly, the seed improvement carried out by Wisconsin canners stimulated other seed companies throughout the country to improve their own production methods, leading to a general improvement in the quality of pea seed.[129] The CSC continued to thrive for decades to come, though it changed form and location, moving to Idaho sometime in the late 1930s.[130]

The work of Wisconsin breeders of canning peas, as a whole, had a successful and lasting legacy. Although the original star of the CSC, the Horal, did not end up being put to much use—because of both its sub-par flavor and its small size—other wilt-resistant varieties that Delwiche developed became dominant throughout the canning industry.[131] By 1942, it was estimated that 71.5 percent of peas grown in Wisconsin originally came from strains that Delwiche had created. Upon his retirement in 1945, the Wisconsin Canners' Association celebrated Delwiche, crediting him with having saved the pea-canning industry of Wisconsin.[132] Delwiche, in turn, made clear that his success was due, in large part, to his industry partnerships. In a 1926 publication he "gratefully acknowledged . . . official representatives of pea canning companies, seed growers, and merchants" who had helped in his pea-breeding work.[133] Beyond the state, pea varieties bred in Wisconsin spread throughout the country and the world. Delwiche saw his own varieties growing in Spokane, Washington, and knew that they had spread to "Europe, Asia, Australia and throughout the American continents where peas are grown."[134] The work of Delwiche, through the Wisconsin Agricultural Experiment Station, was central to the development of the pea-canning industry. And the industry's funding and institutional help, in turn, made his work possible. By the end of the 1920s, the academic and commercial realms were growing ever more intertwined through agricultural research, even as farmers struggled to organize.

· · ·

As Lynn and her family ate their peas during dinner in the 1939 *Pick of the Pod* film, they could not have conceived of the work that had gone into putting those peas on the table. The shiny green peas in the film, butter melting atop, seemed timeless. Yet, they had come far in the last forty years, morphing and adapting to their new canned environment. The industry, in making *Pick of the Pod*, tried to present the canned peas as equivalent to those from the turn-of-the-twentieth-century garden. They tried to make the path from farm to table transparent. However, the new peas were actually a product of industrial funding, scientific manipulation, and agricultural restructuring. The peas the family ate now matured uniformly, had higher yields, grew on straight stems and with larger pods, were resistant to fungal blight, had light-colored blossoms, and tasted relatively sweet and fresh even after several rounds of processing. All of this breeding work had been done to please the consumers of canned food—both with a low price that resulted from an efficient production process and with desirable consumer-end characteristics, like appropriate color and flavor. To win over the trust of consumers in unfamiliar food beneath an opaque metal sheath, canners worked with research scientists and farmers, thereby prompting changes in farming practice and organization.

During the first two decades of the twentieth century, canners went from being fairly independent businessmen to forging ties and relationships with a number of agricultural players. These interdependencies were necessary for the canning industry to keep expanding and building increasing levels of consumption. To build the canned-food market, canners began to invest even more heavily in agricultural research to find solutions to their production problems.

This story of canning agriculture offers us new connections and new ways of seeing old tales about both agriculture and the culture of eating. By bringing food processing into the story of agricultural history, we see the connections among farm, factory, and table more clearly than ever before. Consumers become central to agricultural change because canners' motivations for stimulating research and farmer collaboration were tied so closely to how the canners imagined consumer desires.[135] Canned vegetables clearly became a product both of industry and of the land. This chapter has brought the canning industry into several key stories of agricultural history—industry funding of agricultural experiment station work, the rise of farmer organizations, business involvement in breeding, and the role of Mendelism in developing new plant varieties—highlighting the role that food processors played in these scientific and agricultural dealings. Pea canners were, in fact, one of the earliest businesses to fund agricultural college research for specific industry needs. Overall, these stories offer some understanding of the prewar context by which food processors, as part of a growing agribusiness complex, called on scientists and government to reshape agricultural practice.

This agricultural work lay beneath the growing success of canned food in the second and third decades of the twentieth century. After tackling the technical and organizational problems involved in canned-food production around the turn of the century, canners sought to shore up their success by continuing to improve their products through agricultural research. As we will see in the next chapter, though, concerns emerged about the quality of canned foods in the 1920s, stemming from problems at the processing and marketing levels, far outside the purview of farmers and agricultural researchers. No matter how blight resistant or tender the peas were upon entering the factory, if they were handled improperly once inside, or if harmful bacteria entered the canning process, then the final product a consumer served to her family would not be satisfactory. And in some cases this final product could even be deadly.

3

Poisoned Olives

Consumer Fear and Expert Collaboration

In 1919, just as the canning industry was beginning to find stable footing with investments in agricultural research and advertising campaigns, tragedy struck. Throughout the country, in rare but highly publicized cases, people fell ill and died after eating canned foods, especially ripe black olives. Critics had long blamed canned foods for poisoning and digestive upset. Although many of these former accusations had been unjustified, the string of deaths in 1919–20 was indisputably linked to canned ripe olives, pushing the industry toward crisis.

The first deaths in this epidemic came after a 1919 banquet in Canton, Ohio. Five guests and two waiters died after eating a celebratory feast.[1] Over the course of the next few months, similar deaths occurred in Detroit, Memphis, and New York City, among other locations. These stories all became front-page news. In all the cases, a unifying element was the canned ripe olive.[2] This fruit, typically eaten as an indulgence on special occasions, had been grown and canned—often in glass jars— in the United States since the end of the nineteenth century, with the bulk of production and processing in California.[3] Unfortunately, canning without sufficient heat or an acidic solution made the product highly susceptible to a form of poisoning known as botulism.

It was precisely episodes like these that kept many consumers from trusting canned food as a whole in the early part of the twentieth century, even after the passage of the 1906 Pure Food and Drug Act and the ensuing action by the National Canners Association (NCA).[4] Widespread fear of poisoning, or simply of unpalatable food, meant that many Americans continued to shy away from commercially processed goods. Even those who were familiar with home canning and the resulting colorful transparent jars still felt a level of unease with the opaque containers at their local shop that came from commercial canneries. And although olives themselves were typically packed in glass, they were still as metaphorically opaque as their tinned counterparts, in that their production and distribution processes remained mysterious and unknown. Episodes of botulism deaths exacerbated the lack of trust that had plagued the canning industry since its foundation.

Botulism soon became the center of both widespread media attention and ensuing scientific research programs, as canners sought to deal with this threat to consumer confidence. The Canton, Ohio, deaths and those that followed created a crisis moment for the canning industry, especially in California. But the deaths and crisis also led to far-reaching changes. The botulism outbreak forced canners to contend with the many players in the food system of which they were a part—media, scientists, universities, and government health officials—all in the hopes of establishing trust in their products. Although olives were a marginal part of most Americans' diets and there were relatively few actual deaths, these cases of poisoning provoked consumer fear, prompted by heavy media coverage. Further, because these poisoned olives spread to all parts of the country, they highlighted the dangers inherent in the nationalized food supply that were becoming prominent in the early twentieth century. Canners' nonperishable products stood to benefit from these markets, so the industry had to spring into action to show it was capable of managing the potential dangers. The central actions canners pursued were creating partnerships with university scientists and public health departments, in parallel with those they had developed with agricultural institutions, as described in the previous chapter. These partnerships allowed canners both to reduce the actual recurrence of botulism and to reassure consumers through the perceived authority of science and government. Although canners often downplayed the dangers in published media, they realized how much they needed to reform the industry to save it. The findings of the botulism research would create a new standard for the industry's processing methods in the future.

The botulism outbreak in ripe olives took place at a pivotal moment in the canning industry's development. World War I created high demand for canned food to fulfill government contracts, but when the war ended in November 1918 the canners were left with a huge surplus, which, according to one industry chronicler "hung like a wet blanket over the industry." Rather than decreasing production, the canners optimistically decided to work on increasing demand by improving the industry.[5] In 1919, the NCA launched a campaign of inspection and advertising that they hoped would promote consumer trust through standardized production. The inspection system would ensure that the nation's canneries adhered to uniform trade association standards, which would be rewarded by an official inspection seal. The advertising piece would then aim to convince the public to purchase only those canned foods with the seal.[6] But the highly publicized botulism outbreaks directly thwarted the canners' plans to increase consumer demand.

The NCA, based in Washington, D.C., and the Canners League of California—both trade organizations—were the central groups speaking for the country's canners in response to botulism. California canners were relatively new to the scene, with their canning output doubling between 1915 and 1920.[7] They promised to bring exotic bounty to the whole country through the rise of newly established shipping markets. But they were also in a vulnerable position. During the time of the botulism outbreaks, the state's canners were only beginning to establish themselves as a major force in the national food industry and had more to lose. The California food industry also embodied the fear of widespread food poisoning outbreaks. If the state was producing so much food and sending it out into the far corners of the United States, then no place was safe. The same disconnection from local production that enabled Americans to triumph over geographical limitations also made them vulnerable to extensive food safety problems.[8]

National newspapers emerged as a major threat to the canning industry's success, seizing upon the dramatic botulism stories and broadcasting them widely, taking advantage of the lurid details and the fact that many consumers still had lingering fears about the safety of canned food.[9] Canners realized they needed to wrest control of their public image from the newspapers and find a way to reassure consumers that their products were safe. In responding to consumer fears, canners vacillated between presenting botulism prevention as a responsibility of the individual consumer and as a public health issue. On the one hand, they resisted assuming responsibility because they did not want to reinforce the association between commercially canned food and bacterial contamination. Aside from the ripe olive cases, many newspaper reports described cases of botulism in home-canned food; commercial canners thus wanted to create a clear distinction between their products and these home-canned items. They tried to evade responsibility by blaming their housewife consumers.[10] On the other hand, the canning industry wanted to make use of the authority of public health departments to reassure consumers that the industry was in control of the situation and working to improve.

As knowledge about and fear of germs spread through the United States in the decades before these botulism cases, many Americans had grown increasingly aware of the power of public health campaigns to address disease. A new focus on bacteriology that came with the discovery of germ theory in the 1880s paved the way for the "new public health," which upheld the power of the laboratory in finding diagnostic tests, vaccines, and cures for a variety of diseases—from rabies to diphtheria, from typhoid fever to syphilis. The Progressive Era emphasis on expertise and professionalization also contributed to the rising prestige of public health officials as they made headway in projects like school vaccination programs, rural health work, and maternal and child care. Canners called on the power of physicians and other scientific and state experts to assure consumers that the new industrial food system was as safe as older foodways, in which trust had been based on a social organization that allowed people to have direct relationships with their food producers.[11]

California canners and men of the olive industry joined forces to fund a Botulism Commission of three leading scientists, whose far-reaching scientific investigation yielded important results, producing specific strategies for safely processing olives, which the California State Board of Health made into state law. The findings of the Botulism Commission also led the California canners to fund a permanent statewide cannery inspection service, overseen by the board of health. The collaboration paved the way for even more intertwined research programs in the decades that followed, among university and industry scientists, health officials, and canners.[12] Although these parties did not always see eye to eye, a network emerged as these groups negotiated conflict around the botulism scare. These relationships bolstered the burgeoning canning industry and allowed it to co-opt the authority of science and government to reinforce its position in the eyes of consumers, building trust. Once canners secured this trust, they grew less eager to accept the regulations and loss of independence that came with collaboration, instead opting to control consumer tastes more directly. Around 1920, though, the series of botulism outbreaks made canners seek all the help they could get as they struggled to win over consumers.

BOTULISM AS A RISING CONCERN

Named after *botulus,* Latin for sausage, botulism was known as "sausage poisoning" in the eighteenth and nineteenth centuries because it predominated in processed meat. In 1895, the Belgian physician Emile van Ermengem isolated the bacteria that caused botulism and showed that the toxin the bacillus produced was responsible for the poisoning effect.[13] Before the 1919 outbreaks, laboratory research into botulism had been ongoing for at least six years. In 1913, a Stanford University sorority party came to an unhappy end when twelve young women were stricken with what appeared to botulism poisoning. All those taken ill had eaten some string beans canned in one of the attendees' homes.[14] Although this was a case of botulism poisoning from home-canned, rather than commercially canned, food, the deaths were serious enough to prompt action on the part of medical researchers. Stanford's Ernest C. Dickson, a professor of pathology, took up laboratory study of the botulism bacteria and toxin.[15]

By 1915, Dickson's early research had established that the cold-pack method of putting up vegetables, which was then recommended by the US Department of Agriculture (USDA), was not safe. Simply cooking the vegetables and then packing them into heated jars—without a subsequent reheating in the sealed jars—was not enough to kill the *Bacillus botulinus*.[16] Once he had made this finding through guinea pig trials, Dickson immediately sought to notify the USDA and the American Medical Association (AMA) of his findings, which he considered particularly important because of the recent wartime propaganda encouraging the conservation of food through the home canning of vegetables.

Despite Dickson's findings, botulism cases continued to occur in both home-canned and commercially canned vegetables in the second decade of the twentieth century. The canning industry began to get involved after a 1916 episode of botulism in which five people died after eating vegetables canned in a Kansas factory.[17] In response to this outbreak, the NCA began to fund work on food poisoning, collaborating with the National Research Council and Dr. Milton J. Rosenau of Harvard University.[18] This partnership with government and independent scientists set the stage for the intensive collaboration that emerged after the ripe olive cases a few years later.

Consequently, when the Canton, Ohio, case of botulism in olives occurred in August 1919, botulism was already on the radar of scientists and the canning industry. The prominent episodes in the coming

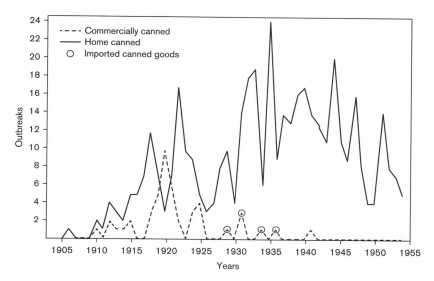

FIGURE 6. Cases of botulism in commercially canned, home-canned, and imported goods, 1905–55. Cases in commercially canned goods peaked around 1920 but remained far outnumbered by home-canned cases. (Courtesy of the Grocery Manufacturers Association.)

months—Detroit in October 1919, New York City in January 1920, and Memphis in February 1920—brought botulism in canned food into the national spotlight (figure 6).[19]

CANNERS AND THE MEDIA

Media reports about the outbreaks played a critical role. The media— and their perceived ability to provoke fear—served both as a central impetus to research and as a tool that the canners employed to combat that same consumer fear. Canners worried that sensational media reports would lead consumers to stop trusting, and therefore stop buying, canned food. Although the market for olives had fallen by 95 percent, so that olive canners had good reason to worry, the market for canned food as a whole remained remarkably consistent between 1918 and 1922.[20] Still, canners behaved with marked concern about the way that botulism deaths would affect housewives' purchasing decisions. While this concern may have stemmed in part from direct communication with worried consumers, it was fueled especially by the lurid stories of canned food deaths that were widespread in the country's newspapers.

We have only a few sources from frightened consumers themselves (discussed in the next section), but we do have access to ubiquitous newspaper reports that likely provoked fear in newspaper audiences. By examining the way media sources depicted botulism and the way scientists and canners responded to these depictions, we can see the role that publicity played in stoking industry anxiety and prompting research. Although there were cases of food poisoning from other kinds of foods and other bacteria—spoiled embalmed beef during the Spanish-American War, typhoid fever spread through food preparation, general "ptomaine" poisoning—the dispersed nature of those accounts softened their impact, or, in the case of embalmed beef, the coverage was part of a larger war narrative.[21] In contrast, following a botulism outbreak, newspapers across the country would post lurid, focused accounts. Media stories presented botulism poisoning as a vicious, frightening occurrence that disrupted the happiest of communal gatherings, leading to anxiety among housewives responsible for the family meal. Canners and the scientists who worked with them resented these dramatic stories because of their potential influence. They tried to correct misinformation—both real and perceived— and to control the message that reached the consuming public. In this way, control of the media became as important a tool in combating the botulism epidemic as did scientific research and government regulation.[22]

Accounts of botulism were frequently reported in newspapers, exaggerating the sense of how often these poisonings actually occurred. This disproportionality was true of other epidemic diseases in the nineteenth and twentieth centuries, often because these diseases were dramatic and visible and created fear, characteristics that media accounts then reinforced. As medical historian Margaret Humphreys has written, "Disease panic and the news media form their own generative circle. The more panic, the more rumors, the more demand for information to be supplied by the newspapers."[23] And in this case, supply they did. Media attention to botulism outbreaks in the United States and elsewhere was relatively intense; in 1919 and 1920, for example, sixteen full-length feature articles appeared in the *Los Angeles Times,* ten in the *Chicago Tribune,* and nine in the *New York Times,* even though there were only nine bacteriologically proven cases in the entire country that year.[24]

Events on the world stage also shaped Americans' sensitivity to botulism fears. For example, one article cited rumors, circulating for several months around December 1917, "probably German inspired, that the thousands of cans of food stuffs preserved by housewives last summer, instead of being valuable food, may contain germs of the deadly bacillus botulinous, which would cause serious illness and possibly death."[25] Whether Americans feared that the Germans themselves were poisoning the country's food supply or simply that the enemy was spreading rumors to produce panic and instability at home, such rumors served to heighten concern. Also, the side-by-side printing of an article about botulism and an article on lingering influenza deaths in January 1920 juxtaposed these two threats to the American public during this time.[26] The 1918 influenza pandemic killed up to fifty million people across the world.[27] People who lived through this outbreak would have watched for symptoms in themselves and in their families, wondering whether that lingering headache might be caused by influenza, botulism, or both. The multiple threats Americans perceived in this era combined with and exacerbated one another.

Journalists further emphasized the terror of botulism by underscoring the intensity of its biological effect. One *New York Times* article made clear just how deadly the toxin could be: "A single molecule may . . . [be] sufficient to cause death . . . . A single molecule is as small compared to a drop as a drop is compared to the water of New York Harbor." The article continued, "If one molecule has the power attributed to it, it would mean that if a gallon of the poison were uniformly mixed in the waters of the ocean, a few drops of water taken from any part of the ocean and injected into the mouse might kill it."[28] Of course, this information might not make consumers any more informed about the threat of botulism, but it certainly brought fear to the table.

Not only did writers frequently publish about botulism and its toxicity, but many authors emphasized the stark contrast between the delight of shared meals and the horror of toxic poisoning, encouraging a sense of fear in public audiences. A 1914 news story with the title "Two Die after Jolly Dinner" describes a "jolly dinner party of seven persons, given last Sunday afternoon at the home of Mrs. J. C. Cunningham in Ocean Park," after which several people died of botulism.[29] Although no details are given on the dinner party or what made it so "jolly," the author seemed to include this descriptor as a way to contrast the levity of the setting with the gruesome outcome. Numerous writers used this sort of contrast, often showing the disparity between the initial peacefulness of a family meal and the dreadfulness of botulism poisoning.

Another article begins the story of the unfortunate Mrs. William Trinner's run-in with botulism by setting the happy scene with "potatoes

... boiling merrily," "fluttering curtains," and a "pot of honey sparkl[ing] invitingly in the warm glow from a shaft of sunlight."[30] The author indulges his poetic urges in telling the tale of this case of botulism, which lends the dramatic material needed for a good story. This romanticized opening vignette, however, contrasts sharply with the horrific turn Mrs. Trinner's story took after she ate some string beans that smelled a little rancid. By the next day, the gas bubbles in the jar of beans seemed to gather into "a menacing cluster [which] merged into a ghostly human hand. . . . The straining fingers—lean, strong, deadly, flexed convulsively, eager to grip tender flesh. It was the hand of a strangler. Closer it crept to her shrinking throat."[31] Such imaginative and grisly embellished narration reinforced the view that botulism was a terrifying occurrence, no matter how rare, and was to be avoided at all costs.

Newspapers served as the main communication source between canners and consumers, as there were rarely direct interactions between the two parties. Besides the still limited advertisements, information on labels, the advice of a grocer, and word of mouth, the only way consumers had any knowledge about what to expect of canned food came through what they read in newspapers.[32] So, canners and researchers paid keen attention to the plentiful stories about botulism in the country's newspapers. Ernest C. Dickson, the Stanford botulism researcher, commissioned Henry Romeike, Inc., "The First Established and Most Complete Newspaper Cutting Bureau in the World," based in New York, to collect all the news reports that came out on botulism in 1920 and 1921. The slogan of this newspaper cutting bureau was a line from Robert Burns: "O wad some power the giftie gi'e us / To see oursel's as ithers see us." This slogan captured the interest of Dickson and his colleagues in monitoring the story around botulism and the information that potential customers were getting through their daily newspapers. The clippings Romeike collected for Dickson came from every corner of the country—from small California newspapers to those from large cities like St. Louis and Philadelphia.[33]

In monitoring the media reports on botulism, Dickson and others often found misleading statements and half truths. "A newspaper," he wrote, "can not be depended upon in matters of this kind."[34] Numerous incidents had given Dickson good reason to suspect "scientific" reports as printed in newspapers. For example, in 1921, a number of Bay Area papers published what purported to be an interview with another botulism researcher, W. V. Cruess. In fact, this interview was falsified, having been cobbled together from extracts of a recent article Dickson had published in the *State Board of Health Bulletin.* Cruess told Dickson that he had actually been in Oregon when the interview had supposedly taken place in California, and added: "Apparently the newspapers are very anxious to play up *B. botulinus.*"[35]

Canners, like scientists, also accused journalists of misrepresenting the botulism situation. C. H. Bentley, from the California Packing Corporation, took issue with an article published in the *San Francisco Chronicle,* which claimed that "botulism was usually found in home-canned fruits."[36] Bentley thought casual readers would interpret this to mean that "it was frequently found in home-canned fruits." In a letter to the newspaper article's author, Bentley claimed that in his forty years in canning he had never seen a case of botulism in canned fruit, with the suggestion that olives were not regarded as fruit by the trade, but instead as pickles or condiments. Of course, Bentley was quick to deny any attempt at misleading on his own part, even though consumers might not know the industry categorization of olives as nonfruit. Bentley wrote to Dickson, perhaps disingenuously, "You may be quite sure that I have no desire to misrepresent the situation and to minimize the serious danger, but I do feel that it is fair to state the truth with regard to our canned fruit business."[37] On both sides, there was a desire to control the way that the story was pitched to the consuming public—depending on whether that public was consuming olives or newspapers.

Scientists and canners actively sought to control media coverage. In 1921, Cruess wrote to Dickson, "I fully realize the damaging effect commercially of any articles in the press on botulism in relation to canned goods and I wish to avoid all such scarehead notices as the one mailed to me by you."[38] Soon after, when the fabricated interview with Cruess was published, he sought to mitigate this damaging effect and wrote to Dickson, "Do you think it would be advisable for us to gently but firmly step on a few of the editors of these respective Bay City papers in order that they will be more discrete [*sic*] in the future?"[39] After conferring with Dickson, Cruess decided to write to his own university's press agent at the University of California-Berkeley, as well as to the publicity department of Dickson's institution at Stanford, to ask them to "advise at least the large dailies to 'go slow' on botulism rumors."[40] It is unclear how much influence universities actually had over these newspapers, or whether this request went through, but these letters do indicate how much researchers were concerned with their media presence.

Canners tried to influence newspaper stories about themselves both overtly and more surreptitiously. C.H. Bentley revealed that the Canners League of California was considering making "the request of the papers that whenever they have an alarming story they endeavor to secure at the same time some statement from the industry to be published . . . with the rest of their story."[41] In this way, the canners thought they could offer another side to the story—whether there was truly another side or not—and lessen the negative impact of reports of botulism outbreaks. These canners also knew that the word *botulism* would draw unwanted media attention. So when olive packers organized a conference in September 1922, they explicitly avoided using the word in any of their printed materials because they suspected that "the newspapers [would] probably give considerable publicity to the meeting" if they advertised the botulism aspect. And even though the canners intended to present precisely on the topic of botulism, the actual topic listed in the program read only "the spoilage of canned fruits."[42]

The memory of this media attention and the harm it caused stayed fresh in the minds of the California food industry for several years after the 1919–20 botulism outbreaks. Six years later, in 1926, the California Department of Agriculture sent a statement labeled "confidential and not for publication" to all those in the state who were involved in the fruit industry. This letter stated that a number of arsenic poisonings had occurred in the fresh fruit industry and that the industry had to work to minimize the publicity around this issue in order to avoid "serious financial injury to the fresh fruit industry [through] the fears and prejudices created in the minds of consumers." The letter continued: "California fruit growers are already familiar with a similar situation in the case of the 'Botulism' scare a few years ago. While the actual facts in this case did not justify any undue alarm, the widespread publicity which was given to it aroused such fears in the minds of the consuming public that the olive industry suffered extreme financial injury from which it has not yet recovered."[43]

This letter testifies to two points. First, even as late as 1926, the agricultural industry of California was attuned to media attention, largely because of the fallout from the botulism scare in ripe olives six years prior. Of course, the main concern was less the media depiction itself than its potential to evoke negative consumer response. Consumers, while often the subject of canner concern, more rarely expressed their own fears about food safety in the public realm. But when they did, it became clear that the canners' worries were substantiated and that some consumers were indeed absorbing the media message about the dangers of canned foods. Second, there were clearly close ties between the state government and the industry. The state department of agriculture took it upon itself to warn the fruit industry of potential financial damages.

CONSUMER CONFUSION

In April 1922, Mrs. Jennie T. Hincks wrote to W. V. Cruess at the University of California with a series of questions about how to treat canned food. "I have become very nervous about the botulinus germ, about which I know very little," she began, "and I come to you for information about it. I do not like to use either the canned goods that I buy at the stores, nor those that I put up myself." But even as Mrs. Hincks harbored these fears, she also dismissed them, writing further, "I realize that it is a very foolish state of mind to be in. . . . I feel that I am really getting morbid over the matter, as, until this winter, I do not think that I should have hesitated to recook and use this canned fruit." This ambiguous sentiment—Mrs. Hincks feared botulism even as she believed her fear to be "very foolish"—reflected the dual information being presented in newspapers.[44] On the one hand, dramatic and frightening accounts were everywhere, with women bearing the brunt of the fear evoked; on the other, experts told housewives not to worry because avoiding botulism was easy, even as scientific uncertainty about the detectability of botulism was rampant.

Another concerned woman, Mrs. H. O. from Oregon, wrote to the "Dr. Wiley's Question-Box" column in *Good Housekeeping* magazine in 1922. Her question read: "Will you please tell me something about the food poisoning called 'botulinus.' I think it comes from canned foods. Is it always possible to tell by the appearance or smell of the product if it is poisonous? Will long cooking or a 20-lb. pressure in a steam cooker render the canned stuff safe? Is there danger of botulinus in any canned food besides green vegetables?"

Mrs. H. O. clearly feared botulism and felt that her lack of knowledge about it prevented her from guarding herself and her family against poisoning. In responding to her, Dr. Wiley—who had been the chief proponent of the 1906 Pure Food and Drug Act before taking his post at *Good Housekeeping*—answered few of her questions but did indicate that botulism was not common and that, when present, it usu-ally had a distinctive odor. "Botulinus poisoning is happily confined to very small areas," he wrote, and could be destroyed by "ordinary heat-ing to the temperature of boiling water."[45] He did not take her worries seriously or use the opportunity to reassure other readers about how to avoid botulism. Wiley's response reveals the deflection of responsibility by scientists onto housewife consumers and the general lack of scientific certainty in the press about how and why botulism toxin developed.

The palpable concern in the written voices of Mrs. Hincks and Mrs. H. O. reflects a number of factors: the widespread nature of the botu-lism epidemic, the prevailing "gospel of germs," and the pressure that doctors and home economists placed on women to protect their families from food poisoning or other contamination. To begin with, the 1919–20 outbreak of botulism in ripe olives was the first major one that saw the effects of transcontinental markets on the scale and distribution of the epidemic. Although botulism outbreaks had occurred in the years before 1919, this scale was something new entirely. As the epidemiolo-gist and pathologist who investigated the Ohio botulism case wrote, "This is especially disturbing, as one can hardly fail to appreciate the possibility of many jars being infected at the same pack, and of the organism being sent broadcast over the country with its attending haz-ards."[46] Earlier botulism cases had emerged from home-canned goods or had been more limited in their reach. This time, though, olives from California had been shipped all the way across the country and had killed people in cities across the Midwest and East Coast, suggesting that these poisoned olives could appear anywhere, anytime.

This omnipresence fed into a larger societal fear about germs. The early twentieth century saw a rise in the public understanding of, fear of, and attempts at protection from invisible microbes that threatened health. Historian Nancy Tomes has written that this movement was motivated by a new "gospel of germs." Scientists and popular media held up women as the protectors of family health. Tomes described how the bacteriological revolution moved from the laboratory to the home, encouraging women to take up the broom, the duster, and also—as this story of botulism illustrates—the sanitary canning jar, all in order to protect themselves and their families from harmful germs. Indeed, as Tomes wrote, "Both scientific and public awareness of microbial food contamination . . . rose steadily in the early 1900s. As a consequence, the need for exacting care in storing and cooking food became a major con-cern of the expanded gospel of germs."[47] Domestic scientists, the new female professionals in a discipline that brought the methods of the laboratory into the home around the turn of the twentieth century, encouraged women to sanitize their kitchens as physicians would their operating rooms, with a particular focus on home canning. Canning manuals often included extensive coverage of microorganisms that infected preserved foods. These detailed discussions likely got many women wondering about what might be growing in a poorly canned batch of summer corn. One home economist, Ola Powell, pointed out how common the discussion of bacteria in home canning had become: "People have gradually acquainted themselves with the ways in which bacteria work for our good or ill, and it is no longer necessary to whisper when discussing their effect on canned goods."[48]

Even if Powell and others had whispered, women would have still heard the message loud and clear: they were responsible for their families' health and safety. Women understood the burden they carried and the risk if something went wrong. The *Journal of the American Medical Association* reported on a 1918 botulism outbreak in Boise, Idaho, that resulted from a salad prepared from cold home-canned asparagus. In that case, when a guest commented about a smell of spoilage from the asparagus, the hostess said, "It can't be; I canned it myself."[49] This defensiveness exemplifies the feeling many women had with regard to the safety of products coming from their kitchens.

Women's responsibility for food safety overlapped with the general responsibility they held for being the guardians of the home. A 1918 cartoon in the *Chicago Tribune* titled "Domestic Dilemma" captured this well, with its depiction of a large balding man sitting in an armchair in a living room reading the newspaper. He has a cigarette hanging lazily from his mouth and he has turned his head halfway toward two women, who are just emerging from a kitchen. The one in front appears to be his wife, while the second is perhaps a maid or cook. The wife is leaning toward the man with a worried look on her face, her hands folded, as she asks, "Whatever can we do? We've finished our gas ration, and the sausages are only half cooked. Shall we risk a prosecution for exceeding the gas allowance—or chance getting botulism?"[50] Because much of this concern about botulism coincided in time with the First World War, American women played double duty when it came to worrying about their domestic and patriotic obligations.

Although botulism outbreaks resulting from these commercial goods were not directly attributable to women's poor kitchen skills, housewives also took responsibility there, as they were expected to monitor the condition of canned foods and to boil all preserved food before serving it, in order to kill any toxins. A *Los Angeles Times* article quoted Ernest C. Dickson: "Any American housewife in this day and age has learned that what offends the nose and the eye should be summarily discarded."[51] Public statements routinely directed women to "use your nose," suggesting that botulism prevention was as simple as that. One California newspaper article made clear who should be responsible for this vigilance: "No economical housewife enjoys disposing of food in this manner, but better many cans of olives or peas or beans in the garbage than one member of the family in the cemetery."[52] In putting the point this way, these statements made it clear that potential deaths would be the fault of the "economical housewife" and her frugality or inability to identify spoiled food.[53]

Although these public statements implied that detecting botulism was a simple matter, there was actually much private debate among scientists as to the obvious presence of a distinct botulism odor. This was a contentious issue because the more strongly that experts claimed spoilage could be detected through the senses, the more they could deflect blame from the packers to the victims. Like the one above, many newspaper articles suggested that botulism nearly always had an obvious, strong smell that housewives could use to guard themselves from danger, if only they used their noses. Behind the scenes, however, the situation wasn't so clear.

One January 1920 exchange between Ernest C. Dickson and Charles Thom of the federal Bureau of Chemistry embodies some of this uncertainty. Dickson first argued that perhaps spoilage was not always obvious. One piece of evidence he drew on was the fact that even when poisoning occurred at a "fashionable hotel" for "moderately well to do people," not all victims had noticed something wrong with their food. On the basis of his own class prejudice, he suggested that perhaps this negligence could be expected among the lower classes but that those who were wealthier would surely notice spoilage if it was indeed obvious.[54] Because of this, Dickson thought it was important not to overstate the amount of decay that was always present in cases of botulism, so that consumers did not assume that lack of visible spoilage meant that there was definitely no botulism. Thom, however, disagreed with Dickson's caution, suggesting that spoilage was important enough an indicator that it was worth emphasizing in the press.

An important difference that emerged between Dickson and Thom in this exchange—and that was also central to the general discussion around food safety in the early twentieth century—was whether this was more an issue of individual responsibility or of public health. In this case, Thom clearly emphasized the former, while Dickson emphasized the latter. Thom wrote, "I am putting the responsibility back on the fellow who opens the can. If you eat hash or salad whose history you do not know, you eat it with blind faith in the fellow who prepares it."[55] Knowing the history of one's "hash or salad" was becoming more and more difficult in this world of industrial food, which raised new problems for public health. Dickson, however, did not believe that the consumer should be held responsible for this increasing distance between consumer and producer. Instead, he hoped that the issue of botulism could "be looked upon as one of importance to the public health, and [that] . . . every physician in the state [could see it as their duty] to aid in preventing outbreaks."[56] Physicians became necessary players in Americans' diets in part because of the rise of a large, commercial, transnational food system that threatened consumers with unknown contamination stemming from unknown places.

Regardless of the scientific debates about responsibility, consumers wanted specific advice about how to behave with regard to canned food. They wanted clear information about the risks of contamination and about what they could do to minimize those risks. Not only were experts unable to reassure consumers about how obvious contamination could be, but they often resisted even admitting that there was danger at all. Many experts—like Harvey Wiley in his response to Mrs. H. O.—emphatically downplayed the danger of botulism. W. V. Cruess, in a March 1920 article entitled "Fear of Canned Olive Is Now Dispelled," was quoted: "I feel that the present fear of canned foods existing in certain localities is entirely unfounded and believe further that the use of canned olives or other canned fruits is no more dangerous than riding on a street car." By drawing this parallel between these two prosaic activities, Cruess suggested that only someone who was unreasonable or unduly anxious would let the thought of botulism affect purchasing decisions.[57]

Judging by Jennie T. Hincks's 1921 letter to Cruess in which she disparaged her own anxiety, calling it "a very foolish state of mind," these messages about the lack of threat were reaching some consumers. But rather than reassuring consumers as the canners intended, these messages created confusion, as they put the responsibility of avoiding botulism onto the housewife but without giving her the proper tools to do so. Given the widespread nature of the 1919–20 botulism epidemic, the fear of germs that many Americans held during this time, and continuing consumer uncertainty, scientists and canners realized that they needed to get a clear message of safety across by giving consumers concrete evidence of industry improvements and resulting regulations.

SCIENTIFIC RESEARCH TO ADDRESS CONSUMER FEARS

Canners may have told consumers not to worry, but when it came to doing research to address the problem of botulism contamination, they invested increasing amounts of money following the 1919–20 outbreaks. By December 1919, within months of the Canton, Ohio, deaths in October, the canners, with the help of the NCA research director Willard D. Bigelow, had established an ambitious research program. Although born of concern on the part of industry, the Botulism Commission was also made possible by the support of government and academic bodies. The *American Food Journal* referred to it as the "first . . . opportunity for intensive collaborative study by a Federal department (U.S. Public Health Service), two of our great universities (California and Stanford), and the California State Department of Health."[58]

At the head of this project was a triumvirate of experts who each had different roles: Karl F. Meyer at the Hooper Research Foundation for Medical Research in San Francisco took on the bacteriological study of the botulinus organism itself; J. C. Geiger of the US Public Health Service began an epidemiological investigation of the field conditions in which the bacteria thrived; and Ernest C. Dickson at the Stanford University Medical School researched how the botulinus spores stood up to the various methods of sterilization used in the preparation of canned foods.[59] These men were all leading scientists who had previously worked on the problem of botulism. The 1919 Botulism Commission, though, differed from early research programs into the bacterial contamination of canned foods in several ways. It was jointly directed by industry, government, and universities; it was in response to consumer fear at a national scale; and it was charged with finding a concrete solution that would then be enforced by state public health departments.

The canners and scientists needed each other, and so cooperated despite the costs to each. Canners wanted to gain information and consumer trust but did not want to lose autonomy and control over their processes. The scientists garnered funding for aspects of their research, as well as the opportunity to contribute to public health. But they stood to tarnish their reputations as independent scientists because of their cooperation with industry. For the canners, though, the risk of consumer distrust and abandonment was strong enough that they welcomed impartial scientific research and the sort of government regulation that they believed would strengthen the industry. And although they tried to shape the recommendations that emerged from this research, they were willing to defer to the Botulism Commission scientists for the sake of gaining the authority and legitimacy of seemingly unbiased science.[60] The olive cases came at a time in American history, at the end of the Progressive Era and after World War I, when the public saw science and the "new public health" as a source of authority and expertise.[61]

The specific groups that funded the Botulism Commission's work were the NCA, the Canners League of California (CLC), and the California Olive Association (COA). These industry groups wanted the help of scientific research not only because of the practical conclusions that could be drawn from it but also because of the confidence conferred by scientific authority. Even if canners considered botulism a relatively insignificant issue as measured by actual number of cases, they realized it was rendered significant by consumer apprehension. Perhaps this apprehension could be alleviated if consumers knew that prominent scientists were on the case. In putting together a press release, olive man J. J. Hoey wrote to canner R. I. Bentley with his thoughts about how to best take advantage of scientific authority: "We will weaken our case by vague reference to 'eminent scientists.' . . . We really need to give names or authoritative sources in order to convince the doctors of the country."[62]

The California canners wanted to work with Dickson, arguably the most eminent botulism researcher in the country, even though a member of his research group, Georgina Burke, had previously called out the canning industry for sponsoring biased research. In that case, John Weinzirl, whose 1918 doctoral work had been funded by a grant from the NCA, produced a report on the bacteriology of canned foods, with which Burke took issue. In the report, Weinzirl reached several conclusions about bacterial activity in cans, the most striking of which was the claim that "food poisoning organisms, such as B. botulinus . . . are not found in commercial canned foods."[63] Although this was before the 1919 outbreaks, Weinzirl's statement was still deliberately misleading and therefore gave consumers a false perception about the safety of canned foods.

Georgina Burke's rejoinder in the *Journal of the American Medical Association* pointed out that Weinzirl's use of the term *commercial* was "restricted and therefore misleading," because he used it to refer only to food that was offered for sale. Since spoiled goods typically were not offered for sale, he did not consider these to be "commercial," even though the general public certainly believed the term to be "synonymous with factory canned foods as opposed to home canned foods."[64] Weinzirl's terminology was clearly deceptive. Burke reproached the industry for their selective scientific research: "The canners and their bacteriologists . . . are not justified in denying the occurrence of botulism from commercially canned foods."[65] Science, she believed, even when done on behalf of industry, had to be clear and honest, even if the scientific facts did not flatter the sponsors of that research. Still, in spite of Burke's reproach, or perhaps because of it, when the NCA sought a reliable scientist to investigate botulism in olives, they turned not to scientists like Weinzirl but to Stanford University and the perceived objectivity of Dickson and Burke.

For the Commission to begin their work, Dickson and his colleague Karl F. Meyer submitted a detailed budget to R. I. Bentley, of the California Packing Corporation. On the whole, for the first year of research, Dickson requested $24,000—of which $7,900 would go to the University of California for Meyer's bacteriological study, $5,000 to Dickson at Stanford for fieldwork, and $11,100 to Dickson at Stanford for laboratory work.[66] These significant sums indicated the importance the canning and olive industries granted to the eradication of botulism.[67] The canners had to mutually agree that this sort of scientific research was worth the large price tag. Meyer later recalled that if the canners had objected to this proposed budget he would have told them, "No money, no research, no salvation of the canning industry."[68] Thankfully for the parties involved, though, the canners chose salvation.

The segment of the nation's canners that most willingly "chose salvation," however, reveals the regional divide that existed around the botulism issue. By April of 1922, the NCA found that its members from the Midwest and the East Coast did not fully support funding the Botulism Commission, in contrast to the Western canners. R. I. Bentley explained the difference this way: "The bulk of the canners in the east do not see, or rather feel, the necessity of action so far as this botulism investigation is concerned, and as you know the coast here has stood the bulk of the expense."[69] Botulism was certainly a national problem, with outbreaks and media reports across the country, but California canners and olive growers were most affected and therefore most motivated to fund scientific research. The board of health of that state, too, was most centrally involved in developing regulations that would prevent further poisonings. Of course, individual eastern canners also engaged with other elements of public health work, such as investigating worker safety in canneries.[70] It was just botulism in olives—a California product—that did not stir them to action. When the processing studies initiated with the olive cases were extended to other products, canners across the country contributed, with the NCA paying a total of $225,000 to several universities over the course of five years.[71]

Once the initial funding had been secured, the Botulism Commission began its work in early December 1919, producing valuable research that led to state regulations. Within a year, in September 1920, J. C. Geiger—of the Botulism Commission and the US Public Health Service—confidently announced to a group of public health officials that although "too much importance was attached to [the early botulism] fatalities, and almost irreparable damage was done to a great industry . . . our experiments have re-established confidence in a great industry and have saved canners of this State $4,000,000 in a single year."[72] One of the major outcomes was that the California State Board of Health passed resolutions with regard to the processing of ripe olives, based on the commission's findings. They stated: "RESOLVED that ripe olives shall be deemed adulterated within the meaning of the California Pure Foods Act unless the same shall have been sterilized at a temperature of 240 degrees Fahrenheit for a period of not less than forty minutes," and further that "the temperature records shall be available at all times to the representatives of the State Board of Health."[73] This statement of required temperature and duration of cooking—240°F for at least forty minutes (240–40)—appeared to be a scientific fact that had been determined by rigorous investigation and that carried with it the weight of unbiased authority. In actuality, as with many regulations, this magic number was a product of negotiation among canners, scientists, and health officials.

Canners intervened all along the way to shape regulations in their favor, a clear example of private industry influencing policy. One of the central issues was that canners preferred a lower temperature—closer to the standard boiling temperature of 212°F—because they wanted to stick to the status quo and because they feared that higher temperatures would leave olives with a scorched taste.[74] Scientists and public health officials, on the other hand, preferred higher temperatures because these were more effective at killing the botulinus bacteria. From the beginning, olive canners sought to influence the temperature ruling.[75] Dickson's preliminary memorandum of July 1920 for the state's olive packers originally read, "Tests . . . warrant the recommendation of a sterilization under pressure at 250 for 50 minutes." The latter part of this sentence, however, had been crossed out by hand and replaced with "240F for at least 40 minutes."[76] While we don't know whether Dickson's choice to reduce the temperature was affected by the olive canners' lobbying or not, it is clear that there was uncertainty and flexibility in this "scientific" determination. Despite this reduced recommendation, the olive canners still encouraged Dickson to lower the temperature even further for the official regulations, in order to protect flavor. Specifically, they requested a 230°F temperature and wrote frequently to Dickson with this suggestion—repeating it in letters on July 20, August 2, and August 6 of 1920. Even as the olive canners exerted verbal pressure, they remained careful to defer to the scientists, writing, "This point [about the 230°F request], however, is subject to the approval of the scientists and no doubt whatever is decided upon by them will be the ultimate schedule."[77] Still, Dickson had the preferences of the industry in mind when he presented the findings that would lead to the ultimate public health ruling. In this situation, it was a matter of neither "pure" nor "corrupt" science but an ongoing set of negotiations.

The suggestion of this 240–40 regulation may have been the most prescriptive of the Botulism Commission's findings, but the research also produced an in-depth review of the documented cases of botulism in the United States and an analysis of its possible cause, distribution, symptoms, and pathology. Among the other notable findings were possible explanations for why there had been a recent increase in the rate of botulism in olives, suggestions for home canning, elucidation of the geographical and seasonal distribution of documented cases, and a discussion of botulism in nonhuman animals. The findings suggested that the increase of botulism could be partly attributed to World War I—"the practice of holding olives during the war years in water or weak brine solutions" likely led to the high rates of spoilage.[78] Because many canneries had shifted their production to meet the war effort during those years, olives that had been prepared before the war apparently sat waiting for the canning of such delicacies to resume after the war. And the increase in overall home canning by those with little experience, in response to the US Food Administration's wartime food conservation program, explained the rise of botulism in home-canned products.

The commission's work further introduced an interesting environmental component to the understanding of the bacteria. The botulinus organism originated in soil, which, when drying to dust, settled on the raw produce that entered the factory for canning. There was also evidence that the bacteria thrived in uncultivated soils. Although the commission emphasized that botulism was not exclusive to California or the Pacific states, this environmental origin of botulism partially explained the higher rates on the West Coast. The dry and dusty soil of California appeared more prone to harboring the bacillus, and the shorter history of California agriculture contributed to the less cultivated condition of some of the state's soils, relative to the Eastern Seaboard.[79]

Some academics did criticize Meyer and Dickson for their work on behalf of industry. Meyer recalled that some of his colleagues considered the industrial research to be a "prostitution of science" but that he "could not see why studies on the behavior of a microorganism under artificial conditions in test tubes in the laboratory constituted 'appropriate' science, while studies on the behavior of bacteria in cans or in nature . . . did not."[80] Indeed, there was a venerable tradition of scientists doing research on behalf of industry, as embodied in the work of Louis Pasteur, the father of the germ theory, who had saved numerous French industries through his work on milk, wine, beer, silk, and other agricultural products.[81] While Meyer saw his work on behalf of the industry as appropriate science, Dickson still insisted on the importance of following the accepted guidelines of scientific research and publishing. He warned canners: "There can be no use of the names of Meyer, Geiger or myself, nor any reference in advertising to the work we are doing until our reports appear in the legitimate medical press."[82] Even though Dickson was working directly on behalf of the industry, he understood his work through a lens of scientific research—with appropriate publishing guidelines—rather than through the lens of industrial research, which sought information for specific ends of practical application or building consumer trust.[83]

Although the canners and scientists did not always have the same views on the practice or applications of scientific research, they joined together in response to the botulism deaths. Canners realized that consumers had greater faith in scientific authority than in the authority of the food manufacturers, so they relied on the work of bacteriologists and public health workers to restore consumer trust after the 1919–20 outbreak of botulism in ripe olives. Further, the California canners took the commission's findings and cooperated with the California State Board of Health in turning these research findings into state-enforced regulations. One industry bulletin suggested that the collaboration marked a "new epoch in public health work in that it represents the combined efforts of three large universities, a government department and a great manufacturing industry."[84]

STATE INVOLVEMENT: THE CANNERY INSPECTION ACT
AND PUBLIC HEALTH

Despite the canners' public deflection of blame from themselves to their housewife consumers, they implicitly assumed responsibility, first in funding the Botulism Commission and then in inviting regulation by the California State Board of Health and a statewide cannery inspection service. In this case, canners clearly accepted canned-food safety as a public health issue in order to get the sanction conferred by the external expertise of government officials and independent regulators. In this way, the botulism outbreaks actually mirrored other outbreaks of rare diseases, in their role as an impetus to public health reform. Historians of epidemic disease have shown how public health activity has often resulted from diseases that were less common, and therefore less familiar and more terrifying, like cholera and yellow fever, rather than the more common tuberculosis or pneumonia.[85]

Botulism emerged in a moment when Americans were experiencing more government oversight in their lives.[86] World War I marked a significant shift in the federal government's size and strength. In mobilizing for war, and in fighting on the home front, the United States dramatically expanded the reach of its federal apparatus. American citizens came to accept the role of government in their daily lives as they took in propaganda from the Committee on Public Information or voluntarily rationed their food purchases on Meatless Mondays and Wheatless Wednesdays.[87] The influenza epidemic of 1918 had also familiarized Americans with public health infrastructure at the state and federal levels. When the botulism epidemic hit, then, canners knew that citizens might look to the government for guidance on health and food safety.

Although in establishing the Botulism Commission canners had been involved with some federal agencies, like the Bureau of Chemistry and the US Public Health Service, they actually worked most closely with public health agencies at the state level. This was in keeping with the larger development of public health oversight in America, which began in the second half of the nineteenth century at the local level, expanded to the state level, and only then reached the federal level.[88]

The California State Board of Public Health was the central organizing body that carried out public health work in response to the botulism outbreak. It was formed in 1870 at the urging of Dr. Thomas M. Logan, who had come west from South Carolina following the population influx after the gold rush of 1848. In its early years, the board oversaw epidemics, sanitation, the gathering of statewide medical statistics, and the establishment of local boards of health. Although other boards of health around the country turned some of their attention to food safety in the mid- to late nineteenth century, it was not until 1907 that California set up a formal state laboratory for the analysis and examination of food and drugs.[89] The state had examined individual cases of adulteration through the state analyst since 1885 but had not done so systematically, with the opening of the state laboratory, until a decade before the botulism outbreak in 1919. The cases refocused the attention of the board of health's Bureau of Food and Drugs to the state's food-processing industry. It was only after the botulism cases that the board even required physicians to report food-poisoning deaths to the state authority.[90]

California canners—who were most threatened by the olive crisis—responded most eagerly to the need for change. They were actually ahead of federal pronouncements of food safety as a public health issue. The federal organization most responsible for oversight of food safety was the Bureau of Chemistry of the USDA, which had overseen the passage of the Pure Food and Drug Act in 1906. But in commenting on the botulism cases in 1922, Charles Thom, chief of the Microbiological Laboratory at the Bureau of Chemistry, rejected federal responsibility: "The packer must use the best known method in putting up food, the dealer must give it intelligent care and scrutiny, but the one who prepares it for the table is the final protector of the life of the consumer."[91] He left no room for the government in this equation, focusing only on the packer, the dealer, and, primarily, the "one who prepares it for the table." California canners may have wanted to agree with Thom, but they considered this deflection of responsibility an unwise move if they were to capture consumer trust. They realized that this strategy did not leave consumers eager to buy canned food and to assume the onus of being the "final protector[s] of life." Instead, the expert seal of approval was necessary. The canners called on the government to help.

The 1906 Pure Food and Drug Act had set a precedent for government regulation of food safety, putting in place a federal system of meat inspection and controlling food adulteration. State and city laws also existed throughout the United States, helping to protect the food supply—especially of milk and meat—and control the spread of any contamination.[92] Indeed, a talk entitled "The Botulism Problem" by R. E. Doolittle of the Bureau of Chemistry remarked with wonder on this level of oversight: "It is almost marvelous, when one stops to think, that when emergencies, such as these outbreaks were, arise, there is at the command of every state, city and federal official an army of trained inspectors and scientists who on almost a moment's notice can be put into the field to investigate shipments and remove from the market suspected products."[93] These inspectors and scientists were employed by the government and, in most cases, were funded by public dollars. California's cannery inspection service, however, was an exception to this rule, as it was funded by the state's canning association.

For the most part, the California canning industry initially welcomed government involvement. Beginning with the 240–40 regulations in September 1920, the California Board of Health enforced a strict ruling for all olives processed in the state. These regulations held without too much resistance for the next few years. By 1924, however, some new work by Botulism Commission scientist Karl Meyer indicated that either a higher temperature or a longer time would be needed for full sterilization, much as Dickson had written in his first drafts of the proposed regulations back in 1920. Meyer recommended a processing time of 250°F for fifty minutes or 240°F for sixty minutes. The California State Board of Health, through its secretary William M. Dickie, communicated this information to the state's packers.

Whereas California canners had mostly come around to the 240–40 regulations in 1920, during a moment of crisis, they were less willing to accept more stringent rules in 1924, when the outbreaks had subsided and consumer distrust was less of an immediate concern. Some canners argued that Meyer's findings were "unjust" and that this higher temperature would destroy the olives. They refused to follow the recommendation. Dickie offered little sympathy to the olive packers and advised that they consider heartier varieties. He emphasized his department's priorities: "We want to do everything we can to help the industry, but we simply cannot have another outbreak if it is humanly possible to prevent it."[94] He further suggested that some of the "reliable packers" could subject different varieties of olives to a range of times and temperatures to test the resulting taste and condition. If this was done, he was sure that they could "get a temperature much higher than we now have. But as it is now, every time there is a change in the temperature or time it seems to throw the fear of God into the packer's hearts, with no definite evidence to either warrant or offset their fears."[95] The board of health sought primarily to protect the public; they therefore considered the canners' resistance irrational.

The state board of health had been involved in botulism investigations even before the 1920 outbreaks, tracking instances of poisoning.

Following the outbreaks, however, they became more centrally involved. An early contribution the board made was to declare botulism a reportable disease in California.[96] This meant that all physicians who saw what they believed to be botulism were required to report this to their local health officer, who then telegraphed the state board in Sacramento. The state would then launch an inquiry, compiling information about the "vehicle of infection," "the history of the implicated food," and any autopsy or other clinical information.[97]

The California Canners League and the state's olive interests largely appreciated the state's help, seeing the involvement of the board of health as a boon. Not all canners were so grateful, however. A 1921 *New York Times* article reported that the Curtis Corporation of California, whose olives were implicated in the first round of outbreaks, brought a million-dollar lawsuit against the Detroit Board of Health. The corporation claimed that its business had been damaged by that amount by the board's seizure of potentially contaminated olives in October 1919, following the death of two Detroit women.[98] Nevertheless, for the most part, California canners believed that state involvement helped more than it harmed—so much so that when a few cases of botulism emerged in canned spinach in early 1921, the state's canners joined together to adopt resolutions dictating time and temperature of spinach processing. They further called for the help of federal and state health inspectors in enforcing these resolutions, writing: "We urgently request [the state] to assist us in policing the industry."[99]

Over the next few years, California took an increasingly active role in the oversight of the canning industry, becoming a true leader in integrating public health concerns into food industry practices. The state created the Division of Cannery Inspection in 1923 and passed the Cannery Inspection Law, Assembly Bill 960, in 1925.[100] A crucial point here is that these inspection programs were funded entirely by canners—testifying to the rising importance canners placed on government regulation around 1920. The programs required each factory to keep detailed production records, copies of which they sent to the state board of health. Additionally, the state dispatched several supervisors to each region of the state to periodically check up on local operations. Although state health officials first focused on olive plants, they soon added spinach to their purview, and by 1925 they were inspecting "all vegetable canned products with the exception of straight tomato products, and sardines and tuna . . . at the request of the packers."[101] The state inspection service inspired similar programs in other states and had a lasting legacy in California, continuing well into the middle of the twentieth century. That this system existed, with industry funding, through at least 1951 attests to the long-standing function and mutual benefit of this collaboration between the canners and the state.[102] While this close oversight by the state provided the tangible benefit of reducing botulism outbreaks through rigorous scrutiny, it also offered the less tangible benefit of giving the industry the stamp of government approval.

Even as canners touted this government approval as a selling point, they also harbored some concerns about the suggestion that their products were dangerous enough to require oversight in the first place. A 1921 announcement about a new advertising campaign read, "Ripe olives as now cured and packed, under the watchful eye of the California state authorities (not, however, that the packers will need watching), are absolutely dependable and may be eaten freely without the slightest danger."[103] The parenthetical aside tried to give the sense that canned olives had the best of both worlds: clear supervision *and* the lack of need for clear supervision. This incongruity put canners in the precarious position of trying to draw on the benefits of government cooperation, while rejecting the idea that such cooperation was needed. Canners were ever mindful of the public image of their products, using governmental oversight as a strategy to reassure consumers only when it served them to do so.

. . .

The crisis of deaths from poisoned olives in October 1919 presaged a far more abstract but complicated crisis among the country's canners, especially those of California. Because death from botulism was so frightening—progressing quickly, causing paralysis, and stemming from the very source that was supposed to offer nourishment and comfort—newspapers found great fodder for their stories in the botulism outbreaks that spread across the United States in early 1920. These reports appeared in great numbers in newspapers throughout the country, despite the relative infrequency of actual deaths. Olive sales took a dramatic nosedive, falling by 95 percent in the months after the first incidents. Canners of all products quickly realized that this fate could befall their sectors as well; the horrific stories in the media could lead to distrust among their existing and potential customers, who still felt concern about the opacity of the tin can.

Although in the public realm the canners were hesitant to take responsibility and often denounced the gravity of the epidemic, behind the scenes they quickly sought the help of government agencies and scientific researchers, funding the Botulism Commission. The findings of this team led to concrete changes in the way that olives were processed—with regulations that required olives to be processed at 240°F for at least forty minutes—and to changes in the view of canned-food safety as an issue of public health. The botulism outbreak prompted California canners to fund a permanent cannery inspection service, carried out by the state board of health, which gave the board the power to regulate and control the production and distribution of canned-food products throughout the state. The canners hoped that these moves would help increase the transparency of their products and of the increasingly industrialized food system.

During this whole process, as canners responded to the botulism crisis, they were moved by an understanding of the power of consumer uncertainty and distrust to undermine their business. Though they might not have had a clear picture of consumer desires, aside from the letters they received from women like Jennie Hincks and Mrs. H. O., they imagined the negative reaction newspaper audiences would have upon reading the numerous and gory accounts of death by olives. Canners and the scientists often emphasized the responsibility of women to protect their families from botulism poisoning. At the same time, however, canners understood that simply blaming consumers would do little to alleviate potential concerns they felt about the safety of canned food. In a time when Americans were coming to accept the role of increased government oversight, especially on issues of health, canners co-opted some of this authority in collaborating with public health agencies.

The botulism cases and ensuing research had a number of lasting effects. When spinach canners experienced some contamination in 1921, they followed in the footsteps of the olive canners, setting their own temperature-time guidelines for processing spinach.[104] Other California canners followed suit, so that by 1925 sardines, tuna, and all vegetable products except tomatoes had standardized methods for production, which were overseen and enforced by the Cannery Inspection Service. Although other states did not establish such rigorous inspection services right away, they became more familiar with the processes of standardization through knowledge of California's innovative activity.[105] The NCA also initiated similar research to establish time-temperature regulations at the national level, under the guidance of Willard D. Bigelow.[106] In 1963, the association reflected on the importance of that earlier research: "So valuable and comprehensive were the findings made between 1919 and 1925, that the conclusions still guide packers today."[107]

In addition to putting stock in scientific research and government regulation, California canners began to invest in new strategies of marketing and advertising, which foreshadowed the direction much of the canning industry would take in the following decades. In response to the 1919–20 botulism outbreak, the associated industries made use of public relations campaigns to encourage renewed consumption. In May 1920, California olive packers decided to raise $100,000 for an advertising campaign, directed at both consumers and grocers, to offset "the unfavorable publicity ripe olives have received through alleged poisoning cases."[108] This large amount was more than three times the budget of the Botulism Commission in its first year of work. As part of this campaign, the California Olive Association, along with the home economics department of the University of California, published a book of recipes that presented a "great many attractive methods" of cooking with olives. Along with the cookbook, representatives of the association were "actively engaged in telling the country of virtues of the California ripe olives" through other means.[109] This focus on reaching out to consumers—rather than simply building confidence by publicizing scientific efforts—gives an indication of where the larger canning industry was headed in its next phase. Canners would soon turn to direct marketing efforts to reach consumers, beginning to reject the need for input from government agencies and seeking a research and regulation agenda that was more securely in their own control.

4

Grade A Tomatoes

Labeling Debates and Consumers
in the New Deal

In the middle years of the 1930s, a can of Campbell's tomato soup sported a red and white label, with fancy white cursive lettering. The label also reported that the soup was made by the Joseph Campbell Company in New Jersey, that it was condensed, and that Campbell's made twenty other varieties of soup. But it gave little information about what was contained inside—no standardized ingredients label or nutrition information, nothing to give consumers a sensory preview of its contents. Instead, there was the familiar logo, the advertising copy with the catchy slogan "M'm! M'm! Good!," and perhaps the cherubic Campbell's Kids who had won over the nation's hearts with their gimmicky rhymes. Consumers had to either rely on the reputation of the brand name and its associated marketing or seek recommendations from store clerks, friends, or domestic advice columnists.

Canning companies did not convey objective quality information directly to consumers, though such quality designations did exist behind the scenes. Consumers encountered canned food on grocery store shelves, or perhaps behind the grocers' counters, or maybe in one of the new self-serve aisles of supermarkets that were popping up all over the country.[1] But if we follow the cans' paths backward, we can also go behind the scenes to see how quality designations functioned outside consumers' line of sight. Let's take a can of tomatoes. Before it made it to the grocery store shelf, it had to be unpacked from a shipping crate in the back of the grocery store. The crate would have had a code marked on the outside, secret and meaningless to an ordinary consumer, but offering full information on quality to the canner and distributor. The crate would have traveled to the grocery store from the cannery, taking a detour at a warehouse, where it would have rested until market time. In compliance with the US Warehouse Act of 1916, trade men used quality codes on crates of canned tomatoes to determine how much they were worth and, accordingly, the amount of collateral the crates represented for financing purposes.[2]

Before the canned tomatoes' stint in the warehouse, the tomatoes themselves passed through the steps of the cannery—being washed and blanched and peeled and packed. And to even make it there, the tomatoes first had to start out as seed, then as fruit in the field, as cargo in the back of a truck or steam engine, and finally as deliveries at the cannery door. When lying in the field, the individual tomatoes might have had tags on them indicating grade and quality, for the use of growers and agricultural experimenters.[3] Once the tomatoes reached the cannery, they would likely have been evaluated by a government-trained inspector, who would grade each tomato as No. 1, No. 2, or cull, according to quality.

As we follow this can of tomatoes, it becomes clear that some form of official grading or quantification was taking place all along the line, except in the final stages. In the end, where we began our story, is the consumer. Although all those before her in the journey of the can of tomatoes—the grower, the agricultural scientist, the canner, the warehouser, the distributor—had quantitative knowledge of the products' grade, the consumer was left without, forced to make decisions about what she fed herself and her family based on incomplete information. But beginning in 1933, government representatives and consumer advocates set out to change that.

That year, as the federal government grew in response to the unprecedented economic shock of the Great Depression, a debate began to rage in Washington, D.C., about the information on canned foods' labels. On one side was the Consumers' Advisory Board (CAB) of the National Recovery Administration (NRA), pushing for grade labels that would offer consumers objective information on quality by grading each can with a grade of "A," "B," or "C." On the other, opposing grade labels, was the National Canners Association (NCA). The former group, in the context of the Great Depression and New Deal, believed that empowered consumers were necessary for a revived economy. Grade labels would offer consumers the power to choose wisely and get the most bang for their buck. They would give consumers a solid foundation for trust, mitigating the opacity of canned food by offering a "window into the can."[4] But the canners pushed against grade labels for a variety of reasons, claiming they were unreliable, difficult to enforce, and not what consumers actually wanted. Each side was steadfast in its view.

The grade-labeling debate helps us understand the complex and changing relationships among the canning industry, consumers, and scientific and governmental experts in the 1930s. This decade brought a turning point in these interrelationships and set the canners on a path that would lead them toward the modern food industry. Whereas canners had previously complied with regulation that modified industrial and agricultural practices in the name of gaining consumer trust, by the 1930s the canning industry began to resist this intrusion. Instead, the industry came to rely more on its own strengthened position in the American economy to push for autonomy in winning over consumers. The canners turned to the ascending fields of marketing, advertising, and branding to more directly influence their audiences. The burgeoning consumer movement of the 1930s contributed both to the New Deal government's special attention to consumer issues and to canners' new perception of consumers as a particular demographic who could be known and directly addressed. In the fight against grade labeling, canners saw an opportunity to claim the right to speak for the consumer.

This story shows the centrality of consumers in the changing political economy of the New Deal era, a period in which the federal government sought to boost and reform the economy through a series of social programs.[5] During this period between 1933 and 1938, questions of labor and capital were central to federal decision making. But consumers also played a crucial part in the configuration of the 1930s economy. The "concrete daily economic experiences" of shopping—in the words of New Dealer Caroline Ware—played a central role in shaping the actions of consumer product industries, which then reverberated throughout the economy.[6] How and why a consumer chose a can of tomatoes had far-reaching consequences beyond the family dinner table. Consumers organized to elevate concerns about food quality and transparency, making them deeply political and social issues. Organized consumers fought long and hard to get representation in New Deal agencies.[7] The canners' waning willingness to cooperate with these organizations and with external regulation followed from the fact that by the 1930s business was booming. More and more consumers were buying and eating canned food. They were coming to trust canned food. The canners therefore found themselves on more stable ground, less in need of external affirmation.

THE NEW DEAL AND THE "AWAKENING CONSUMER"

The stock market crash of 1929 and the subsequent Great Depression rocked the United States to the core. At the lowest point, a quarter of Americans were out of work. Banks failed, countless people defaulted on their loans, drought savaged the farms of the Great Plains, and newly homeless citizens crowded the streets. Twelve million Americans were unemployed and had to turn to charity or government support to find their next meal. Soup kitchens emerged to feed the hungry, and breadlines stretched endlessly.[8] Despair and psychological upheaval went hand in hand with economic collapse.

Although the immediate years after the crash yielded optimism and a hope that the economy would quickly right itself, by 1933 the Depression was calling into question the foundations of American capitalism and of the industrial order that had been so fruitful in previous decades. Perhaps a reliance on the market and the laws of supply and demand was not enough to keep the country chugging along in prosperity? Perhaps regulation was needed to reduce cutthroat competition and to ensure that different interests were represented? Although the canning industry had been particularly open to government involvement in the fight for pure foods at the turn of the century and the fight against botulism in the 1920s, many other industries had stood firm in their independence and faith in the free market.[9]

In the early days of the Depression, the country's industries were among the most optimistic about the economic situation and most dismissive of the idea that government interference was needed. This was matched by President Herbert Hoover's commitment to finding a solution to depression through industry, local government, and charity rather than through the federal government. But as citizens, workers, and consumers banded together to voice their struggles and to make clear that this was not just a minor hiccup, businesses and the federal government began to take notice.

When Franklin D. Roosevelt was elected president in 1932, he quickly got to work, looking for solutions to the economic crisis. Although some of his early measures reflected the same basic economic philosophy of his predecessor Hoover, at the beginning of the New Deal in 1933 Congress passed a slew of initiatives that signaled new directions. Among the mix of new agencies devoted to public works, relief, and regulation, the most important initiative of the first "hundred days" of the New Deal was the establishment of the NRA.[10] The NRA set out to develop a series of codes for the country's industries, which would encourage the formation of trade associations and minimize negative competition, thereby leading to recovery. The codes regulated a wide range of industrial and labor practices, including price fixing, wages, unionization, and collective bargaining, for over three hundred industries. On the whole, the NRA proposed to promote consumption by encouraging all industries to raise wages without raising prices, in the hopes that this would increase consumer spending potential. In the case of consumer products industries, like canned food, the codes also had provisions for quality labeling to give consumers more information and increase their purchasing power.

In an unprecedented move for the federal government, many of the agencies created by the New Deal had sections within them devoted to the interests of consumers. The NRA had the CAB, the Agricultural Adjustment Administration had the Consumers' Counsel, and the National Emergency Council had the Consumers' Division. One contemporary noted that these represented "an entirely new departure by the Federal Government in behalf of the consumer."[11] While modern Americans of the twenty-first century may now take it for granted that businesses and the government alike cater to consumers, this was not the case in the 1930s. Never before had the government recognized consumers as a distinct entity with their own interest, separate from that of the public in general.

The consumers' divisions argued that the "public" was divided into three groups: producers, laborers, and consumers. Since the former two groups were well organized and well represented by trade organizations and labor unions, respectively, this left consumers in need of their own representative group to speak on their behalf. And government funding for consumer support seemed fair considering the funds offered to the country's businesses. The CAB's Committee on Standards wrote, "If our national economy is to be sufficiently directed at both ends—in its making and in its spending—the consumer will have to be helped in some wholesale fashion comparable to the $50,000,000 of annual help" that the government gave to industry.[12]

Although these consumer organizations may have been new within the federal government, they took as their foundation a wider consumer movement that had been spreading throughout the country by the 1930s, seeking to harness the power of consumption to improve society and the economy. Some contemporaries called this period the era of "the Awakening Consumer."[13] In February 1934, Lena M. Phillips of the National Council of Women said, "We have a new consumer consciousness in psychology, that is increasing very rapidly in our country."[14] President Roosevelt, in his 1934 State of the Union Address, alluded to this "slowly growing impulse among consumers to enter the industrial marketplace equipped with sufficient organization to insist upon fair prices and honest sales."[15] And sociologist Robert Lynd, author of the *Middletown* studies, wrote, "There is a 'consumer problem' of national proportions, and it is here to stay as a large white elephant on the doorstep of business."[16]

These impulses toward consumer organization in the 1930s were helped along by a series of popular muckraking books on consumption, beginning with the 1927 book *Your Money's Worth* by Stuart Chase and F.J. Schlink. Other books by Schlink that followed, such as *100,000,000 Guinea Pigs* and *Eat, Drink, and Be Wary,* further sparked consumers' desire to know more about industrial products and their recognition of the power of everyday consumption. Chase and Schlink also formed Consumers' Research in 1929, the first "professional consumer organization," which grew to have fifty-eight thousand subscribers by 1935.[17]

However, Consumers' Research and similar organizations weren't so popular among the nation's businesses, which saw consumer activism as a threat to the established economic order. One *Business Week* article referred to Consumers' Research as "Advertising's Enemy No. 1," which was responsible for "the current wave of consumer distrust."[18] Although some historians have argued that consumer tactics were complicit with capitalist culture—that, in effect, these business had nothing to worry about—many others have pointed out the ways in which consumer activism offered a critique of capitalism, bolstering the welfare state and the idea of social citizenship.[19] On the whole, during this era, consumers considered themselves central actors in a democracy, using their purchasing practices to exert power and shape business practices and the economic order. This idea is embodied by the idea of the "citizen consumer" and is evidenced by consumer representation within New Deal agencies.[20]

Of the many arenas in which consumers demanded change, the purchasing of food—and canned food in particular—was central. In a 1930 address, the president of the NCA remarked on the increase in communication from consumers. Previously, he said, most complaints had come through newspaper reports, and "very few complaints came direct from consumers. In the past three years particularly there has been a marked change."[21] Whereas in earlier decades consumers had pushed for food safety, now shoppers began to petition for clear labeling, higher quality, and fair prices. Historian Tracey Deutsch points to the growing demand for "such changes as graded canned goods and standardized sizes of products" as a central marker of the growing consumer movement.[22] As consumers claimed more of a national spotlight, women began to ask grocers, canning-industry home economists, and federal government food officials for clearer information on which to base their purchasing decisions and their allocations of trust.

These demands for information led not only to altered consumption practices on the individual level but also to a changing relationship with the federal government. In protesting what they saw as unfair food prices for the given quality, consumers shifted away from their earlier tactics of comparison shopping and bargain hunting and toward asking government officials to assess proper food prices and to share pricing information. From this emerged a new public attachment to Washington, D.C., such that consumers looked to the government for information to fuel their local activism.[23] In this way, the federal government, consumers, and the food industry laid the groundwork for an integrated relationship. It was these concerns of consumers that led the NRA's CAB to take up grade labeling as a central cause. Consumer groups took an interest in labeling well before politicians proposed ideas around labeling in the New Deal. Indeed, popular support led to federal policy debates.

THE CONSUMER UNDER THE NATIONAL RECOVERY ADMINISTRATION

Grade labeling in the canning industry offers a perfect case to examine how consumer demand for information about food products, federal government intervention, and the food industry's response affected public policy during the New Deal. Grade labeling proposed an intervention into the daily economic experiences of consumers, giving the "awakening consumers" of the New Deal a concrete opportunity to channel into their own lives the abstract ideas of consumer empowerment that were floating around in popular and political culture. This grade-labeling plan—proposed by the NRA's CAB—was a clear illustration of the changing relationships among consumers, producers, and the government in the 1930s.

The NRA sought to regulate the country's industries by setting a minimum wage and a maximum work week across the board, and also by requesting that each individual industry establish its own "code of fair competition," which dictated how the industries would operate to promote economic recovery. These codes were voluntary agreements, established through public hearings, which dictated aspects of production, like increased wages, pay rates, price-fixing, and hours. Of course, this would only work if *all* businesses gave up full initial profits. Otherwise, cutthroat competitors would benefit from others' sacrifice and would leave the poor consumer to either pay higher prices while on a lower income or support unscrupulous business practices. This is where the CAB came in. According to its founding document, the CAB was "responsible for watching every agreement and every hearing to see that nothing is done to impair the interest of those whose daily living may be affected by these agreements."[24] In this way, the CAB would try to ensure both that industries increased wages without inflating prices and that this was uniformly done, by all businesses.

The CAB was composed of a diverse group of economists, sociologists, consumer advocates, commercial purchasing agents, and representatives from several government agencies.[25] It was a departure from the disparate strands of consumer activism that had immediately preceded it. The chair of the board, Mary Harriman Rumsey, was a friend of Eleanor Roosevelt and came from a distinguished family—daughter of railroad magnate E.H. Harriman and sister to one-time New York governor W. Averell Harriman. Throughout her life, until her tragic death from a horse-riding accident in December 1934, she fought for consumer representation in government. The executive director of the board was Dexter M. Keezer, a renowned economist who served as president of Reed College between his time with the CAB and his return to Washington in 1942 to serve as deputy administrator of the Office of Price Administration.[26] Through the work of Rumsey, Keezer, and the board, consumers finally had hope of government representation to balance the attention given to industry trade organizations and labor unions.

Despite the existence of the CAB, many observers considered the NRA to be serving only the interest of business or labor. From the start, the NRA was subject to so many competing demands that forward movement was difficult. Producers and business wanted profits, laborers wanted higher wages, and consumers wanted lower prices. And although these varying interest groups weren't always fully distinct, producers were first and foremost representatives of their respective industries and only secondarily consumers themselves.[27] Industries had more power, both financially and organizationally, and, as a result, the CAB often had to devote time to "picking itself up off the floor after being knocked down and around by high test pressure groups."[28] But even the country's businesses were not always happy with the work of the NRA.

Observers also continued to doubt the board's ability to meet consumer hopes. According to CAB executive director Dexter M. Keezer, many people saw the NRA as "a sort of steam roller designed to flatten the consumer" and were skeptical of a program that expected consumers to buy more when their "taxes have gone up, living costs have gone up, and salaries gone down." When Keezer wrote an article entitled "The Consumer under the National Recovery Administration," some of his "delightful skeptics" suggested that the title held a double meaning, indicating "that the NRA is just one more of those insupportable burdens which are constantly being heaped upon that long-suffering subject of economic abuse—the consumer."[29] These critics were skeptical that the NRA could actually do anything to help consumers, given its industrial focus and the larger economic trends. And indeed, the CAB buckled under the weight of bureaucratic bungling, an impossibly large task, and a lack of power to enforce its recommendations. To give just a taste of the vast scope of the task, the board hoped to develop codes for several hundred industries, all at top speed, with a minimal budget. For comparison, the US Tariff Commission typically spent $25,000 in doing a cost study of just one single product.[30] The CAB had a herculean job to do.

Some economists questioned the idea upon which the New Deal agencies' consumer councils were founded, arguing that most Americans were more invested in their role as producers than as consumers. Ultimately, only those whose primary role was consumption should care more about the consumer's interest than that of the producer. This directed consumer agencies' spotlight squarely at American housewives. Although nearly a quarter of women worked outside the home in the 1930s, women were still generally pictured primarily as homemakers, responsible for consumer decisions and less concerned with production.[31] Thus much of the New Deal conversation about consumers—and certainly about grade labeling—focused primarily on American housewives who did not work outside the home. This was a convenient way of collapsing a more complicated body of consumers into a single stereotype, which was easy to make assumptions about as a target of marketing and economic policy.

While the NRA may not have succeeded in its goal of curtailing chaotic competition, the CAB did succeed in advancing one of its primary reforms: quality labeling. There was a concern that if industries had to raise wages without raising prices, the quality of the goods would suffer, leaving the consumer paying the same amount for lower-quality items. The answer to this problem? Quality standards, to be regulated by the government, and communicated to consumers by clear grades printed on labels. If the consumer could make an informed decision about what she was buying, based on clear information right there on the label, she would be better able to hold industries to higher standards without relying on the price to indicate grade. Beyond canned food, the board worked with a range of industries in the hopes that they would develop quality standards—across consumer products like blankets, dresses, and fabrics.[32]

The CAB's work on informative labeling was tied to the larger consumer movement of the 1930s, which encouraged public education and sought to reform economic citizenship. This interest in grade labeling among consumers had begun in the 1920s and had also been picked up by a number of governmental agencies, like the Bureau of Home Economics, in previous years.[33] By 1933, the CAB, under the guidance of renowned sociologist Robert S. Lynd, began research into quality standards, seeing this work as essential to consumer protection and to the development of well-rounded codes of fair competition.[34]

In many ways, it might seem that the CAB's research targeted only individual action, rather than calling for any structural changes in economic or political foundations. But in fact these individual actions added up to a larger challenge to the existing workings of the marketplace. Manufacturers maintained the idea that price indicated quality and that consumers could therefore get higher-quality items by paying higher prices. But the issuing of standards undermined this assumption, suggesting that government standards were necessary beyond the assurances brand names carried. Understandably, the biggest manufacturers, who had invested in building their brands, worried that grade labels would expose their falsehood. Brand names cost more, but not always because they were of a higher quality. In this way, basic decisions of consumption became part and parcel of new relationships among business, consumers, and the state. Indeed, as political historian Meg Jacobs grandly claims, "Fights over canned peaches stood at the center of a new conception of American political economy."[35] The grade on a can of peaches or tomato soup—or the standards for any consumer product—armed shoppers with the power to turn their individual action into structural change, forcing producers to supply quality goods.

THE GREATEST TEST CASE: THE CANNING CODE

Of the hundreds of industries the CAB worked with to develop codes of fair competition, the board had its greatest hopes set on developing grade labeling within the canning industry. According to consumer advocate Persia Campbell, the canning code "was considered a test case by the C.A.B.," its importance indicated by the presence of CAB chair, "Mrs. Rumsey herself," at the first public hearing for the canning industry.[36] The reasons for this focus on the canning code were twofold: first, quality labels seemed most needed for canned food, and second, they seemed most likely to succeed in this particular industry, relative to other consumer products.

Grade labels for cans were especially needed because canned foods were of a fundamentally different nature than other consumer products, like coats or curtains. While a consumer could judge a coat in the store by trying it on, touching it, or looking at it, she could not do this with a can of tomatoes, with its contents hidden within the tin can. And even if she knew one brand had served her well last time, there was no certainty that the next can would meet the same standards. The only ways she could judge the quality of the tomatoes before opening the can were to use price as an indicator, to trust descriptive words on the label, to believe in the value of the brand name, or to be lured by a catchy slogan. But none of these was sufficient. Numerous studies by the Federal Trade Commission and other organizations found that price did not correspond to quality. Brand names had more to do with advertising budgets than with a food's flavor. And there was no oversight for labeling, beyond the assurance that the food was not adulterated. What cans needed, what grade labels could supply, was a "window into the can."

The CAB had great hopes for the establishment of grade labels within the canning industry. These hopes lay in the fact that canners had been working with some kind of grading system for over ten years, had welcomed previous labeling plans, and already had a working grade-labeling system in Canada. All of these factors gave the CAB reason to believe that their plans would be successful in this arena. And if they didn't work here, it was likely that quality labels on the whole were doomed to failure.

Previously, canners had worked with grades under the US Warehouse Act and in grading raw produce. The Warehouse Act passed in 1916, allowing farmers to use their stored staple crops, and later, canned food, as collateral for Federal Reserve Bank loans.[37] But in order to calculate the worth of their collateral, the producers in each case had to estimate the value of the goods stored in their warehouses. Among the canners, this led to the development of a grading system, carried out by the US Department of Agriculture (USDA), which categorized different canned foods according to quality so that the canners could receive a higher loan amount for higher-quality canned goods.[38] By 1926, the USDA had successfully established criteria that placed a value on canned goods based on characteristics of color, size, and firmness. But, to be clear, these grades were used only in the factory and in the warehouse, not in the actual retail outlets where consumers interacted with canned food. That is, the grades would be prominently displayed on the boxes and crates in which cans of tomatoes were shipped, but not on the can labels that were visible to consumers in the grocery store aisles.

The Warehouse Act grades were also used for trade dealings among canners, brokers, and grocers. Those who bought and sold canned foods benefited from as clear a description of quality as possible so that they were paying and receiving fair prices. Government purchasing agencies, in addition to private agents, bought canned food on the grade. Later, consumer advocates would point out the hypocrisy of using information among businessmen and government officials that was withheld from the average consumer.

The second case in which canners worked with grades, grading raw produce intended for canning, began by the late 1920s under the guidance of Fay C. Gaylord at the Purdue University Agricultural Experiment Station in Indiana. Gaylord started out by convincing tomato canners in his area that buying on a graded basis would be more advantageous than the flat basis on which most canning produce had been purchased.[39] Typically, canners would contract with growers at the beginning of the season, promising a certain price per pound of produce. Unfortunately, quality didn't always correlate with weight, and this system failed to reward growers for delivering high-quality produce. As Gaylord wrote in 1930, "The grower who delivers tomatoes that just pass and the one with a load of really fine quality are paid the same price per ton." This led to the packing of low-grade tomatoes and a "resultant decrease in per capita consumption" of canned goods.[40]

To combat this, Gaylord worked with the US Bureau of Agricultural Economics to set up a tiered system of grading in which tomatoes were separated into No. 1, No. 2, and culls, to be evaluated by government-trained inspectors. No. 1 tomatoes were "firm, ripe, well-colored, well-formed, free from molds and decay and from damage caused by growth cracks, worm holes, cat-faces, sun-scald, freezing injury, or mechanical or other means." No. 2 tomatoes were those that didn't meet the above criteria but were better than the culls, which were typically green or rotten.[41] The same inspectors also worked with individual growers early in the season to teach them how to identify tomatoes by grade. This system worked, at least in the case of Indiana tomatoes, and the number of culls delivered to the canneries decreased substantially. Growers appreciated this system because they both got support in producing better tomatoes and were rewarded monetarily for their improved practices. Canners, for the most part, were happy with this system of grading and the resulting relationship with the federal government. One representative canner testimonial reported, "When buying tomatoes on a graded basis was first talked [about] we were dead against it. We followed it and studied it. In 1929 we used it, and one year has convinced us of its merits—of its fairness to both grower and canner. We now are as radically for it as we were against it."[42] Canners welcomed standards and quality designations when these were used on the production side.

The CAB had high hopes for canned food grading not only because canners had accepted these previous instances of grading but because canners had been happy to comply with other instances in which the federal government had imposed labeling requirements. They hoped this situation would be no different. In addition to canners' cooperation with the 1906 Pure Food and Drug Act, the NCA had been central in the passage of the McNary-Mapes Amendment in 1930. This amendment to the original 1906 Act offered a "substandard" label for canned foods that were below a minimum quality but still legal under the guidelines for adulteration. In this case, canners not only had cooperated with the regulation but had in fact instigated it, asking the secretary of agriculture to pass the amendment.[43] The canners worked with the USDA to develop minimum standards for tomatoes, peas, peaches, pears, apricots, and cherries, in each case determining which characteristics—size, color, texture, firmness, et cetera—would be used to judge quality.[44] These standards made the CAB confident that "sufficient work had already been done to permit the establishment without delay of three grades for canned goods above the McNary-Mapes substandard level."[45]

Besides canners' previous experience with grading and with labeling, a final reason the CAB saw the inclusion of grade labeling in the canning code as a safe bet was the example set by their neighbors to the north. Canada had had a system of quality labeling for canned food in place since 1927, when the Canadian Meat and Canned Foods Act of 1907 had been amended accordingly.[46] Members of the CAB, along with representatives from the Bureau of Agricultural Economics and the USDA, visited relevant Canadian parties—important canneries, plant managers, retailers, wholesalers, government officials, and members of the press—to judge the success of grade labeling in Canada. They found that "the obligatory statement of quality on all labels serves both to promote orderly marketing and to protect consumers." What's more, the delegates found that Canadian canners fully supported the system and that none of the canners interviewed "would willingly abandon the system."[47] The CAB studied many of the US canners' claims about the potential dangers of grade labeling and found that none of them had materialized in Canada. This gave the CAB confidence that their plan for the US canners was, indeed, a sound one.

The CAB had ample reasons to believe that the canning code would successfully incorporate grade labeling. The great need for labels to serve as a window into the can, along with the precedents in both grading and labeling, made the government board hopeful that quality standards could be quickly established and enforced. Unfortunately, things did not work out exactly as they had hoped.

"TWO ARMIES DUG IN FOR A WAR OF ATTRITION"

Despite how likely it seemed that grade labeling for canned food would succeed, the topic provoked major disagreement—according to one industry source, more disagreement than nearly any other consumer protection topic.[48] One trade editorial remarked, "The canning industry and the NRA Consumers Advisory Board resemble nothing . . . so much as two armies that have dug in for a war of attrition."[49]

The canning industry began working on its code of fair competition as soon as the NRA was established in June 1933. The NRA held the public hearings for the canning industry in February 1934, and by April the canning industry had approved what they thought would be a final code. In a section titled "Standards and Grades," they agreed that "the

FIGURE 7. A comparison of the grade-labeling and descriptive-labeling models, as depicted by the *Canner* trade journal in 1935. (Courtesy of the Grocery Manufacturers Association.)

consumer is entitled to truthful information on the label, [which] should be required to be as informative as practicable," and proposed that the canners would work with the government to establish a scientific consumer grade.[50] Within a month, President Roosevelt followed up on the NRA's recommendation and provisionally approved the code, so long as the industry set up a committee to formulate standards of quality that would enable compulsory grade labeling. The NRA's suggestion, under the CAB's guidance, was for canners to develop grades of A, B, and C, for several major vegetables and fruits, which would be clearly posted on the can labels and would indicate relative quality ratings to consumers.

By September 1934, the canners' committee countered the NRA's suggestion with their own suggestion of *descriptive* labeling, rather than *grade* labeling (figure 7). They agreed that consumers needed information, but they wanted this to be qualitative rather than quantitative.

For example, in proposing descriptive labeling, P. L. Gowen of the Campbell Soup Company said that cans of tomatoes should carry objective terms speaking to three different factors of appearance: style of the pack, proportion of solid material to the liquid, and the color as an indication of ripeness. A label on a can of tomatoes might read, "whole pack, "solid pack," and "red-ripe," along with the weight of the contents and an indication of whether any salt was added. The label would also carry a statement that described what each of these terms meant.[51] The NRA administrator, however, did not believe that descriptive labeling met the goals of the CAB's push for quality labeling and rejected the canners' suggestion. Throughout the end of 1934 and the beginning of 1935, the NRA and the canners' committee went back and forth many times on the labeling question, each side unwilling to budge.[52] The debate finally ended in a stalemate in May 1935 when the US Supreme Court deemed the whole NRA project unconstitutional for its assumption of legislative power by the executive branch.[53] With the NRA now defunct, the consumer advocates no longer had the backing to continue this particular fight.

Before describing the specific arguments that each side used to defend its position, let's step back a moment to consider how each pictured the consumer—the implicit driving force of this whole acrimonious debate. Despite new surveying techniques, the consumer remained mostly a mysterious figure, and her motivations were unknown. For the most part, both the government and the canners conceived of average consumers as "middle-class women thought to be irrational and endlessly suggestible."[54] Women were both assumed to be the natural audience for consumer issues and dismissed when it came to substantive issues of political power.[55] But what did these women want? CAB director Dexter Keezer wrote that there was "confusion over the scope and nature of the consumer interest" and that the consumer "is all things to all men, and accordingly subject to grave vicissitudes of definition."[56] Another CAB member complained that the consumer interest "cannot be reduced to a get-at-able question."[57] Consumer's Research founder Frederick J. Schlink memorably described the consumer as a "shy and elusive being."[58]

Despite all this hand-wringing about the unknowability of the consumer, canners and government officials alike were happy to speak on behalf of the consumer, confidently representing her desires. Consumers in these cases were pictured as women—typically white housewives who had no producer status.[59] Paul M. Williams, of the USDA's Bureau of Agricultural Economics, described how the consumer housewife would use different grades of canned foods: "Once in a while the housewife wants an extra fine grade, say, of canned whole tomatoes, if she is entertaining. For ordinary table grades she usually selects a middle grade. And for making soup or gravy . . . she can use the standard or even the substandard grade."[60] This was the picture of the average consumer, with uniform preferences and practices.

Those who were against grade labeling also forged ahead in speaking from the consumer's point of view. The NCA committee that supported descriptive labeling proclaimed, "Such labeling is the kind wanted by the consumer and the kind that would be of real value to her . . . related directly to some particular purpose for which the consumer desires the product."[61] H. W. Phelps, the president of the American Can Company, spoke directly to women through a 1934 CBS radio broadcast. "Stripping the A-B-C of the glamor of Government indorsement [sic], and the blind faith that it induces, who of you who hear me will be able to know what those grades mean?" he asked. "Will you, as a busy housewife, take the trouble to get a copy of the NRA standards? . . . Wouldn't you much prefer to have the label on the can that you hold in your hand tell you in plain, terse English just what is in the can?" In posing these questions, Phelps was not so much asking women what they would do as presuming on their behalf.[62]

The CAB did hear statements in favor of grade labeling from representatives of many organizations like the Consumers' Counsel of the Agricultural Adjustment Administration, the General Federation of Women's Clubs, the National League of Women Voters, and the National Council of Women. These latter women's groups, while having different missions—community voluntarism, political advocacy, and human rights, respectively—largely represented white, educated, middle- to upper-middle-class American women.[63] The canners made some overtures in the direction of research and surveys to actually collect consumer opinion. But on the whole these were biased in their execution, served only the interest of producers, or took so long to develop that the crucial results weren't found until years later—as was the case with the 1941 Elmo Roper survey, described below. As one agricultural economist put it, although there had been studies of consumers, "These studies have not been made by nor initiated at the request of consumers. . . . [The consumer] has been considered more as a possible contributor to the welfare of certain groups of producers than as one whose own satisfaction should be increased."[64]

To give one taste of the biased informal surveys being carried out by canners, Nell B. Nichols, the associate editor of *Woman's Home Companion,* traveled around the country talking to women about canned-food labels. Her aim was to discover whether the "professional spokesmen for the consumer [who] have insisted that housewives would be heart-broken if grade labeling were not adopted" were right. Nichols's quest to talk to housewives began after she listened to a group of grade-labeling advocates talk about women's eagerness for ABC grades. These advocates, Nichols pointed out, were all professional home economists, and few of them had families of their own. Nichols questioned the ability of these professional women to fairly represent the desires of housewives like those of her native Sunflower State of Kansas. So she went out and talked with over a hundred "honest-to-goodness" housewives in seventeen states and found that all of them were eager for descriptive labels once she explained what they were. She argued that these women had voted for grade labeling in their various women's clubs only because they'd been told that this was a good idea and that they had blindly followed their leaders (who were presumably the same childless professional homemakers with whom she had begun her essay). She was, of course, less reflective about the ways in which her *own* explanations and advocacy of descriptive labeling had swayed the opinions of these housewives.[65]

The reasons canners gave for their opposition to grade labeling were many: they claimed that food quality was too hard to measure, that it was too costly, that it would lead to a decrease in overall quality, that women wouldn't buy low grades, and that women weren't educated enough to even understand the grades in the first place. Many outside observers thought that large, successful canners were actually just trying to protect their brand identities. And although canners sometimes mentioned this motivation, they downplayed this mercenary reason in favor of much more grand claims, like those about the irreducibility of food quality to measurement. Unlike other industries that dismissed NRA demands outright, the canners knew that something was needed to appease the consumer demand for information. However, they wanted to set their own terms, rather than merely giving in to the government proposal in this case. Also, many canners were bolstered in their resistance by their cooperation with other industries, such as the wholesale grocers, the advertising agencies, and the publishers, all of whom pushed back against grade labeling in a campaign spearheaded by the NCA and the Grocery Manufacturers Association.[66]

One of the major opposition points was that quality could not be measured objectively. Practically, canners feared expensive litigation that would result from discussions about whether an item of food conformed to the grade on its label.[67] The canners' Committee on Labeling suggested that quality grades could not be fully accurate and were therefore deceptive.[68] Canners posited that even if grades could be determined, enforcing the labeling would be prohibitive in terms of both cost and variability in interpretation. An American Can Company representative questioned the ability of inspectors across the country to follow guidelines uniformly. Each of the inspectors, he wrote, "has a copy of the NRA standards. But, the inspector in Pennsylvania reads them one way, the man in Ohio another way, the man in Wisconsin another way, etc. That's only inevitable because of the human equation. . . . It's confusion worse confounded!"[69]

Beyond the supposed practical problems, there were claims about how grade labels would attempt to "impound the imponderable," in reducing a wide range of qualities to a single letter grade.[70] NCA president Howard A. Orr put it this way, "Standardized grades contemplate a standardized humanity. . . . Surely we have no such situation."[71] H. J. Carr of the Canning Machinery and Supplies Association commented, "No one would be more delighted, I believe, than the canner, if nature would turn out fruits and vegetables plainly labeled 'A. B. C.,' which he might pack and label as such. Since nature, however, does not accept the principle of such regimentation, any attempt by legislative means to impose such designations will prove to be unworkable."[72] Now, we have seen that the canning industry typically thrived on uniformity and indeed *did* label fruits and vegetables A, B, and C, as in the case of grading tomatoes in Indiana. But in the case of ABC canned food labels, the manufacturers rebelled against this rigid notion that ostensibly presupposed a standardized food production system. The characteristic that most embodied the "imponderability" of food quality was flavor, which was of "so elusive or subjective a nature as to defy physical measurement by any scientific method."[73] Many canners claimed that since flavor could not be measured objectively, any grade offered would not sufficiently capture the overall goodness of the food and would mislead consumers, since "few women would understand . . . a quality grade which does not include the element of flavor."[74]

Canners furthered asserted that grade labeling would actually undermine consumer trust in canned food, which had been steadily increasing in recent years. Some unscrupulous packers would be tempted to exaggerate the quality of their goods, leading to mislabeling. When the public paid more for grade A cans, only to find that the quality inside was more like grade B, or grade C, they would feel betrayed, and the "reputation of the entire canning industry would seriously suffer."[75] Of course, since they had already argued that grades would be unenforceable and not subject to oversight, canners could now easily claim that this kind of mislabeling would be rampant.

The industry continued its attack by arguing that even if grades could be determined and enforced, they would still fail when they reached the grocery store and the hands of consumers. Women either wouldn't want to buy the lower grades or wouldn't understand the distinction among the grades in the first place.[76] One industry observer wrote, "Not understanding its limitations, the majority of women would at first be deceived by [grade labeling]."[77] In suggesting women's incompetence, the NCA grade-labeling committee contrasted them with the "experts" with whom they used grades on the production and trade side of things. Grading in those situations was possible, they wrote, "because dealings within the trade are between experts, each of whom is capable of appraising for himself the claim of the other."[78] Housewives, clearly, were *not* seen as experts.

Some outside observers believed the canners' objections came mostly from larger canners who had developed name recognition through their national brands and feared losing some of this cachet in the face of grade labeling. Because some canners, like Campbell's Soup Company, had invested so much in promotional advertising to build up their brand, they relied on this "intangible equity and competitive advantage" and feared that grade labels "would destroy much of the goodwill value of a brand name."[79] Canners also made some mention of brands as a reason for their opposition, though they generally downplayed this factor, perhaps because it seemed too self-interested.[80]

Even as canners widely rejected grade labeling, they acknowledged that something needed to be done to give consumers more information. In fact, relative to many other industries, the canners were remarkably cooperative. The Chemical Manufacturing Industry, for example, simply reveled in its subversion of the NRA codes process. In sarcastic and arrogant tones, the chemical manufacturers' code committee urged its trade organization members to ignore what was included in the code or to find ways around it. They bragged that they "put a lot of boloney" into the code to appease the "poor goofs in Washington" and that they planned to take the expense of running the code "out of the hide of Kid Consumer." These industry men openly flouted the code process, treating it all as a ridiculous joke.[81]

The canners, meanwhile, worked to find alternate means of giving consumers the "window into the can" that grade labeling promised. The opacity of the can had long been a barrier for convincing new consumers to try canned food. Many advertisements tried to use images to show what was inside, displaying tasty meals behind the veneer of a graphically transparent can. One company, Visual Display, Inc., tried to make a profit out of this problem by creating a gadget of curved glass that fit on top of the can and had a small sample of what was inside (figure 8). Of course, the food inside the glass had to be "treated chem-

One woman tells another. The visual display sells because it tells the customer what is inside the can.

Visual Display Fixture Proves Selling Ability

FIGURE 8. This 1933 image depicts efforts of some canners to provide a literal window into the can with a "visual display fixture" that they hoped would help consumers overcome the opacity of the can. (Courtesy of the Grocery Manufacturers Association.)

ically to fix its color" and a "crystal-clear jelly [had to be] employed to hold [the food] firmly in place," methods which presumably were *not* used inside the can.[82]

The descriptive labeling that canners proposed, too, was a way of showing the can's contents without using ABC grades, by listing factors of appearance, like size, color, or solidity. But as one *Consumer Notes* article stated, "While this suggestion is hopeful as showing a rising interest on the part of the industry in being frank with consumers, it still definitely avoids stating the facts in such a way that buyers could compare qualities."[83]

Despite all the canners' arguments against grade labeling, there were many well-founded reasons that the CAB was in favor of the system. Beyond the literal opacity of the can, many other barriers prevented the consumer from knowing her food. Julia K. Jaffray of the General Federation of Women's Clubs pointed to the structural barriers of the new food system: "It is difficult for homemakers to know when they are getting fair value for their money, because they are often thousands of miles from their food producers, do not know them, and never see the many hands through which foods pass to reach the grocers' shelves."[84] In highlighting this disconnect between producer and consumer, Jaffray lamented women's diminishing opportunities to know where their food came from. Foods were further cloaked in mystery upon reaching the grocery store, as consumer advocate Persia Campbell described: "It is difficult in these times to judge the quality of goods bought, since the display is so varied, so highly fabricated, so elegantly and securely wrapped or canned."[85] Grades promised to cut through all these layers of obscurity and to communicate directly with the consumer in the way she deserved.

The methods that consumers typically used to choose among different cans—brands and prices—were both insufficient. To illustrate the scope of the problem, C. T. Schmidt of the Consumers' Counsel of the Agricultural Adjustment Administration observed, "When the consumer in 1928 wanted a can of corn, he had to choose from among 4500 brands. And all of them labeled with equally glowing and meaningless description of their quality."[86] Brands were often unreliable, with companies offering varying quality from season to season and labeling products of different canneries, with different practices, under a uniform brand. As Schmidt bluntly put it, "Manufacturers and distributors oppose standards and grades because they profit from the consumer's ignorance."[87] At the same time that they might have profited from the consumer's ignorance and faith in brand labels, the manufacturers themselves were not willing to be subject to the same ignorance. Lena M. Phillips, the president of the National Council of Women, turned the tables on the canners:

> You are asking us to do something which you, yourself, I believe, would not do. If the producers drove up to your cannery and said, "Well, I have got my crop here; I want you to take it." And you would say, "All right, I will come out and look at it." He would say, "Oh, no you don't. I have got a fine label on it, that says 'Sunset Glow', and you have to take it as it is. It is all right. It has got all sorts of things on the label, except what the property is like." You would laugh at him. Now, the consumer can laugh at you, too.[88]

Phillips skewered both the meaninglessness of typical brand name labels and the hypocrisy present when canners wanted something from their producers that they would not offer to their own consumers.

Beyond the emptiness of the brand name, price also failed to fairly indicate quality. Given the complexity of economic and production factors, price could not be relied upon to be a meaningful guide. Many consumers' councils, the Tri-State Packers, the Federal Trade Commission, home economists, and others undertook simple studies in which they taste-tested a range of commercially available cans to determine the correlation between price and quality. To give just one example, when the Consumers' Council of the Agricultural Adjustment Administration analyzed forty-seven cans of peas, they found that the three most expensive contained peas that had characteristics corresponding to the "C" grade on the ABC scale. And the only one that met the standards of an "A" grade was among the least expensive.[89]

If consumers could rely neither on brands nor on prices to ascertain quality, grades seemed to be the answer. The CAB believed that grades not only were needed but would be easy to establish. They did not buy the canners' claims of "imponderability" and instead believed that quantification and its associated costs should be no problem, as grading was already in place at many levels of production. Wells A. Sherman of the Bureau of Agricultural Economics said that his agency had been "working with the grades for cotton, for livestock, for grain, for fruits and vegetables, for dairy products and poultry products, [long enough] to know that grading of food and farm products is not an occult science." Further, he wondered why it was possible to grade all these other agricultural products but not canned food, the very food that is intended for human consumption and must be purchased "sight unseen."[90] Other government officials referenced the precedent set by the US Warehouse

Act and other business dealings, which required canning companies to grade their products in order to get bank loans: "If these grades are so reliable as to be used as a basis for lending money, they should give the consumer effective help in getting his money's worth."[91] If canned goods could be graded for trade, why not offer the consumer this same information? Proponents of grade labeling argued that the overall cost of administering grades would be relatively small, especially since it would be balanced by consumer savings.

Finally, the CAB was bolstered in its support of grade labeling by the support of the constituency they were charged with representing: the consumers themselves. Consumer representatives from across the country—from professional groups like Consumers' Research to governmental groups like the Food and Drug Administration, to women's groups like the General Federation of Women's Clubs, to labor groups like the American Federal of Labor—all came together at a February 1934 hearing to speak in favor of grade standards for canned goods.[92] The reasons for their support were many. Some suggested that canners would suffer under the competition of home canning and of fresh products if they didn't offer consumers a clearer sense of quality, since turning to those alternatives was the present tendency of consumers who did not trust canned foods.[93] And indeed, an increase in glass jar sales around 1931, along with a drop in sales of canned goods around the same time, did indicate that some women were replacing commercial cans with those produced by their own labor.[94] Consumers wanted their options to remain open and wanted commercially canned goods to be a viable, easy-to-understand alternative.

Nearly all those speaking on behalf of grade labeling spoke of their desire for knowledge. Mrs. John Boyle of the Washington, D.C., Consumers Council described her situation: "When I go to the grocery store, I see some cans that say 'fancy,' other say 'selected.' . . . The label of none of them tells me what grade I am buying, I do not know until I get home and open the can just what grade I have bought."[95] Agnes Wilkinson, speaking on her own behalf "as a housewife and a mother," called for standards: "Often, [the housewife] will pay for a good grade, or for a medium grade, where she could have got the other grade, and it seems that there should be some standard set, so we would know what we are getting for the purpose for which we want to use it."[96] Miss Lena M. Phillips, president of the National Council of Women, admitted that she had not spoken with each of the five million women who made up her organization but claimed that they were generally in favor of grade labeling. For them, grade labeling was "not a controversial matter in any sense." She appealed to a sense of history in telling the canning industry it owed consumers the knowledge of what they were buying. "I appeal to you gentlemen of the industry," she began, "because after all, you got this industry from us. It belonged to your grandmothers, your great-grandmothers, in the home, as you know, and so we feel a sort of a proprietary interest in it, and I appeal to you for fair play."[97] While the story of canning, as we have seen, was never so straightforward as a transition from female-dominated home canning to male-dominated commercial canning, Phillips's appeal offers insight into the attitudes some female consumers had toward the industry. Fair play depended on grade labels.

Despite all these arguments, on both sides, for and against grade labeling, consumers never got the "fair play" they were hoping for. Grade labeling under the New Deal ultimately failed across all industries, not just for canned food, for reasons that had to do much more with governmental reorganization than with the intrinsic merits of the arguments. Even before the Supreme Court deemed the NRA unconstitutional in May 1935, the enforcement of quality standards lagged.[98]

Still, both consumer organization at the federal level and efforts toward grade labeling continued in the years to come. Upon the termination of the NRA, the Consumers' Division was transferred to the Department of Labor and continued in its focus on grading.[99] By this time, the county consumer councils had spread to "two hundred counties that collectively represented forty-two million people, or thirty-four percent of the country."[100] The movement jump-started by the New Deal had assumed a life of its own. As for federal pushes for quality standards, they reemerged prominently in 1938, during the passage of the Federal Food, Drug, and Cosmetic Act, and again during the Second World War, when the Office of Price Administration considered grade labeling in order to help enforce maximum prices. In the latter case, the country's industries—led by fruit and vegetable canners—again fought vigorously against it, and won. This time, the enforcing agency collected testimony only from industrial representatives and took no statements from consumer agencies, indicating a shift in the relative valuation of industrial and consumer representation.[101] Grade labeling had been defeated.

Finally, in the years after the NRA, the canning industry did eventually carry out a nationwide survey of consumer attitudes toward grade labeling, making an attempt at concretizing the mysterious consumer, rather than simply speaking on behalf of imaginary consumers. Signaling the increasing importance of market research, in 1941, the NCA hired Elmo Roper to determine consumer needs relative to can labels. Roper was a reputable public opinion expert who worked for *Fortune* magazine and who had honed his surveying technique while conducting presidential polls. In a publication on canned-food labels, the canners presented Roper's results so as to make grade labeling seem unwanted: "Eighty-five per cent of the women of the country have no difficulty in picking out the quality or kind of canned food they want and most people are not aware of the absence of any important information on the labels of canned foods."[102] In publishing only this piece of his work, the canners directly contradicted Roper's warning at the beginning of his report: "The reproduction of isolated portions of this report, out of their context as part of Mr. Roper's findings as a whole, is . . . expressly forbidden." A closer look at Roper's full report, in context, offers a more nuanced view. He found that while most housewives were satisfied with canned foods, "There are enough instances of unsatisfactory quality to indicate the need for continued vigilance in the industry." Further, while housewives may not have actively clamored for grade labeling, once Roper introduced them to the subject, over half "showed a receptivity," and one-third even said that grade labeling was "necessary and should be done."[103] This case—both the canners' investment in market research and the fact that they misconstrued the findings in ensuing reports—indicates the industry's growing confidence and desire to shape its own image in the 1940s and into the postwar years.

TAKING CONTROL OF CONSUMERS

On the surface, canners offered many reasons for their opposition to grade labeling—reasons that ranged from practical to theoretical and were often inconsistent with one another. If we look beneath the surface, however, we find that much more lay beneath these purported reasons. Considering the canning industry as a dynamic entity with its own life cycle, we can begin to see the 1930s as a turning point in its relationship with consumers and outside expertise. There was much more at stake in the grade-labeling debate than simply whether there would be ABC letters on the outside of a can: the power to speak for the consumer; the deference of industry to scientific and governmental involvement; the means by which trust in canned food would be developed. This was a time when the place of the consumer in American society was shifting, when corporations were growing ever larger, and when businesses were beginning to take advantage of the new tools of advertising, marketing, and branding that were at their disposal. The grade-labeling debate magnifies a larger set of issues about how the canning industry began to respond less to external expertise and instead to take more direct control of shaping consumer preferences.

The canning industry had been growing in strength and size since its days of technological development after the Civil War and its national organization in the first decade of the twentieth century. Addressing the joint problems of agricultural production and bacterial contamination in the 1920s had given the canners confidence as consumers' own confidence in canned foods had grown. Between 1915 and 1930, canned-food production had doubled, growing from about 80 million cases to 190 million cases. But in the next span of fifteen years, between 1930 and 1945, production more than tripled, from 190 million cases to 600 million cases.[104] Although this dramatic change was partly due to production for the war effort, the statistics clearly signal a rapid increase in consumers' exposure to and consumption of canned foods. By the mid-1930s, a chain-store researcher could speak, if somewhat hyperbolically, of a new generation of "can-opener cooks" who preferred opening a commercially produced can from the grocery store to cooking their own meals with fresh foods. It is important to note that, even as canned-food production was indeed increasing rapidly, most Americans still ate much more fresh foods than canned items.[105] But producers for the fresh market still worried about the dramatic increase in consumption of canned and frozen foods, with one expert fearfully asking in 1951, "Are we building a race of processed food eaters?"[106]

This strengthening of the canning industry was part of a broader expansion of business in the American economy of the 1930s. The majority of the country's central industries had come to be dominated by huge corporations, with assets of upwards of $90,000,000. Almost half of the country's corporate wealth was controlled by less than 0.0007 percent of the corporations.[107] A 1932 study, *The Modern Corporation and Private Property*, by Adolph Berle and Gardiner Means, shed light on the tremendous power of the country's largest corporations.[108] Berle and Means described how corporations' increasing size had allowed them to distance themselves from their shareholders' interests, leading to decreased accountability. Historian David Blanke points to the "price controls, oligarchies, standardized trading practices, national branding and retailing, and a host of other rationalizations" of this era as factors that made large corporations more dominant.[109] All of this led to what contemporary consumer advocate Persia Campbell described as the "progressive loss of consumer bargaining power."[110] Consumer purchases came to reflect manufacturers' desires as much as their own, if not more so.

At the same time that corporations grew in size, so did the focus on marketing, advertising, and branding. These fields gave commercial producers access to consumer preferences and, at the same time, tools to influence those preferences.[111] This changed how businesses communicated with consumers. In the case of the canning industry, rather than relying on the middlemen of scientists and government regulators to offer external stamps of approval to convince consumers that new products were trustworthy, producers could build this trust more directly. Many of the figures in the history of advertising who played increasingly important roles in the postwar years began to come together in the 1930s in opposition to the New Deal.[112] Although there had been some initial attempts at market research as early as the 1790s, marketing began to organize as a discipline in the first decades of the twentieth century.[113] Campbell's Soup developed its first sales research department with a home economics unit by the late 1930s, dedicated to determining housewives' preferences with regard to food products and to encouraging the consumption of Campbell's soup.[114] Marketing had grown into an important discipline, employed by many of the country's leading industries.

Beyond market research to find out consumer desires, industries began to make use of advertising to *create* desires. As one tobacco advertiser put it in 1936, "The old sales bywords 'know your customer's needs' have been remolded to 'know what your customer should need and then educate him on those needs.'"[115] Of course, many studies of consumer agency undermine this simple idea of manipulation, yet advertising certainly began to have a more commanding influence over consumers in the 1920s and '30s.[116] The dominant presence and cultural influence of national advertising grew in the 1920s and continued to spread many of the same messages into the Great Depression.[117] The Campbell's Soup Company was among the most prolific and successful advertisers from its early days. Although the soups were first advertised through streetcar cards—images on small cards passed around and posted on streetcars—by 1914 Campbell's had shifted mostly to magazine advertising, finding this to be the most effective medium. By 1926, Campbell's had peppered women's magazines with full-color ads, which was still unusual at a time when most illustrations were in black and white.[118] This reflects Campbell's large advertising budget, which had grown from $10,000 in 1899 to $1,000,000 (5 percent of sales) by 1920. One Campbell's chronicler writes that, although such large advertising spending may be routine in the twenty-first century, this strategy "was at the time revolutionary."[119]

Nearly all Campbell's ad campaigns were directed toward middle-class women, with the assumption that they were the exclusive group who purchased and prepared food. This ignored the realities of women's labor, especially during the Great Depression, when economic exigency brought more women into the workforce.[120] Campbell's used a variety of tactics to convince consumers to buy their soups, a number of which were coercive in their messaging. Historian Katherine Parkin argues that the stridency of these messages increased in the 1930s as the canning industry's entrenchment made Campbell's more confident in demanding women's allegiances. A number of ads challenged women's authority in the kitchen, suggesting that no housewife could make a better soup than those produced in the expert company kitchen. A 1936 Campbell's ad stated, "Women everywhere are cheerfully admitting that Campbell's beat them at soup making. The better the cooks, the more ready they are to admit it." Other ads further suggested that if a woman did try to make her own soup, or to serve an inferior brand, she would bring shame upon herself in serving the lesser product to her family or to company. These advertisements attempted to play up women's insecurities in order to reinforce brand identity and force participation in the marketplace.[121] And as advertising came to have a more prominent role in food manufacturing, the canners elevated some consumers over others, targeting the audience they most desired—well-heeled white women.

Campbell's relied on advertising to build brand recognition. Brands were becoming an increasingly important aspect of consumption (figure 9). In the absence of grades or other objective indicators of quality, consumers turned to brands to make decisions about the relative reliability of different products. The 1941 Elmo Roper survey revealed that 70.8 percent of women made choices about which canned foods to buy by picking a certain brand, while only 11.2 percent read the label information.[122] Advertising and branding campaigns had successfully fostered brand loyalty, at least among consumers of canned food. This loyalty was precisely one of the major reasons for the objections of many canners to grade labeling. If consumers knew that the brand to which they were devoted was actually grade "B," while another, potentially cheaper brand, was grade "A," it would be unlikely that their loyalty would remain steadfast in the face of this new information. Campbell's, with its

FIGURE 9. An emphasis on branding and labeling within the canning industry predominated in the 1930s. (Courtesy of the Grocery Manufacturers Association.)

iconic label, almost made it irrelevant for the consumer to see what was inside the can because the label itself was the relevant part. The company's power came not from showing what was inside the can but exactly the opposite.

The major players in the canning industry—those who were the leading members of the NCA—thrived on a branding system because it fostered a kind of competition in which these major players had the advantage. The NRA's plan to cartelize this industry, however, would reduce competition in order to promote the mutual interest of all canners. Having uniform, relatively objective canned-food grades might well serve the average interest of all canners by putting them on equal footing, but it would undermine the interest of the largest canners who had developed brand loyalty among their consumers and who wanted to preserve competition. Had grade labeling been proposed in an earlier era, when canners were less segregated by size and scope and more desperate for consumer approval, it might well have succeeded, at least in the canning industry. But in the middle of the 1930s, when the brand had come to be dominant, any encroachment on the brand's success could be viewed as a threat to the foundation that the leading canners had managed to build.

Even as the canners resisted grade labeling by claiming that consumers did not want this system or that it was impractical to quantify nature in this way, much of what they were really saying was that they, the canners, had earned the right to dictate how their industry would communicate with consumers and now had the strength to defend this right. The growth of the canning industry and of industrial power in the United States more broadly gave canners an increasing confidence that made them no longer as deferential to governmental authority as they had been in earlier decades. The new tools of marketing and advertising, along with the increasing strength of brand names, gave canners a more direct way to create consumer trust, rather than working through the proxy of laboratory expertise. Branding had grown to be such an important aspect of the leading canners' strategies that they had to resist grade labeling, which threatened to mitigate the strength of the brand.

GRADES AS MARKERS OF POWER

At first glance, letters and numbers—those posted on the surfaces of tomatoes or on crates holding cans of tomatoes, and those noticeably absent from the cans themselves—seem so simple. Yet in the 1930s they represented not only grade designations but also markers of power. Those who had access to these letters and numbers were the "experts," while those without were consumers with incomplete information. For a brief period of time, the decisions that these consumers made every day at the grocery store were imbued with the potential to change the country's economic infrastructure.[123] The swelling consumer movement of the 1930s reminded businesses that daily economic decisions could be important and could offer a challenge to the capitalist order, if only at a small scale.

The CAB of the NRA believed that posting grades on consumer product labels would increase consumer purchasing power, which was the ultimate goal. Unfortunately for this plan, the industries that the CAB most needed to convince did not agree about the value of grade labels. Though consumers wanted more knowledge of their foods and found both brand labels and price guides insufficient, the NCA maintained the impracticability and undesirability of grade labels, offering the limited descriptive labels instead. Many consumer advocates pointed to the hypocrisy of canners welcoming grades in the field and the warehouse but denying them in the marketplace. This highlighted the intermediate position of the canners—they were themselves consumers relative to growers but were producers relative to housewives. When they assumed the consumer role they wanted the information that grades provided, but when they were in the producer role they did not want to extend this courtesy to their own consumers.

Although the grade-labeling controversy ended without much resolution when the NRA disbanded in 1935, it had enduring consequences for the story of canned food and the rise of the modern food industry. In previous decades canners had deferred to the authority of scientific and governmental expertise—for technological development, for agricultural production, for bacteriological control—all in the interest of courting consumers. Beginning with this grade-labeling case, however, canners pushed back against external intrusion, taking more direct control of how they interfaced with consumers. In previous decades, in the memorable phrase of one CAB member, consumers had not seemed "get-at-able" except through the intermediaries of scientists and government officials, with whom many consumers already had a relationship of trust. Beginning in the 1930s, however, consumers began to seem far easier to reach, for a number of reasons: the increasing stability of the canning industry; the increasing visibility of the consumer movement; and the rise of marketing, advertising, and branding. Canners began to substitute the knowledge of quality that might come through grade labels with the illusion of quality that came through rich advertisements. They tried to make the opacity of the can a positive attribute instead of a negative one, offering consumers fantastic visions of what was inside, rather than a more realistic window into the can. These visions came to be associated with specific brands, which companies believed would be undermined by grade labels that cut across brand distinctions.

This transformation signaled a turn in the direction of the modern food system, with its resistance to government regulation and its emphasis on advertising and consumer manipulation. The next phase of this story explores the canned-food industry as it became more deeply embedded in the American diet, following it into the postwar years, through the era of corporatization and consolidation within the food industry and into another wave of consumer activism.

5

Fighting for Safe Tuna

Postwar Challenges to Processed Food

In 1970, Dr. Bruce McDuffie made a startling discovery. In his lab at the State University of New York in Binghamton, he and his students found that common canned tuna fish contained high levels of toxic methylmercury, often more than twice as much as the US Food and Drug Administration (FDA) limit of 0.5 parts per million (ppm). Because canned tuna fish was a popular American staple, McDuffie quickly publicized his findings. He contacted the FDA with his alarming laboratory tests and urged the agency to take action. The FDA followed up by issuing a nationwide recall of contaminated fish, pulling some 12.5 million cans of tuna from grocery store shelves.

Despite this action, the FDA insisted that canned tuna was still safe to eat and that the recall was just a precautionary measure. Nevertheless, consumers heard a different message. For example, one shopper said, "I love tuna fish, but I'm not going to buy it anymore. . . . Everything we eat is poisoned." The recall had a big impact not only on consumers but also on canners, who lost around $84 million and a crushing 40 percent of their market in some areas. The tuna-canning industry tried to make use of the recalled tuna, either as pet food, or as an export to countries with less regulation. In addition, the National Canners Association (NCA), along with the tuna industry's advocacy group the Tuna Foundation, launched a battle to convince the FDA to raise the limit of how much mercury was considered safe and to investigate more closely the details of mercury's danger to human health.[1]

By the 1970s, canners realized that the technical methods they had used to build trust in earlier eras were no longer sufficient. Consumer advocates and environmentalists were calling into question the authority and benign nature of science.[2] Following practices set in motion by the New Deal grade-labeling debate, canners of the postwar era began to rely less on tools of the laboratory and more on new tools of the developing social sciences. No longer were improved technologies, agricultural practices, and bacteriological findings sufficient as primary methods of winning over consumers. Instead, postwar canners tried to hold on to an increasingly skeptical consumer base by employing motivational research, increasing their advertising budgets, and investing in political lobbying. The technical fixes that earlier had served to appease consumer fears even began to contribute to new fears. For example, technological improvement in the food-processing factories yielded a monolithic food system from which many consumers felt detached. A desire to improve raw crops gave way to a system of industrial agriculture reliant on aggressive breeding, pesticides, and chemical fertilizers. Additives and processing techniques intended to reduce spoilage led to concerns about nutrition.[3] As a result, new tools were needed to address these new fears. The opaque nature of canned food had shifted—the unfamiliar and unknowable aspects now had less to do with the preservation process itself than with the larger system of processed food.

One of the reasons that consumers of the 1960s had come to doubt the food system was that the industrial model now dominated production, making clear both its benefits and its drawbacks. Between the 1930s and 1960s, canners had succeeded in gaining a market share they had only dreamed of in the early twentieth century. By 1959, around 90 percent of consumers ate canned food weekly.[4] And canned food was joined by a proliferating supply of other processed foods, from TV dinners to powdered cake mixes, all of which built on the foundation of the older canning industry. Canners and food processors came to frequently speak with a single voice, so that the story of the canning industry becomes the story of processed food more broadly.

Perhaps no product better exemplifies the rising popularity of canned food in postwar America than tuna. While the average American ate 0.2 pounds of tuna in 1926, that figure had grown to 3.1 pounds by 1976, an increase of 1300 percent. During that same time, tuna's proportion among canned-fish products also grew dramatically, from 7 percent of the canned-fish market in 1926 to 65 percent fifty years later.[5] This growth reflected the broader entrenchment of processed foods. There are several reasons that tuna rose in popularity—the appeal of the big fish to sport fishermen, new processing techniques that preserved the fish's white flesh, new advertising campaigns, and the rise of sushi in the 1960s. But one of the central reasons for its new popularity was that food producers found ways to incorporate tuna into homey processed-food-based recipes that appealed to changing American tastes. Canned tuna became inextricably bound with other major brand names through linked marketing campaigns. Campbell's Cream of Mushroom Soup became an irreplaceable part of tuna noodle casserole beginning in the 1940s; Hellman's Mayonnaise promoted tuna salad; and Kraft's Velveeta processed cheese seemed most at home atop a tuna melt sandwich. Canning companies distributed free recipe books, printed recipes on their products' labels, and published suggested uses in women's magazines.[6] These all became crucial dishes in the repertoire of the 1950s housewife, alongside other processed delights.

But events of the 1960s and 1970s began to threaten this dominance, both of canned tuna and of other processed foods. A small outbreak of botulism in canned tuna fish in 1963 joined with recent fears about additives and pesticides to undermine consumer confidence. By the time concerns about mercury in canned tuna surfaced with McDuffie's research in the 1970s, the consumer and environmental movements had swelled, bringing with them critiques of industrialized food. Food processors found themselves once again struggling to gain consumer confidence, only now new concerns required new approaches. While early canners had celebrated their laboratory research and reliance on biological science, later canners were less forthright about their investment in marketing research and political lobbying. These interventions were more discreet, contributing to the opacity of the late twentieth-century food system.

"THE GOLDEN AGE": CONSUMER CONFIDENCE IN PROCESSED FOODS

After a century of worrying about how to win over consumer confidence, by the 1950s canners were happy to sit back and observe a trusting nation awash in canned foods. This era was one that culinary historian Harvey Levenstein describes as "the Golden Age of Food Processing," during which canned food, frozen food, fast food, TV dinners, Betty Crocker, food additives, television advertising, and baby boomer housewives reshaped the American food system.[7] Many of the investments in the industrialized food sector that the US military made during World War II carried over into the domestic context after the war, including the entrenchment of canned food and the development of the frozen-food industry. As we will see, increased levels of consumption, the growth of agribusiness, the rise of suburban supermarkets, an emphasis on convenience, and celebration of the nuclear family as the bulwark of democracy came together to provide a perfect home for processed food.

Before the golden age, at the time of the United States' entry into the Second World War in 1941, Americans were eating more canned food than ever before—50 percent more than a decade earlier, and getting closer to rates of fresh fruit and vegetable consumption.[8] But because prices were low, the canning industry was struggling to make a profit. The war brought increased demand for canned goods as the federal government bought supplies to provision troops, which revived the industry, as it raised prices and provided a market for the industry's products. The Columbus Canning Company in Wisconsin, for example, sold its entire stock of canned corn and tomatoes to the army for several years.[9] Troops abroad relied on canned food for two-thirds of all their military rations. Government research laboratories also sponsored several improvements that transitioned to civilian food production, helping to strengthen the processed-food industry—from designing stronger boxes for shipping to building larger cannery storage spaces.[10]

On the whole, business and government came to work closely in wartime, building off new power-sharing relationships developed during the New Deal. Even as canners benefited from military purchases, however, they still rejected governmental involvement. The opposition of canners to grade labeling that had marked the mid-1930s continued into the next decade, as the Office of Price Administration (OPA)—which handled domestic price fixing and rationing—tried to impose grade labeling for the benefit of government purchases.[11] Canners also had other reasons to complain about the federal government. By 1943, farm labor shortages meant that some canners had difficulty finding farmers with whom to contract at a sufficient scale to meet wartime demands. But because the OPA set flat price ceilings, canners were unable to raise the prices they offered to farmers in order to convince them to contract. As a result, according to one leading Wisconsin canner, many canning men felt "that all government men are alike—petty tyrants, little men in big jobs, who are arrogant, domineering, demanding and utterly lacking in understanding."[12] Canning leaders who worked more directly with government men, however, acknowledged that many of the bureaucrats sought to understand the industry's problems, even if they couldn't always fix them.

Regardless of the average canner's attitude toward the government, federal financial support of the canning industry paved the way for a golden age of processed food by the late 1940s and 1950s. Changes in culture, agriculture, and business practices also contributed to this new food system. The war had freed a struggling nation from the grip of economic depression, leading to higher incomes for the average American. The United States exported more of its wares, taking advantage of the reduced production of war-torn nations abroad. Economic growth also came from increased defense spending by the federal government in the face of the Cold War. The gross national product grew from about $200 billion before the war to $300 billion in 1950, and then to over $500 billion in 1960.[13] The postwar years also saw population growth as the baby boom generation was born. More Americans with more money meant that levels of consumption increased significantly. Women also went to work in greater numbers, creating a demand for processed foods that a harried mother could throw together at a moment's notice. The appeal of standardized, prepared foods was highlighted by advertising through the new medium of television, which emphasized consumer abundance and the homogeneity of middle-class American values.[14]

During the 1950s, as a backdrop for the rise of processed foods, both business and agriculture grew bigger and more consolidated. Calpak, which began in 1899 as the California Fruit Canners Association and later took the name Del Monte, underwent a wide range of acquisitions and mergers in the postwar years. It became a full-scale multinational corporation—canning tuna in Puerto Rico, vegetables in Italy, peaches in South Africa, and tomatoes in Mexico, and growing bananas in the Caribbean and pineapples in Thailand and Kenya.[15] The canning industry served as the foundation for the new frozen food industry, with the leading trade journal the *Canner* changing its name to the *Canner and Freezer* in November 1955. At the same time, the country's farms became more dependent on chemical inputs—a wide array of fertilizers, pesticides, herbicides, antibiotics, and hormones—produced by former wartime munitions factories. Wealthier farmers who could afford machinery also turned to mechanical harvesters, dusters, and irrigation lines. These required a large financial investment but then drove down production costs, lowering prices for farm crops. Many smaller farms could not afford to compete with the large farms and were swallowed up by corporate agribusiness.[16] Canners also played a part in this changing face of American agriculture, contributing to mechanization and chemical dependence. The field men employed by canners advised growers on the best pesticides and herbicides to use. And many canners loaned harvesters, crop dusters, and power sprayers to small growers who otherwise could not afford such expensive equipment.[17] Many large canners took over farm production as well, leading to vertical integration—with a single company controlling everything from seed to table—that came to define many leaders in the processed-food industry.

These broad changes also led to fundamental shifts in the way that American people ate. Convenience became a highly touted value, helping give rise to fast food and standardized supermarkets.[18] Although early fast-food restaurants like White Castle had gained some popularity in urban areas by the late 1920s, it wasn't until the 1950s that suburbanization and the new car culture gave rise to omnipresent fast-food hamburger chains. McDonald's and Burger King created successful franchises throughout the country, catering to a fast-paced modern America. As these chains became deeply rooted in American culture, they had far-reaching effects—boosting the beef industry and paving the way for the ensuing rise of feedlots.[19] Between 1946 and 1953, the number of supermarkets grew from ten thousand to seventeen thousand, benefiting from suburbanization and the rise of the automobile. With their long, well-stocked aisles and their lack of grocers to mediate purchases, supermarkets promoted unplanned, impulse buys. As a result, food processors invested more heavily in attractive packaging, paying more attention to wooing the consumer at the point of purchase than to shaping the preconceived notions with which she entered the store.[20]

Although canned foods—by now the old standbys—took up a full third of supermarket shelves, thousands of new products emerged, many of them made possible only through the magic of modern chemistry.[21] During the 1950s, chemists created over four hundred new additives to use in processed food.[22] This chemical ferment had several causes. For one, World War II drove the need for cheap shelf-stable foods, leading to the creation of a wide range of preservatives and flavorings that carried over into the postwar years. Further, new discoveries in the field of nutrition and vitamin research spawned a slew of nutritional additives that were added to everything from cereals to orange juice. New food colorings, flavors, emulsifiers, stabilizers, hydrogenated fats, and preservatives paved the way for popular foods of the 1950s like Cool Whip whipped topping, marshmallow salad, and shelf-stable Cheez Whiz. This power of chemistry allowed the food industry to imagine that all American cooking could one day be based on pre-packaged items. One 1954 trade article read, "Fresh produce for retail consumption is a thing of the past."[23]

All of these transitions in postwar food boosted consumption and left the industry more secure about consumer confidence than ever before. In addition to the new fabricated foods, the frozen-food industry expanded dramatically in the 1940s and '50s. Because tin was rationed during the war, many consumers who otherwise relied on canned food were motivated to try frozen food for the first time. Processors had been trying to freeze foods for decades, but the market grew slowly until after World War II because of a lack of small freezers for storing frozen foods and a lack of consumer interest. Just as with canned food, the federal government boosted the production of frozen food during World War II by investing in research that optimized the industry.[24]

Frozen food piggybacked on the existing infrastructure and methods of the canning industry. The pattern was more one of consolidation than competition. One of the major farms that supplied Birdseye with its early produce was Seabrook Farms in New Jersey, which had already developed along an industrial model in supplying crops for area canneries. In Wisconsin, many canneries began adding freezing capabilities to their production lines, but they relied on the same growers and the same produce.[25] The frozen-food industry's advertising campaigns also mimicked canning slogans, touting the magical ability of food preservation to flatten space and time. One Birdseye advertisement exclaimed, "Here is the most wondrous magic of all! June peas, as gloriously green as any you will see next summer. Red raspberries, plump and tender and deliciously flavored. . . . Imagine having them all summer-fresh in March!"[26] Between 1954 and 1976, the production of frozen vegetables more than doubled, from 890 million pounds to 2,156 million pounds. In addition to fruits and vegetables, frozen food reached its pinnacle through the TV dinner, made most popular by the Swanson Company in the mid-1950s.[27]

Even as these new packaged foods emerged, canned food, now of long-standing familiarity, remained the most commonly purchased packaged-food item across class divides. A US Department of Agriculture (USDA) source wrote that, by 1959, 86 percent of low-income, 91 percent of middle-income, and 90 percent of high-income households ate canned foods weekly.[28] New canned items—like baby foods, juices, citrus, and tuna fish—rose in popularity in the interwar years, helping cement the dominance of the industry in the postwar era. Canned goods became more affordable, as their prices remained stable against a back-drop of rising costs. Canned corn, for example, cost exactly as much in 1952 as it had in 1919, even though the cost of other foods, like coffee and potatoes, had doubled during the same period.[29]

Along with its affordability, canned food offered the increasingly touted virtue of convenience for American women. It had what postwar marketers called "built-in maid service," freeing young housewives from the grunt work of the kitchen and allowing all Americans to live like the upper class, complete with a housemaid.[30] Poppy Cannon, who wrote the popular *Can-Opener Cookbook* in 1952, referred to the can opener as "the open sesame to freedom . . . from tedium, space, work, and your own inexperience."[31] The president of Campbell's Soup suggested that the young housewife of 1957 "doesn't regard slaving in the kitchen as an essential of a good wife and mother," as she might have in earlier eras.[32] Despite this claim, some industry psychologists found that, although cooking from scratch might have become less essential, many women still wanted to feel as if they were part of the cooking process. Thus canned foods were advertised for use as ingredients in slightly more complex meals. Canned soup became not only a soup but also a quick sauce that the "creative housewife" could use to show her own investment in her family's meal. This is where the tuna noodle casserole or the green bean casserole, made of the contents of different cans dumped together, was born.[33]

These changes had distinct gender, racial, and class dimensions. Advertisers and producers nearly always imagined white housewives in their kitchens as the target audience for processed foods. Men in the food business frequently referred to "Mrs. Consumer," used the female pronoun for discussions of their customers, and featured drawings of finely dressed white women in their publications. This dominant image of the stay-at-home housewife ignored the rising percentage of working women in the postwar era, who were no doubt among the consumers of packaged foods.[34] Mass-produced foods of the 1950s overrode many social distinctions, as they were enjoyed by working women and upper-middle class families alike.[35]

By the early 1960s, canned food had become part of—and had helped to produce—a much larger processed-foods industry, rooted in American postwar culture. Broader changes in the economic, cultural, agricultural, and business landscape had created a setting in which processed food thrived. Canning leaders celebrated the centrality of their products to the American diet, calling them an "indispensable staple" and "a necessity of life."[36] By 1963, canned food made up a tenth of the nation's food supply. One industry publication proudly calculated that "if all the food cans Americans open in a year were laid end to end, they would stretch a distance equivalent to three round trips to the moon."[37] Andy Warhol's iconic pop art depictions of Campbell's soup cans, first produced in 1962, testified to the ubiquity of this commonplace item. According to some accounts, Warhol painted the cans on the suggestion of his friend Muriel Latow, who encouraged him to paint "something you see every day and something that everybody would recognize."[38] Canned food had become that omnipresent object. With such a wide reach, canners now felt that they had earned the consumer confidence and trust that they had fought for over the last century, even as they continued to mobilize science and technology to protect that growth.

"FROM LIBEL TO LABEL": CANNERS FOCUS ON RESEARCH AND MARKETING

In 1963, the NCA Research Laboratory celebrated its fiftieth anniversary. This commemoration included many events and articles glorifying the industry and all that it had accomplished (figure 10).[39] One publication read, "Many people believe that the laboratories have been instrumental in making canned foods universally popular; this is an age of science and science has proved the safety and excellence of canned foods to a once unbelieving public."[40] Another piece, entitled "Fifty Years of Winning Public Confidence through NCA Research," described how the early canning industry had devoted attention to battling libelous claims by improving their processing methods, whereas now the canning industry did not have to worry about such claims and could instead focus on topics like label design. The author wrote, "The shift in emphasis from libel to label . . . summarizes the successful history of the canning industry during this century."[41]

Indeed, when botulism struck olives in 1920, canners had cried "Libel!" and had hurried to both contain media attacks and carry out bacteriological research to solve the processing problems. But when another case of botulism struck canned tuna in 1963—the first significant outbreak in commercially canned foods in forty years—canners instead turned to the "label," as they invested most heavily in advertising campaigns, trusting that those would suffice to maintain the industry's image. When two Detroit women died in March 1963 after a lunch of canned tuna fish salad sandwiches, health officials did employ some

FIGURE 10. The National Canners Association laboratory celebrated its fiftieth anniversary in 1963 by inviting a group of influential female publishers and press representatives to see its state-of-the-art technology. (Courtesy of the Grocery Manufacturers Association.)

of the same methods as they had in 1920.[42] They traced the deaths to botulism and to specific brands of canned tuna, which had been caught in Pacific waters, frozen in Japan, shipped to the United States, and commercially canned by the Washington Packing Corporation in San Francisco, California. The FDA seized the offending cans and forced the cannery to close. Consumers, too, had similar reactions—panicking and reducing their tuna purchases by 35 percent nationwide.[43]

But canners, for their part, turned less to bacteriological research and public health oversight than to assuring consumers that this kind of problem was insignificant and would not happen again.[44] They were still confident in the industry's processing methods, and the canners now had new marketing tools at their fingertips that they could deploy. The editor of the *Canner/Packer*, though he acknowledged the "tragedy of the two families," had what he called a "typical reaction" upon hearing the news: "We thought as every food processor must have thought: 'What kind of fuss will it raise? How will it affect sales?'" The main concern of the canning industry was its market and the media portrayal of the incident. Newspapers, funded in large part by food industry advertisements, went easy on the canners.[45] One trade observer commented, "The newspapers didn't play the potency of the toxin. They treated the two cans of tuna, as just two cans." Still, processors understood that "the reputation of the entire food industry is dependent on each of those same cans," so they launched an expensive campaign to shore up that reputation.[46]

This was not a problem just for the tuna industry, or even for the larger canning industry. This was now a problem of the nation's entire food industry. And so, at a June 1963 meeting of the Grocery Manufacturers Association (GMA), the nation's canners, distributors, and retailers organized the Tuna Emergency Committee with a $10 million advertising campaign. The committee sent retailers "tuna telegram" advertisements and encouraged them to promote tuna in special sales by cutting wholesale prices. The industry also worked with the federal government—the US Departments of Agriculture and the Interior endorsed tuna as a healthy food on TV, on the radio, and in their publications. Related industries, like celery, mayonnaise, and mushroom soup, whose success was intimately tied to the consumption of tuna fish in sandwiches and casseroles, widely advertised the indispensability of tuna to the American diet.[47] The canning industry, now part of a much larger consolidated food industry, was more media-savvy and had greater resources at its disposal than in 1920. Canned food was much more deeply rooted in the American diet, so the industry could simply bolster its existing strength.

Of course, laboratory research remained central to the industry as a whole. After establishing a Washington, D.C., laboratory in 1913, the NCA went on to open branch laboratories in Seattle in 1919 and in San Francisco in 1926. These laboratories carried out thousands of studies throughout the twentieth century on a wide range of topics. Paul B. Dunbar, the FDA commissioner of Food and Drugs in 1949, named the NCA a pioneer in food technology, as "the first national trade association to establish a laboratory purely for its own research and technical service problems."[48] Drawing on the ranks of many canning scientists, the Institute of Food Technologists (IFT) was founded as a professional organization in 1939. Soon after, the IFT began awarding the Nicholas Appert Award for outstanding contributions to the field of food technology, named after the "father of the canning industry."[49] This reliance on science characterized the canning industry throughout the twentieth century, leading to a broader food supply based on processing and packaging.

By the 1950s, canners had already begun much of the research that would become particularly relevant in the highly charged atmosphere of the following decades. They studied standardization, vitamins, pesticides, radiation, and water pollution, just to name a few. All of these topics would become areas of concerns for consumer and environmental activists, who later sought to reform the food industry. As described in the previous chapter, canners had been working with the federal government on establishing standards of identity, for agricultural and warehousing purposes, since the 1920s. During the same decade, with the recent discovery of vitamins, canners had begun extensive research into the subject, publishing one 1937 study by E. F. Kohman that suggested that food processing destroyed vitamins no more than regular cooking.[50] In fact, many nutritionists and home economists, on the industry's dime, suggested that so-called "fresh" produce might even be less nutritious than canned foods, since the former was often shipped across the country for days on end, while the latter was sealed in an airtight container within hours of harvesting. The canning industry was, as one publication put it, "not a Johnny-come-lately in the field of nutrition research."[51] Further, by the 1930s, with the introduction of synthetic pesticides, the NCA was studying and giving guidance on pesticide residues, with specific research on DDT begun in 1946, the same year that that soon-to-be controversial chemical was introduced into agricultural practice.[52]

A significant change that food science experienced in the mid-twentieth century was the internalization of research and funding structures. This change made laboratory science less visible and transparent to consumers. The trade organization of the GMA created the Nutrition Foundation in 1941 to offer grants to researchers on topics relevant to food products. By the 1950s, the leading tuna canners—StarKist, Bumble Bee, Chicken of the Sea—formed the Tuna Research Foundation to promote work that benefited the industry in legislative or regulatory matters.[53] And in 1961, the NCA created its own research foundation, to provide funds for food science studies. This foundation accepted "grants from such agencies as the AEC [Atomic Energy Commission] and the Public Health Service, as well as from private sources."[54] Research, too, became more internal and privately controlled. Large food corporations like Borden and General Foods, along with can makers like the Continental Can Company, created their own laboratories in the postwar period.[55] The 1950s saw the growth of in-house laboratories partly because companies grew big and wealthy enough in the Golden Age of Processed Food to support such internal research.[56]

Just as changes in the industry's scientific practices were taking place in the years leading up to the 1960s, so too were changes in its relationship with the federal government. On the whole, canners around this time maintained a mostly amiable relationship with federal agencies like the FDA. At the fiftieth anniversary of the NCA Laboratories in 1963, the FDA commissioner George P. Larrick commended the canners for their work, saying: "Our confidence in their scientific competence and integrity is so great that their results are taken most seriously by our people."[57] Soon after, the industry trade journal returned the favor, indicating canning leaders' "increasing respect for the FDA and their inspection teams," despite some packers still showing "suspicions toward the FDA." And the journal editor wrote that although he, too, was sometimes "in there yelling with the rest about 'government encroachment,'" he was now more inclined to give the federal agency the benefit of the doubt, seeing as he did a change for the better in its oversight.[58]

But this amiability wasn't to last long. The years around 1960 saw renewed action among regulatory agencies, both on topics like additives and pesticides—discussed further below—and on agricultural policy. This renewed action worried canners. For example, as part of the Agricultural Act of 1961, President John F. Kennedy supported production and price controls to maintain farm income.[59] *Canner/Packer* editor El Stark called the act an "arbitrary, undemocratic, inefficient, socialistic, unconstitutional measure" and wrote that it was "so little concerned with the rights of the hundreds of thousands of Americans who make their living from processed food packing."[60] Canners were prone to viewing actions like the Farm Bill as incursions especially because of the uncertain future of the canning industry. One 1962 article, entitled "Commercial Canning: What Does the Future Hold?," cited a number of challenges, such as a small decrease in the number of canneries, the rise of other processed foods that competed for shelf space, and the increased labor costs on the farm and factory since World War II.[61] Such anxieties about the future of the industry, even as the present industry thrived, encouraged canners to seek ways of boosting their market.

This was the context in which the NCA shifted its attention toward the label and the emphasis on marketing that it represented. Food processors in the middle decades of the twentieth century realized that their packaged products offered a unique opportunity to let the label act as a "silent salesman" and the "window of the can."[62] Processing companies launched public relations campaigns targeted at restaurants, public schools, and the average consumer. But by the early 1960s they also began to invest more heavily in marketing research. This research helped food processors understand consumer motivation, so that the industry could design more appealing labels and advertising campaigns, as well as modify their products.[63]

Canners and other businessmen had employed marketing before this era, but it now took a new form. Marketing science saw a shift toward scientific formalization in the postwar years.[64] Earlier work had been mostly practical, stimulated by the introduction of branded and processed agricultural products, canned foods central among them. George Gallup introduced the scientific methods of polling beginning in the mid-1930s, and food processors soon took advantage of the diffusion of telephones to use Gallup's methods and survey audiences after advertisements were aired on radio, and later television.[65] Canners began to make use of some early survey research in the grade-labeling debate of the 1930, but it wasn't until the postwar years that mass consumption prompted a formalization of the marketing system.[66] Motivational research, the science of understanding the underlying psychological principles that shaped consumer choice, rose in popularity. Among the most prominent practitioners who worked frequently with the food industry was Ernest Dichter. Industries throughout the country employed the new techniques—rooted in the social sciences of sociology, economics, and psychology—to promote their business practices.[67] As Vance Packard, author of the 1957 exposé *The Hidden Persuaders,* put it, "Many of the nation's leading public-relations experts have been indoctrinating themselves in the lore of psychiatry and the social sciences in order to increase their skill at 'engineering our consent to their propositions.'"[68]

This priority placed on labels, advertising, and market research was on clear display in the canning industry's response to the 1963 botulism outbreak in canned tuna. Rather than battling libel or changing factory processes, canners and their food industry partners invested $10 million in an advertising campaign aimed at restoring consumer confidence and reminding Americans of their love for tuna fish. The investment paid off, as the National Association of Retail Grocers could announce that after the June 1963 formation of the Tuna Emergency Committee, "tuna sales have climbed steadily ever since," regaining the 35 percent of the market lost after the initial outbreak. By November of that year, a *Time* magazine headline declared, "Tuna Back in Favor."[69]

CONCERNS BREWING: FALTERING CONSUMER
CONFIDENCE IN THE 1960S

Much of the research and focus of the canning industry before the early 1960s was based on what the industry thought was needed to woo consumers and to streamline and optimize production. It was largely proactive, rather than reactive, relative to expressed consumer preferences. As the 1960s progressed, however, canners grew more and more reactive in their priorities, as consumers began to voice their complaints and desires more forcefully. As consumer and environmental movements emerged and grew in influence, the processed-food industry had to grapple with the threats posed by activists. The technological and scientific foundations of the industry came under attack for their contributions to what consumer and environmental activists considered a chemical-ridden, misleadingly marketed, environmentally hazardous food supply. Canners thus had to deal with the growing image problem that lay at the heart of an industrialized food system. During the 1960s, the food-processing industry still generally believed and acted as if it held the confidence of most consumers. By the following decade, however, the industry grew more concerned with new strategies for boosting consumption as it saw consumer confidence on the decline.

The resurgence of consumer activism in the 1960s picked up on some of the trends of the debates about pure food legislation around 1900 and grade labeling in the 1930s. Many historians periodize American consumer movements into three broad epochs along these lines: the first situated within Progressive Era reform; the second within the consumer advocacy groups of the 1930s New Deal government; and the third within the social upheaval of the 1960s and '70s. Consumer historian Lizabeth Cohen has characterized this third wave as a backlash against what she calls the "Consumers' Republic," an era in the postwar years in which the "economy, culture, and politics [were] built around the promises of mass consumption, both in terms of material life, and the more idealistic goals of greater freedom, democracy, and equality."[70] This consumption consensus of the 1950s came under attack as the activists of the following decades questioned the dominance of big business, unrestrained capitalism, and conformist culture.[71] The processed-food industry was a central target of these complaints.

An early sign of the consumer movement's third wave was Senator Estes Kefauver's call for a federal Department of the Consumer, in

1959, drawing upon his history of antimonopoly action. This department was intended to give consumers a voice in the federal government, alongside the official representation that groups like businesspeople, farmers, and workers had through the Departments of Commerce, Agriculture, and Labor, respectively. Although there had been calls for something like this dating back to the 1920s, new circumstances made such a department particularly needed in the second half of the twentieth century. As Senator Warren Magnuson expressed it, these new circumstances included the "recent explosion in consumer buying and credit and the changing conditions in technology and marketing."[72] The increasing systematic and technological complexity of modern production challenged consumers' ability to make informed choices about food and other consumer goods. By 1962, President John F. Kennedy had appointed a Consumer Advisory Council, and had presented a consumer bill of rights, which included rights to safety, information, choice, and being heard.[73]

The canning industry joined many other businesses in denouncing the proposal for the Department of the Consumer, which they called "as American as borsch." The *Canner/Packer* editor wrote in 1961, "U.S. processed foods today are the best the world has ever seen—and need self-appointed watchdogs as you and I need three heads." The editorial protested the idea that "experts" in Washington could police the industry better than the food processors themselves, or better than "Mrs. Consumer," who voted every time she made a purchase. The canners also bristled against the restraint on free enterprise, which they believed best served the consumer through competition and incentives toward efficiency. Foretelling an increasing involvement of the food industry in politics, the *Canner/Packer* editor made clear that he and his colleagues would "keep our business associates, our congressmen and other interested persons aware of our opinions."[74] The trade journal expressed similar distaste for Kennedy's Consumer Advisory Council. When a member of that council, David W. Angevine, spoke before the IFT, some members of his audience suggested that "sometimes it is better to stay home" than to listen to the opinions of consumer advocates.[75]

Three major issues relevant to the processed-food sector that occupied the consumer movements in the 1960s were food additives, pesticides, and packaging standards. The many new food additives introduced by the industry in the 1950s led to concerns about their health effects, and eventually the passage of the Food Additive Amendment of 1958, which regulated the use of chemicals. The food industry considered this amendment overly restrictive, writing in 1965, "We're still smarting under the effective interpretation [of the amendment]. . . . Under this ruling the FDA appears to be willing to wreck an industry— or at least threaten it—amid great publicity." Despite complaints like these, the amount of additives that went into food still increased dramatically during the 1960s. Historian Warren Belasco writes that the legislation "served mainly to validate the existing food supply. . . . Technologists could point to the list as evidence that additives were safe and that the government was taking care of everything."[76] Though the amendment did not reduce suspicion of chemicals in the long run, it gave the food industry a temporary cover for the addition of new additives.

Spurred on by the finding of carcinogenic pesticide on cranberries in 1959 and the publication of Rachel Carson's book *Silent Spring* in 1962, consumers turned to pesticides as another major area of concern in the 1960s.[77] *Silent Spring,* which criticized the dominance of pesticide chemicals in agriculture, helped launch the modern environmental movement but was heavily opposed by the chemical industry and others.[78] Canners made use of the public outcry in response to the book to highlight the good deeds of their own industry in using pesticides responsibly. Roy G. Lucks, NCA vice president, pointed out that Carson had made no mention of canned foods in her book. This might be, he wrote, because "canners were concerned about the possibility of contamination of their product long before Miss Carson's work was written. They were concerned, and they did something about it." Lucks told his audience that canners could be proud of the way their industry had handled pesticide concerns like those raised by *Silent Spring,* "whether you consider that book a compendium of sensational half-truths, or whether you consider it a monument of scientific accuracy and prophesy [*sic*], or whether you consider it something in between."[79]

A third category of consumer concern about the food industry was packaging and labeling. After taking testimony for more than a year, Senator Philip A. Hart introduced a "Truth-in-Packaging Bill" to Congress in September 1962.[80] The bill was intended to give consumers full information about packaged products so that they could make informed decisions. The NCA joined the GMA in vigorously opposing the legislation, putting forth a resolution that the Hart Bill was "unnecessary and unwarranted interference with the labeling and packaging of canned foods [and] an undesirable delegation of legislative power, contrary to the best interest of the consumer."[81] Echoing arguments from the 1930s grade-labeling debate, canners claimed that the bill would reduce competition and that it was demeaning to the housewife, in that it framed her as "incapable of decisions, incapable of knowing when she is cheated." One 1963 trade article displayed a box of blueberry muffin mix as it would have to be marketed under the Hart Bill. Instead of displaying cooked blueberry muffins, golden and moist, it showed a small mound of dry muffin mix, with a few dried blueberries lying next to it. "Want truth in packaging?" the article taunted. "Then this is the kind of mediocre label that you will get."[82] After years of testimony and negotiation with industry, consumer groups, and government agencies, the bill was resubmitted in a watered-down version in 1966. It passed easily through Congress, going into effect as "the Fair Packaging and Labeling Act" (FPLA) on July 1, 1967.[83] The FPLA ended up requiring food manufacturers only to list net contents, identity of commodity, and name and place of business, along with some vague language about preventing consumer deception. In the final version, few canners opposed it, as it did not go far beyond the McNary-Mapes Amendment of 1930, which already specifically regulated canned food packaging.[84]

The canners of the early 1960s were secure in the "universal use and acceptance of canned foods by the American public." They wrote that housewives used cans "with a trust which is complete—and completely justified." They spoke of "public confidence" and "universal popularity."[85] This kind of confidence carried canners through the trials of the early and mid-1960s—through botulism outbreaks and legislative battles around pesticides, additives, and packaging. But by the early 1970s, the battle-weary canning industry began to speak in more measured tones. Although consumers were buying canned goods in the same significant quantities that they had for a decade, canners began to worry about how society saw their business. The *Canner/Packer* editor, after happening upon a Vietnam antiwar rally in 1970, noted the activists' harsh attacks on American industrialists, who were blamed for everything from the war to air pollution. Realizing that these attacks implicated the processed-food industry, the editor asked, "What can we do to improve our own credibility?"[86] Food processors acknowledged "the hectic pace of science and the impersonal pressure of feeding the world, along with the growth of the corporate image."[87] Canners, and the larger food industry in which they were now embedded, saw the consumer movement and emerging environmental movement as a real threat to the values that had led to the food industry's growth throughout the century.

These challenges would only grow stronger in the 1970s, leading canners to manage the backlash behind the scenes, covertly shaping consumer preferences through market research and shaping government regulation through political lobbying, contributing to a food system that was increasingly difficult for consumers to understand and trust.

PUSHBACK: CONSUMER AND ENVIRONMENTAL MOVEMENTS OF THE 1970S

The critiques of the 1970s were more trenchant than those of the previous decade, now rooted in new concerns about health and nutrition, a larger cultural movement emerging from the New Left, and an environmental movement that more deeply condemned the corporate enterprise.[88] Concerns about industry takeover of food science research, truth in advertising, nutrition, animal welfare, and the culture of eating dominated consumer advocates' attention. By 1977, the program cover of the IFT's convention announced, "Remember when 'consumerist' was a misspelled word? And remember when regulations were mostly standards of identity? Well, forget it, because the emphasis has changed."[89]

These consumerists—as consumer advocates were called by the 1970s—were part of separate but frequently converging groups. One of the most prominent advocates among the group of organized, politicized consumers was Ralph Nader, who had come to national attention in 1965 with his exposé of General Motors, *Unsafe at Any Speed*. In 1969, he published a wide-ranging critique of the American food system, *The Chemical Feast*, which called on the federal government to protect the public's food supply. Following in Ralph Nader's footsteps was Michael Jacobson, a microbiologist who founded the Center for Science in the Public Interest in 1971 and wrote many influential books—*Food for People, Not for Profit* (1975) central among them. Jacobson dismissed the dominant use of scientific research by industry and argued that research should benefit the public interest.[90]

Other critiques of the 1970s food industry originated with antiwar protesters and members of the New Left. They harbored a general distrust of large corporations and big government alike, seeing the FDA as serving the needs of industry rather than of consumers. Frances Moore Lappé, in her famous book *Diet for a Small Planet* (1971), does not specifically target canned foods—she lists canned tomatoes and tuna fish as pantry staples, along with kidney and garbanzo beans "only when I am really rushed and have used up my freezer store of leftover cooked beans." But she clearly attacks the larger problem of corporate control, of which the canning industry was coming to be a central part.

In the book's introduction, she writes, "When I went to a supermarket, I felt at the mercy of our advertising culture. My tastes were manipulated. And food, instead of being my most direct link with a nurturing earth, had become mere merchandise by which I fulfilled my role as a 'good' consumer."[91]

Lappé's reference to food as a link to the earth, along with the New Left's critique of unrestrained growth, fit neatly into the environmental activism that also came to define the era. Environmentalism, which had been growing as a movement throughout the 1960s, emphasized the interconnectedness of humans and nature. Expanding their scope beyond romantic ideas of wilderness, many within the movement came to see the courtroom and the legislative arena as key sites of furthering their agenda, leading to a flurry of legislation. Many environmentalists called into question the technological optimism and celebration of economic growth that ignored environmental limits.[92] Although mainstream environmental groups did not pay much attention to food beyond pesticides and additives, books like *Diet for a Small Planet* and the rise of "natural foods" among cultural protesters made food a topic of environmental interest. As historian Warren Belasco describes, the counterculture of the late 1960s and 1970s rejected mainstream society by adopting a diet that eschewed chemicals, pesticides, and food processing.[93]

All three of these intersecting groups—consumer organizations, New Left radicals, and environmentalists—shared a number of basic critiques of the food industry. These complaints hit at the foundation of the industrialized food system, preventing the industry from addressing these complaints by going about business as usual. Although many of the critiques were targeted more at "fabricated foods" like fortified cereal and snack cakes than at canned food, the activists certainly included canned fruits and vegetables in their complaints. In the critics' eyes, these packaged foods stripped away nutrients, were filled with salt and sugar, created a troubling disconnect between people and seasonal cycles, and led to an unhealthy culture.[94] These objections could not be simply addressed by a turn to the laboratory or the field station.

Food activists of the 1970s attacked the food industry for its model of corporate monopoly and its ties with universities and government agencies. One sourcebook offered the following statistics in 1975: "Of 32,500 food processors in the United States, 100 account for 71 percent of all processing profits. . . . Campbell's controls 90 percent of the canned soup business. More than 60 percent of the baby food market belongs to Gerber. Agribusiness controls over 70 percent of all vegetable production in California."[95] Because of this corporate power, consumer advocates called for federal intervention. But numerous studies found that government agencies and many prominent universities had disturbing reciprocal relationships with the food industry. Ralph Nader's *The Chemical Feast* made visible the revolving door between the FDA and major food companies—offering evidence that thirty-seven of forty-nine top FDA officials took industry jobs after leaving the federal government.[96] Michael Jacobson's article "Professors on the Take" showed how heavily the food industry funded nutrition departments, and also reported that the industry hired people to serve as "expert witnesses" in congressional hearings.[97] Findings like these combined with Vietnam protests, the Watergate scandal, and episodes of domestic spying to encourage a general feeling of uneasiness toward and desire for reform of the federal government in the 1970s.[98]

Reformers also took issue with the actual food spilling from the maw of the food companies. By the late 1970s, new foods designed in food laboratories were everywhere. As the director of corporate research at the General Foods Corporation put it, "Mother Nature is far from perfect when it comes to supplying optimum nutrition in the foods people want to eat. . . . We accept the obligation to put nutrition in the foods they like, wherever possible. . . . A direct improvement on nature through control by man."[99] This kind of "improvement" led to the creation of products like Hostess Astrofood, in 1976. This "fortified, baked product with a crème filling" was designed to be fed to schoolchildren for breakfast. When eaten with eight ounces of milk, Astrofood "provided the nutrients equal to those of 4 ounces of orange juice, 2 slices of bacon, 1 egg, 1 pat of butter, and one slice of bread." The product had initial success in some cities but was phased out after controversy arose over feeding children packaged snack cakes for breakfast.[100]

Beneath the political and health problems that the consumer advocates identified was a more fundamental criticism of the culture of eating promoted by the processed-food industry. The editors of *Food for People, Not for Profit* wrote, "We can often save time by using convenience foods, but occasionally we should take a moment or two of that time to reflect on what we are losing when we use them."[101] They described the values of family togetherness, ethnic identity, quiet reflection, and diversity conveyed by home-cooked food, traditional recipes, and shared meals. In 1974, *Washington Post* columnist Tom Donnelley quoted French gourmand Auguste Escoffier: "The history of the table of a nation is a reflection of the civilization of that nation." Donnelley continued, "If Escoffier, wherever he may be, is in a position to survey the history of the table of the US, I'll bet he would pronounce Watergate an eminently fitting reflection of our civilization at this point in time."[102] In the views of these critics, modern packaged foods symbolized a bereft culture, a corrupt nation.

By the mid- to late 1970s, these criticisms piled up, leading industry representatives to lament the loss of consumer confidence in canned and processed foods, although certainly these criticisms represented just one sector of society, as most Americans continued to buy processed foods. One food scientist blamed the news media for trumpeting unconfirmed criticisms and "destroying [consumers'] faith in our foods." Another called for education to "counteract increasing consumer mistrust of 'processed foods.'" He further pointed to "lost confidence" among consumers as a major reason not to allow more "regulations to feed the already massive legal animal," for fear of a crushed industry through combined distrust and over-regulation.[103] The issues that 1970s consumerists raised struck at the heart of the food industry, questioning technological optimism, the fruits of laboratory research, and an increasingly complex industry.

"THE OVERWHELMING BLANKET OF REGULATORY PEOPLE": THE FOOD INDUSTRY RESPONDS

The activism of the 1960s and 1970s also contributed to an increase in government regulation. The food industry reacted with hostility. Fritz C. Friday, a Wisconsin cannery vice president speaking at the 1976 NCA convention, said, "If you sense a note of bitterness and frustration in my remarks, so be it. . . . Dealing daily with the overwhelming blanket of regulatory people taxes my patience to the extreme."[104] Processors like Friday blamed consumer advocates, in part, for this suffocating regulation, as they believed the advocates misrepresented the food business, undermining ordinary consumers' trust.

Despite their anger, many canning leaders tried to tackle their problems in a constructive manner—conducting market research and launching public relations campaigns, developing their own environmental initiatives, and becoming involved in federal politics. By the end of the decade, canners were fully engaged in a broader food industry. As the *Canner/Packer* trade journal already said of its title in 1974, "We serve the canners, glass-packers, pickle packers, dry mixers, sausage stuffers, ham boners, shrimp peelers, cheese makers, pet food packers, freezers, preservers, and others in the general category of food producers—but you can't put all of that on the cover of the book."[105] These many kinds of food producers came together, bringing their combined strength to the project of overcoming consumer criticism.

Throughout the 1970s, food processors considered so-called "consumerism"—that is, consumer advocacy—to be their biggest problem. They felt that they were suffering under stringent regulations because consumerists had raised red flags about topics that would otherwise be low-priority items. James J. Albrecht, vice president at the Libby, McNeill, and Libby Food Company, wrote in 1974, "To hear [the advocates] tell it, consumers are dropping like flies because of unsafe foods; consumers are malnourished because of unavailable good nutritious foods; and the food industry is stuffing its pockets with all sorts of profits beyond the limits of reason. None of these issues could be further from the truth!" Albrecht posited that the food industry as a whole made an average profit of only 3 percent, and the canning industry less than 2 percent.[106]

Processors further attacked consumer advocates for their lack of scientific knowledge and for claiming to represent all individual consumers. Food technologists railed against Ralph Nader's appearance at their 1970 convention, pointing to his "massive ignorance."[107] One canning scientist wrote, "The calibre of so-called technical data offered by consumer advocates and academicians is so low that if such data were submitted by a graduate student he or she would probably be asked to leave the university."[108] They bristled at the idea that consumerists used scientific findings in misleading ways and that consumers fell for it.

In response, canners became even more reliant on a different kind of scientific enterprise: market research. This field, rooted in the social sciences, sought to determine the average consumer's actual preferences, rather than deferring to consumer representatives.[109] Professionalized market research grew around 1970, with American Marketing Association membership growing from less than four thousand in 1950 to nearly seventeen thousand by 1980, and with the first "marketing science" conference in 1979.[110] Canners made use of the popularity of consumer research to gaze deeper into their audiences' preferences. For example, in 1974, the NCA commissioned an expensive national study of consumer "eating and food buying habits" from Sindlinger & Co., then used these findings to launch public relations campaigns to "acquaint the public with the record—the sustained and outstanding record—of the canning industry."[111]

The field of marketing science, along with the fields of nutrition and food science, tended to be male dominated. This meant there was a shift in who could claim expertise over areas of consumption in the 1960s and beyond. Professional home economists, most of them women, contributed less to this phase of the consumer movement, in part because the American Home Economics Association disagreed about political involvement. Other organizations who spoke for consumers, like the National Consumers' League and the Consumers Union, also found their allegiances split as they took on more diverse issues and disagreed over strategies. As a result, even though consumers were commanding more attention from lawmakers and manufacturers in this era, they also became less effective in pushing for greater regulation in any one area, such as canned food.[112]

In addition to blaming consumerists for undermining the authority of science and inspiring public distrust, the food industry held them responsible for increased government regulation.[113] Canners considered themselves to be especially burdened by oversight: "The food processing industry operates in more of a goldfish bowl than any other in the United States. . . . What other industry has to cope with regulations of the USDA and the FDA, EPA and FTC, to say nothing of OSHA?" The complex and multifaceted nature of food processing meant that the industry had to comply with rules for agriculture, food safety, the environment, business, and workplace safety.[114] In many cases, processors believed they had more relevant expert knowledge about how to efficiently and safely do business than the federal government in Washington, D.C., rejecting the notion that all protection "comes through the munificent benefit derived by washing our tax dollars in the Potomac."[115] One canner in 1976 claimed that he spent 15 percent of his time dealing with the logistics of managing rules and regulations and that his company had had to increase sales by 36 percent to stay in business. He therefore considered the "constant and . . . almost despairing . . . chorus of criticism" among food processors about government action to be justified.[116]

One major target of that chorus of criticism in the 1970s was regulation of energy and the environment. The temporary ban on oil sales by the Organization of Petroleum Exporting Countries (OPEC) during the winter of 1973–74 led to a dramatic increase in oil prices.[117] The 1974 NCA annual convention was "held in an atmosphere of crisis" as food processors struggled to obtain fuel and keep costs down.[118] The food industry—along with many Americans—berated Congress for its inability to develop a constructive energy policy in the years to come. Further, in 1976, the Federal Energy Administration found that the food industry was one of the country's major energy consumers and urged the industry to adopt voluntary monitoring. Industry leaders were incensed that their right to fuel was being questioned, as they considered their business of food production to be the most essential.[119] Despite all the grousing about energy restrictions, canners did initiate some environmental projects of their own accord, dedicating conference sessions to the theme of "Man and His Environment," instituting voluntary energy conservation measures, and cooperating with the Environmental Protection Agency on issues of water pollution (figure 11).[120]

Although food processors had had some representation in Washington, D.C., through lobbying efforts since the late 1960s, levels of political participation increased significantly over the next decade. Amendments to the Federal Election Campaign Act after Watergate in 1974 led to an overall increase in Political Action Committees (PACs). Food processors were highly represented among these PACs, tending to contribute to candidates who supported corporate interests.[121] In 1976, R. Burt Gookin, CEO of the H. J. Heinz Company, attested to the growing desire of business to become involved in politics. He wrote, "Our food industry trade associations—NCA, GMA, SMI, NAFC, NAWGA—and others—are increasingly effective vehicles in the political arena and need our continuing personal participation and support."[122] A 1977 study determined that roughly 612 individuals and 460 groups were lobbying on food and nutrition issues, usually on behalf of producers.[123] Major food processors, and their marketing partners, had come to accept government regulation as a new part of the industrial landscape and now sought to shape that regulation in their favor, rather than denouncing it outright.

In November 1977, the trade journal *Canner/Packer* changed its name to *Processed Prepared Food,* to reflect the long-standing expanded focus of its audience members. Accordingly, the next year, the National Canners Association—so named since its founding in 1907—changed its name to the National Food Processors Association.[124] These changes exemplified increasing consolidation in the food industry as one strategy for mounting a stronger campaign against political incursion. In 1976, a food industry adviser had warned food processors: "The industry as a force is significant but it is not a cohesive force. . . . There is not enough time to coordinate and consolidate concerns. Regulatory concerns are dumped into the lap of the various trade associations (Grocery Manufacturers Assn., National Canners Assn., Meat and Livestock

recycle wastewater

FIGURE 11. *The Canner* trade journal of the 1970s featured many advertisements for products that would help canners lessen their environmental impact, suggesting some industrial response to consumer concern. This ad for a "C-E Bauer Hydrasieve screen" promised to help canners reclaim wastewater. (Courtesy of the Grocery Manufacturers Association.)

Board, etc.). . . . The food industry must unite."[125] The name changes, then, were an active attempt to streamline and unite the various concerns within the food industry for greater effectiveness.

Similarly, by 1977, the NCA claimed that it sought to "work with the Carter Administration to demonstrate that its goals are in harmony with those of consumers" by instituting voluntary nutritional labeling and other bridge-building efforts.[126] Just as the industry's engagement with politics was largely rooted in self-interest and an awareness of the changing business landscape, so too was this nod toward consumer partnership connected to the changing position of the consumer and environmental movements by the end of the 1970s. The difficult economic situation of the 1970s, along with the proliferation of conflicting consumer groups, led to a weakening of activist energy. After nearly two decades of effort and many near misses, the fight for a Consumer Protection Agency within the federal government took its last breath in 1979, in part because of lobbying by the food industry.[127] The environmental movement similarly stalled, partly because of the public's perception that environmental regulation was to blame for the economic downtown that followed the OPEC energy crisis. President Jimmy Carter's call for austerity measures in July 1979 was widely ridiculed, leading to the marginalization of environmental and conservation efforts. As historian Gary Cross observed, "Consuming patterns that freely used energy were too closely associated with freedom itself."[128] And so, regulation by 1980 largely turned away from the movements that encouraged measured consumption and interactions with the natural world. Against this backdrop of weakened government intervention, the NCA had less to fight against and could more easily, if disingenuously, offer cooperation.

Despite the consumer activism and the "overwhelming blanket" of regulation, the processed-food sector reached the end of 1970s with better business than ever. A stalled consumer movement combined with the food industry's active efforts to turn new forms of expertise in its favor and give the industry the upper hand once more. Social science–based consumer research, political lobbying, and united food trade groups bolstered the industry. The newly titled *Processed Prepared Food* journal, in its first issue in 1977, congratulated the industry on its "tremendous growth," offering these glowing statistics: "Processed meats, fruits, vegetables, prepared foods and frozen specialties grew from $65 billion in 1972 to just over $107 billion this year. And it's projected to be $234 billion by 1985."[129]

. . .

The story of the canning industry between 1940 and 1980 can be told as one of consumer confidence gained, consumer confidence lost, and finally consumer confidence—or at least the consumer market—regained once more. These fluctuations were embedded in changes and connections among the third-wave consumer movement, environmentalism, and the growing food industry in postwar America. By the mid-1960s, consumers' concerns about an industrialized food system and its impact on the natural environment led them to mistrust the technological foundations of the processed food industry. Canners of the 1970s combated this mistrust and the resulting government regulation by uniting with other food trade groups and using their considerable budgets to shape advertising and federal intervention.

As the pitch of consumer complaints intensified, food processors responded not by abandoning research and technological development but by investing in different forms of expertise. But the 1970s were not the first time that the canning industry struggled with consumer distrust. Indeed, the first 120 years after the invention of canning had been one long struggle, in which the canners worked proactively to improve their industry and convince consumers to trust the safety and desirability of their products. When dealing with the problems of metal toxicity, agricultural production, and bacterial contamination in the early twentieth century, canners responded by turning to the laboratory sciences of toxicology, genetics, entomology, and bacteriology. But when new and complex problems of public discontent and government regulation emerged in the 1960s, canners responded reactively by expanding their repertoire to also make use of the human and social sciences—of psychology, marketing, and political engagement. The story of this chapter reveals that the forms of expertise in play changed alongside shifts in government, business, and cultural concern. This new strategy for managing consumer concern set a course for the food industry's path into the twenty-first century.

6

BPA in Campbell's Soup

New Threats to an Entrenched Food System

In 2011, Kelly Lanham of Annapolis, Maryland, signed a Change.org petition calling on Campbell Soup Company to remove the chemical Bisphenol-A, or BPA, from its can linings. She wrote, "I am signing this petition because I have 4 children and I often use Campbell's as the soups help stretch our tight budget. I had no idea BPA was in the cans. I only buy plastics which are BPA free."[1] Lanham was just one of over twenty thousand people who signed this petition to Campbell Soup over a six-month period.

At first, in reply to the petition, Campbell spokesman Anthony Sanzio maintained the safety of BPA in can linings.[2] But by March 2012 the company responded to the huge outpouring of concern by announcing that it would begin work to phase out the chemical. Though Campbell still claimed BPA was safe, Chief Financial Officer Craig Owens indicated that the company's long record of addressing consumer concerns justified the move to BPA-free cans: "We believe that current can packaging is one of the safest options in the world; however, we recognize that there is some debate over the use of BPA. The trust that we have earned from our consumers for over 140 years is paramount to us."[3] Despite this stated commitment to consumer trust, for four years Campbell failed to indicate a timeline or clarify which products were making the transition. Finally, in March 2016, the company announced a more specific plan for the elimination of the chemical and set a target date of mid-2017.[4]

In defense of the four-year time lag, Campbell publicly pointed to the lengthy testing process required to find an affordable, safe substitute, suggesting that they had been actively engaged in the project since their first announcement in 2012. Privately, however, Campbell spokesmen admitted that the company's foot-dragging had more to do with a desire to appease consumers without making real change. According to *Forbes,* David Stangis, Campbell's vice president of corporate social responsibility and sustainability, said in 2012: "There are concerns, emotional concerns. . . . You don't win over anyone with a fact based science argument. We believe BPA is safe. But how can we be scientifically credible without appearing to be ignoring our consumers? . . . Despite what's been reported in the press [about finding a substitute], we're not there yet."[5] In essence, Campbell believed its consumers were misguided in their concern about BPA, but because its marketing efforts were so firmly based on a "customer is always right" mentality, the company projected an attitude of responsiveness to consumer concern. This rather insulting, and disingenuous, response mirrors the long history of how manufacturers have disparaged their consumers even as they professed their desire to serve them.

It is difficult to know what actually went on behind the closed doors of the Campbell research laboratories and boardrooms between 2012 and 2016 because so much of this information is considered proprietary. But what is clear is that Campbell was deeply, fundamentally concerned about how it was perceived by consumers. During this same period, the company took on new leadership and invested heavily in ambitious consumer research initiatives and neuromarketing technologies to try to increase its flagging popularity. It became more invasive than ever before, entering people's homes through consumer surveys and bodies through brain mapping—all in an effort to capture consumer taste. The 1980s, 1990s, and 2000s saw the canning industry get swallowed up by a larger processed-food industry and then face its increasingly out-of-date reputation in an age of farmers' markets and foodie blogs. Even though canned-food sales have not changed dramatically, leading canners still fear being maligned in the public image, in the eyes of the tastemakers. Just as we've seen throughout the history of the canning industry, concerns about consumer distrust drive research to capture and fulfill the desires of the elusive consumer.

At its foundation, the problem of BPA in canned food is a technical one. How to get this chemical out of the materials that come in contact with our food? But the kinds of research that canners have embraced in the last half century focus less on the technical than on the social—less on the problem itself than on the managing the perception of the problem. Since the mid-twentieth century, when canners felt they had solved most of the technological, bacteriological, and agricultural problems that plagued the early industry, they have worked to build the brand and public reputation of their products. When BPA arose, it threatened to force a return to older strategies, forcing the industry to reexamine the very container on which it was built and disrupting the technical stability that had been considered a given.

Even as Campbell committed to addressing the BPA problem in its laboratories, it put more of its effort into maintaining the image projected to its consumers. But the narrative for public consumption often differed significantly from what was happening behind the scenes. In public, Campbell took consumer concerns about BPA seriously, while privately it used its trade organization to push against BPA legislation. This two-faced aspect characterizes food companies particularly, because their brand names are at stake in the consumer marketplace. Other industries implicated in the case of BPA—chemicals, plastics— did not deal in consumer goods and so got away with a more straightforward resistance to change. The consumer-focused Campbell had to remain more malleable and work out of sight in its resistance. This double-dealing nature of many food companies has led to modern calls for transparency in the food system. To see through the object and see not only what is painted on the front but also what is going on behind the scenes, consumers want to make the industry transparent.

One of the great barriers in achieving this transparency has been the deep connection between industry and federal regulatory bodies. In the case of BPA, the agencies in charge are the US Food and Drug Administration (FDA) and the European Food Safety Authority. Both of these organizations, however, have lagged in their regulation of BPA. When they have ruled, as with the removal of BPA from baby bottles in 2012, the decisions have often followed the actions of industry rather than directing those actions. Further, many of the FDA's guidelines privilege the industries that are often the interested parties in a particular determination of a chemical's safety. They rely on "competent scientists" to designate a chemical as "generally regarded as safe," without defining what "competent" means and while allowing these scientists to be hired by the chemical companies themselves. To accept a scientific study into consideration, the FDA requires that the study be conducted using "Good Laboratory Practices," which are restrictive guidelines that effectively rule out the majority of peer-reviewed, replicable, independent scientific studies in favor of industry-funded ones. All of these tactics pose obvious conflicts of interest and call into question the reliability of the organizations the public looks to for guidance.

So in the absence of trustworthy regulatory bodies, consumers have turned inward, emphasizing the power of individual action. They have tried to buy less canned food, to can their own tomatoes in glass mason jars, to buy direct from the farmer. They have also started online petitions and have looked for "BPA-free" products. But the power of consumer activism is limited; consumers are often all too easily appeased by half measures. A company can make empty promises. An alternative "BPA-free" plastic may be found to be just as toxic. To be sure, many of the vocal critics of the food system, both from the 1960s and 1970s counterculture and from today, *have* led food companies like Campbell's to make changes. But many of the gains of the food movement have occurred at the margins, while the core of the food system remains. In the absence of federal support, it is difficult for individual consumers to make real change.

The BPA story in the twenty-first century is a complicated one, involving conflicting scientific findings, corporate lobbying efforts, strategic marketing campaigns, biased media, consumer activism, and bureaucratic regulations. But this smaller story of Campbell Soup serves as a case study, capturing the essence of the broader narrative. Campbell's situation embodies the ongoing struggle of food processors to rise above technological and health limitations, by whatever means necessary, to preserve a place for their products in kitchens across America.

FOOD SYSTEM CHANGES AFTER 1980

To place the BPA story in context, we must understand the position of the canning industry during this time. When the National Canners Association changed its name to the National Food Processors Association in 1978, it signaled a circling of the wagons as the canning industry deepened its connections with other segments of the processed-food industry in order to shore up its strength for the battles to come. The canners had long had alliances with other food manufacturers and now wanted to make those ties official.

By 1980, canners and their trade organization had become part of a much larger, consolidated, and powerful institution. The canning industry had given way to a broader processed-foods industry, a behemoth that would have an increasing influence on American health, environment, and politics. Although the efforts of the consumer and environmental movements of the 1960s and 1970s did have some lasting impacts on the food system, they did not fundamentally transform production. The increasing involvement of business at all levels of government meant that many political agendas were directed in support of processed food. The industry's 1970s critiques of regulators as overbearing tyrants who were destroying the economy worked. They stuck around and continued to shape ideas of "big government" throughout the late twentieth century and into the twenty-first. The election of Ronald Reagan in 1980 led to a contraction of the federal government, with weakened consumer and environmental regulations.[6]

Many commentators also point to the late 1970s as the origin of today's obesity epidemic, a time when cheap carbohydrates and sugars began to flood the markets, and a focus on nutrients at the expense of whole foods came to dominate. These events were partly the result of changes in agricultural subsidies under the US Department of Agriculture (USDA), at the urging of producers in agribusiness. As journalist Michael Pollan has shown, the cheap corn that was the legacy of these subsidies has become the foundation of our modern diet. More processed-food products, based on this cheap corn, have emerged in the later twentieth century than postwar "golden age" consumers could ever have imagined. The ubiquity of high-fructose corn syrup, a processed sugar from corn, has contributed to the increasing rates of obesity and type 2 diabetes in America. As Pollan writes, "Sweetness became so cheap that soft drink makers, rather than lower their prices, super-sized their serving portions and marketing budgets." Food processors added the cheap fructose to an amazing array of foods, from canned soups to chicken nuggets, from Gatorade to hamburgers.[7]

Another significant political change that reshaped the food system during the early 1980s was the weakening of antitrust law. This allowed for the consolidation of many food companies under one banner, with increasingly large budgets to influence consumer trust through advertising and legislation through lobbying. To give just one example, in 1979, the tobacco giant R. J. Reynolds Corporation purchased the Del Monte Corporation, which had begun in 1899 as the California Fruit Canners Association. Reynolds then went on to buy snack company Nabisco Brands in 1985, forming RJR Nabisco. In 2000, RJR Nabisco split and sold its Nabisco holdings to another cigarette company, Philip Morris, which already owned both General Foods and Kraft Foods.[8] Although these companies have divided and merged and spun off in the years since, this kind of trading among the world's largest food processors gives some sense of the scale at which these acquisitions are occurring. Today, most American food, including organic brands, is produced by just twenty companies.[9] This corporate consolidation has led to a modern food industry with significant political power. As one example of its political involvement, during the 2000 election cycle industries related to agribusiness contributed $60 million to campaigns and $78 million to lobbying efforts. The food sector, in turn, received $23 million in public subsidies around the same time.[10]

Such a concentration of power has also characterized food trade groups. After 1978, the new National Food Processors Association later became the even more general Food Products Association (FPA). Then, in 2007, the FPA became part of the Grocery Manufacturers Association (GMA), creating the largest food trade group in the world, with over three hundred members representing every major food manufacturer in the United States and exerting inordinate influence on policy, science, and consumer access. Of those three hundred members, nearly all those with the earliest dates of establishment began as canning companies.[11]

The food trade has leveraged its significant size and power to defend itself against consumer complaints. In recent years, many consumers have grown concerned about emerging issues—not just BPA but also genetically modified foods, high-fructose corn syrup, supersized sodas, junk food in schools, and others.[12] One strategy many food processors have taken is to co-opt the language of consumer protection toward their own ends. The benignly named Center for Consumer Freedom, for example, is entirely funded by the food industry, in an effort to frame scientific findings around health and nutrition in a way that supports processed food and minimizes concerns around issues like childhood obesity. Another group, the American Council on Fitness and Nutrition, which might seem to be a public health advocacy group, instead has among its central constituents such major organizations as Campbell Soup, Del Monte, Heinz, and the GMA.[13] The industry has figured out ways to use food science and the language of consumer advocacy to direct policy and public opinion in its favor.

Following the legacy of the consumer and environmental movements, the food industry adopted for its own purposes many of the tactics of the counterculture's food efforts. When marketing surveys revealed that an affluent class of American consumers would pay higher prices for "natural" foods, the industry began to use this term widely. In many cases, the term was more a marketing strategy than an indication of genuine change. But in other cases companies did revise their existing products and offerings, using whole grains or reducing the amount of refined sugar. And many of the hippies' "natural foods"—like yogurt, whole wheat bread, and granola—came to dominate the mainstream marketplace over the next several decades. Further, the activism of groups like Michael Jacobson's Center for Science in the Public Interest did lead to concrete changes in nutritional labeling, as with the passage of required sodium labeling in 1982.[14] Although these changes by no means reversed the industrializing trend in the American food system, they did reflect the continuing efforts of food processors to maintain consumer trust by appearing responsive.

Similar to the activism of the 1970s, today a flourishing food movement is prioritizing organic production, local sourcing, and ethical practices. And although this movement is still limited in size and scope, terms like *food miles* have become broadly familiar, and products from Haagen-Dazs ice cream to Lay's potato chips are flaunting the fact that their ingredient lists are short and pronounceable.[15] These movements are building on those that came more than forty years before, even if those earlier movements have become part of a forgotten history. Consumer activists then and now have railed against the opacity of the food system, though the degree of that opacity has changed substantially.

Contemporary critics point to a number of factors that shroud the food industry in mystery: the manipulation of scientific research, the use of advertising to influence consumers, misleading nutritional labeling, the revolving door between big companies and government agencies, and the high degree of processing that introduces synthetic chemicals and renders ingredients unrecognizable.[16] The food movement's push for transparency seeks to reverse some of these disturbing trends. But these characteristics have become so central to the modern food industry that addressing them may require fundamentally dismantling the current system.

CANNED FOOD IN A FOODIE WORLD

Even as the canning industry became embedded in the larger processed-food industry, it faced unique challenges. Between 1970 and 2005, at the same time that more Americans were eating fruits and vegetables, the percentage of those foods that were in a canned form dropped. The consumption of canned fruit per person fell by 37 percent, and the portion of total fruit made up by canned fruit decreased from 11 percent to

6 percent. As for vegetables, while the per person amount marginally increased, the portion of total vegetables decreased from 30 percent to 25 percent.[17] Not dramatic numbers, but still a clear indication that, as Americans have heeded federal advice to eat their fruits and veggies, they have turned away from canned items and toward fresh produce. And this trend has been especially pronounced in the first decade of the twenty-first century, with a decrease of 7.5 percent in all canned foods between 2003 and 2013.[18]

Still, many Americans continue to make use of canned foods. A 2013 survey found that more than 60 percent of respondents used canned foods at least weekly.[19] And the FDA reports that some people get up to 17 percent of their daily nutrition from canned food. On the whole, though, the market for canned food is quite segmented, by age, race, and income, among other factors. Canned foods are the staples of venues that depend on nonperishable foods, often serving marginal audiences: food banks, food drives, or underground bunkers. And older consumers tend to prefer canned foods. In one study, the USDA found that in households headed by someone younger than forty, the average spent on canned vegetables per person per year is $11.35, and $4.91 for canned fruits. In homes where the head of household is over the age of sixty-four, however, the average spent on canned vegetables is $18.24 (61 percent more) and on fruits, $10.74 (118 percent more).[20] For these older consumers, canned food plays on the nostalgia factor. As one brand consultant wrote, "Campbell's soup transports us back to our childhood and reminds us of a time when a bowl of tomato soup and a grilled cheese sandwich was the height of fine dining. . . . We continue the tradition by serving Campbell's to our children today—with organic sourdough croutons, of course."[21]

The nod to "organic sourdough croutons" points to a significant trend in American cuisine that has pushed against the popularity of canned food. These croutons might embody the so-called "foodie" culture that has emerged in the last several decades. Many commentators give restaurant critic Gael Greene the credit for coining the term *foodie* in a 1980 *New York Times* article. She used it to describe a group of people who "were obsessed with food, taking cooking classes, competing to cook complicated perfect dinners, making the rounds of three-star restaurants in France." Further, she explicitly contrasted them with the majority of New Yorkers at the time, who "were not especially fussy about what they ate—an overcooked lamb chop and canned peas were fine."[22] Already in 1980, Greene used canned peas to symbolize the opposite of foodie tastes. In making this link, she presaged the decline in popularity of canned foods alongside the increasing interest in food as a marker of culture. Canned food had become decidedly lowbrow.

The canning industry has also come to see the historical quality of canned food as a liability. For some, this historic nature can read as "old-fashioned." Authors Joseé Johnston and Shyon Baumann, who have written about the "foodie" phenomenon, argue that consumers maintain interest in a product when it is new and rare.[23] Canned food does not pass the test. Leading canning companies recognize this problem and have been working to address it. Brent Bailey of Del Monte Foods, a company founded in 1891, sought to reframe the image of its products: "This is not your grandmother's Del Monte," he said.[24] In its focus groups, Campbell Soup Company found that many of its customers expressed the view that "I grew up with Campbell's, but [it] didn't grow up with me."[25] That is, they had a deeply rooted attachment to the brand but no longer felt that it met their needs as twenty-first-century consumers.

A deepened interest in nutrition and food-related health issues has also led to avoidance of canned foods. To combat the commonly held view that the canning process destroys nutrients, the canning industry has taken to funding and promoting studies that argue otherwise. In 2015, the Can Manufacturers Institute (CMI) funded research on nutrient intake and canned food consumption at the University of California-Davis. The author also received consulting fees from CMI. The study found that frequent consumption of canned food was positively correlated with a more nutrient-dense diet. Other studies have analyzed specific canned foods themselves and have found that their nutrient levels are not diminished.[26] Canning companies have also developed new low-sodium varieties of their products, even garnering the support of the American Heart Association, to address consumer concerns that canned foods are full of salt.[27] Despite initiatives like these, many consumers continue to think of food from cans as nutritionally inferior to fresh.

Along with an explicit concern about nutrient density, many savvy shoppers today seek indicators that their foods are less processed. They look to rules of thumb inspired by Michael Pollan: "Avoid food products containing ingredients that no ordinary human would keep in the pantry," and "Shop the peripheries of the supermarket and stay out of the middle."[28] Both of these rules push against the consumption of canned food. One of Campbell Soup Company's most successful products of the last decade is their Select Harvest line of soups, which avoids ingredients like "hydrolyzed vegetable protein and MSG" in favor of "farm fresh vegetables." Senior brand manager Jeff Jackson indicated that this product appealed to "Americans' focus on real ingredients and transparency" and their view of "the back of the label as the new front of the label."[29]

Younger consumers, of the so-called millennial generation, also treat money differently from their parents.[30] Whereas previous generations may have reined in their food budgets when faced with a backlog of debt, an inability to pay rent, and low wages, millennials actually spend more at restaurants and on organic foods. In the past, the canning industry expected increased demand for its inexpensive products during periods of economic downturn. Now, this association has weakened. Some millennials have begun to see food as one area in which they can exert some control, in contrast to the huge forces outside their sphere of influence—like economic recession, terrorism, and fears of global climate change. According to writer Eve Turow, these consumers shy away from technologically complex processed foods: "Because you [Big Government] are not telling us how they [these foods] work, even if I can't get a job, even if I can't get a date, gosh darn it I can control what I'm eating three times a day."[31] For some young consumers, canned food just doesn't fit the bill, regardless of the low price.

CAMPBELL'S "UNCANNED" APPROACH

Many canning companies have developed multipronged campaigns to address their diminishing appeal to twenty-first-century consumers. Campbell Soup Company has been among the most active. The company markets food under many brands—Prego, V-8, Godiva, Pace, and Pepperidge Farms—but its line of soups has been its mainstay since its founding in 1869. As the market for soup has declined, Campbell has gone to great lengths to reach and win over the elusive consumer, giving a sense of the vulnerable position of Campbell in the years surrounding the campaign against BPA in can linings.

Around 2009, Campbell invested heavily in a new method of market research called neuromarketing. Traditional forms of market research, like focus groups and questionnaires, assume that consumers behave rationally and are able to faithfully report why they choose to buy what they do. Neuromarketing, in contrast, uses brain-imaging technologies to go straight to the source. By studying brain processing, this method claims to be able to capture unconscious emotional responses. After finding in 2005 that their ad campaigns did not translate to increased sales, Campbell wanted a new strategy. The company wanted to figure out which specific elements of their soup labels did or did not push the "buy-me" button in consumers' brains. They enlisted three neuromarketing firms in two years of study, which led to a redesign of their labels.[32]

Campbell Soup, thanks in large part to Andy Warhol's pop art of the 1960s, has one of the most deeply iconic and recognizable logos in the American food landscape. Since the late nineteenth century, the cursive font and the red and white color scheme have remained unchanged. The company made some changes to its label in 1999, introducing a photo of a bowl of soup, among other tweaks.[33] But the most significant changes came in 2010, reflecting the neuromarketing research findings. The photo of the bowl of soup remained, but the spoon holding a bite of soup in the foreground was removed, as brain imaging data revealed that people "had little emotional response" to the spoon. Graphic designers added steam rising from the bowl, to make the soup appear warm, which allowed consumers to feel "more emotionally engaged." The logo was moved to the bottom of the label because studies that tracked consumer eye movement suggested that a logo at the top made different varieties hard to distinguish.[34]

To gain these insights, Campbell invested large sums in neuromarketing. Some experts suggest the fMRI scans and interpretation cost around $3,000 per subject.[35] But it's actually not at all clear that this expensive technique is effective. Many analysts are skeptical of the value of this new method. Detractors say that a savvy graphic designer could determine the need to remove a spoon, add steam, and move a logo without the heavy investment required for complicated medical technologies. Other critics point not only to the unproven efficacy of this method but also to the questionable ethics involved. Gary Ruskin, of the nonprofit organization Commercial Alert, has written that neuromarketing furthers the existing "epidemic of marketing-related diseases . . . obesity, type 2 diabetes, anorexia, bulimia, and pathological gambling." He has also highlighted the "totalitarian implications" of the behavior control that follows from the use of neuroscience for marketing purposes.[36] Given these criticisms—the expense, uncertain state, and moral issues of the neuromarketing field—Campbell's willingness to give it a try speaks volumes about its deep desire to make sense of consumer preference. Desperate times call for desperate measures.

On the heels of the neuromarketing effort and other innovations, Campbell CEO Doug Conant stepped down to pursue an independent career. His successor, Denise Morrison, took over in 2011. She decided even more drastic change was necessary. Even though Campbell soup is still quite popular—finding a home in 80 percent of US cupboards—the company worried its main audience was aging and slipping away.[37] As one journalist put it, "If your lunch still consists of a bowl of Campbell's tomato soup and a grilled cheese sandwich, chances are you grew up using a typewriter."[38] Thus the company's new approach was an attempt to bring the familiarity and fond memories of Campbell into the twenty-first century, to build a new kind of trust among consumers.

In order to attract younger consumers, Campbell launched an ambitious consumer research initiative. Around 2010, the company sent executives to "hipster hubs" like Portland, Austin, San Francisco, and London, where they observed favorite food trucks and neighborhood restaurants. The company recruited young people for "eat-alongs," in which researchers ate meals in consumers' homes, accompanied them to the grocery store, asked them to display their favorite pantry items, and observed their menu choices. Campbell's chefs were sent to grocery stores and spice shops, and "In Boston, they even ducked into an Urban Outfitters clothing store, just to get a better sense of the overall mindset of Millennials."[39] CEO Morrison emphasized the company's deep attention to the consumer: "Consumers today crave . . . foods that help them feel alive, engaged and connected. No company is connected to consumers' lives quite like Campbell."[40]

All of this consumer research revealed that young people wanted seemingly contradictory things: adventurous ethnic flavors *and* meals that could be popped right into the microwave without so much as the twist of a can opener. They wanted the taste of elaborate cooking without the work to get there. These results manifested in the August 2012 introduction of several new lines of products and flavors. In a departure from its reliance on cans, Campbell launched a new line of "Go! Soups" in microwavable plastic packages, featuring flavors like "Coconut Curry with Chicken & Shiitake Mushrooms" and "Creamy Red Pepper with Smoked Gouda."[41] Although the bodies of the packages themselves are still opaque like tin cans, they do feature a clear bottom panel explicitly designed to give a peek at the food inside. The pouches feature modern graphics, young models from a variety of ethnic backgrounds, and humorous taglines. As a *Consumerist* article put it, the soups seem "to be based on a checklist of 'what the kids today like.'"[42] The Go! Soups website was initially designed in the style of popular websites Tumblr and Pinterest, featuring animated kitten GIFs and encouraging viewers to create Spotify music playlists inspired by the new soup flavors. Campbell's chief executive Denise Morrison said herself that these more adventurous, "globally-inspired" products were an explicit response to a changing consumer base and a desire to cater to a younger generation.[43]

There is some indication that these new efforts worked. Campbell reported an 8 percent sales increase in the first quarter after the Go! Soups' introduction.[44] But many commentators also skewered these initiatives. The consumer affairs blog *Consumerist,* after describing the food trucks that had inspired Campbell's, commented, "What they're missing, of course, is that eating food from your neighborhood restaurants and food trucks is about eating food that's local, seasonal, and made right in your neighborhood. Not trucked cross-country in a non-biodegradable plastic pouch and microwaved."[45] An author on the media blog *Gawker* added, "Thank god the 'DIY' ethos so prized by my generation has been co-opted by a massive corporation, for which I am now serving as a walking symbol of obfuscation!"[46] Although the campaign may have appealed to its less visible consumer base, when it came to the hipster millennial audience the company sought, Campbell had swung and missed.

Some of these same criticisms underpinned the many comments on the Change.org petition against BPA that begins this chapter. At the same time that Campbell was trying to make tweaks at the margins in order to win over young consumers, the BPA crisis rose to a fever pitch, undermining their efforts and pointing to a much more deeply rooted problem. Millennial consumers, it turns out, care far more about their reproductive health than about whether steam is pictured on a can label. When Healthy Child Healthy World and the other environmental nonprofit organizations behind the anti-BPA cause chose Campbell as target of their 2011 campaign, they identified a company whose vulnerability was obvious. Nearly all major canning companies use BPA in their can linings, but few are so historic, brand dependent, and eager to please as Campbell's. The company's reaction to the concerns about BPA embodied the larger canning industry's ongoing efforts to secure consumer trust in moments of unease. It also made clear that canners have seen certain kinds of consumers as more desirable, and more deserving of attention, over time.

INTRODUCING AND REGULATING BISPHENOL-A

Until the mid-twentieth century, canned food was packed in all-metal cans. In the early days of the canning industry some of these metals posed health concerns, as with lead poisoning or fears of "salts of tin."[47]

Canning-industry scientists experimented with various enamels and lacquers to create a barrier between the metal and the food. But until the 1950s, these early linings were unpalatable, unaffordable, or inflexible. When plastics came on the scene in the 1950s, they were heralded as a miracle that could solve many industrial problems, including those of the canners. Derived from petroleum, plastic was the new material of the age, creating a wide range of consumer products that were inexpensive, lightweight, and easy to clean. As historian Jeffrey Meikle writes, "Plastic not only offered a perfect medium for this material proliferation. It conceptually embodied and stimulated it."[48]

Canners discovered that polycarbonate and epoxy resins from plastic were tasteless and easy to apply. They could be brushed onto the inside of metal cans to prevent leaching and corrosion, providing the durability and temperature tolerance of metal along with the advantages of plastic linings. One of the elements of these resins was the chemical Bisphenol-A, or BPA. This synthetic chemical was first created in 1891 but came to wider use in the 1930s, when scientists discovered that it mimicked the hormone estrogen in the human body. It was first considered for use in estrogen replacement therapies but became widely used several decades later as a component of plastic that provides strength and flexibility.[49] By the early 1960s, the FDA approved plastics made with BPA for food packaging as part of its food additive regulations.[50]

Although the estrogenic properties of BPA as an isolated molecule have long been known, it was only in the late 1980s that it became clear that BPA in plastic could leach out into the adjacent fluid. Several scientists made this discovery by accident in the laboratory, when they found abnormal cell growth in their experiments. BPA was leaching out of the plastic tubes and flasks and having estrogen-like effects on the biological material.[51] It followed that food eaten from plastic containers, or plastic-lined metal containers, would likely be contaminated as well.

Within a few years, leading scientists coined the term *endocrine disruptors* to capture the class of chemicals, of which BPA was a part, that mimicked hormones in the human body and interfered with the endocrine system. The 1991 Wingspread Statement, led by scientist Theo Colborn, established the scope of concern relative to endocrine disruption. "Unless the environmental load of synthetic hormone disruptors is abated and controlled," the Statement read, "large scale dysfunction at the population level is possible."[52] The authors especially pointed to threats to developing fetuses, whose growth and maturation are directed by a delicate balance of hormones. Damage could be done to all bodily processes that depend on the endocrine system—resulting in everything from learning disabilities to breast cancer, from diabetes to sexual development problems. This foundation of concern led to hundreds of scientific studies on endocrine disruptors in the following years, with a central focus on BPA.[53]

Endocrine disruptors were especially unsettling because they did not fit previous understandings of chemical risk. Although synthetic chemicals had come to be an accepted part of the industrial and cultural landscape since the 1950s, regulators and scientists felt they had a handle on managing the inherent risks of those older chemicals. All they had to do was establish a limit to minimize exposure—how many parts per million before a chemical became dangerous? The "dose makes the poison" became the reigning ideology. But endocrine disruptors did not work that way. When they came on the scene in the 1990s, scientists found that these compounds could cause serious damage at very low levels by signaling a change in the endocrine system. As historian Sarah Vogel writes, they "fundamentally undermined the long held logic of safety and revealed that there is more to defining risk than the dose."[54]

Since BPA first rose to public consciousness around 2005, countries and organizations around the world have taken action: Canada banned BPA in baby bottles in 2008; the European Union followed suit in 2011; and France became the first country to ban BPA in all food packaging, effective 2015. In the United States, thirteen states have adopted legislation to regulate BPA, particularly in baby bottles and sippy cups. The FDA also announced its own ban on BPA in infant cups in 2012 but has resisted any movement in food packaging. Much of this legislation has been the result of concerted consumer activism, against coordinated resistance from industry.[55] A coalition of environmental, consumer, health, and parenting groups have come together to demand change in the marketplace, as with the Healthy Child Healthy World petition that opened this chapter.[56]

Although there has been movement at the state level, most industry players want to keep regulation at the federal level because they have more lobbyists and clout in Washington. Further, federal environmental laws typically set a minimum standard, which states can exceed if they choose.[57] The FDA itself admits, however, that its "regulatory structure limits the oversight and flexibility of FDA."[58] Currently, BPA is on a list of chemicals considered "indirect food additives" that were approved in the early 1960s on the basis of the science of the era. Once a compound is on that list, companies can use it without interference. What's more, to make it on the list and be designated "generally regarded as safe"

(GRAS), a chemical simply has to be deemed so by "competent scientists." Studies have shown, however, that these scientists are typically hired by the very companies seeking the evaluation, leading to obvious conflicts of interest.[59] Even chemicals that have been approved since 2000, when more stringent requirements were established, are still not tested for endocrine-disrupting properties at low doses—the primary danger of BPA.[60]

Even in the face of ongoing consumer pressure, international movement, and state-level regulation, the FDA has stubbornly held on to the reference dose, or maximum daily exposure, of 50 µg/kg/day, established by the Environmental Protection Agency (EPA) in 1988. The EPA came to this number by simply dividing by 1,000 the lowest dose at which adverse effects were seen in laboratory animals. The problem was that no experiments were done to see if this lower level could also cause adverse effects. Since then, more than a hundred peer-reviewed studies have indeed shown health effects at lower doses. But the federal government continues to uphold its 1988 reference dose in food packaging.[61]

Until 2010, the FDA held fast to its assessment that BPA was largely safe at the regulated levels. But this determination was based on just two industry-funded studies.[62] In 2010, the FDA, along with the National Toxicology Program (NTP), modified its earlier position, voicing "some concern" about BPA toxicity. Rather than making any moves to label or limit BPA use, the FDA called for more research, touting a recent pledge of $30 million for the study of BPA from the National Institute of Environmental Health Sciences.[63] But legislators and activists want action now. The "Ban Poisonous Additives (BPA) Act of 2014" and the "BPA in Food Packaging Right to Know Act" of 2015 were introduced to Congress in an effort to get the FDA to move more quickly on this issue of public health, but they have not gained traction.[64]

Much of this question of BPA hinges on the question of authority. Whom do we trust?[65] How can consumers know if their food supply is safe or not? Industry spokesmen repeatedly point to the appraisals of the FDA and the corresponding European Food Safety Authority (EFSA) in choosing not to restrict the use of BPA. Indeed, the statements of these federal bodies are often taken to be the final word on issues of food safety. Yet many scientists and public health activists express concern about the methods used by the FDA to make its determinations. Investigative journalism has revealed the deep influence of industrial lobbying in the regulatory process.[66] A 2009 statement by thirty-six leading scientists from elite institutions around the world identified the core problem with the selection criteria that FDA and EFSA use to choose studies for their determination of BPA's safety. These scientists argued that federal rules for defining "Good Laboratory Practices" (GLP) are unnecessarily restrictive and lead FDA away from including many crucial studies by experts in the field.[67]

At its foundation, GLP is a set of well-intentioned guidelines for laboratory research, addressing everything from caring for research animals to maintaining facilities and equipment, from collecting data to laboratory inspections.[68] Despite its good intentions, though, GLP can end up being more restrictive than necessary, while also not providing for the best means to detect BPA. Because FDA weighs GLP more highly than other factors, industry-funded scientists shape their studies to these practices—unnecessarily large numbers of research animals, for example—while avoiding the methods used by independent and academic studies, like sensitive assays, independent replication, and peer review. But these latter characteristics, while not valued by GLP, are actually fundamental to identifying the true threat of BPA in order to make informed public health decisions. In the words of the 2009 statement by leading BPA scientists, "FDA and EFSA have mistakenly assumed that GLP yields valid and reliable scientific findings (i.e., 'good science'). . . . Public health decisions should be based on studies using appropriate protocols with appropriate controls and the most sensitive assays, not GLP."[69] Considering all this, the question becomes, if the agencies with the authority to designate BPA as "safe" or "unsafe" are themselves using unreliable methods, where do consumers turn for guidance?

INDUSTRIAL AND CONSUMER RESPONSES TO BPA

Industry responses have been many and varied. Not just canning companies are implicated in this movement against BPA but also the plastics, chemical, and packaging industries—a vast network of power. How closely tied each of these is to its consumer base has determined how resistant each has been to phasing out BPA. The more familiar the brand, the more they are willing to change. Those companies with an established, trusted brand name have more to lose. When the Change. org petition targeted Campbell soup, it targeted the company's 140-year legacy, its familiar red and white label, and its vulnerability in the face of changing consumer tastes. Campbell's response also reflects its long history of marketing and consumer engagement. By quickly making public pledges to phase out BPA while privately doubting its need or ability to do so, Campbell displayed an approach to managing consumer confidence even in the face of lack of investment in new technologies and research.

While Campbell capitulated to consumer demand, at least in its public statements, other implicated industries have been far more defiant. Extensive reporting from the *Milwaukee Journal Sentinel, Mother Jones,* and other publications has shown that in its fight to protect BPA the chemical industry has co-opted not only the tactics of the tobacco industry, but also its specific consultants and scientists.[70] Chemical companies have funded research that has found BPA safe and that has been published in journals like *Regulatory Toxicology and Pharmacology.* This journal, while presenting itself as a dispassionate and peer-reviewed publication, is funded by the Weinberg Group, a notorious industry mouthpiece. It routinely publishes work funded by industrial groups without disclosing conflicts of interest.[71] As of 2001, a review of the one hundred studies on low-dose BPA that were in print revealed that 90 percent of those authored by government scientists found serious danger, while not even one industry-funded study did so. Throughout their counterattack, plastics manufacturers have claimed that more research needs to be done—this despite the fact that some researchers have called BPA one of the "most studied chemicals on the planet." A 2006 panel convened by the National Institute of Environmental Health Sciences brought together thirty-eight scholars to evaluate more than seven hundred studies on the topic.[72] Chemical trade groups have also suggested that, even if BPA were unsafe, regulation would be too costly.[73]

The packaging industry has done its part to fight anti-BPA activism by maintaining secrecy. When journalist Jonathan Waldman made his way into "Can School," run by Ball Canning Company, and began asking question about BPA, Ball revoked Waldman's invitation to attend. When Waldman questioned a corrosion engineer about BPA, he "stammered so . . . that he lost his train of thought."[74] Eden Foods, a pioneer in BPA-free canned foods, reached out to its can suppliers in the 1990s in order to explore the safety of its linings. Upon contacting the Can Manufacturers Institute and the American Canning Association, Eden reported that they showed a "seemingly orchestrated collusion amongst them to spin and dismiss." The can producers gave "half information and half answers" and insisted that the composition of their can linings was a "trade secret."[75]

Alongside this secrecy, a trade group for can producers, the North American Metal Packaging Alliance (NAMPA), goes above and beyond in openly responding to BPA fears. It devotes a considerable portion of its website to BPA, and publishes incredibly detailed responses to any media coverage of BPA concerns. For example, an April 2016 editorial from the *Bangor Daily News* was met with a point-by-point refutation, with each comment highlighted using the "track changes" feature of a word-processing program. Among the comments from NAMPA directed at the editorial's writers: "You may want to make that 'in my uneducated opinion.'"[76] In responding to a blog post with no stated author, from a website entitled Seattle Organic Restaurants, NAMPA made twenty-five comments in a three-page article, including "This entire section is WRONG." These are just two examples from a broader trade organization effort to battle those who raise questions about BPA. The ire with which NAMPA addresses these naysayers, and the defensiveness revealed by the line-by-line breakdown, suggest a real fear on the part of industry that consumers will abandon canned goods to avoid BPA.

Food companies have also gotten involved in the campaign to protect BPA. But as has historically been the case, they have used the mantle of the trade association rather than their more familiar brand names. This has given them both a way to build strength in numbers and a way to create distance from consumer recognition. The major trade association of the canning industry today, which the National Canners Association was folded into, is the GMA. This group has over three hundred members, among them Campbell Soup Company. In May 2009, the GMA and representatives from the American Chemistry Council and NAMPA came together for a meeting of what they called the BPA Joint Trade Association. The goal: "Prolong the life of BPA." The minutes of this meeting, which were leaked to the media, document the group's intention to "manipulate the legislative process"; its use of "fear tactics" to play up the "impact of BPA bans on minorities (Hispanic and African American) and poor"; and its hope of finding a "holy grail spokesperson" of "a pregnant young mother" since they doubted a "scientific spokesperson" would be attainable.[77] In all of the group's machinations at this meeting, there was no discussion of whether BPA was actually safe or not, only how they would convince consumers to believe it to be safe.

At the same time, individual food companies *are* eager to please their consumers, and are therefore actively seeking alternatives to BPA. Coating manufacturers are investing heavily in research toward this end. The problem is that, so far, the majority of alternatives have not proven to be safe or effective. Tritan, one of the leading alternative plastics that has been marketed as safe, shows clear estrogenic properties in independent studies. (Eastman Chemical, the maker of Tritan, has gone on the offensive, suing the researchers behind these studies).[78] A 2016 report from the Breast Cancer Fund and other nonprofit organizations tested the coatings on cans marketed as BPA-free. It found that some of the alternative linings contained PVC or polystyrene, both composed of known carcinogens. The formulation of other coatings was impossible to determine, given the proprietary nature of this information. Additionally, the same report found that, despite many companies' claims about moving away from BPA, 67 percent of cans tested contained BPA. Of the fifteen cans from Campbell that were tested, 100 percent contained BPA-based epoxy, even as the company announced its progress toward a BPA-free goal.[79]

Although many canning companies have done little to actively move away from BPA, they have remained vividly aware of their public image. Campbell may be struggling to go BPA-free, but the company has identified BPA as one of a larger set of issues that concerns consumers. The fundamental problem is that consumers do not trust their food suppliers. As has been the case throughout history, consumers once again fear what lurks beneath the literally opaque walls of the tin can and the metaphorically opaque food system of which canned food is a part. Even beyond the BPA issue, Campbell has made an effort to increase transparency. In July 2015, the company launched its website www. whatsinmyfood.com, with the statement, "We are proud of the food we make. But we know you may have questions about ingredients we use. We've tried to answer some of those here."[80] Six months later, in January 2016, Campbell made the remarkable move of calling for mandatory labeling of genetically modified organisms (GMOs), even ahead of federal standards, and even as its trade organization lobbied heavily *against* GMO labeling. CEO Denise Morrison wrote that this call came despite Campbell's confidence in the "science behind GMOs [and] their safety." She wrote that the reason for this decision was that "GMO has evolved to be a top consumer food issue reaching a critical mass of 92% of consumers in favor of putting it on the label. In addition, we have declared our intention to set the standard for transparency in the food industry."[81] Campbell sought transparency, for marketing purposes, wherever they could find it—if not around BPA, then around GMOs.

In absence of industrial change or federal regulation, many commentators call on consumers to take individual action. Shoppers concerned about BPA are encouraged to soak and cook their own beans instead of buying canned, buy more fresh produce, replace their plastic containers with more expensive glass or stainless steel, and even brew their own beer.[82] Of course, each of these steps requires more attention, time, and money. The groups that are most at risk for BPA exposure are the very same who have the least amount of energy, time, and money to pressure-cook their own kidney beans. Studies have shown that low-income groups have the highest BPA concentrations, likely because low-income neighborhoods are often "food deserts" with little access to fresh foods.[83]

But even for those consumers who are already conscious of environmental health risks and have the means of moving away from canned foods, things aren't so simple. The same folks who shop at farmers' markets and buy organic have moved away from eating food from cans in order to limit their BPA exposure. But some studies suggest that even these consumers are still ingesting endocrine-disrupting chemicals. The University of Washington's Sheela Sathyanarayana carried out a controlled study in which one group of consumers ate only catered meals that shunned plastics and used largely fresh, local, organic ingredients— avoiding canned food. But after five days on this diet, the group surprisingly showed *increased* levels of BPA and of DEHP, another highly toxic chemical that mimics hormone action. Sathyanarayana went back to the catering company and found high DEHP in their dairy products and their spices, even though the milk was bottled in glass at a local farm, and the spices were certified organic. The spices were also imported, which meant that, despite their organic certification, almost nothing is known about how they were processed. As for the locally produced milk, while it's not certain how the endocrine disruptors got into the milk, Sathyanarayana speculated that the soft plastic tubing that was used to funnel warm milk from the cows' udders may have been to blame.[84] This surprising finding highlights consumers' lack of control in the face of the modern food system, dependent as it is on processing technology. As journalist Tom Philpott wrote, in response to this study, "Independent of choices we make as consumers . . . processing is taking place beyond our view that can contaminate our food. . . . When individual consumers can't protect themselves through reasonable means, collective action—i.e., regulation—is the only remedy."[85] Philpott called on the FDA to regulate plastics in food processing, even beyond a focus on BPA or the canning industry.

. . .

In response to the changing landscape of food preferences in the last several decades, Campbell Soup Company launched a wide range of new products and initiatives to win consumer trust: low-sodium varieties with American Heart Association endorsement; the Select Harvest line of soups without MSG and with "all-natural chicken"; investment in neuromarketing to fuel a label redesign; market research in "hipster hubs" to develop a line of ethnic-inspired Campbell's Go! soups in microwavable plastic bags; a call for mandatory GMO labeling; the launch of www.whatsinmyfood.com to promote product transparency. In all of these areas, Campbell has acted ahead of government regulation or consumer boycott in assessing the pulse of consumer preference and searching for a way to satisfy new tastes (even as it has sometimes missed the mark).

But as consumers asked for BPA-free cans, Campbell has been less willing to enact meaningful change. The company first promised in 2012 to phase out the chemical but privately admitted that it was in no rush to do so. Four years later, an analysis of Campbell's cans in grocery stores found that 100 percent of them still contained BPA linings. In March 2016, Campbell renewed its commitment to ridding its packages of the endocrine disruptor and set a time line toward this end. The search for safe alternative linings, however, has been fraught.

BPA has caught the canning industry off guard in a way that few other technical issues have in nearly a century. Since canners and can makers seemingly perfected the can in the early twentieth century, the central health concerns around canned food have been bacterial. The can itself seemed unimpeachable. Stretching back to the botulism-in-olives cases of the 1920s, canners developed techniques to address food safety issues. These methods held strong for most of the twentieth century. But BPA called for something else altogether. The problem couldn't be fixed by cooking the cans at a different temperature or for a different length of time. It couldn't be fixed by ramping up inspection and being vigilant for cleanliness. It was resistant to changes in agriculture or processing. And BPA, as an endocrine disruptor, wasn't easily regulated by the traditional dogma of toxicology that "the dose makes the poison."

In the past several decades, the canning industry has joined forces with the broader processed-food industry, through consolidation and the merging of trade organizations. As the food industry grew stronger and more powerful, it had the clout to push back against government regulation, make use of agricultural subsidies, and co-opt the use of scientific research toward corporate ends. But this strength has also been met with another phase of consumer resistance. Young consumers today have called for a food movement that seeks transparency. More members of this generation push against the food system that was launched by the canning industry over 150 years ago, putting canning companies in a particularly vulnerable position.

Among the many reasons that the slow action on BPA is concerning is that this chemical is only the first in an onslaught of endocrine disruptors that are on the horizon. The EPA, among many other health organizations, is developing screening programs for endocrine disruptors, which are likely to soon reveal a whole host of chemicals that have similar effects.[86] The American government's response to BPA will set the course for how it responds to the other chemicals soon to be uncovered. This will create a model for how regulatory agencies and federal governments protect their citizens in a synthetic age.

For now, the protections that exist for consumers are those they enact themselves. Individuals are encouraged to shop and cook differently, making use of expensive and laborious products and processes to avoid endocrine-disrupting plastics. This is only possible for the most educated and privileged consumers. And even for that class of Americans, unexpected sources of endocrine disruptors emerge in a food system rife with plastic and with so many unknown, unregulated corners of production. Beyond any change that an individual can make, there exists a vast network of companies and laboratories and boardrooms that determine what and how we eat. We consumers can push and push against this system, can buy frozen foods instead of canned, can ferment our own yogurt and buy our milk direct from the farmer, but at the end of the day, we are firmly embedded within something much bigger. To change what we eat, we must change the institutions that feed us.

Conclusion

Over the past several years, as I've spoken with friends, family members, and passersby about this project, I've often gotten the question, "So, should I eat canned food?" After reading the book, you probably can imagine that the answer I offer is never short and sweet. In the contemporary context, considering the story of BPA in can linings, canned food appears fundamentally flawed and embedded within a regulatory system that fails to fix those flaws. BPA, and the fears that it and other endocrine disruptors raise, have led some consumers to abandon canned food altogether or to search for BPA-free versions. But as we have seen, this does not always fix the problem. Individual dietary change is often limited by the larger infrastructure that dictates our daily lives. This means that transforming our food choices at the individual level requires structural, institutional change.

Pointing to "structures" and "institutions," though, can conjure images so vast and vague that it often leaves consumers feeling powerless. Can these huge impersonal entities even be changed? One of the central aims of this book has been to dive down into the trade associations, government agencies, and other bodies that have shaped the canning industry and to see the individual decisions that these important players have made over time. Meeting the leaders of the National Canners Association, the consumer advocates, the agricultural breeders, and the regulators gives a sense of how decisions and motives all along the chain add up to our present reality. It becomes clear that this industry has been built through the efforts of specific businessmen and producers who are involved in constant negotiations to win over consumers. They make decisions in response to their shareholders' economic concerns and their consumers' environmental, health, and social concerns. Over the course of the twentieth century, consumer activism has emerged in key moments to reshape industry priorities as food corporations have struggled to gain or regain consumer trust.

Although the food industry and the federal government are beginning to pay more attention to issues like environment and health, processed foods are more central to the American diet than ever before. Even as companies adopt new products and methods, they typically make only incremental changes within the existing structure. Large food processors could not continue to remain viable at their present scale without the manufactured, packaged, and consolidated system on which they now rely. This system was built for profit and output, with the unavoidable side effects of a lack of transparency, resistance to regulation, and complicated machinations beyond the view of consumers.

Today, apart from the issue of BPA, canned food is not often the primary culprit in discussions of our problematic food system. Instead, other forms of processed food are highlighted: the high-fructose corn syrup in soda, the trans fats and refined flour of commercially produced baked goods, the empty calories of so-called diet foods. But the methods of food engineering, marketing, and politicking that have brought these "edible foodlike substances" to our diets were first pioneered by the canners.[1] Canned food was the first nationally marketed processed, packaged food. Understanding how canners cultivated trust in this new kind of food gives us a sense of the building blocks of our modern food system.

· · ·

In the opening phases of the canning industry, consumers were discouraged by the literal opacity of the tin can and the metaphorical opacity of the food preservation method that incomprehensibly seemed to make seasons stand still. Because consumers could not see inside the solid walls of the can, they had no way of knowing in advance exactly what lay inside and no way of understanding how it had come to be. As canned food moved from serving people on the move—explorers, sailors, and soldiers—to serving people in their homes, the founding canners struggled against this unfamiliarity. They also grappled with concrete problems of production like technological limitations, metals leaching into the food, spoilage and bacterial contamination, and agricultural pests. Canners in the late nineteenth and early twentieth centuries adopted a number of strategies for overcoming these roadblocks and winning over consumers, even without making their packaging more physically transparent. Among the most important tools that these early canners used was a reliance on relationships with external experts—everyone from universities and agricultural experiment stations, to scientists and government regulators, to media outlets and advertisers.

These relationships laid the foundation for a well-integrated and flourishing industry by the middle of the twentieth century. Its collaborations were central to the development of public trust in processed food. Canners' contracts with the Union Army in the Civil War gave the crucial jump-start to consumer exposure and factory growth. During the first years of the twentieth century, canners formed strategic partnerships with pure food advocates, pushing for legislation that would give their products a governmental seal of approval. They followed up by recruiting independent scientists to solve problems of leaching salts of tin and bacterial spoilage, hoping to reassure consumers through the burgeoning authority of laboratory science and medicine. Relationships with scientists only intensified into the 1920s, with canners enlisting agricultural experiment stations to breed canning crops that would better conform to the factory environment. Elsewhere, they funded public health research and oversight, as in the case of California olive canners' responses to the botulism outbreak in 1919–20. The resulting interactions not only transformed the canning industry and its reach into the consumer marketplace but also supported scientific institutions through funding, recognition, and business collaboration. Notably, the canners' partnerships with external experts also reshaped systems of labor—both in the factory and on the farm—as technological and agricultural improvement created new expectations, needs, and contractual obligations. The growth of a processed-food system had effects that reverberated throughout the American economy and society.

Beginning in the 1930s, and accelerating in the postwar years, the forms of expertise that canners drew on to build and maintain consumer trust shifted. Because canned food had become a staple of the modern American diet by midcentury, canners were less concerned about gaining consumer trust through improved methods than about raising rates of consumption of existing products. With its increasing power, the canning industry was less willing to defer to external scientific and governmental expertise and more eager to speak directly to its public. A rising consumer movement in the 1930s also made it easier for the industry to target consumers directly rather than relying on the proxy of external approval. Whereas early canners had seen scientific improvement as a primary pathway to consumer confidence, later canners began to see this confidence as more of a public relations issue and to see science as something that took place behind the scenes. Earlier, science had been deployed as a kind of branding, in which canning companies touted their scientific engagement as a mark of status. But by the 1930s brand names and labels came to stand on their own, representing symbolic desirability beyond scientific improvement.

Although scientific research began to move away from the spotlight, canners continued to make use of experts, even as the kinds of expertise changed with the emergence of new tools. The burgeoning social sciences made possible new forms of marketing research, such as consumer surveys and nationwide focus groups. Just as the elucidation of germ theory in the late nineteenth century made food spoilage understandable in terms of bacteria, so did market research make consumer purchases more understandable in terms of unexpressed desires. Canners thus began to build relationships not only with laboratory and agricultural scientists but also with psychologists, economists, and advertising specialists. They made use of new political experts as they developed private foundations and lobbied for government regulation in their own favor. But while the industry might have touted its earlier collaborations with laboratory scientists, its work on motivational research and political lobbying was kept more in the background, further contributing to a food system that functioned in ways unknowable to the consumer.

A final reason that canners shifted the kinds of expertise they emphasized, from the laboratory toward the social arena, was that some of the earlier tools and solutions had in fact created new problems that required new responses. For example, canners' attempt to overcome the literal opacity of tin had led them to employ ever more colorful and creative labels in the hopes that these could offer a window into the can. But these labels served as an facade that further obscured the actual products and processes that went into the container. Consumers by the 1960s and 1970s began to feel as though they were being asked to judge a book by its cover because of the potential inadequacies of the book's inner contents. Similarly, some of the earlier agricultural work—with breeding, pesticides, and funding of experiment station research—that canners had initiated to improve their products and thereby increase consumer trust now had unintended consequences of environmental contamination. These innovations of the 1920s contributed to the groundwork for the agro-industrial complex that grew to dominate the food system in the postwar era and that began to alienate consumers. The industrialized food system of the second half of the twentieth century obscured the origins of American food, making it more opaque than ever, despite the canners' initial intentions. The industry had to win back newly distrustful consumers, not by undoing the system that had been built, but by reassuring them through clever advertising campaigns and industry-sponsored science that their fears—about nutrition, the environment, or toxicity—were unwarranted.

Canners' attitude toward regulation also underwent a marked change over the course of the twentieth century. They began the century welcoming the Food and Drugs Act of 1906, seeing it as a way of assuring consumers of their products' purity. The industry cooperated with state public health officials in the 1920s and with the McNary-Mapes Amendment to the Food and Drugs Act that was passed in the early 1930s. But canners soon pushed back against external involvement. The increasing stability of their business, the rise of advertising, decreasing competition through consolidation, and the heightened visibility of the consumer made canners seek more direct access to the public, rather than working through government mediation. By the end of the 1970s, most canners saw federal regulation as a significant intrusion and invested in political lobbying to minimize oversight. By the time BPA emerged as a significant issue in the twenty-first century, canners had joined forces with others in the food, plastics, and chemical industries to direct the practice of science and regulation at the federal level.

Since the opening years of the nineteenth century, the humble discovery in Nicolas Appert's makeshift laboratory has grown into a huge industry offering products entrenched in the American diet. Even amid the many changes, there has also been continuity among the canners' central aims and approaches. They have consistently sought to shape their reputations, through media engagement and branding. They have battled the opacity of the tin can and of the canning process, working to win consumer trust—if often with a stereotyped image of who that consumer actually was. And canners have served as intermediaries along the chain from production to consumption throughout the two hundred years of the industry's existence.

· · ·

This history can offer some lessons for the contemporary food system. Transparency has become an ideal for many commentators seeking to address the toll of industrial food production on human health, animal welfare, the environment, workers, and the flavor of food itself. Michael Pollan, along with many others, has called for Americans to have a closer relationship with the farmers who grow their food so that they can monitor production practices beyond a reliance on labels like "organic." There has been a widespread call for food companies to open up their methods to scrutiny and for consumers to get closer to the source of their food. Renewed interest in gardening, home canning, shopping at farmer's markets, signing up for Community Supported Agriculture (CSA) farm shares, and home cooking has emerged.

Transparency in the food system is certainly a worthy ideal, and one that I find personally compelling. I have been right in there with my home garden and my refrigerator stocked with local produce all these years. I have cooked and blogged about food, have taught school kids how to make sun-dried kale and hand-ground pesto, have lobbied for reform in the school lunch program. I've canned my own tomatoes, baked my own bread, and fermented my own kimchi. I have felt the power of individual action in terms of reclaiming control in my little area of influence and feeling not quite so hopeless. I do think that individual choices of consumption matter and that there is value in voting with our forks.[2] At the same time, though, the foregoing story of canners gives me pause.

Over the last century and a half, consumers have had an off-again, on-again relationship with canned food. All these years, canners have sought ways to overcome public mistrust of their opaque containers and methods and to convince consumers to let down their guard. To make canned food more legible in the first part of the twentieth century, canners used science to improve their products and symbolize their progress. And it helped—consumers felt more confident about what was in the can. But as time went on, the canners grew stronger and more buoyed by the rising success of processed food. As a result, they pushed concrete improvements aside in favor of marketing strategies and political influence, making the process opaque once again. In turn, consumer movements reemerged to assert their preferences and push for change. And they have been able to make progress, but it has been incremental at best. Canners laid the foundation for this behemoth of a food industry that is resistant to deep-rooted change, even as consumers call for concrete improvements.

So individual consumer action matters, but it has serious limits on a number of fronts. First, as long as the broader system is under-regulated, trying to avoid one problem can just lead us into another. In the previous chapter's example, even when consumers shifted away from canned foods in favor of an all-local diet featuring farmers' market produce and milk delivered in glass bottles from a nearby dairy, they still exposed themselves to endocrine-disrupting chemicals. Yes, they avoided the BPA of canned foods, but they increased their exposure to chemicals that had leached out of the plastic tubing used to funnel milk from the cows' udders into the glass bottles. The failure was not on the part of the consumers but on the part of the regulatory structure that allowed these chemicals into food contact materials in the first place.

Another reason that expecting change at the personal level is problematic is that it presupposes a certain class-based level of access. Not everyone has the time, tools, or knowledge to cook from scratch with fresh produce.[3] Inexpensive, filling meals offer a way out of hunger for many Americans on limited budgets. Canned foods are already chopped and cooked, are nonperishable, and can be stored anywhere. This means that people who have insecure housing without steady access to refrigeration, or who simply do not have the time or materials to prep fresh ingredients, can still eat relatively healthful meals. Canned fruits, vegetables, and fish would be welcome additions to the food deserts of many low-income areas, which otherwise provide highly processed, sugary, and fatty foods with little nutritional quality.[4] Relatedly, the rejection of canned food—especially among members of a younger generation who hail from middle- and upper-class backgrounds—has implicit class biases. Cans were once a symbol of modernity in the United States but now are seen as poverty food.[5] If we are to expect a fresher, perhaps healthier, way of eating to spread to all people, we must create economic and regulatory systems that make that possible.

Finally, calling for people to change the way they eat in response to political or environmental concerns ignores the more deeply rooted emotional reasons that we all eat the way we do. Our food preferences are shaped in early childhood, based on experiences we have with food when our tastes are just developing.[6] Particular kinds of canned and processed foods have strong emotional resonances for many consumers. To suggest that, because of the BPA in the lining, people should stop eating Campbell's chicken noodle soup is to discount the comfort and pleasure some may associate with that bowl of broth. Food choice is deeply tied to memory and emotion. The risks we may subconsciously calculate when we make food decisions inevitably take these intangibles into account. This does not mean that people cannot change their preferences or create new, less positive associations with those beloved foods, but it does mean that those original associations must be taken into account. Fundamentally, we cannot profitably change the food system without an informed historical and cultural awareness.

· · ·

Canned food today, and the modern food system built on its foundation, is in need of reconsideration and reconfiguration. But its history reminds us how context specific this evaluation is. In a different time and place, canned food was a miracle, changing the way that people thought about food and the kinds of foods they had access to. The monotonous diets of starch, meat, and dried or stored root vegetables that dominated American food until the early twentieth century were enlivened by canned fruits, vegetables, and fish. In a time when nutrition researchers and domestic scientists were just discovering vitamins, the introduction of canned fruits and vegetables was a real boon. The rise of canned foods and premade meals significantly reduced preparation time, easing the housekeeper's burden. But even more than the tangible changes in diet, canned foods brought a fundamental shift in how Americans thought about access to foods in and out of season, from near and far locales. Cans helped to transform consumers' imagination of what was possible.

Understanding the history of canned food and the many ways in which it has been celebrated and condemned gives a sense of how food processors have responded to wavering consumer confidence over time. For those American consumers who seek a more healthy, sustainable, and equitable food supply, this history provides a chance to pause and reflect on the paths not taken and the ones still available in the future.

Acknowledgments

This book is the result of the labor of many who have supported me, in a variety of critical ways, as I produced it. I am grateful I have so many such people in my life.

At the University of Wisconsin, where I began this project, the mentorship of Gregg Mitman, Bill Cronon, and Judy Leavitt taught me how to be a historian, a writer, an engaged scholar, and an advocate. They always gave lovingly of their time and incredible expertise. Russ Shafer-Landau, Jess Gilbert, Jack Kloppenburg, Nan Enstad, Eric Schatzberg, and Judy Houck also counseled me at crucial moments. The Center for Culture, History, and Environment (CHE) offered me a place of intellectual and social belonging like no other. Andrew Stuhl, Andrew Case, Brian Hamilton, Kevin Gibbons, Travis Tennessen, Kristoffer Whitney, Nic Mink, Alex Rudnick, Megan Raby, Rachel Gross, Amrys Williams, Meridith Beck Sayre, Kate Wersan, Andy Davey, Peter Boger, Kellen Backer, Christine Vatovec, and many others offered friendship and true understanding through the sometimes difficult days of getting this project off the ground. Adam Mandelman and Jake Fleming read almost every one of these chapters in their early phases, offering suggestions, good humor, and sustenance.

Many other Madison friends and colleagues also provided needed words of encouragement, expressions of interest, and shared meals and laughter: Rachel Mallinger, Nancy Rydberg, Dave Strasfeld, Dave Ullman (and his parents), Tom Yoshikami, Ariana Stuhl, Micah Hahn, Maggie Grabow, Daniel Crow, Katlyn Arnett, Robbie Gross, Joelle Lomax, Josh and Sadie Barocas, Ben Morris, Erin and Matt and James Barker, Heather Swan, and Sarah Camacho. Other communities, too, helped balance out and enrich my writing days: Nathan Larson and Community GroundWorks; UW GreenHouse; Team Hot Stuff; and Brenda Baker and the Madison Children's Museum.

Conevery Bolton Valencius was my earliest mentor in studying history and has turned out to be among my most enduring, cheering me on from the start. Others who have helped shape this project include Kendra Smith-Howard, Gabriella Petrick, and Jim Feldman. Intellectual connections on the conference circuit—with Helen Curry, Marty Renner, Gregory Rosenthal—have bloomed into friendships. Old friends have provided nourishment of all sorts, as they tend to do. Helen Rubinstein has been my sounding board and kindred spirit. Dana Burshell, Nazneen Bahrassa, Abigail Myers, Kendl Winter, Sarah Farmerie, Josh Segal, Deepani Jinadasa, Emiliano Huet-Vaughn, Katy Rivlin, John Brueck, Michelle Costello, Ryan and Cate Collins, Ben Schatz, Alex Barcham, Mike Roy, and Stacey Vucko have known me in many different manifestations of myself and have lifted me up through all of them.

In my three years at Oklahoma State University I have been fortunate to find a great department and very supportive colleagues, with special thanks to Laura Belmonte, Doug Miller, Richard Boles, Lesley Rimmel, Brian Frehner, and Elizabeth Williams. Beyond the office, Ari Eisenberg and Charles Hughes first made this place feel like home, and many others, especially our Saturday morning brunch crew, have helped to perpetuate that feeling.

Kate Marshall at the University of California Press had confidence in this book from the very beginning, and working with her and Bradley Depew to see it from proposal to final manuscript has been a sincere pleasure. The very thoughtful reader reports and additional feedback I received from Tracey Deustch, Andrew Haley, and three anonymous readers have deeply improved this work, and I am grateful to them.

I am indebted to the following sources for helping to fund this work: the National Science Foundation Graduate Research Fellowship; the UW University Fellowship; the Mellon-Wisconsin Summer Fellowship; and the Public Humanities Fellowship funded by the Andrew W. Mellon Foundation. Many archivists and librarians have also helped me to find the material so crucial to any historian's practice, among them Jane Linzmeyer, Drew Bourn, Jeff Barach, David Oberhelman, Kevin Dyke, and Suzanne Reinman. Thanks to Audrey Rubio of the Grocery Manufacturers Association and Richard Straub of the University of Wisconsin College of Agricultural and Life Sciences for helping to secure image permissions.

As I wrote in my dedication, my father has inspired me from the very beginning. He was a consummate intellectual, deeply thoughtful, eccentric, and iconoclastic, and we admired each other. The path I have trodden is nothing if not the one he laid down for me, and I miss him terribly. My mama, too, has provided her unyielding support, love, and devotion, teaching and learning with me all along the way. Aaron, Amy, Jeremy, Max, and Abby have offered many insightful questions, study breaks, play sessions, and adorable FaceTime conversations. Nancy and Jim Horn have taken me in as their own, and I only wish Nancy were still here to see the fruits of my work.

I couldn't be more grateful that Justin Horn has been my partner for nearly all of my adult life. We have been through so much together that I have a hard time distinguishing my accomplishments from his own; they have been shared in the most meaningful sense. Through his incredible sensitivity, communication, and deep understanding of who I am, he has given me strength. Most importantly, he has given me Nancy and Mira, our daughters, whose essential goodness, curiosity, and adoration make me feel whole. I hope someday they like this book as much as they love their bedtime stories.

Notes

INTRODUCTION

1. David Edgerton offers this argument in *The Shock of the Old: Technology and Global History since 1900* (Oxford: Oxford University Press, 2007).

2. Food history is itself a relatively new field within the discipline of history, though it has produced a range of scholarship in the last decades, following pioneers like Warren Belasco and Harvey Levenstein. Although canning has been largely understudied, several unpublished dissertations have taken up the topic: Edward F. Keuchel, "The Development of the Canning Industry in New York State to 1960" (PhD diss., Cornell University, 1970); Mark W. Wilde, "Industrialization of Food Processing in the United States, 1860–1960" (PhD diss., University of Delaware, 1988); Gabriella Petrick, "The Arbiters of Taste: Producers, Consumers, and the Industrialization of Taste in America, 1900–1960" (PhD diss., University of Delaware, 2006); Gregg Pearson, "The Democratization of Food: Tin Cans and the Growth of the American Food Processing Industry, 1810–1940" (PhD diss., Lehigh University, 2016). Petrick's dissertation and her other published pieces, in particular, offer useful insights on some of the broad questions of industrial food and consumption.

3. Gabriella M. Petrick, "Industrial Food," in *The Oxford Handbook of Food History*, ed. Jeffrey M. Pilcher (New York: Oxford University Press, 2012), 258–78.

4. Arthur I. Judge, ed., *A History of the Canning Industry* (Baltimore: Canning Trade, 1914): 6; John A. Lee, *How to Buy and Sell Canned Foods* (Baltimore: Canning Trade, 1914), 8.

5. Ann Vileisis, *Kitchen Literacy: How We Lost Knowledge of Where Food Comes From and Why We Need to Get It Back* (Washington, DC: Island Press/Shearwater Books, 2008), 77–78.

6. This book links canners' efforts to meet changing consumer tastes with the increasing industrialization of American food. It builds on the work of other scholars, across a variety of disciplines, who have engaged with ideas around food and changing consumer preferences. Some of these include Tracey Deutsch, *Building a Housewife's Paradise: Gender, Politics, and American Grocery Stores in the Twentieth Century* (Chapel Hill: University of North Carolina Press, 2010); Susanne Freidberg, *Fresh: A Perishable History* (Cambridge, MA: Harvard University Press, 2009); William Cronon, *Nature's Metropolis: Chicago and the Great West* (New York: W. W. Norton, 1991); Laura Shapiro, *Something from the Oven: Reinventing Dinner in 1950s America* (New York: Viking Press, 2004); Amy Bentley, *Inventing Baby Food: Taste, Health, and the Industrialization of the American Diet* (Berkeley: University of California Press, 2014); Doug Sackman, *Orange Empire: California and the Fruits of Eden* (Berkeley: University of California Press, 2005); Gary S. Cross and Robert N. Proctor, *Packaged Pleasures: How Technology and Marketing Revolutionized Desire* (Chicago: University of Chicago Press, 2014); Bartow J. Elmore, *Citizen Coke: The Making of Coca-Cola Capitalism* (New York: W. W. Norton, 2014); Carolyn de la Peña, *Empty Pleasures: The Story of Artificial Sweeteners from Saccharin to Splenda* (Chapel Hill: University of North Carolina Press, 2010); Gabriella M. Petrick, "'Purity as Life': H. J. Heinz, Religious Sentiment, and the Beginning of the Industrial Diet," *History and Technology* 271, no. 1 (2011): 37–64; Roger Horowitz, *Putting Meat on the American Table: Taste, Technology, Transformation* (Baltimore: Johns Hopkins University Press, 2006); Shane Hamilton, *Trucking Country: The Road to America's Wal-Mart Economy* (Princeton, NJ: Princeton University Press, 2008).

7. Vileisis, *Kitchen Literacy*. Suzanne Freidberg makes clear that even "fresh" food, as it came to rely on technologies like refrigeration to extend the period of edibility, confounded consumers. Advertisers had to convince consumers to accept "technology's power over the perishable" (*Fresh*, 15). But the can's opaque container deepened this sense of alienation, relative to fresh foods.

8. This metaphorical opacity is not exclusively tied to the literally opaque tin can; it also extends to the industrial production of food in glass jars. Not all home-canned food is packed in glass, and not all commercially canned food is packed in tin. For one key example of commercially canned food in glass jars, see Bentley, *Inventing Baby Food*.

9. Wenonah Hauter, *Foodopoly: The Battle over the Future of Food and Farming in America* (New York: New Press, 2012).

10. Courtney I. P. Thomas also explores trust in the American food system in *In Food We Trust: The Politics of Purity in American Food Regulation* (Lincoln: University of Nebraska Press, 2014).

11. Michael Pollan, *The Omnivore's Dilemma: A Natural History of Four Meals* (New York: Penguin Press, 2006), 10–11; "McDonald's Transparency Campaign Continues with Questions You Never Thought the Chain Would Answer," *Huffington Post*, August 2, 2012, www.huffingtonpost.com/2012/08/02/mcdonalds-transparency-campaign_n_1733676.html; Dan Charles, "Can Big Food Win Friends by Revealing Its Secrets?," *The Salt*, December 25, 2015, NPR,

www.npr.org/sections/thesalt/2015/12/25/460304899/can-big-food-win-friends-by-revealing-its-secrets.

12. Eve Turow, author of *A Taste of Generation Yum: How the Millennial Generation's Love for Organic Fare, Celebrity Chefs and Microbrews Will Make or Break the Future of Food,* explores this idea in relation to food. She "cites the economic recession alongside the inability to control political wars, climate change, and technological privacy violations as historic events that have caused several millennial Americans to see their food as a way to exert some dominance and structure of their own lives." Quoted in Matthew Sedacca, "How 'Foodie' Culture Survived the Recession," *Eater,* May 19, 2016, www .eater.com/2016/5/19/11705966/foodie-millennials-recession.

13. For more on other middle parties, see Warren Belasco and Roger Horowitz, eds., *Food Chains: From Farmyard to Shopping Cart* (Philadelphia: University of Pennsylvania Press, 2008).

14. Originally Grocery Manufacturers of America. See Michele Simon, *Appetite for Profit: How the Food Industry Undermines Our Health and How to Fight Back* (New York: Nation Books, 2006).

15. GMA, "History: A Century of Leadership," n.d., accessed August 13, 2017, www.gmaonline.org/about/history/; Joseph Mercola, "Grocery Manufacturer's Association Overtakes Monsanto as 'Most Evil Corporation on the Planet,'" Mercola, January 28, 2014, http://articles.mercola.com/sites/articles /archive/2014/01/28/gma-evil-corporation.aspx. In 1978, the NCA changed its name to the National Food Processors Association, then to the Food Products Association (FPA). In 2007, the FPA joined the existing GMA, creating the largest food trade group in the world. For one example of the influence the GMA has had on contemporary debates, see its role in the current discussions over labeling genetically modified organisms in food: GMA, "GMA: Congressional Biotech Report Should Aid Effort to Dispel Fear, Misinformation," April 13, 2000, posted at Polluter Watch, www.documentcloud.org/documents/1350514-grocerymanufaco1564.html.

16. The history of capitalism as a subdiscipline has gotten increased attention in recent years, as scholars have incorporated its insights into ever-broader fields. For a review of some of this recent work, see Seth Rockman, "What Makes the History of Capitalism Newsworthy?" *Journal of the Early Republic* 34, no. 3 (Fall 2014): 439–66; Sven Beckert et al., "Interchange: The History of Capitalism," *Journal of American History* 101, no. 2 (2014): 503–36.

17. Information from NCA, *The Canning Industry: A Series of Articles Furnishing Information on the History, Organization, Methods and Products of the Industry, with Selected List of References* (Washington, DC: NCA, 1939), and from the 1952, 1963, and 1971 editions of the NCA's *The Canning Industry: Its History, Importance, Organization, Methods, and the Public Service Values of Its Products* (Washington, DC: NCA) and from US Department of Commerce, *Census of Manufactures: Industry Statistics, Preserved Fruits and Vegetables* (Washington, DC: Bureau of the Census, 1914).

18. For more on Progressive reformers, see, for example, Michael McGerr, *A Fierce Discontent: The Rise and Fall of the Progressive Movement in America,*

1870–1920 (New York: Oxford University Press, 2005). Thanks to Andrew Case for helping me develop this connection.

1. CONDENSED MILK

1. Letter from David Coon, July 1864, in Civil War Letters, 1864, Wisconsin Historical Society, Madison.

2. Thanks to the journal *Repast* for permission to reprint the section on canned food in the Civil War: Anna Zeide, "Building Taste and Trust: The Civil War's Influence on the U.S. Canning Industry," *Repast: Quarterly Publication of the Culinary Historians of Ann Arbor* 29, no. 1, Civil War Sesquicentennial Series, pt. 4 (Winter 2013): 4–7.

3. Ruth Schwartz Cowan, "The Consumption Junction: A Proposal for Research Strategies in the Sociology of Technology," in *The Social Construction of Technological Systems: New Directions in the Sociology and History of Technology*, ed. Wiebe E. Bijker, Thomas Parke Hughes, and T. J. Pinch (Cambridge, MA: MIT Press, 1987).

4. The classic work on the effects of food on industrial economies is Sidney W. Mintz, *Sweetness and Power: The Place of Sugar in Modern History* (New York: Penguin Books, 1986).

5. In looking at these interdependent aspects of the canning industry, my work adds to growing literatures within the history of technology that focus on consumption, everyday use, and consumer agency within technological and industrial development. See, for example, Ronald R. Kline, *Consumers in the Country: Technology and Social Change in Rural America* (Baltimore: Johns Hopkins University Press, 2000); Susan Strasser, "Making Consumption Conspicuous: Transgressive Topics Go Mainstream," *Technology and Culture* 43, no. 4 (October 2002): 755–70.

6. Ruth Schwartz Cowan, *A Social History of American Technology* (New York: Oxford University Press, 1997), 151.

7. Other historians have explored environmental history and history of technology in tandem—at the "envirotech" intersection: for example, Jeffrey K. Stine and Joel A. Tarr, "At the Intersection of Histories: Technology and the Environment," *Technology and Culture* 39, no. 4 (1998): 601–40; Martin Reuss and Stephen H. Cutcliffe, eds., *The Illusory Boundary: Environment and Technology in History* (Charlottesville: University of Virginia Press, 2010).

8. Nicolas Appert, *The Art of Preserving All Kinds of Animal and Vegetable Substances for Several Years: A Work Published by Order of the French Minister of the Interior, on the Report of the Board of Arts and Manufactures*, 2nd ed. (London: Black, Perry and Kingsbury, 1812).

9. Allen Long, "Chef Founds Canning Industry," *Science News-Letter* 62, no. 16 (October 18, 1952): 250–51; National Canners Association (hereafter NCA), *The Canning Industry: Its History, Importance, Organization, Methods, and the Public Service Values of Its Products*, 6th ed. (Washington, DC: NCA, 1971), 5, accessed from the NCA Archives at the Grocery Manufacturers Association headquarters in Washington, DC (hereafter GMA Library); J. C.

Graham, "The French Connection in the Early History of Canning," *Journal of the Royal Society of Medicine* 74 (May 1981): 374–81.

10. Edward S. Judge, "American Canning Interests," in *1795–1895: One Hundred Years of American Commerce*, ed. Chauncey M. Depew (New York: D. O. Haynes, 1895), 396; Tom Geoghegan, "The Story of How the Tin Can Nearly Wasn't," *BBC News Magazine*, April 21, 2013, www.bbc.co.uk/news /magazine-21689069.

11. Peter Durand coined the term *can*, Bryan Donkin and John Hall set up the first cannery to use metal cans, and William Underwood brought the process to the United States. Long, "Chef Founds Canning Industry," 250.

12. Hugh S. Orem, "Baltimore, Master of the Art of Canning," in Arthur I. Judge, preface to *History* (Baltimore: Canning Trade, 1914), 8; Edward F. Keuchel, "The Development of the Canning Industry in New York State to 1960" (PhD diss., Cornell University, 1970), 20.

13. Frederick Gamble, *Observations on the Preservation of Animal and Vegetable Substances; with an Account of Appert's Process, and the Subsequent Improvements of That Invention; and Also a Description of the Various Modes Adopted for the Extraction of the Gelatine from Bones. Submitted for the Consideration of the Members of the Royal Dublin Society* (Dublin: Milliken and Son; London: Longman, 1839), vii–viii.

14. Arthur I. Judge, preface to *History*, 5.

15. Janet Macdonald, *Feeding Nelson's Navy: The True Story of Food at Sea in the Georgian Era* (London: Frontline Books, 2014).

16. James Lind, *Treatise on Scurvy: A Bicentenary Volume Containing a Reprint of the First Edition of "A Treatise of the Scurvy"* (Edinburgh: Edinburgh University Press, 1953).

17. Scott Cookman, *Ice Blink: The Tragic Fate of Sir John Franklin's Lost Polar Expedition* (New York: Wiley, 2001); Richard Bayliss, "Sir John Franklin's Last Arctic Expedition: A Medical Disaster," *Journal of the Royal Society of Medicine* 95, no. 3 (March 2002): 151–53.

18. Bayliss, "Sir John Franklin's Last Arctic Expedition." Others point to botulism or scurvy as potential causes of death. B. Zane Horowitz, "Polar Poisons: Did Botulism Doom the Franklin Expedition?," *Journal of Toxicology— Clinical Toxicology* 41, no. 6 (2003): 841–47; S. Mays, G. J. R. Maat, and H. H. de Boer, "Scurvy as a Factor in the Loss of the 1845 Franklin Expedition to the Arctic: A Reconsideration," *International Journal of Osteoarchaeology* 25, no. 3 (May 1, 2015): 334–44.

19. Bayliss, "Sir John Franklin's Last Arctic Expedition."

20. "Poisonous Food," *New York Times*, March 14, 1886.

21. Jacqueline B. Williams, *Wagon Wheel Kitchens: Food on the Oregon Trail* (Lawrence: University Press of Kansas, 1993).

22. Peter Browning, *To the Golden Shore: America Goes to California, 1849* (Lafayette, CA: Great West Books, 1995), 73.

23. Jane Busch, "An Introduction to the Tin Can," *Historical Archaeology* 15, no. 1 (January 1, 1981): 95–104.

24. Walter Prescott Webb, *The Great Plains* (Boston: Ginn, 1931), 320.

25. Orem, "Baltimore," 10.

26. William C. Davis suggests that the Civil War had little impact on soldiers' food habits and preferences once they returned home. Though this conclusion may apply to the rat meat and hardtack he describes, it does not extend to the canned food soldiers encountered. William C. Davis, *A Taste for War: The Culinary History of the Blue and the Gray* (Lincoln: University of Nebraska Press, 2011), 125–27. Other historians have written about the impact of wars on the American diet, most notably in the context of World War II. See E. M. Collingham, *The Taste of War: World War Two and the Battle for Food* (London: Allen Lane, 2011); Kellen Backer, "World War II and the Triumph of Industrialized Food" (PhD diss., University of Wisconsin-Madison, 2012).

27. Ray B. Browne and Lawrence A. Kreiser, eds., *The Civil War and Reconstruction* (Westport, CT: Greenwood Press, 2003), 82; Tom Dicke, "Red Gold of the Ozarks: The Rise and Decline of Tomato Canning, 1885–1955," *Agricultural History* 79, no. 1 (Winter 2005): 1–26; Mark McWilliams, *Food and the Novel in Nineteenth-Century America* (Lanham, MD: Rowman and Littlefield, 2012), 129.

28. For an early autobiographical account of Gail Borden, see Clarence Wharton, *Gail Borden, Pioneer* (San Antonio, TX: Naylor, 1941).

29. "Startling Exposure of the Milk Trade of New York and Brooklyn," *Frank Leslie's Illustrated Newspaper*, May 8, 1858.

30. Andrew F. Smith, *Eating History: 30 Turning Points in the Making of American Cuisine* (New York: Columbia University Press, 2009), 66–73. For more about the history of milk and concerns about purity, see E. Melanie DuPuis, *Nature's Perfect Food: How Milk Became America's Drink* (New York: New York University Press, 2002); Daniel R. Block, "Public Health, Cooperatives, Local Regulation, and the Development of Modern Milk Policy: The Chicago Milkshed, 1900–1940," *Journal of Historical Geography* 35, no. 1 (2009): 128–53; Kendra Smith-Howard, *Pure and Modern Milk: An Environmental History since 1900* (Oxford: Oxford University Press, 2013).

31. Joe Bertram Frantz, *Gail Borden, Dairyman to a Nation* (Norman: University of Oklahoma Press, 1951), 254.

32. Southeast Museum (Brewster, NY), "Borden's Milk: New York Milk Condensary," 1997–99, www.southeastmuseum.org/SE_Tour99/SE_Tour/html/borden_s_milk.htm.

33. Earl Chapin May, *The Canning Clan: A Pageant of Pioneering Americans* (New York: Macmillan, 1938), 177; Wharton, *Gail Borden,* 197.

34. To see a description of the standard rations and more details on the commissary department, see An Officer, "The Quartermaster's Department, 1861–1864," in *Annals of the Army of the Cumberland* (Philadelphia, 1863), www.qmfound.com/quartermaster_1861-63.htm.

35. Dorothy Denneen Volo, *Daily Life in Civil War America,* 2nd ed. (Santa Barbara, CA: Greenwood Press, 2009), 143.

36. "The Siege of Charleston: The Siege Progresses Well," *New York Times,* August 5, 1863. For more on sutlers, see, for example, Scott Reynolds Nelson and Carol Sheriff, *A People at War: Civilians and Soldiers in America's Civil War* (New York: Oxford University Press, 2007), 217–18.

37. "Labors of the Sanitary Commission," *New York Times,* July 30, 1863; Judith Ann Giesberg, *Civil War Sisterhood: The U.S. Sanitary Commission*

and Women's Politics in Transition (Boston: Northeastern University Press, 2000).

38. Sanitary [Commission], "Northwestern Fair: Eighty Thousand Dollars Raised—What Has Been Done with It," *Chicago Tribune,* January 12, 1864.

39. Andrew F. Smith, *Starving the South: How the North Won the Civil War* (New York: St. Martin's Press, 2011), 82.

40. Orem, "Baltimore," 10; May, *Canning Clan,* 26.

41. Ezra J. Warner, "Can Opener," US Patent 19,063, January 5, 1858; William W. Lyman, "Improvement in Can Openers," US Patent 105,346, July 12, 1870.

42. Mary E. Creswell and Ola Powell, *Home Canning of Fruits and Vegetables: As Taught to Canning Club Members in the Southern States,* Farmers' Bulletin / US Department of Agriculture 853 (Washington, DC: Government Printing Office, 1917); Sue Shepard, *Pickled, Potted, and Canned: How the Art and Science of Food Preserving Changed the World* (New York: Simon and Schuster, 2006); Volo, *Daily Life,* 273; John Landis Mason, Canning Jar Exterior Thread and Metal Cap, US Patent 22,186, November 30, 1858. Another significant date in the development of home-canning technologies is Frank C. and Edmund B. Ball's founding of the Ball Corporation in 1880. Frederic Alexander Birmingham, *Ball Corporation, the First Century* (Indianapolis, IN: Curtis, 1980).

43. Davis, *Taste for War.*

44. Waverly Root and Richard De Rochemont, *Eating in America* (New York: Morrow, 1976), 187.

45. US Census Office, *Ninth Census of the United States, 1870, Industry and Wealth* (Washington, DC: Census Office, 1872); Keuchel, "Development," 42; Mark W. Wilde, "Industrialization of Food Processing in the United States, 1860–1960" (PhD diss., University of Delaware, 1988), 31. Women have long been an important source of labor for the seasonal canning industry. See Vicki L. Ruiz, *Cannery Women, Cannery Lives: Mexican Women, Unionization, and the California Food Processing Industry, 1930–1950* (Albuquerque: University of New Mexico Press, 1987).

46. See Philip Scranton, *Endless Novelty: Specialty Production and American Industrialization, 1865–1925* (Princeton, NJ: Princeton University Press, 1997).

47. A. Judge, preface to *History.*

48. Orem, "Baltimore," 8.

49. NCA, *Canning Industry,* 10–11.

50. F. W. Schultz, "A Retrospect," in A. Judge, *History,* 6.

51. The canning industry grew alongside and ahead of other industries that relied on mechanization, many which notably focused on food, such as flour production (Oliver Evans's automatic flour mill, introduced around 1790) and meatpacking (the "disassembly line," which began around 1867). Smith, *Eating History;* Lawrence Goldstone, *Drive! Henry Ford, George Selden, and the Race to Invent the Auto Age* (New York: Ballantine Books, 2016), 322; David Hounshell, *From the American System to Mass Production, 1800–1932: The Development of Manufacturing Technology in the United States* (Baltimore: Johns Hopkins University Press, 1984).

52. For example, the calcium chloride caused external corrosion on the cans, along with dangerously high internal pressures, which sometimes led to explosions. S. L. Prescott and W. L. Underwood, "Microorganisms and Sterilizing Processes in the Canning Industry," *Technology Quarterly* 10 (March 1897): 183–99.

53. Orem, "Baltimore," 10.

54. May, *Canning Clan,* 11–12. This early canning industry was heavily reliant on the tinplate industry, which produced thin sheets of steel or iron coated with tin. Before the McKinley Tariff of 1890, nearly all tinplate was produced abroad. The tariff, however, encouraged domestic production, which expanded rapidly in the years after 1890. See Douglas A. Irwin, "Did Late-Nineteenth-Century U.S. Tariffs Promote Infant Industries? Evidence from the Tinplate Industry," *Journal of Economic History* 60, no. 2 (June 1, 2000): 335–60.

55. W. H. H. Stevenson, "Cans and Can-Making Machinery," in A. Judge, *History,* 8–11.

56. NCA, *The ABC's of Canned Foods* (Washington, DC: NCA, 1961), 31.

57. For more on this American shift toward a disposable society, see Susan Strasser, *Waste and Want: A Social History of Trash* (New York: Metropolitan Books, 1999).

58. Martin Brown, Jens Christiansen, and Peter Philips, "The Decline of Child Labor in the U.S. Fruit and Vegetable Canning Industry: Law or Economics?," *Business History Review* 66, no. 4 (December 1, 1992): 723–70; Greg Hall, "The Fruits of Her Labor: Women, Children, and Progressive Era Reformers in the Pacific Northwest Canning Industry," *Oregon Historical Quarterly* 109, no. 2 (July 1, 2008): 226–51.

59. Martin Brown and Peter Philips, "The Decline of the Piece-Rate System in California Canning: Technological Innovation, Labor Management, and Union Pressure, 1890–1947," *Business History Review* 60, no. 4 (December 1, 1986): 743.

60. Martin Brown and Peter Philips, "Craft Labor and Mechanization in Nineteenth-Century American Canning," *Journal of Economic History* 46, no. 3 (1986): 743–56. This mechanization within the canning industry was taking place against a backdrop of larger industrial conflict and frequent strikes by workers who were agitating for better treatment. See, for example, Philip Sheldon Foner, *The Great Labor Uprising of 1877* (New York: Pathfinder Press, 1977). For a specific story of labor relationships in a cannery in a later era, see Robert Bussel, "'Business without a Boss': The Columbia Conserve Company and Workers' Control, 1917–1943," *Business History Review* 71, no. 3 (Autumn 1997): 417–43.

61. For more on the Cox Capper, see John D. Cox, "The Evolution of Tomato Canning Machinery," in A. Judge, *History,* 83; Arthur I. Judge, "The Past, Present and Future of the Canned Food Industry," in A. Judge, *History,* 55.

62. *Mukwonago Chief,* November 1898, cited in Frederick Arthur Stare, *The Story of Wisconsin's Great Canning Industry* (Baltimore: Canning Trade, 1949), 34.

63. E. Judge, "American Canning Interests," 400.

64. In 1908, the Sanitary Can Company was bought by the American Can Company, the country's largest can manufacturer, which had formed in 1901

when sixty smaller firms joined together. In 1913, the federal government sued the American Can Company, as part of the trust-busting measures of the Progressive Era. The suit charged that the so-called Tin Can Trust, which was then worth $88 million, was guilty of restraining trade through a monopoly. "Government Sues American Can Co.," *New York Times,* November 30, 1913. By 1922 the old hole-and-cap was practically obsolete. The story of the American Can Company also deserves more attention.

65. Max Ams Machine Company, *The Seal of Safety: Year Book of the Max Ams Machine Co.* (Mount Vernon, NY: Max Ams Machine Company, 1914), 17.

66. Stewart M. Brooks, *Ptomaine: The Story of Food Poisoning* (South Brunswick, NJ: A. S. Barnes, 1974).

67. French scientist Louis Pasteur and German scientist Robert Koch were central to the elucidation of germ theory. René J. Dubos, *Pasteur and Modern Science,* Science Study Series S15 (Garden City, NY: Anchor Books, 1960); Christoph Gradmann, *Laboratory Disease: Robert Koch's Medical Bacteriology* (Baltimore: Johns Hopkins University Press, 2009).

68. NCA, *Appert Was the Precursor of Pasteur* (Washington, DC: NCA, 1937), 3, GMA Library.

69. H. L. Russell, "Gaseous Fermentation in the Canning Industry," *Annual Reports of the Wisconsin Agricultural Experiment Station* 12 (1895): 227–31.

70. For more on the relationship between Prescott and Underwood and their impact on the canning industry, see Gabriella Petrick, "The Arbiters of Taste: Producers, Consumers, and the Industrialization of Taste in America, 1900–1960" (PhD diss., University of Delaware, 2006).

71. May, *Canning Clan,* 100.

72. Katherine Leonard Turner, *How the Other Half Ate: A History of Working-Class Meals at the Turn of the Century* (Berkeley: University of California Press, 2014), 51–53.

73. As cited in May, *Canning Clan,* 325.

74. Max Ams Machine Company, *Seal of Safety,* 7–8.

75. See David Edgerton, *The Shock of the Old: Technology and Global History since 1900* (Oxford: Oxford University Press, 2007), for a similar argument.

76. As late as 1918, the Federal Trade Commission described the canning industry as being composed of many small rural canneries, because of low barriers to entry, as cited in Wilde, "Industrialization of Food Processing," 40.

77. "Food Preservers Working for National Legislation," *New York Times,* November 1, 1903.

78. Thomas A. Bailey, "Congressional Opposition to Pure Food Legislation, 1879–1906," *American Journal of Sociology* 36 (July 1930): 52.

79. May, *Canning Clan,* 324.

80. "Sandpaper" quote from Iowa canner William Ballinger is cited in ibid., 334; Wiley's praise is cited in ibid., 326.

81. James Harvey Young, *Pure Food: Securing the Federal Food and Drugs Act of 1906* (Princeton, NJ: Princeton University Press, 1989), 175–76.

82. Benjamin R. Cohen, "Analysis as Border Patrol: Chemists along the Boundary between Pure Food and Real Adulteration," *Endeavour* 35, no. 2–3

(June 2011): 66–73; Susanne Freidberg, *Fresh: A Perishable History* (Cambridge, MA: Harvard University Press, 2009); Aaron Bobrow-Strain, *White Bread: A Social History of the Store-Bought Loaf* (Boston: Beacon Press, 2012); Nancy F. Koehn, "Henry Heinz and Brand Creation in the Late Nineteenth Century: Making Markets for Processed Food," *Business History Review* 73, no. 3 (1999): 349–93; Gabriella Petrick, "'Purity as Life.'": H.J. Heinz, Religious Sentiment, and the Beginning of the Industrial Diet," *History and Technology* 271, no. 1 (2011): 37–64.

83. Young, *Pure Food;* Lorine Swainston Goodwin, *The Pure Food, Drink, and Drug Crusaders, 1879–1914* (Jefferson, NC: McFarland, 1999); Clayton A. Coppin and Jack C. High, *The Politics of Purity: Harvey Washington Wiley and the Origins of Federal Food Policy* (Ann Arbor: University of Michigan Press, 1999). Federal regulation was the focus because a patchwork of state and municipal food regulations of food already existed, however inadequate they may have been.

84. Mark Sullivan, *Our Times: The United States, 1900–1925*, vol. 2 (New York: C. Scribner's Sons, 1926), 236.

85. Upton Sinclair, *The Jungle* (New York: Doubleday, 1906). The American public had been sensitized to sensational outcries of this kind with the embalmed beef scandal of the Spanish-American War several years earlier. During the war, preserved beef from Chicago packing plants caused the deaths of many American soldiers from food poisoning. "The Army Meat Scandal," *New York Times,* February 21, 1899. Sinclair focused particularly on occupational health issues among meatpacking workers. Cannery laborers, too, suffered from occupational health problems, related to hearing loss, repetitive motion, and other injuries.

86. See Young, *Pure Food.*

87. For a valuable analysis of working-class diets around 1900, see Turner, *How the Other Half Ate.*

88. Keuchel, "Development," 219.

89. May, *Canning Clan,* 157.

90. For specific examples of how the law affected New York State canners, see Keuchel, "Development," 248–50.

91. Alfred D. Chandler, *The Visible Hand: The Managerial Revolution in American Business* (Cambridge, MA: Belknap Press, 1977). For one challenge to the Chandlerian model, see Naomi R. Lamoreaux, Daniel M.G. Raff, and Peter Temin, "Beyond Markets and Hierarchies: Toward a New Synthesis of American Business History," *American Historical Review* 108, no. 2 (April 1, 2003): 404–33. For an overview of the literature on industrialization and food, see Gabriella Petrick, "Industrial Food," in *The Oxford Handbook of Food History,* ed. Jeffrey M. Pilcher (New York: Oxford University Press, 2012), 258–78.

92. The Baltimore Canned Goods Exchange organized in 1883, the Western Canned Goods Packer's Association in 1885, and the Atlantic States Canned Goods Packers' Association in 1894. New York, New Jersey, and Virginia, among other states, had created state associations during the 1880s and 1890s. Arthur I. Judge, "A History of the First National Association, the National Association of Canned Food Packers," in A. Judge, *History,* 59–66.

93. May, *Canning Clan,* 324–25.

94. Arthur I. Judge, "The Development of the Present National Organization, the National Canners' Association," in A. Judge, *History,* 75.

95. NCA, *Canning Industry,* 42.

96. For a description of the emergence of ethnic entrepreneurs in the packaged-food industry, see Donna R. Gabaccia, *We Are What We Eat: Ethnic Food and the Making of Americans* (Boston: Harvard University Press, 2000).

97. Edward Wiley Duckwall had opened the first canners' research laboratory in Aspinwall, Pennsylvania, in 1902, where he would address problems that canners wrote to him about. Max Ams Machine Company, *Seal of Safety,* 14; and Robert C. Alberts, *The Good Provider: H.J. Heinz and His 57 Varieties* (Boston: Houghton Mifflin, 1973), 168; Columbus Food Corporation Records, 1901–46, Wisconsin Historical Society, University of Wisconsin-Madison, Microfilm Reel 1. For an example of Duckwall's work, see Petrick's analysis of his correspondence with the Edgett-Burnham canner in "Arbiters of Taste," chap. 1.

98. A. Judge, "Development," 74; May, *Canning Clan,* 160.

99. For more, see, for example, Deborah Kay Fitzgerald, *The Business of Breeding: Hybrid Corn in Illinois, 1890–1940* (Ithaca, NY: Cornell University Press, 1990).

100. General Electric is credited with establishing the first industrial research laboratory in 1901. Leonard S. Reich, *The Making of American Industrial Research: Science and Business at GE and Bell, 1876–1926* (New York: Cambridge University Press, 1985).

101. A. Judge, "Development."

102. Walter J. Sears to Mr. Jan Westervelt, September 5, 1910, NCA Historical Records, in "Salts of Tin," GMA Library.

103. Ibid.

104. All the foregoing dialogue is reprinted in "Some Important Work Well Done," *Canning Trade,* January 1911, in "Salts of Tin," GMA Library.

105. Frank E. Gorrell to Mr. Theo Whitmarah, September 14, 1910, in "Salts of Tin," GMA Library.

106. Frank E. Gorrell, "Minutes of Meeting of the Executive Committee of the National Canners Association," held in Washington, DC, September 20, 1910, in "Salts of Tin," GMA Library.

107. "Chairman's Report of the Work of the Research Committee of the National Canners Association," 1913, in "Salts of Tin," GMA Library; Harvey W. Wiley, "Don't Be Afraid of Canned Goods," *Good Housekeeping,* April 1913, 539. See also "The Dirt We Eat," *Los Angeles Times,* February 20, 1913, editorial.

108. Memo on Tin Salts to Mr. Gorrell from W.D. Bigelow, October 21, 1921, in "Salts of Tin," GMA Library.

109. Ibid.

110. For a description of the canners' attempts to find noncommercial scientists, see Memorandum to Mr. Gorrell from W.D. Bigelow, April 19, 1924, in "Salts of Tin," GMA Library. For a description and list of the scientific studies, see Memorandum to Mr. Gorrell from W.D. Bigelow, October 13, 1925, and

E. W. Schwartze and W. F. Clarke, "Some Observations upon the Pharmacology of Tin," March 22, 1927, both in "Salts of Tin," GMA Library.

111. NCA Information Letter No. 329, October 26, 1929, Washington, DC, in "Salts of Tin," GMA Library.

112. A. Judge, "Development," 74–75. John Tyndall (1820–93) was an Irish physicist who worked on properties of heat. Joseph Lister (1827–1912) was an English surgeon who invented antiseptic surgical techniques.

113. NCA Information Division, "Fifty Years of Winning Public Confidence through NCA Research," press release, May 21, 1963, 2, GMA Library.

114. Orem, "Baltimore," 9.

115. Roland B. Page, "A History of the Milk Canning Industry," in A. Judge, *History*, 45.

116. A. Judge, "Past, Present and Future," 58.

117. Martin Brown and Peter Philips, "The Evolution of Labor Market Structure: The California Canning Industry," *Industrial and Labor Relations Review* 38, no. 3 (1985): 392–407; Ruiz, *Cannery Women;* Harry Bridges Center for Labor Studies, University of Washington, "Waterfront Workers History Project: Cannery Workers and Their Unions," n.d., accessed February 25, 2017, http://depts.washington.edu/dock/canneries_intro.shtml.

2. GROWING A BETTER PEA

1. *Pick of the Pod* (California Packing Corporation, 1939), www.archive.org/details/Pickofth1939.

2. The statistics come from National Canners Association (hereafter NCA), *The Canning Industry: A Series of Articles Furnishing Information on the History, Organization, Methods and Products of the Industry, with Selected List of References* (Washington, DC: NCA, 1939), 8.

3. Charles G. Summers Jr., "'Cooperation between Canner and Grower,' Address at the Joint Meeting Growers and Canners," in *Report of the Maryland Agricultural Society* (College Park: Maryland Agricultural Society, 1917), 184.

4. Gabriella Petrick, "Industrial Food," in *The Oxford Handbook of Food History*, ed. Jeffrey M. Pilcher (New York: Oxford University Press, 2012), 269.

5. Lenna Cooper, *How to Cut Food Costs* (Battle Creek, MI: Good Health Publishing, ca. 1917); Gertrude T. Spitz, *Food for the Worker: The Food Values and Cost of a Series of Menus and Recipes for Seven Weeks* (Boston: Whitcomb and Barrows, 1917).

6. By 1907, the state was packing a third of the country's canned peas. Glenn Cyrus Sevey, *Peas and Pea Culture* (New York: Orange Judd, 1911). On Wisconsin's prominence within agricultural research, see Deborah Kay Fitzgerald, *The Business of Breeding: Hybrid Corn in Illinois, 1890–1940* (Ithaca, NY: Cornell University Press, 1990), 109. For more on the history of agricultural research, see Kathy J. Cooke, "Expertise, Book Farming, and Government Agriculture: The Origins of Agricultural Seed Certification in the United States," *Agricultural History* 76, no. 3 (2002): 524–45; R. Douglas Hurt, *American Agriculture: A Brief History*, rev. ed. (Lafayette, IN: Purdue University Press,

2002); Jack Kloppenburg, *First the Seed: The Political Economy of Plant Biotechnology,* 2nd ed. (Madison: University of Wisconsin Press, 2005); Barbara A. Kimmelman, "Mr. Blakeslee Builds His Dream House: Agricultural Institutions, Genetics, and Careers, 1900–1915," *Journal of the History of Biology* 39, no. 2 (July 1, 2006): 241–80.

7. Jim Hightower, *Hard Tomatoes, Hard Times: A Report of the Agribusiness Accountability Project on the Failure of America's Land Grant College Complex* (Schenkman, 1973); Pete R. Daniel, *Breaking the Land: The Transformation of Cotton, Tobacco, and Rice Cultures since 1880* (Urbana: University of Illinois Press, 1986).

8. There are a number of important studies of the food-processing sector, but they could more deeply engage with the agricultural research aspect of the industries. See, for example, Mark W. Wilde, "Industrialization of Food Processing in the United States, 1860–1960" (PhD diss., University of Delaware, 1988); Derek Oden, "From Cob to Can: The Development of Iowa's Canning Industry in the Late Nineteenth and Early Twentieth Centuries," *Annals of Iowa* 63 (Fall 2004): 390–418; Roger Horowitz, *Putting Meat on the American Table: Taste, Technology, Transformation* (Baltimore: Johns Hopkins University Press, 2006).

9. This supports the arguments of Alan L. Olmstead and Paul Rhode in *Creating Abundance: Biological Innovation and American Agricultural Development* (New York: Cambridge University Press, 2008).

10. Several historians have argued for the limited value of Mendelism around 1900. Delwiche's case is perhaps an exception because he was working with the pea plant, Mendel's original model. See Diane B. Paul and Barbara A. Kimmelman, "Mendel in America: Theory and Practice, 1900–1919," in *The American Development of Biology,* ed. Ronald Rainger, Keith R. Benson, and Jane Maienschein (New Brunswick, NJ: Rutgers University Press, 1988), 281–310; Fitzgerald, *Business of Breeding,* 109.

11. This work follows the model of William Cronon, *Nature's Metropolis: Chicago and the Great West* (New York: W. W. Norton, 1991), in tracing the pathways out of town in order to understand the connections between urban consumption and rural production. For work on the agency of rural consumers, see Ronald R. Kline, *Consumers in the Country: Technology and Social Change in Rural America* (Baltimore: Johns Hopkins University Press, 2000).

12. Office of the Dean and Director, College of Agriculture, University of Wisconsin, "Finding Aid, Industrial Fellowships, 1923–1942," University of Wisconsin Division Archives 9/1/1–12.

13. Many historians have used "the Golden Age of Agriculture" to describe this time when agricultural prices and the value of farmland were at an all-time high. See, for example, Richard Hofstadter, *The Age of Reform: From Bryan to F.D.R.* (New York: Knopf, 1955), 109–10; Carrie A. Meyer, *Days on the Family Farm: From the Golden Age through the Great Depression* (Minneapolis: University of Minnesota Press, 2007).

14. Wisconsin established its experiment station in 1883, four years before the 1887 Hatch Act funded stations in every state. For more on federal agricultural programs, see Hurt, *American Agriculture.* For more on the Wisconsin story, see Vernon Carstensen, "The Genesis of an Agricultural Experiment

Station," *Agricultural History* 34, no. 1 (January 1, 1960): 13–20; Merle Eugene Curti, *The University of Wisconsin: A History, 1848–1925* (Madison: University of Wisconsin Press, 1949); Wilbur H. Glover, *Farm and College* (Madison: University of Wisconsin Press, 1952).

15. This quote is from Justin Smith Morrill, the founder of the Morrill Act, which established land-grant colleges throughout the United States. For more, see William Belmont Parker, *The Life and Public Services of Justin Smith Morrill* (Boston: Houghton Mifflin, 1924).

16. See Thomas A. Woods, *Knights of the Plow: Oliver H. Kelley and the Origins of the Grange in Republican Ideology* (Ames: Iowa State University Press, 1991).

17. H. L. Russell, *Report of the Director, 1911–1912*, Bulletin 228 (Madison: University of Wisconsin, Agricultural Experiment Station, 1913), 3. For more on farmers' antagonism to professional agricultural experts, see Roy Vernon Scott, *The Reluctant Farmer: The Rise of Agricultural Extension to 1914* (Urbana: University of Illinois Press, 1971).

18. Kathy J. Cooke explores how agricultural scientists depended on the knowledge of farmers' practical breeding efforts in her article "From Science to Practice, or Practice to Science? Chickens and Eggs in Raymond Pearl's Agricultural Breeding Research, 1907–1916," *Isis* 88, no. 1 (March 1997): 62–86.

19. For more on science and politics at leading state institutions of agriculture, see Fitzgerald, *Business of Breeding*; Charles E. Rosenberg, *No Other Gods: On Science and American Social Thought* (Baltimore: Johns Hopkins University Press, 1997).

20. Carstensen, "Genesis," 20; Joseph Schafer, *A History of Agriculture in Wisconsin* (Madison: State Historical Society of Wisconsin, 1922), 159.

21. When establishing New Deal agricultural policies in the 1930s, the US Department of Agriculture (USDA) used the conditions of this golden age, the years 1909 to 1914, as a baseline measurement, since it was during this time that farmers achieved price parity, in which farm goods and nonfarm goods were equal in value. R. Douglas Hurt, *Agricultural Technology in the Twentieth Century* (Manhattan, KS: Sunflower University Press, 1991).

22. US Bureau of the Census, *Thirteenth Census of the United States, 1910: Agriculture, 1909 and 1910* (Washington, DC: Government Printing Office, 1913), 27–29.

23. Rosenberg, *No Other Gods*, 176.

24. David B. Danbom, "The Agricultural Experiment Station and Professionalization: Scientists' Goals for Agriculture," *Agricultural History* 60, no. 2 (Spring 1986): 251.

25. For more on the politics of agricultural experiment stations, see John L. Shover, *First Majority, Last Minority: The Transforming of Rural Life in America*, Minorities in American History (DeKalb: Northern Illinois University Press, 1976), 232–33.

26. Extension Service of the College of Agriculture, University of Wisconsin, *The Story of the Babcock Test* (Madison, WI: Extension Service, 1938); Fitzgerald, *Business of Breeding*. This unbalanced relationship only increased as the century progressed. By the mid-twentieth century, angry critics bemoaned the

corporate takeover of the land-grant system. The 1973 report *Hard Times, Hard Tomatoes* alleged that the federal agricultural system directed $750 million a year toward agribusiness projects rather than supporting the country's average farmer. Hightower, *Hard Tomatoes*.

27. Wyman Smith, "7000 Miles of Peas," *Bean Bag* 3, no. 8 (January 1921): 34–36, describes how the Wisconsin College of Agriculture worked to establish a pea-canning industry in the northern regions of the state in order to boost the local economy. J. A. Hagemann and W. E. Nicholoy, "University Service to the Pea Canning Industry," *Wisconsin Alumni Magazine* 26, no. 7 (May 1925): 255–57, attests to the university's long-standing interest in supporting the state's pea canners.

28. Schafer, *History of Agriculture*; Richard Nelson Current, *Wisconsin: A History* (Urbana: University of Illinois Press, 2001), 85; Agricultural Experiment Station, University of Wisconsin, *Canning Peas in Wisconsin*, Bulletin of the University of Wisconsin Agricultural Experiment Station 444 (Madison: Agricultural Experiment Station, University of Wisconsin, 1939).

29. Several sources describe the fit between the Wisconsin environment and pea-growing needs: William Henry Mylrea, *Home-Making Opportunities in Wisconsin* (Chicago: National Farm Land Congress, 1909); Arthur I. Judge, preface to *A History of the Canning Industry* (Baltimore: Canning Trade, 1914), 18; Smith, "7000 Miles of Peas." Current, *Wisconsin*, 87, describes how pea-growing practices were brought to Wisconsin by European immigrants.

30. Frederick Arthur Stare, *The Story of Wisconsin's Great Canning Industry* (Baltimore: Canning Trade, 1949), 40; B. L. Wade, "Breeding and Improvement," in *Yearbook of Agriculture, 1937*, 252; E. J. Delwiche, "History of Pea Breeding and Cultural Work in Wisconsin," in Stare, *Story*, 199.

31. Seed peas were those that were grown for the explicit purpose of seed production and then sold to pea growers and canners throughout the country, rather than to consumers for eating. Stare, *Story*, 27; Current, *Wisconsin*, 87.

32. US Bureau of the Census, "Canning and Preserving," in *Census of Manufactures 1914*, vol. 2 (Washington, DC: Government Printing Office, 1919), 366–67.

33. *Mukwonago Chief*, November 1898, cited in Stare, *Story*, 34. Historian Deborah Fitzgerald notes a similar dynamic in Iowa, "Eating and Remembering [Presidential Address]," *Agricultural History* 79 (2005): 397.

34. Frederick Arthur Stare, "Wisconsin's Canning Industry, Past and Present," *Wisconsin Magazine of History* 36, no. 1 (Autumn 1952): 36.

35. Theodore Macklin, *Cost of Canning Wisconsin Peas*, Bulletin 327 (Madison: Agricultural Experiment Station, University of Wisconsin, 1921), 2.

36. George P. Hambrecht, *Women in Industry: Proceedings of the Seventh Annual Convention of the Association of Governmental Labor Officials of the United States and Canada*, Bulletin of the US Bureau of Labor Statistics, no. 266 (Washington, DC: Government Printing Office, 1920), 62.

37. Macklin, *Cost of Canning*, 12.

38. A May 10, 1900, issue of the *Canner* trade journal reported that the East Wisconsin Canning Company of Manitowoc "intends to open up and conduct

in connection with its new canning factory an up-to-date experiment station," as cited in Stare, *Story,* 43.

39. E. Delwiche, "History of Pea Breeding," 195.

40. H. L. Russell, "Gaseous Fermentation in the Canning Industry," *Annual Reports of the Wisconsin Agricultural Experiment Station* 12 (1895): 227–31; Nancy Tomes, *The Gospel of Germs: Men, Women, and the Microbe in American Life* (Cambridge, MA: Harvard University Press, 1998).

41. Hagemann and Nicholoy, "University Service," 256.

42. Russell, *Report of the Director,* 5.

43. Vaughan joined Professor L. R. Jones, who had already been studying blight upon the request of the Columbus Canning Company. E. Delwiche, "History of Pea Breeding," 196.

44. The Columbus Canning Company was not unique in growing its own crops. Major processor H. J. Heinz also kept company control over agriculture; see Gabriella Petrick, "Purity as Life: H. J. Heinz, Religious Sentiment, and the Beginning of the Industrial Diet," *History and Technology* 271, no. 1 (2011): 44.

45. Russell, *Report of the Director,* 49; Clyde Morse Shields, *The Pea Growing Areas and the Pea Canning Industry in Wisconsin in Their Relation to Natural Environment* (Madison: University of Wisconsin, 1928), 29–30.

46. Russell, *Report of the Director,* 49.

47. By 1924, there were 135 plants canning peas in Wisconsin, processing the raw crops from about 102,000 acres. F. R. Jones and M. B. Linford, *Pea Disease Survey in Wisconsin,* Bulletin 64 (Madison: Agricultural Experiment Station, University of Wisconsin, 1925).

48. For a biographical overview of E. J. Delwiche, see an account written by his son Richard Delwiche, *E. J.* (Green Bay, WI: n.p., 1963), E. J. Delwiche Biographical File, University of Wisconsin Archives, along with many other newspaper clippings and biographical press releases in his UW Archives Biographical File.

49. Ibid., 60.

50. E. Delwiche, "History of Pea Breeding," 199.

51. Fitzgerald, *Business of Breeding,* 104.

52. Both quotes in E. Delwiche, "History of Pea Breeding," 202.

53. Paul and Kimmelman, "Mendel in America," 295.

54. Paolo Palladino, "Wizards and Devotees: On the Mendelian Theory of Inheritance and the Professionalization of Agricultural Science in Great Britain and the United States, 1880–1930," *History of Science* 32 (1994): 411; Cooke, "From Science to Practice."

55. E. J. Delwiche and E. J. Renard, *Breeding New Varieties of Canning Peas,* Research Bulletin 70 (Madison: Agricultural Experiment Station of the University of Wisconsin, 1926), 2.

56. R. Delwiche, *E. J.,* 70.

57. E. Delwiche and Renard, *Breeding New Varieties;* Wade, "Breeding and Improvement." Despite the early promise of peas as genetic subjects, they later proved not to be so ideal as model organisms for a variety of biological reasons, as described in Wade, "Breeding and Improvement," 268.

58. For more on specific pea varieties and their characteristics, see E. Delwiche and Renard, *Breeding New Varieties;* Wade, "Breeding and Improvement"; Stare, "Wisconsin's Canning Industry," 28.

59. But other states followed suit in later years too. Wade, "Breeding and Improvement," describes work in 1937 to develop *Fusarium* wilt resistance at the California Agricultural Experiment Station, in collaboration with the USDA.

60. Mary Swartz Rose, *Everyday Foods in War Time* (New York: Macmillan, 1918), 37.

61. See Susanne Freidberg, *Fresh: A Perishable History* (Cambridge, MA: Harvard University Press, 2009). She describes how vegetable growers sought to capture some of the virtues of canned food—"sturdy, standardized, and seasonless"—while also highlighting the nutrition and "moral superiority" of fresh, unprocessed vegetables (159).

62. Ibid., 255–56.

63. E. Delwiche and Renard, *Breeding New Varieties,* 22.

64. Wade, "Breeding and Improvement," 256.

65. E. Delwiche and Renard, *Breeding New Varieties,* 30.

66. See an image of this poster in Charles Lathrop Pack, *The War Garden Victorious* (Philadelphia: J. B. Lippincott, 1919), 16. For more on food in World War I, see Helen Zoe Veit, *Modern Food, Moral Food: Self-Control, Science, and the Rise of Modern American Eating in the Early Twentieth Century* (Chapel Hill: University of North Carolina Press, 2015).

67. Hambrecht, *Women in Industry,* 63.

68. Edward C. Hampe and Merle Wittenberg, *The Lifeline of America: Development of the Food Industry* (New York: McGraw-Hill, 1964), 125.

69. "Roman Speaks of the Early Incidents in the Canning Industry," *Rome NY Daily Sentinel,* January 26, 1925.

70. John H. Sherburne, Charles H. Adams, and John D. Willard, *Report of the Massachusetts Commission on the Necessaries of Life . . .* (Boston: Wright and Potter, 1920), 74.

71. E. Delwiche, "History of Pea Breeding," 204.

72. "Report of the Grand Jury Empaneled in the United States District Court for the Northern District of Illinois at Chicago at the June Term, A.D. 1917, as to Conditions of Trade in Food Products. Canned Goods," *Monthly Review of the U.S. Bureau of Labor Statistics* 5, no. 2 (1917), 56.

73. Lawrence B. Glickman, *Buying Power: A History of Consumer Activism in America* (Chicago: University of Chicago Press, 2009).

74. This transition happened at different times in different states, but largely during the first two decades of the twentieth century. In New York, for example, most peas, corn, and tomatoes were grown under contract as early as 1908. New York State Department of Labor, *Report of Bureau of Factory Inspection* (New York: Bureau of Labor Statistics, 1908), 403. Even within Wisconsin, the transition was incremental, with large packers moving to a contract system before small packers, as described in a letter from the Columbus Canning Company to the *Canner,* October 21, 1911, Columbus Food Corporation Records, 1901–46, Wisconsin Historical Society, University of Wisconsin-Madison

(hereafter Columbus Records), Reel 1. But by 1919, 80 percent of canning peas in Wisconsin were cultivated by farmers, the remaining 20 percent by canners. Macklin, *Cost of Canning,* 4.

75. "State News," *Oshkosh Daily Northwestern,* July 29, 1913.

76. William C. Leitsch to *Canner,* March 9, 1917, Columbus Records, Reel 1.

77. Schafer, *History of Agriculture,* 164. Despite this commentary, some dairy improvers also faced challenges in getting dairy farmers to adopt business principles. Kendra Smith-Howard, *Pure and Modern Milk: An Environmental History since 1900* (New York: Oxford University Press, 2013).

78. Columbus Canning Company to Mr. James J. Mulligan, editor, *Canner and Dried Fruit Packer,* August 5, 1912, Columbus Records, Reel 1. Fred A. Stare was also the father of Frederick J. Stare, who came to be seen as American's foremost nutritionist and who had a close relationship with the food industry, promoting sugar, Coca-Cola, and other processed foods. "Frederick Stare Obituary," *Economist,* April 18, 2002, www.economist.com/node/1086689.

79. William C. Leitsch to *Canner,* March 9, 1917, Columbus Records, Reel 1.

80. Columbus Canning Company to *Canner,* October 21, 1911, Columbus Records, Reel 1.

81. Other Wisconsin canneries that had feeding operations included the Waterloo Canning Company, the Chippewa Falls Canning Company, and the Randolph Canning Company. Stare, *Story,* 52.

82. Columbus Canning Co. to Department of Animal Husbandry, March 3, 1911, Columbus Records, Reel 10, Slide 545.

83. Columbus Canning Co. to Department of Animal Husbandry, September 20, 1911, Columbus Records, Reel 10, Slide 549.

84. Hugh S. Orem, "Address at the Joint Meeting Growers and Canners," in *Report of the Maryland Agricultural Society* (College Park: Maryland Agricultural Society, 1917), 192.

85. Walter J. Sears, "The Farmer and the Canner," *Canning Age,* May 1920, 30.

86. Agriculturist, "Outsider's View."

87. Macklin, *Cost of Canning,* 3.

88. Ibid., 3, 5; statistics for 1923 are given in "Features of Farm Production in Wisconsin during 1923," *Wisconsin Crop and Livestock Reporter* 3, no. 1 (November 1924), http://digicoll.library.wisc.edu/cgi-bin/WI/WI-idx?type=article&did=WI.CLRv03.i0001&id=WI.CLRv03&isize=M.

89. Robert Paarlberg and Don Paarlberg, "Agricultural Policy in the Twentieth Century," *Agricultural History* 74, no. 2 (April 1, 2000): 136–61.

90. Many pea-canning plants packed other kinds of foods at other times of year. They typically employed women, children, and seasonal farm laborers who could work with uncertain and intermittent schedules. Macklin, *Cost of Canning,* 19.

91. May, *Canning Clan,* 381; Hampe and Wittenberg, *Lifeline of America,* 125. The French canning industry developed slowly for a number of reasons: canned products were expensive; French foodways contradicted the convenience and standardization of packaged foods; and safety problems continued through the 1920s. Martin Bruegel, "How the French Learned to Eat Canned Food,

1809–1930s," in *Food Nations: Selling Taste in Consumer Societies,* ed. Warren James Belasco and Philip Scranton (New York: Routledge, 2002), 113–30.

92. Macklin, *Cost of Canning,* 10.

93. W. M. Wright, "Address at the Joint Meeting of Growers and Canners," in *Report of the Maryland Agricultural Society* (College Park: Maryland Agricultural Society, 1917), 182.

94. Sears, "Farmer and the Canner," 32.

95. NCA, *Agricultural Research Relating to Canning Crops* (Washington, DC: NCA, 1936), 2; Sears, "Farmer and the Canner," 25–30.

96. "Co-operative Movement Encouraging," *Canning Age,* May 1920, 24.

97. Summers, "Cooperation," 184.

98. Hampe and Wittenberg, *Lifeline of America,* 125.

99. Campbell Soup Company, "Grower-Canner Agreements: An Abuse of Mass Standardized Contracts," *Yale Law Journal* 58, no. 7 (June 1, 1949): 1161–71; "Tomato Growers: A Meeting at Hamilton—Advance Prices Demanded," *Canadian Horticulturist* (1903); New York State Department of Labor, *Report of Bureau,* 402; Stare, *Story,* 47.

100. For more on contentious relationship between farmers and contractors, see Monica Richmond Gisolfi, "From Crop Lien to Contract Farming: The Roots of Agribusiness in the American South, 1929–1939," *Agricultural History* 80, no. 2 (Spring 2006): 167–89.

101. Sears, "Farmer and the Canner," 25.

102. Fred A. Stare, "Permanent Pea Packing Records; Their Value and Use," *Canner* 55, no. 24 (December 9, 1922): 32.

103. Sears, "Farmer and the Canner," 32.

104. "Raising Prices for Canning Crops," *Market Growers Journal,* February 1, 1919, 95.

105. Nancy K. Berlage, "Organizing the Farm Bureau: Family, Community, and Professionals, 1914–1928," *Agricultural History* 75, no. 4 (October 1, 2001): 406–37.

106. Victoria Saker Woeste, *The Farmer's Benevolent Trust: Law and Agricultural Cooperation in Industrial America, 1865–1945* (Chapel Hill: University of North Carolina Press, 1998).

107. "New York Notes: Canning Crops," *Market Growers Journal,* May 1, 1919, 14.

108. "Notes from New York: Canning Crops Organization," *Market Growers Journal,* November 15, 1920, 7.

109. Theodore Macklin, "Marketing Canning Peas," in *The Road to Better Marketing,* Wisconsin Bulletin 136 (Madison: Extension Service of the College of Agriculture, University of Wisconsin, 1921), 14.

110. "Co-operative Movement Encouraging." Canning crop grower cooperation did not take hold nationally, perhaps because growers of canning crops often had other roles and identities as well.

111. NCA, *Agricultural Research,* 3.

112. C. G. Woodbury, "Address Delivered before Vegetable Growers' Association of America, at Albany," *Market Growers Journal* 30, no. 1 (January 1, 1922): 28.

113. NCA, *Agricultural Research.*

114. Natural Resources Planning Board, *Research—A National Resource, II. Industrial Research* (Washington, DC: Government Printing Office, 1940), 94.

115. Willis L. Crites, "Problems of Agriculture," *Canner* 50, no. 5 (January 31, 1920): 37–39.

116. As an explanation of this coverage, the Industrial Fellowships Finding Aid reads, "It is possible that there were no formal files before 1923. It is not known why they end in 1942." Office of the Dean, "Finding Aid," University of Wisconsin Division Archives 9/1/1–12. Farmers with other kinds of crop interests collaborated with experiment stations in the early decade, as Deborah Fitzgerald describes for a federal field station established in 1917 with the Funk Brothers Seed Company, in cooperation with the Illinois station. Fitzgerald, *Business of Breeding,* 112.

117. See letters between John E. Dudley Jr. and the Columbus Canning Company, Columbus Records, Reel 10. Hagemann and Nicholoy, "University Service," 256–57; "Pea Packers of Wisconsin Are Planning," *Oshkosh Daily Northwestern,* June 20, 1924.

118. Fitzgerald, *Business of Breeding,* 109.

119. Campbell Soup Company was breeding tomato varieties by the 1920s. Hampe and Wittenberg, *Lifeline of America,* 73.

120. Crites, "Problems of Agriculture," 38.

121. Wade, "Breeding and Improvement," 258; R. Delwiche, *E.J.*

122. E. Delwiche and Renard, *Breeding New Varieties,* 6.

123. And farmers and canners were typically too busy and without space in their own fields to produce their own seed. R.E. Vaughan, "Peas an Important Crop," *Bean Bag* 3, no. 12 (May 1921): 21.

124. Ibid., 22; "Pea Packers of Wisconsin."

125. Stare, *Story,* 253.

126. Ibid., 254. The CSC charter stated that it was not "a profit earning corporation primarily." Stare, *Story,* 253. And indeed, during the Great Depression, in 1932, the CSC recognized "a duty to feed people of the nation" and decided to "continue operations on a normal basis whether or not they prove[d] profitable." "State Canners Not to Curb Operations," *Manitowoc Herald News,* February 5, 1932.

127. W.E. Nicholoy to CSC stockholders, December 21, 1925, Columbus Records, Reel 12, Slide 31.

128. Wade, "Breeding and Improvement," 258.

129. E.J. Holden to Fred Stare, September 25, 1948, Columbus Records, Reel 4, Slide 410–11.

130. Stare, *Story,* 255. As late as 1977, the corporation was still in operation, under the management of Paul H. Deniger, likely a grandson of J.W. Deniger, one of Wisconsin's early canning leaders. "Elm Center Includes Eight Offices," *Post-Register,* March 21, 1977.

131. Maurice B. Linford, "A Fusarium Wilt of Peas in Wisconsin," *Report of the Agricultural Experiment Station of the University of Wisconsin, Madison* 85 (June 1928): 42.

132. R. Delwiche, *E.J.,* 69.

133. E. Delwiche and Renard, *Breeding New Varieties,* 32.

134. E. Delwiche, "History of Pea Breeding," 202, 206.

135. For more on the idea of the "imagined consumer," see Regina Lee Blaszczyk, *Imagining Consumers: Design and Innovation from Wedgwood to Corning* (Baltimore: Johns Hopkins University Press, 2002).

3. POISONED OLIVES

1. Chas Armstrong, R. V. Story, and Ernest Scott, "Botulism from Eating Canned Ripe Olives," *Public Health Reports* 34, no. 51 (December 19, 1919): 2877–2905.

2. James Harvey Young has written about these botulism cases in ripe olives, with special attention to the early 1920 outbreak in New York City. He focuses most on the immediate response to the outbreak by local health officials and the activities of the federal Bureau of Chemistry. His article provides valuable information that fleshes out the details of some of the outbreaks mentioned in this chapter. James Harvey Young, "Botulism and the Ripe Olive Scare of 1919–1920," *Bulletin of the History of Medicine* 50 (1976): 372–91. Gabriella Petrick has also connected botulism cases in canned food with canners' investment in bacteriological research. Gabriella Petrick, "An Ambivalent Diet: The Industrialization of Canning," *OAH Magazine of History* 24, no. 3 (July 2010): 35–38.

3. Judith M. Taylor, *The Olive in California: History of an Immigrant Tree* (Berkeley, CA: Ten Speed Press, 2000).

4. For more background on the general context of concerns over purity in American food, see Susanne Freidberg, *Fresh: A Perishable History* (Cambridge, MA: Harvard University Press, 2009); Benjamin R. Cohen, "Analysis as Border Patrol: Chemists along the Boundary between Pure Food and Real Adulteration," *Endeavour* 35, no. 2–3 (June 2011): 66–73; Aaron Bobrow-Strain, *White Bread: A Social History of the Store-Bought Loaf* (Boston: Beacon Press, 2012).

5. Frederick Arthur Stare, *Story of Wisconsin's Great Canning Industry* (Baltimore: Canning Trade, 1949), 95.

6. Edward F. Keuchel, "The Development of the Canning Industry in New York State to 1960" (PhD diss., Cornell University, 1970), 351–53.

7. *Western Canner and Packer* 12 (August 1920), cited in Steven Stoll, *The Fruits of Natural Advantage: Making the Industrial Countryside in California* (Berkeley: University of California Press, 1998), 82. The opening of the Panama Canal in 1914 also allowed the California canning industry to grow by giving it more direct access to the ports of Europe. Isidor Jacobs, "The Rise and Progress of the Canning Industry in California," in *A History of the Canning Industry,* ed. Arthur I. Judge (Baltimore: Canning Trade, 1914), 39. Soon after, in 1916, the California Packing Corporation formed, consolidating production by operating farms, canneries, and brokerage firms throughout the West, leading to a national market for its products under the Del Monte Brand. Dean Witter and Co., *California Packing Corporation: A Study of Impressive Progress* (San Francisco: Dean Witter and Co., 1950).

8. Although the country had been linked by transcontinental railroad since 1869, shipping fruit from California remained difficult. See Stoll, *Fruits of*

Natural Advantage. Widespread cases of foodborne illness are all too common in today's world, but the 1919 botulism outbreak was one of the first times that bacterial contamination from food spread throughout the country in such a publicized way.

9. Sensationalistic press—"yellow journalism"—had characterized many newspapers since the turn of the twentieth century. John D. Stevens, *Sensationalism and the New York Press* (New York: Columbia University, 1991).

10. The impulse to blame individual housewives for botulism was part of a larger expectation of housewives to solve all sorts of food-related problems. See, for example, the expectation that women consumers should "solve" inflation by simply not buying expensive or overpriced goods, or should "solve" economic exploitation by changing those with whom they traded. Tracey Deutsch, *Building a Housewife's Paradise: Gender, Politics, and American Grocery Stores in the Twentieth Century* (Chapel Hill: University of North Carolina Press, 2012).

11. Many historians have written about this rising authority of public health after the discovery of germ theory in the 1880s. Judith Walzer Leavitt, *Typhoid Mary: Captive to the Public's Health* (Boston: Beacon Press, 1996); Nancy Tomes, *The Gospel of Germs: Men, Women, and the Microbe in American Life* (Cambridge, MA: Harvard University Press, 1998). For an examination of the changing relationships of consumers to those who produced their food, see Ann Vileisis, *Kitchen Literacy: How We Lost Knowledge of Where Food Comes From and Why We Need to Get It Back* (Washington, DC: Island Press/Shearwater Books, 2008).

12. The canning story parallels the more familiar story of the tobacco industry in America, as both began to fund large public relations campaigns, research projects, and government collaborations in response to public health scares. Allan M. Brandt, *The Cigarette Century: The Rise, Fall, and Deadly Persistence of the Product That Defined America* (New York: Basic Books, 2007).

13. Ernest C. Dickson, "Botulism, an Experimental Study: A Preliminary Report," *Journal of the American Medical Association* 65, no. 6 (August 7, 1915): 492–96.

14. Ray Lyman Wilbur and William Ophuls, "Botulism: A Report of Food-Poisoning Apparently Due to Eating of Canned String Beans, with Pathological Report of a Fatal Case," *Archives of Internal Medicine* 14, no. 14 (October 1914): 589–604. Gabriella Petrick also describes this case in "Ambivalent Diet."

15. Albert D. Sabin, *Karl Friedrich Meyer, 1884–1974: A Biographical Memoir* (Washington, DC: National Academy of Sciences, 1980), 288.

16. Ernest C. Dickson to Wilbur A. Sawyer, August 8, 1917, Box 1, Folder 5, Ernest Charles Dickson Papers, 1881–1939, Acc. # MSS 21, Box 1, Folder 6, Lane Medical Archives, Stanford University Medical Center (hereafter cited as Dickson Papers). *Bacillus botulinus* was the taxonomic designation for botulism before the olive outbreak spurred a taxonomic reclassification to *Clostridium botulinum.*

17. Walter L. Dodd, "Botulism," *American Food Journal* 15, no. 2 (February 1920): 13. The first time commercial canned food was linked with botulism

was in 1907. "Report of Three Cases of Fatal Ptomaine Poisoning," *Southern California Practitioner* 22 (1907): 370–72, cited in Young, "Botulism," 374.

18. "Scientists Advance in War on Botulism," *American Food Journal* 17, no. 11 (November 1922): 19–20. For an analysis of Rosenau's research into canned food, see Gabriella Petrick, "Arbiters of Taste: Producers, Consumers, and the Industrialization of Taste in America, 1900–1960" (PhD diss., University of Delaware, 2006), chap. 1.

19. Charles G. Jennings, Ernest W. Haas, and Alpheus F. Jennings, "An Outbreak of Botulism: Report of Cases," *Journal of the American Medical Association* 74, no. 2 (January 10, 1920): 77–80; J. C. Geiger, E. C. Dickson, and K. F. Meyer, *The Epidemiology of Botulism,* Public Health Bulletin No. 127 (Washington, DC: Government Printing Office, 1922), 39–41.

20. See *Almanac of the Canning Industry, 1922* (Baltimore, MD: Canning Trade, 1922), 56, 60.

21. Edward F. Keuchel, "Chemicals and Meat: The Embalmed Beef Scandal of the Spanish–American War," *Bulletin of the History of Medicine* 48, no. 2 (1974): 249–64; Stewart M. Brooks, *Ptomaine: The Story of Food Poisoning* (South Brunswick, NJ: A. S. Barnes, 1974); Leavitt, *Typhoid Mary.*

22. Scholars have explored media attention to and misrepresentation of science beginning in the late nineteenth century—first in newspapers, magazines, and popular books and later across radio and television. John C. Burnham, *How Superstition Won and Science Lost: Popularization of Science and Health in the United States* (New Brunswick, NJ: Rutgers University Press, 1987); Dorothy Nelkin, *Selling Science: How the Press Covers Science and Technology,* rev. ed. (New York: W. H. Freeman, 1995); Marcel C. LaFollette, *Science on the Air: Popularizers and Personalities on Radio and Early Television* (Chicago: University of Chicago Press, 2008).

23. Margaret Humphreys, "No Safe Place: Disease and Panic in American History," *American Literary History* 14, no. 4 (Winter 2002): 847.

24. The statistics for publication rates come from a search for "botulism" or "botulinus" and a scan for olive topics in Proquest Historical Newspapers; the outbreak statistics are from Geiger, Dickson, and Meyer, *Epidemiology of Botulism,* 49.

25. "Discount Food Poison Tales," *Los Angeles Times,* December 30, 1917, sec. II.

26. "Airplane Fails; Death Is Victor," *Los Angeles Times,* January 18, 1920.

27. For more on the 1918 influenza, see Alfred W. Crosby, *America's Forgotten Pandemic: The Influenza of 1918* (Cambridge: Cambridge University Press, 1989); Nancy K. Bristow, *American Pandemic: The Lost Worlds of the 1918 Influenza Epidemic* (New York: Oxford University Press, 2012).

28. "Botulism Called Deadliest Poison," *New York Times,* October 1, 1922, Proquest Historical Newspapers.

29. "Two Die after Jolly Dinner," *Los Angeles Times,* August 1, 1914, sec. II, 1, Proquest Historical Newspapers.

30. Dodd, "Botulism." 12.

31. Ibid.

32. Many industries were beginning to understand the power of communicating with—and influencing the preferences of—their consumers via advertisements in major media sources by the early twentieth century, but newspaper stories remained a crucial source for the stereotypes, assumptions, hopes, and fears that consumers associated with canned foods. For more on the rise of this consumer culture and attendant advertising, see William Leach, *Land of Desire: Merchants, Power, and the Rise of a New American Culture* (New York: Basic Books, 1993); Jackson Lears, *Fables of Abundance: A Cultural History of Advertising in America* (New York: Basic Books, 1994); Susan Strasser, *Satisfaction Guaranteed: The Making of the American Mass Market* (Washington, DC: Smithsonian Institution Press, 1995).

33. For the slogan, see clipping attached to "2 Sailors Die, 4 Ill from Eating Olives," *New York Sun*, December 20, 1920, Box 1, Folder 6, Dickson Papers. A collection of these clippings is in the Dickson Papers, Box 4, Folder 1.

34. Ernest C. Dickson to R.I. Bentley, May 9, 1921, Box 1, Folder 7, Dickson Papers.

35. W.V. Cruess to E.C. Dickson. January 24, 1921, Box 1, Folder 10, Dickson Papers.

36. For more on Bentley and his brother R.I., both crucial players in the early twentieth-century canning industry, see Earl Chapin May, *The Canning Clan: A Pageant of Pioneering Americans* (New York: Macmillan, 1938), 230.

37. C.H. Bentley to Ernest C. Dickson, October 27, 1920, Box 1, Folder 6, Dickson Papers.

38. W.V. Cruess to E.C. Dickson, January 12, 1921, Box 1, Folder 10, Dickson Papers.

39. W.V. Cruess to E.C. Dickson, January 24, 1921, Box 1, Folder 10, Dickson Papers.

40. Wm. V. Cruess to Ernest C. Dickson, January 28, 1921, Box 1, Folder 10, Dickson Papers.

41. C.H. Bentley to Ernest C. Dickson, October 27, 1920, Box 1, Folder 6, Dickson Papers.

42. W.V. Cruess to E.C. Dickson. September 5, 1922, Box 1, Folder 10, Dickson Papers.

43. G.H. Hecke, director of California Department of Agriculture, to state agriculturists, June 24, 1926, California State Archives, Sacramento, CA, Inventory of the Records of the Department of Public Health, Collection Number R384 (hereafter cited as Cal. Dept. Pub. Health), Food and Drug Inspection Files, 1918–39: Botulism, Box 2, Folder 22.

44. Mrs. J.H. Hincks to Prof. Cruess, April 17, 1922, Box 1, Folder 10, Dickson Papers.

45. "Dr. Wiley's Question-Box," *Good Housekeeping*, May 1922, 88.

46. Armstrong, Story, and Scott, "Botulism," 2878.

47. Tomes, *Gospel of Germs*, 102.

48. Ola Powell, *Successful Canning and Preserving*, 3rd, rev. ed. (Philadelphia: J.B. Lippincott, 1917), 12.

49. C. Thom, R.B. Edmonson, and L.T. Giltner, "Botulism in Canned Asparagus," *Journal of the American Medical Association* 73 (1919): 907,

reprinted as "Report 67" in Geiger, Dickson, and Meyer, *Epidemiology of Botulism*, 43.

50. "Domestic Dilemma," *Chicago Daily Tribune,* June 17, 1918, 6, Proquest Historical Newspapers.

51. "Discount Food Poison Tales," A1.

52. "Use Your Nose," *Riverside Press* (Riverside, CA), February 5, 1920, Box 4, Folder 1, Dickson Papers.

53. This follows what historian Thomas Stapleford calls a "schizophrenic" discourse around the housewife as an expert on consumption. She is expected to be both a rational actor in her management of the home and also a "confused woman desperately in need of expert guidance." Thomas A. Stapleford, "'Housewife vs. Economist': Gender, Class, and Domestic Economic Knowledge in Twentieth-Century America," *Labor: Studies in Working-Class History of the Americas* 1, no. 2 (2004): 89–112; Angie M. Boyce, "'When Does It Stop Being Peanut Butter?': FDA Food Standards of Identity, Ruth Desmond, and the Shifting Politics of Consumer Activism, 1960s–1970s," *Technology and Culture* 57, no. 1 (2016): 54–79.

54. Ernest C. Dickson to Dr. Chas. Thom, January 13, 1920, Box 1, Folder 9, Dickson Papers.

55. Charles Thom to Dr. E. C. Dickson, February 7, 1920, Box 1, Folder 9, Dickson Papers.

56. Ernest C. Dickson to Dr. Charles Thom, February 26, 1920, Box 1, Folder 9, Dickson Papers.

57. "Fear of Canned Olive Is Now Dispelled," *Ventura Free Press* (Ventura, CA), March 12, 1920, Box 4, Folder 1, Dickson Papers.

58. "Scientists Advance," 19. The Bureau of Chemistry began as the Division of Chemistry within the USDA. In 1927, its name was changed to the Food, Drug, and Insecticide Administration, and in 1930 to the Food and Drug Administration (FDA). "Significant Dates in U.S. Food and Drug Law History," FDA, November 6, 2012, www.fda.gov/AboutFDA/WhatWeDo/History/Milestones/ucm128305.htm.

59. K. F. Meyer and Ernest C. Dickson, "Outline of a Proposed Investigation of Botulism as It Occurs in California," statement submitted to R. I. Bentley, December 3, 1919, Box 1, Folder 5, Dickson Papers.

60. This also echoed the search for academic scientists without a "taint of commercialism" for the salts of tin research described in chapter 1.

61. Allan M. Brandt, *No Magic Bullet: A Social History of Venereal Disease in the United States since 1880* (New York: Oxford University Press, 1985); Karen Deane Ross, "Making Medicine Scientific: Simon Flexner and Experimental Medicine at the Rockefeller Institute for Medical Research, 1901–1945" (PhD diss., University of Minnesota, 2006); John Parascandola, *Sex, Sin, and Science: A History of Syphilis in America* (Westport, CT: Praeger, 2008).

62. J. J. Hoey to R. I. Bentley, November 28, 1921, Folder 1, Box 7, Dickson Papers.

63. John Weinzirl, "The Bacteriology of Canned Foods," *Journal of Medical Research* 39, no. 3 (January 1919): 411.

64. Georgina S. Burke, "Spoiled Canned Foods and Botulism," *Journal of the American Medical Association* 73, no. 14 (October 4, 1919): 1078.

65. Ibid., 1079.

66. Ernest C. Dickson, memo attached to letter to R.I. Bentley, December 26, 1919, Box 1, Folder 5, Dickson Papers.

67. For comparison, the entire budget of the federal Public Health Service in 1915—for all research expenditures for social security, welfare, and health functions—was $416,000. A. Hunter Dupree, *Science in the Federal Government: A History of Policies and Activities to 1940* (Cambridge, MA: Belknap Press of Harvard University Press, 1957).

68. Sabin, *Karl Friedrich Meyer,* 290.

69. R.I. Bentley to Ray Lyman Wilbur, April 13, 1922, Folder 1, Box 7, Dickson Papers.

70. Keuchel, "Development." Because public health regulation at the city level originated on the East Coast, most notably with the creation of New York City's Metropolitan Board of Health in 1866, eastern canners undoubtedly came into close contact with well-established health departments in the late nineteenth and early twentieth centuries. Charles E. Rosenberg, *The Cholera Years: The United States in 1832, 1849, and 1866* (Chicago: University of Chicago Press, 1987); Judith Walzer Leavitt, "'Be Safe, Be Sure': New York City's Experience with Epidemic Smallpox," in *Sickness and Health in America: Readings in the History of Medicine and Public Health,* ed. Judith Walzer Leavitt and Ronald L. Numbers, 3rd ed. (Madison: University of Wisconsin Press, 1997), 407–17.

71. Research Committee, *What Every Canner Should Know,* Bulletin No. 89A (Washington, DC: NCA, 1922), 3, NCA Archives at the Grocery Manufacturers Association headquarters in Washington, DC (hereafter GMA Library).

72. "Industry Saved by Guinea Pigs," *Los Angeles Times,* September 22, 1920, sec. II.

73. "Resolutions of the California State Board of Health in Regard to the Processing of Ripe Olives," September 3, 1920, Box 1, Folder 4, Dickson Papers.

74. Even before the conversation began about processing standards, the olive packers pushed back against government suggestions (from the federal Bureau of Chemistry) that they stop packing olives in glass, in early March 1920. As cited from FDA Records in Young, "Botulism," 387.

75. Dr. Ernest C. Dickson to Frank Simonds, April 13, 1920, Box 1, Folder 6, Dickson Papers.

76. Ernest C. Dickson, "Memorandum to the Olive Packers of California," July 14, 1920, Box 1, Folder 4, Dickson Papers.

77. Frank Simonds to Prof. E.C. Dickson, August 2, 1920, Box 1, Folder 2, Dickson Papers.

78. Geiger, Dickson, and Meyer, *Epidemiology of Botulism,* 105.

79. Sabin, *Karl Friedrich Meyer,* 291. James Harvey Young writes that this set of findings suggested that botulism was a "disease of civilization." Young, "Botulism," 384.

80. Sabin, *Karl Friedrich Meyer,* 290.

81. Louis Pasteur, "On the Extension of the Germ Theory, to the Etiology of Certain Common Disease," in *Medicine and Western Civilization,* ed. David J. Rothman (New Brunswick, NJ: Rutgers University Press, 1995), 253–57. There was also a long tradition of industrial research in Germany, back to the 1870s and 1880s. John Beer, "Coal Tar Dye Manufacture and the Origins of the Modern Industrial Research Laboratory," *Isis* 49 (1958): 124. Such research grew increasingly common in the 1920s, but some of it apparently still carried a stigma. See Leonard S. Reich, *The Making of American Industrial Research: Science and Business at GE and Bell, 1876–1926* (New York: Cambridge University Press, 1985).

82. Ernest C. Dickson to R. I. Bentley, December 3, 1921, Box 1, Folder 7, Dickson Papers.

83. Many historians have written about the conflicts that emerged when professional scientists began to work for industry in the early twentieth century as they struggled to adapt their research and publication practices to a new setting. George Wise, "A New Role for Professional Scientists in Industry: Industrial Research at General Electric, 1900–1916," *Technology and Culture* 21, no. 3 (July 1, 1980): 408–29; Leonard S. Reich, "Edison, Coolidge, and Langmuir: Evolving Approaches to American Industrial Research," *Journal of Economic History* 47, no. 2 (June 1, 1987): 341–51.

84. Research Committee, *What Every Canner Should Know,* 3. Businesses were involved in public health in a variety of ways during the early twentieth century, from creating foundations for public health research to dealing with workplace safety issues. But the canning industry was unusual in its use of science and regulation in winning the trust of consumers, relative to its own products. John Ettling, *The Germ of Laziness: Rockefeller Philanthropy and Public Health in the New South* (Cambridge, MA: Harvard University Press, 1981); David Rosner, *Deadly Dust: Silicosis and the Politics of Occupational Disease in Twentieth-century America* (Princeton, NJ: Princeton University Press, 1991); Christopher C. Sellers, *Hazards of the Job from Industrial Disease to Environmental Health Science* (Chapel Hill: University of North Carolina Press, 1997); John Farley, *To Cast Out Disease: A History of the International Health Division of the Rockefeller Foundation (1913–1951)* (Oxford: Oxford University Press, 2004).

85. David Rosner, ed., *Hives of Sickness: Public Health and Epidemics in New York City* (New Brunswick, NJ: Rutgers University Press, 1995); Nayan Shah, *Contagious Divides: Epidemics and Race in San Francisco's Chinatown* (Berkeley: University of California Press, 2001); Howard Markel, *When Germs Travel: Six Major Epidemics That Have Invaded America since 1900 and the Fears They Have Unleashed* (New York: Pantheon Books, 2004).

86. The first decades of the twentieth century saw an increase in the size of the federal government, with legislation like the Pure Food and Drug Act regulating more aspects of American business and consumer products. This dovetailed with the rise of federal oversight of public health programs. All of these movements prepared Americans for the dramatic growth in the government under the New Deal. James Harvey Young, *Pure Food: Securing the Federal*

Food and Drugs Act of 1906 (Princeton, NJ: Princeton University Press, 1989); David M. Kennedy, *Freedom from Fear: The American People in Depression and War, 1929–1945* (New York: Oxford University Press, 2004).

87. David M. Kennedy, *Over Here: The First World War and American Society*, 25th anniversary ed. (New York: Oxford University Press, 2004).

88. Before the 1912 US Public Health Service, public health at the federal level largely oversaw medical inspection of immigrants, in conjunction with the Marine Hospital Service. Amy L. Fairchild, *Science at the Borders: Immigrant Medical Inspection and the Shaping of the Modern Industrial Labor Force* (Baltimore: Johns Hopkins University Press, 2003). The establishment of the New York City Metropolitan Board of Health in 1866 marks early assumption of public health responsibility on the part of municipal governments. Rosenberg, *Cholera Years*.

89. Wilton L. Halverson, "History of Public Health in California," *Bulletin of the Medical Library Association* 37, no. 1 (1949): 59–61; "Agency History" and "Records of the Bureau of Food and Drug Inspections, 1933–1956," Inventory of the Records of the Department of Public Health, Collection Number R384, California State Archives, Online Archive of California, www.oac.cdlib .org/. Many historians have written about general public health oversight in California, especially as related to contagious disease. See, for example, Susan Craddock, *City of Plagues: Disease, Poverty, and Deviance in San Francisco* (Minneapolis: University of Minnesota Press, 2000).

90. California had made provisions for a state analyst in 1885, who could use laboratory procedures to determine the composition of processed foods and thereby prevent adulteration. The law was entitled "An Act to Provide for Analyzing the Minerals, Mineral Waters, and Other Liquids and the Medicinal Plants of the State of California, and of Food and Drugs, to Prevent the Adulteration of the Same," March 9, 1885. Stephanie Fuglaar Statz, "California's Fruit Cocktail: The Industrial Food Supply, The State, and the Environment of Northern California" (PhD diss., University of Houston, 2012); "Botulism a Reportable Disease in California," *Public Health Reports* 35, no. 17 (April 23, 1920): 997.

91. Charles Thom, "Botulism from the Regulatory Viewpoint," *American Journal of Public Health* 12, no. 1 (January 1922): 50.

92. Stuart Galishoff, *Safeguarding the Public Health: Newark, 1895–1918* (Westport, CT: Greenwood Press, 1975); Judith Walzer Leavitt, *The Healthiest City: Milwaukee and the Politics of Health Reform* (Princeton, NJ: Princeton University Press, 1982); Mitchell Okun, *Fair Play in the Marketplace: The First Battle for Pure Food and Drugs* (Dekalb: Northern Illinois University Press, 1986); Leavitt, *Typhoid Mary*; Ronald F. Wright and Paul Huck, "Counting Cases about Milk, Our 'Most Nearly Perfect' Food, 1860–1940," *Law and Society Review* 36, no. 1 (January 1, 2002): 51–112; Kendra Smith-Howard, *Pure and Modern Milk: An Environmental History since 1900* (New York: Oxford University Press, 2013).

93. R. E. Doolittle, "Botulism Problem in the United States," paper presented at the 25th Annual Convention of the Association of Dairy, Food, and Drug Officials, *Canner/Packer* 53, no. 25 (December 1921): 30.

94. W. M. Dickie to Mr. B. B. Meek, December 1, 1924, Cal. Dept. Pub. Health, Box 2, Folder 22.

95. W. M. Dickie to Mr. B. B. Meek, December 4, 1924, Cal. Dept. Pub. Health, Box 2, Folder 22.

96. "Botulism a Reportable Disease," 997; California State Board of Health, "Some Suggestions Dealing with the Methods of Investigation of Food Poisoning Outbreaks," Cal. Dept. Pub. Heath, Box 2, Folder 22.

97. California State Board of Health, "Some Suggestions."

98. "Canners Sue for Million," *New York Times,* June 11, 1921.

99. Preston Mckinney to the Canners League of California members, April 1, 1921, Box 1, Folder 8, Dickson Papers.

100. The Division of Cannery Inspection is mentioned in W. M. Dickie to Glenn D. Wiles, November 18, 1925, Cal. Dept. Pub. Health, Box 2, Folder 22; the Cannery Inspection Law in Frank Simonds to W. M. Dickie, September 15, 1925, Cal. Dept. Pub. Health Box 2, Folder 22.

101. For the spinach regulations, see Preston Mckinney to the Canners League of California members, April 1, 1921, Box 1, Folder 8. For the quotation, see W. M. Dickie to Glenn D. Wiles, November 18, 1925, Cal. Dept. Pub. Health, Box 2, Folder 22.

102. Canners League of California, "Request for $151,449 from General Fund," March 28, 1951, Cal. Dept. Pub. Health, Box 2, Folder 22. In this letter, the Canners League requested that the state take over some of the cost of cannery inspection. We have no record of the outcome.

103. "Ripe Olives to Be Advertised," *Canner* 53, no. 20 (November 1921): 41.

104. Canners League of California, Bulletin No. 228-A, April 1, 1921, Box 1, Folder 7, Dickson Papers.

105. The USDA began a more focused study of time-temperature relations for different fruits and vegetables in the wake of the botulism research. USDA, "A Study of the Factors Affecting Temperature Changes in the Container during the Canning of Fruits and Vegetables," Bulletin 956, cited in "Temperature at Center of Can Important in Canning," *Canner* 53, no. 11 (September 1921): 28.

106. "What Canners Are Doing to Gain Confidence of Consumer," *Canner* 53, no. 20 (November 1921): 31. Other researchers, like M. J. Rosenau, A. W. Bitting, and George Thompson also carried out work on time-temperature controls and heat penetration. See Petrick, "Arbiters of Taste," chap. 1; George E. Thompson, "Temperature-Time Relations in Canned Foods during Sterilization," *Journal of Industrial and Engineering Chemistry* 11 (July 1919): 657–64.

107. NCA Information Division, "NCA Laboratories Perform Vital Educational Function for Canning Industry Members," press release, May 21, 1963, 3, GMA Library.

108. "California Olive Packers Planning Big Publicity Campaign," *Canner* 50, no. 20 (May 1920): 54.

109. W. V. Cruess, "Making the Olive Palatable," *American Food Journal* 16, no. 10 (October 1921): 7–10; "Offer Ripe Olive Recipes," *American Food Journal* 16, no. 7 (July 1921): 46.

4. GRADE A TOMATOES

1. On the rise of supermarkets as a product of the politics of mass consumption and women's work, see Tracey Deutsch, *Building a Housewife's Paradise: Gender, Politics, and American Grocery Stores in the Twentieth Century* (Chapel Hill: University of North Carolina Press, 2012).

2. US Department of Agriculture, Bureau of Agricultural Economics, Regulations of the Secretary of Agriculture under the United States Warehouse Act, as Amended Regulations for Warehousemen Storing Canned Foods, September 1926.

3. The country's main tomato-growing state, Indiana, carried out a series of agricultural experiments in the 1930s, in which individual fruits were tagged for quality. Fay C. Gaylord, "Buying Tomatoes on Grade: Facts and Figures from Nineteen-Thirty," *Canner* 72, no. 11 (February 28, 1931): 17–20.

4. This evocative phrase was used throughout canning trade journals and elsewhere, especially in the 1930s. For one example, see F. M. Shook, "What Is in 7 Billion Cans," *Journal of Home Economics* 30, no. 7 (1938): 455.

5. Historian Lizabeth Cohen has offered the major contributions on consumers in the New Deal, in her *Making a New Deal: Industrial Workers in Chicago, 1919–1939* (Cambridge: Cambridge University Press, 1990) and *A Consumers' Republic: The Politics of Mass Consumption in Postwar America* (New York: Vintage, 2004). Another crucial work is Meg Jacobs, *Pocketbook Politics: Economic Citizenship in Twentieth-Century America,* Politics and Society in Twentieth-Century America (Princeton, NJ: Princeton University Press, 2005).

6. Caroline F. Ware, *The Cultural Approach to History* (New York: Columbia University Press, 1940).

7. Susan Strasser, Charles McGovern, and Matthias Judt, eds., *Getting and Spending: European and American Consumer Societies in the Twentieth Century* (Washington, DC: German Historical Institute, 1998); Landon R. Y. Storrs, *Civilizing Capitalism: The National Consumers' League, Women's Activism, and Labor Standards in the New Deal Era* (Chapel Hill: University of North Carolina Press, 2000); L. Cohen, *Consumer's Republic;* Charles McGovern, *Sold American: Consumption and Citizenship, 1890–1945* (Chapel Hill: University of North Carolina Press, 2006); Jacobs, *Pocketbook Politics.*

8. Jane Ziegelman and Andrew Coe, *A Square Meal: A Culinary History of the Great Depression* (New York: Harper, 2016).

9. David M. Kennedy, *Freedom from Fear: The American People in Depression and War, 1929–1945* (New York: Oxford University Press, 2004); Ellis W. Hawley, *The New Deal and the Problem of Monopoly: A Study in Economic Ambivalence* (Washington, DC: Fordham University Press, 1995). Michael Bernstein has written about how the sudden contraction in credit and demand during the Depression kept emerging industries, like canning, from gaining traction, thus prolonging the Depression. Michael A. Bernstein, "Why the Great Depression Was Great: Toward a New Understanding of the Interwar Economic Crisis in the United States," in *The Rise and Fall of the New Deal Order, 1930–1980,* ed. Steven Fraser and Gary Gerstle (Princeton, NJ: Princeton University Press, 1989), 32–54.

10. Alan Brinkley, *The End of Reform: New Deal Liberalism in Recession and War* (New York: Alfred A. Knopf, 1995).

11. Dexter M. Keezer, "The Consumer under the National Recovery Administration," *Annals of the American Academy of Political and Social Science* 172 (March 1, 1934): 97.

12. Persia Campbell, *Consumer Representation in the New Deal* (New York: Columbia University Press, 1940), 171.

13. Joseph Gaer, *Consumers All: The Problem of Consumer Protection* (New York: Harcourt, Brace, 1940); McGovern, *Sold American;* Jacobs, *Pocketbook Politics.*

14. US National Recovery Administration Consumers' Advisory Board, *Testimony on standards for consumer goods at canning industry hearing, before Deputy Administrator Walter White* (Washington, DC: Government Printing Office, 1934), 12.

15. Franklin D. Roosevelt, *State of the Union Addresses of Franklin D. Roosevelt* (Teddington, Middlesex: Echo Library, 2007), 7.

16. Robert S. Lynd, foreword to Campbell, *Consumer Representation,* 10.

17. Stuart Chase, *Your Money's Worth: A Study in the Waste of the Consumer's Dollar* (New York: Macmillan, 1927); Arthur Kallet, *100,000,000 Guinea Pigs; Dangers in Everyday Foods, Drugs, and Cosmetics* (New York: Grosset and Dunlap, 1933); F. J. Schlink, *Eat, Drink and Be Wary* (Washington, NJ: Consumers' Research, 1935); Lawrence Glickman, "The Strike in the Temple of Consumption: Consumer Activism and Twentieth-Century American Political Culture," *Journal of American History* 88, no. 1 (June 2001): 12.

18. "CR: Comedy Relief," *Business Week* (October 12, 1935): 30, cited in Glickman, "Strike in the Temple," 107.

19. Margaret Mary Finnegan offers the former story, in showing how suffragists in the early twentieth century bought into capitalist ideas in promoting their cause, in *Selling Suffrage: Consumer Culture and Votes for Women* (New York: Columbia University Press, 1999); Sheryl Kroen, in contrast, explores how consumer activism offered an alternative to pure capitalism in "A Political History of the Consumer," *Historical Journal* 47, no. 3 (2004): 709–736. Glickman, "Strike in the Temple."

20. L. Cohen, *Consumers' Republic.*

21. Frank E. Gorrell, *Annual Report of Secretary, Twenty-Third Annual Convention of the National Canners Association* (Chicago, January 1930), 12, NCA Archives, Grocery Manufacturers Association headquarters in Washington, DC (hereafter GMA Library).

22. Tracey Deutsch, "From 'Wild Animal Stores' to Women's Sphere: Supermarkets and Mass Consumption, 1930–1950," *Business and Economic History* 28, no. 1 (Fall 1999): 145.

23. Meg Jacobs, "'Democracy's Third Estate': New Deal Politics and the Construction of a 'Consuming Public,'" *International Labor and Working-Class History* 55 (Spring 1999): 42–43.

24. National Recovery Administration, press release no. 2, June 25, 1933; Ben W. Lewis, "The 'Consumer' and 'Public' Interests under Public Regulation." *Journal of Political Economy* 46, no. 1 (February 1, 1938): 97–107.

25. Keezer, "Consumer," 93.

26. "Mary Harriman Rumsey Obituary," *Consumer Notes,* December 29, 1934; Alfonso A. Narvaez, "Dexter M. Keezer Is Dead at 95; Economist Gauged U.S. Outlook," *New York Times,* June 25, 1991.

27. Lewis, "'Consumer' and 'Public' Interests," 103–5.

28. Dexter M. Keezer, "Review of Consumer Representation in the New Deal by Persia Campbell," *American Economic Review* 31, no. 3 (1941): 675.

29. Ibid., 88–89.

30. Ibid., 95.

31. Susan Ware, *Holding Their Own: American Women in the 1930s* (Boston: Twayne, 1982).

32. Campbell, *Consumer Representation,* 168.

33. Jessie V. Coles, "Compulsory Grade Labeling," in *Marketing: The Yearbook of Agriculture* (Washington, DC: Government Printing Office, US Department of Agriculture, 1954), 164. Home economics centrally shaped discourse about diet and nutrition in the first half of the twentieth century. See Carolyn M. Goldstein, "Part of the Package: Home Economists in the Consumer Products Industries, 1920–1940," in *Rethinking Home Economics: Women and the History of a Profession,* ed. Sarah Stage and Virginia B. Vincenti (Ithaca, NY: Cornell University Press, 1997), 271–96.

34. Keezer, "Consumer," 93.

35. Jacobs, "'Democracy's Third Estate,'" 39. Jacobs explores the broader questions of how prices drove American political conflict in the twentieth century in her book *Pocketbook Politics.*

36. Campbell, *Consumer Representation,* 175.

37. US Department of Agriculture, Farm Service Agency, "The United States Warehouse Act," n.d., accessed August 13, 2017, www.fsa.usda.gov/Internet /FSA_File/aboutuswa.pdf.

38. Faith M. Williams and Ethel D. Hoover, "Measuring Price and Quality of Consumers' Goods," *Journal of Marketing* 10, no. 4 (April 1946): 354–69.

39. Fay C. Gaylord, "Buying Tomatoes on Graded Basis: The Mechanics of Grading," *Canner* 70, no. 13 (1930): 13; Fay C. Gaylord, "Buying Tomatoes on Graded Basis: Three Years' Results," *Canner* 70, no. 14 (1930): 17; Fay C. Gaylord, "Buying Tomatoes on Graded Basis: Dangers Ahead," *Canner* 70, no. 15 (1930): 15; Gaylord, "Buying Tomatoes on Grade: Facts and Figures."

40. Gaylord, "Buying Tomatoes on Graded Basis: The Mechanics," 13.

41. Ibid., 14.

42. Gaylord, "Buying Tomatoes on Graded Basis: Three Years' Results," 19.

43. Coles, "Compulsory Grade Labeling," 164.

44. Howard R. Smith, *Historical Summary of Standards for Canned Foods* (Washington, DC: National Canners Association, March 1955), 6, GMA Library.

45. Campbell, *Consumer Representation,* 174.

46. CAB, "Grade Labeling of Canned Foods: A Report Made by the Consumers Advisory Board to Division Administrator Armin W. Riley, December 21, 1934," in folder "Canning Code, Labeling Question," General Correspondence, September 1933–January 1936, 1935 C, Box 16, Entry 358, Records of

the Industrial Advisory Board, Records of Advisory Bodies; Records of the National Recovery Administration, Record Group 9, National Archives at College Park, College Park, MD, p. 18553–6.

47. Ibid., 18553–2. However, instead of A, B, and C, Canadian canners used "Fancy" "Choice," and "Standard" to denote the same levels. This still offered the distinct, "graded" divisions of the grade-labeling plan, rather than the descriptive-labeling plan's suggestion of identifying each can according to a variety of characteristics.

48. NCA, *Canned Food Labels That Meet Consumer Needs* (Washington, DC: NCA, 1941), 2, GMA Library.

49. "The Labeling Front," *Canner* 79, no. 21 (1934): 21.

50. H. Smith, *Historical Summary,* 10.

51. "Tomato and Tomato Products Section, 28th Annual Convention of the National Canners Association and Meetings of Allied Groups at Chicago," *Canner* 80 (February 9, 1935): 41.

52. In the back-and-forth of this debate, many new factors emerged that the NRA thought would push the canners in the direction of grade labeling. For example, the country's largest chain, A&P, released its own line of grade-labeled goods in November 1934. The Bureau of Home Economics hoped that the NCA would follow suit. "Economics Bureau Presses Campaign for New Labeling," *Journal of Commerce and Commercial Bulletin,* November 30, 1934, in folder "Canning Code, Labeling Question," General Correspondence, September 1933–January 1936, 1935 C, Box 16, Entry 358, Records of the Industrial Advisory Board, Records of Advisory Bodies. Records of the National Recovery Administration, Record Group 9, National Archives at College Park, College Park, MD.

53. A. L. A. Schechter Poultry Corp. v. United States Citation. 295 U.S. 495, 55 S. Ct. 837, 79 L. Ed. 1570, 1935 U.S. New Deal Network. FDR and the Supreme Court, http://newdeal.feri.org/court/295US495.htm.

54. Jacobs, "'Democracy's Third Estate,'" 27.

55. See Deutsch, *Building a Housewife's Paradise.*

56. Keezer, "Consumer," 676.

57. Walton H. Hamilton, "The Consumer's Front," *Survey Graphic* 24 (November 1935): 524–28, cited in Lawrence B. Glickman, *Buying Power: A History of Consumer Activism in America* (Chicago: University of Chicago Press, 2009), 190.

58. M. C. Phillips and F. J. Schlink, *Discovering Consumers* (New York: John Day, 1934), 7, cited in Glickman, "Strike in the Temple," 100.

59. Women had long been considered responsible for shopping, and especially for buying food. See, for example, Dana Frank, "Housewives, Socialists, and the Politics of Food: The 1917 New York Cost-of-Living Protests," *Feminist Studies* 11, no. 2 (July 1, 1985): 255–85; Jeanne Boydston, *Home and Work: Housework, Wages, and the Ideology of Labor in the Early Republic* (New York: Oxford University Press, 1990).

60. "'Get Government Out of Business,' Committee Tells Congress," *Canner* 76, no. 10 (n.d.): 10.

61. NCA, Committee on Labeling, "Final Report of the Committee on Labeling, Appointed Pursuant to the Executive Order of May 29, 1934 to

the Administrator for Industrial Recovery," September 26, 1934, 7, GMA Library.

62. H. W. Phelps, "The Consumer and Canned Food Labels," *Canner* 79, no. 25 (1934): 8.

63. Kathleen A. Laughlin and Jacqueline L. Castledine, eds., *Breaking the Wave: Women, Their Organizations, and Feminism, 1945–1985* (New York: Routledge, 2011).

64. Don S. Anderson, "The Consumer and the Agricultural Adjustment Administration," *Journal of Marketing 1*, no. 1 (July 1936): 3.

65. Nell B. Nichols, "What Kind of Labeling Do Housewives Favor?," *Canner* 80, no. 18 (1935): 7–8.

66. Campbell, *Consumer Representation,* 175–76.

67. Ibid., 178.

68. NCA, Committee on Labeling, "Final Report," 5.

69. Phelps, "Consumer," 20.

70. NCA, Committee on Labeling, "Final Report," 7.

71. "Address of Howard A. Orr," *Canner* 80, no. 10 (1935): 19.

72. "Address of H. J. Carr," *Canner* 80, no. 10 (1935): 17.

73. NCA, Committee on Labeling, "Final Report," 4.

74. Ibid., 5.

75. Ibid.

76. Campbell, *Consumer Representation,* 178.

77. NCA, Committee on Labeling, "Final Report," 5.

78. Ibid., 6.

79. Campbell, *Consumer Representation,* 168, 178.

80. Coles, "Compulsory Grade Labeling," 169.

81. "Suggested Letter to Be Written by the Chemical Alliance, Incorporated to the Members of the Chemical Manufacturing Industry Giving Them the Lowdown on the Chemical Manufacturing Industry Code," 1934, File 19, Willis F. Harrington Papers, Hagley Museum and Library, Wilmington, DE, cited in *Major Problems in American History, 1920–1945: Documents and Essays,* ed. Colin Gordon (Boston: Houghton Mifflin, 1999), 305–7. Kim Phillips-Fein has written about an influential group of American businessmen who fought against New Deal liberalism, paving the way for conservative politics in the later twentieth century: *Invisible Hands: The Businessmen's Crusade against the New Deal* (New York: W. W. Norton, 2009).

82. "Display Unit Shows the Buyer Just What's in the Can," *Canner* 76, no. 18 (April 15, 1933): 20.

83. "Canned Goods Grading: A Summary," *Consumer Notes,* December 29, 1934, 5.

84. "Testimony on Standards," 7.

85. Campbell, *Consumer Representation,* 168–69.

86. "Testimony on Standards," 6.

87. Ibid., 7.

88. Ibid., 11.

89. "What Relation Has the Price of Canned Foods to Quality?," *Canner* 79, no. 9 (1934): 10.

90. "Testimony on Standards," 5.

91. Ibid., 6.

92. There were twenty-one groups in all. "Testimony on Standards."

93. Ibid., 8, 11.

94. Gordon, *Major Problems*, 282.

95. "Testimony on Standards," 9.

96. Ibid., 11.

97. Ibid.

98. Keezer, "Consumer," 93; Coles, "Compulsory Grade Labeling."

99. Director of the Consumers' Division, "Memorandum to the Readers of the Consumer," *Consumer* 1, no. 6 (January 1, 1936): i.

100. Jacobs, "'Democracy's Third Estate,'" 44.

101. Ibid., 167–68. Coles, "Compulsory Grade Labeling," reports that a congressional committee investigated grade labeling in 1943, taking testimony from many industries but not from any consumer representatives. Amy Bentley, *Eating for Victory: Food Rationing and the Politics of Domesticity* (Urbana: University of Illinois Press, 1998), engages with World War II food conservation and rationing.

102. NCA, *Canned Food Labels*, 9.

103. Elmo Roper, "A Study of Certain Attitudes of Women toward Canned Fruits and Vegetables," NCA, June 1941, GMA Library.

104. Edward C. Hampe and Merle Wittenberg, *The Lifeline of America: Development of the Food Industry* (New York: McGraw-Hill, 1964), 130.

105. Carl Schmalz, "Why the Food Chains Need Research," *Chain Store Age, Administration Edition* 13 (1937): 38, cited in Deutsch, "From 'Wild Animal Stores,'" 147; US Bureau of the Census, *Historical Statistics of the United States, Colonial Times to 1970* (Washington, DC: US Department of Commerce, 1975).

106. Helen E. Goodrich, "Processed Foods Gain Vital Issue," *Western Grower and Shipper* 22 (1951): 25+, cited in Susanne Freidberg, *Fresh: A Perishable History* (Cambridge, MA: Harvard University Press, 2009), 185.

107. Keezer, "Consumer," 92. The statistics that Keezer gives are for the year 1929. There were three hundred thousand nonbanking corporations, with two hundred of them controlling half the wealth.

108. Adolf A. Berle and Gardiner C. Means, *The Modern Corporation and Private Property* (New York: Commerce Clearing House, 1932).

109. David Blanke, "Consumer Choice, Agency, and New Directions in Rural History," *Agricultural History* 81, no. 2 (April 1, 2007): 189.

110. Campbell, *Consumer Representation*, 23.

111. Scholars in business history and the history of capitalism have written about the story of branding to show the power these new schemes to transform production and consumption in the early twentieth century and after. See, for example, Douglas Ward, *A New Brand of Business: Charles Coolidge Parlin, Curtis Publishing Company, and the Origins of Market Research* (Philadelphia: Temple University Press, 2009); Nancy Koehn, *Brand New: How Entrepreneurs Earned Consumers' Trust from Wedgwood to Dell* (Cambridge, MA: Harvard University Press, 2001).

112. Kroen, "Political History," 729. See also Charles McGovern, "Consumption and Citizenship in the United States, 1900–1940," in Strasser, McGovern, and Judt, *Getting and Spending,* 56.

113. Paul D. Converse, "The Development of the Science of Marketing: An Exploratory Survey," *Journal of Marketing* 10, no. 1 (July 1, 1945): 19–22.

114. Douglas Collins, *America's Favorite Food: The Story of Campbell Soup Company* (Harry N. Abrams, 1994), 138–39.

115. Peter B. B. Andrews, "The Cigarette Market, Past and Future," *Advertising and Selling* (January 16, 1936), 27, cited in Allan M. Brandt, *The Cigarette Century: The Rise, Fall, and Deadly Persistence of the Product That Defined America* (New York: Basic Books, 2007), 77–78.

116. For examples of rural consumer agency, see Ronald R. Kline, *Consumers in the Country: Technology and Social Change in Rural America* (Baltimore: Johns Hopkins University Press, 2000).

117. Roland Marchand, *Advertising the American Dream: Making Way for Modernity, 1920–1940* (Berkeley: University of California Press, 1985); Jackson Lears, *Fables of Abundance: A Cultural History of Advertising in America* (New York: Basic Books, 1994); Pamela Walker Laird, *Advertising Progress: American Business and the Rise of Consumer Marketing* (Baltimore: Johns Hopkins University Press, 2001).

118. Collins, *America's Favorite Food,* 90–91.

119. Andrew F. Smith, *Souper Tomatoes* (New Brunswick, NJ: Rutgers University Press, 1999), 96–97.

120. Alice Kessler-Harris, *Out to Work: A History of Wage-Earning Woman in the United States* (New York: Oxford University Press, 1982).

121. Parkin cites the 1936 ad in Katherine Parkin, "Campbell's Soup and the Long Shelf Life of Traditional Gender Roles," in *Kitchen Culture in America: Popular Representations of Food, Gender, and Race,* ed. Sherrie A. Inness (Philadelphia: University of Pennsylvania Press, 2001), 59. See also Katherine Parkin, *Food Is Love: Food Advertising and Gender Roles in Modern America* (Philadelphia: University of Pennsylvania Press, 2006).

122. Roper, "Study of Certain Attitudes."

123. For more on this idea, see McGovern, *Sold American.*

5. FIGHTING FOR SAFE TUNA

1. Consumer quotation from "Mercury: Why Tuna Is Crossed Off the Shopping List," *New York Times,* December 20, 1970; Richard D. Lyons, "Mercury in Tuna Leads to Recall: F.D.A. Head Says They Don't Imperil Health; Millions Cans of Tainted Tuna Recalled," *New York Times,* December 16, 1970. This battle actually continues into the present; see Jane M. Hightower, *Diagnosis Mercury: Money, Politics, and Poison* (Washington, DC: Island Press/Shearwater Books, 2009), 185–252.

2. In this era, many Americans lost trust in the authority of science and medicine, as well as in government. Allan Mazur, "Public Confidence in Science," *Social Studies of Science* 7, no. 1 (February 1, 1977): 123–25; Susan Reverby, *Examining Tuskegee: The Infamous Syphilis Study and Its Legacy*

(Chapel Hill: University of North Carolina Press, 2009). For more on how the disenchantment with science connected to environmentalism, see Linda J. Lear, *Rachel Carson: Witness for Nature* (New York: Henry Holt, 1998); Adam Rome, "'Give Earth a Chance': The Environmental Movement and the Sixties," *Journal of American History* 90, no. 2 (September 2003): 525–54.

3. To twenty-first-century readers, all of these concerns may seem much more of their own era, connected to critiques of modern food activist Michael Pollan and others. See Michael Pollan, *The Omnivore's Dilemma: A Natural History of Four Meals* (New York: Penguin Press, 2006) and *In Defense of Food: An Eater's Manifesto* (New York: Penguin Press, 2008). But many of these same concerns were central among the complaints voiced by 1970s food activists, decades before the modern food movement. Industrialized food and its attendant cultural associations came under attack as part of the broader consumer and environmental movements of the 1960s and 1970s.

4. Janet Murray and Ennis Blake, "What Do We Eat?," in *Food: The Yearbook of Agriculture,* ed. US Department of Agriculture (hereafter USDA) (Washington, DC: Government Printing Office, 1959), 608.

5. Letitia Brewster and Michael F. Jacobson, *The Changing American Diet* (Washington, DC: Center for Science in the Public Interest, 1978). Tuna was first canned in 1903 but grew so dramatically in popularity that by the end of World War II it had eclipsed salmon as Americans' favorite canned fish for the first time. By the 1950s, tuna began its "fall," as Japan sent frozen tuna to the United States and as environmental problems like dolphin bycatch and mercury contamination plagued the industry. Andrew F. Smith, *American Tuna: The Rise and Fall of an Improbable Food* (Berkeley: University of California Press, 2012).

6. Campbell Soup Company, *Easy Ways to Good Meals: 99 Delicious Dishes Made with Campbell's Soups* (Camden, N.J: Campbell Soup Company, 1941), 16; A. Smith, *American Tuna,* 79.

7. See chap. 7 of Harvey A. Levenstein, *Paradox of Plenty: A Social History of Eating in Modern America* (New York: Oxford University Press, 1993). This was also the era when beverages, from beer to soda, began to be canned, with the introduction of aluminum cans in 1957. Quentin R. Skrabec, *Aluminum in America: A History* (Jefferson, NC: McFarland, 2016). By 1975, the technology to open cans had also evolved, from the church-key opening to pull tabs to the stay-put tabs we have today. Henry Petroski, *The Evolution of Useful Things: How Everyday Artifacts—From Forks and Pins to Paper Clips and Zippers—Came to Be as They Are* (1992; repr., New York: Vintage, 1994); Henry Petroski, *Invention by Design: How Engineers Get from Thought to Thing* (Cambridge, MA: Harvard University Press, 1996).

8. USDA, *Consumption of Food in the United States, 1909–52,* USDA Handbook 62 (Washington, DC: Government Printing Office, 1953), 147; Gabriella Petrick, "Industrial Food," in *The Oxford Handbook of Food History,* ed. Jeffrey M. Pilcher (New York: Oxford University Press, 2012), 258–78.

9. Kellen Backer, "World War II and the Triumph of Industrialized Food" (PhD diss., University of Wisconsin-Madison, 2012), 49, 157.

10. Ibid., 161, 159. See also Anastacia Marx de Salcedo, *Combat-Ready Kitchen: How the U.S. Military Shapes the Way You Eat* (New York: Penguin, 2015).

11. Howard R. Smith, *Historical Summary of Standards for Canned Foods* (Washington, DC: NCA, March 1955), 6, NCA Archives, Grocery Manufacturers Association headquarters in Washington, DC (hereafter GMA Library).

12. Frederick Arthur Stare, *The Story of Wisconsin's Great Canning Industry* (Baltimore: Canning Trade, 1949), 298–300.

13. Nathan Balke and Robert J. Gordon, "Appendix B: Historical Data," in *The American Business Cycle: Continuity and Change*, ed. Robert J. Gordon (Chicago: University of Chicago Press, 1986), 783.

14. Stephanie Coontz, *The Way We Never Were: American Families and the Nostalgia Trap* (New York: Basic Books, 1992); Laura Shapiro, *Something from the Oven: Reinventing Dinner in 1950s America* (New York: Viking Press, 2004); Elaine Tyler May, *Homeward Bound: American Families in the Cold War Era*, rev. and updated 20th anniversary ed. (New York: Basic Books, 2008); Sarah T. Phillips and Shane Hamilton, *The Kitchen Debate and Cold War Consumer Politics: A Brief History with Documents* (Boston: Bedford/St. Martin's, 2014).

15. William Braznell, *California's Finest: The History of the Del Monte Corporation and the Del Monte Brand* (San Francisco: Del Monte Corporation, 1982).

16. Edmund Russell, *War and Nature: Fighting Humans and Insects with Chemicals from World War I to Silent Spring* (Cambridge: Cambridge University Press, 2001); Deborah Kay Fitzgerald, *Every Farm a Factory: The Industrial Ideal in American Agriculture* (New Haven, CT: Yale University Press, 2003).

17. Allen Long, "Chef Founds Canning Industry," *Science News-Letter* 62, no. 16 (October 18, 1952): 250–51.

18. Crucially, the rise of trucking during the 1950s and 1960s allowed for goods to be shipped to supermarkets, giving food processors a more direct path to their consumers. Shane Hamilton, *Trucking Country: The Road to America's Wal-Mart Economy* (Princeton, NJ: Princeton University Press, 2008).

19. See Eric Schlosser, *Fast Food Nation: The Dark Side of the All-American Meal* (Boston: Houghton Mifflin, 2001); Theodore Steinberg, *Down to Earth: Nature's Role in American History* (Oxford: Oxford University Press, 2002), 190–205; Nicolaas John Mink, "The Restaurant: Food, Power, and Social Change" (PhD diss., University of Wisconsin-Madison, 2010).

20. Tracey Deutsch, *Building a Housewife's Paradise: Gender, Politics, and American Grocery Stores in the Twentieth Century* (Chapel Hill: University of North Carolina Press, 2012).

21. A. Smith, *Eating History*, 71.

22. "How Pure Is Your Food?," *U.S. News and World Report*, December 7, 1959.

23. Trade article quote from B. E. W. Williams, "Frozen Foods 2000 A.D.: A Fantasy of the Future," *Quick Frozen Foods*, February 1954, 108. For more on food chemistry and additives, see Levenstein, *Paradox of Plenty;* Shapiro, *Something from the Oven;* Institute of Food Technologists, "Our History," n.d., accessed March 12, 2013, www.ift.org/about-us/our-history.aspx.

24. Shane Hamilton, "The Economies and Conveniences of Modern-Day Living: Frozen Foods and Mass Marketing, 1945–1965," *Business History Review* 77, no. 1 (April 1, 2003): 33–60; Backer, "World War II"; Mark Kurlansky, *Birdseye: The Adventures of a Curious Man* (New York: Doubleday, 2012); Jonathan Rees, *Refrigeration Nation: A History of Ice, Appliances, and Enterprise in America* (Baltimore: Johns Hopkins University Press, 2013).

25. Kurlansky, *Birdseye*, 191. *Wisconsin Canners and Freezers Association 75th Anniversary: November 12, 13, 14, 1979* (Madison: Wisconsin Canners and Freezers Association, 1979), 7.

26. Kurlansky, *Birdseye*, 182.

27. *Wisconsin Canners and Freezers Association*, 21; Kurlansky, *Birdseye*, 172.

28. Minnie B. Tracey, "The Present Status of Frozen Food Marketing," *Journal of Marketing* 13, no. 4 (April 1, 1949): 470–80; Murray and Blake, "What Do We Eat?," 608.

29. NCA, *The ABC's of Canned Foods* (Washington, DC: NCA, 1961), 6.

30. Although there is some evidence that women actually did spend less time on food preparation—with one source citing the figure less than twenty hours in 1968 compared to the average twenty-three hours in 1926—they also spent more time on general housework by the 1950s. Ruth Schwartz Cowan, *More Work for Mother: The Ironies of Household Technology from the Open Hearth to the Microwave* (New York: Basic Books, 1983); Laura Schenone, *A Thousand Years over a Hot Stove: A History of American Women Told through Food, Recipes, and Remembrances* (New York: W. W. Norton, 2004).

31. From *Life* magazine, 1954, cited in Thomas Hine, *Populuxe* (New York: Knopf, 1986), 24.

32. *U.S. News and World Report*, February 15, 1957, cited in Levenstein, *Paradox of Plenty*, 108.

33. Shapiro, *Something from the Oven*; Katherine Parkin, *Food Is Love: Food Advertising and Gender Roles in Modern America* (Philadelphia: University of Pennsylvania Press, 2006); Stefan Schwarzkopf and Rainer Gries, *Ernest Dichter and Motivation Research: New Perspectives on the Making of Post-war Consumer Culture* (Basingstoke: Palgrave Macmillan, 2010).

34. Kathleen G. Donohue, "What Gender Is the Consumer? The Role of Gender Connotations in Defining the Political," *Journal of American Studies* 33, no. 1 (April 1, 1999): 19–43; Jennifer Scanlon, ed., *The Gender and Consumer Culture Reader* (New York: New York University Press, 2000); Levenstein, *Paradox of Plenty*, 105–6; Schenone, *Thousand Years*; Parkin, *Food Is Love*; Nancy C. Unger, *Beyond Nature's Housekeepers: American Women in Environmental History* (Oxford: Oxford University Press, 2012).

35. Coontz, *Way We Never Were*; Parkin, *Food Is Love*.

36. NCA Information Division, "Today's Soup Stock Is in the Cupboard, Not on the Stove," press release, May 21, 1963, 2, GMA Library; NCA Information Division, "Preparing Today's Baby Food Is No Strain, Thanks to the Canning Industry," press release, May 21, 1963, 1, GMA Library.

37. NCA, foreword to *The ABC's of Canned Foods*.

38. Andy Warhol, *Campbell's Soup Cans*, synthetic polymer paint on thirty-two canvases, 1962, Museum of Modern Art; Gary Comenas, "The Origin of

Andy Warhol's Soup Cans or the Synthesis of Nothingness," *Warhol Stars,* 2010, www.warholstars.org/art/warhol/soup.html.

39. See, for example, the collection NCA Research Laboratories, *50 Years of Research, 1913–1963* (Washington, DC: NCA, 1963), GMA Library.

40. NCA Information Division, "Ask the National Canners Association," press release, May 21, 1963, 3, GMA Library.

41. NCA Information Division, "Fifty Years of Winning Public Confidence," press release, May 21, 1963, 1, GMA Library.

42. Ralph W. Johnston, John Feldman, and Rosemary Sullivan, "Botulism from Canned Tuna Fish," *Public Health Reports* 78, no. 7 (July 1963): 561–64. See chapter 3 for an analysis of the botulism outbreak in ripe olives in 1919–20.

43. "Marketing and Selling: The Tuna Scare," *Time,* April 26, 1963; "Mystery of the Tainted Tuna," *Life,* April 26, 1963; Gordon A. Eadie et al., "Type E Botulism: Report of an Outbreak in Michigan," *Journal of the American Medical Association* 187, no. 7 (February 15, 1964): 496–99.

44. Because there were cases of botulism in other kinds of fish also in 1963, the outbreaks led to increased investigations of the growth of the bacteria in fishery products, among those outside the canning industry. An international conference on botulism was held in Moscow in 1966. M. Ingram and T. A. Roberts, eds., *Botulism 1966: Proceedings of the Fifth International Symposium on Food Microbiology, Moscow, July 1966,* International Association of Microbiological Societies (London: Chapman and Hall, 1967); E. Emil Marcel Mrak, George Franklin Stewart, and C. O. Chichester, *Advances in Food Research* (New York: Academic Press, 1976), 137.

45. "Look Who's Feeding the Food Editors," *Changing Times: The Kiplinger Magazine,* July 1981; Levenstein, *Paradox of Plenty,* 18–19.

46. All quotations in this paragraph from Dennis H. Murphy, "Nobody Cares What a Canner Thinks," *Canner/Packer* 132, no. 5 (May 1963): 58.

47. National Association of Retail Grocers of the United States, "Canned Tuna Is Making Real Progress," *NARGUS Bulletin* 50 (1963): 28; "Marketing and Selling: Tuna Back in Favor," *Time,* November 29, 1963.

48. NCA Information Division, "NCA Laboratories Perform Vital Educational Function for Canning Industry Members," press release, May 21, 1963, 4, GMA Library.

49. Samuel A. Goldblith, *Samuel Cate Prescott, M.I.T. Dean and Pioneer Food Technologist,* vol. 1 (Trumbull, CT: Food and Nutrition Press, 1993); Institute of Food Technologists, "Our History."

50. E. F. Kohman, *Vitamins in Canned Foods,* Bulletin No. 19-L, 4th rev. (Washington, DC: NCA Research Laboratory, December 1937); NCA Information Division, "Fifty Years," 4.

51. NCA, *The Canning Industry: Its History, Importance, Organization, Methods, and the Public Service Values of Its Products* (Washington, DC: NCA, 1971), 38. One of the eminent nutritionists who spoke on behalf of the high vitamin content of canned food was none other than Dr. Fredrick J. Stare, of the Harvard University Department of Nutrition, the son of Fred A. Stare, of the Columbus Canning Company, who was an important figure in the agricultural research story of chapter 2. D. Mark Hegsted, "Fredrick John Stare

(1910–2002)," *Journal of Nutrition* 134, no. 5 (May 1, 2004): 1007–9. See also Levenstein, *Paradox of Plenty*, 15.

52. NCA Information Division, "NCA Foundation Concentrates on Long-Range Research," press release, NCA, May 21, 1963, 1, GMA Library.

53. Hightower, *Diagnosis Mercury*, 186; A. Smith, *American Tuna*, 152.

54. NCA Information Division, "NCA Foundation," 2.

55. Edward F. Keuchel, "The Development of the Canning Industry in New York State to 1960" (PhD diss., Cornell University, 1970), 362; V.S. Troy, J.M. Boyd, and J.F. Folinazzo, *Spoilage of Canned Foods Due to Leakage*, Metal Division, Research and Development Department (Chicago: Continental Can Company, 1963), GMA Library.

56. Scientific culture of the mid-twentieth century still encouraged scientists to remain impartial, so that when the tobacco industry sought to find a scientific director in 1954 many prominent scientists were suspicious of the offer. The food industry was thus a pioneer in this area. Allan M. Brandt, *The Cigarette Century: The Rise, Fall, and Deadly Persistence of the Product That Defined America* (New York: Basic Books, 2007); Robert Proctor, *Golden Holocaust: Origins of the Cigarette Catastrophe and the Case for Abolition* (Berkeley: University of California Press, 2011). Another example of industry cooptation of scientific research is the case of polyvinyl chloride research in the chemical industry: Gerald Markowitz and David Rosner, *Deceit and Denial: The Deadly Politics of Industrial Pollution* (Berkeley: University of California Press, 2002).

57. George P. Larrick, "The Teamwork of Research between NCA and Government Agencies," NCA press release, May 21, 1963, 2, GMA Library.

58. Dennis H. Murphy, "Maybe We Should Learn How to Milk the Cows, Too," *Canner/Packer* 134, no. 11 (October 1965): 62.

59. See chap. 8 of R. Douglas Hurt, *American Agriculture: A Brief History*, rev. ed. (West Lafayette, IN: Purdue University Press, 2002).

60. El Stark, "The Farm Bill Is a Very Bad Bill, Indeed," *Canner/Packer* 130, no. 7 (July 1961): 64.

61. Carlos Campbell, "Commercial Canning: What Does the Future Hold?," *Journal of Marketing* 26, no. 2 (April 1, 1962): 44–47. Even as Campbell bemoaned these changes, in 1963, there were still some 2,200 canning plants in the United States across forty-nine states, with about 15 percent each in New England and the South, 25 percent in the Upper Midwest, and 45 percent on the Pacific Coast. NCA, *The Canning Industry: Its History, Importance, Organization, Methods, and the Public Service Values of Its Products*, 5th ed. (Washington, DC: NCA, 1963), 27, GMA Library.

62. NCA, *ABC's of Canned Foods*, 28.

63. Although there had been advertising and promotion efforts before the war, the postwar efforts occurred at a larger scale. *Wisconsin Canners and Freezers Association*, 10; "Consumer and Trade Relations Program Continued," *Wisconsin Canners Bulletin*, February 27, 1959, 15; "NCA Inaugurates Restaurant Bulletin Series," *Wisconsin Canners Bulletin*, September 18, 1959, 95. Some of this research also affected the preparation of the product itself. See Robert J. Lenz, K.G. Weckel, and Antonieta Liwanag Gaddi, *Effects of Salt and Sweeteners on Quality Properties of Canned Peas*, Research Report, University

of Wisconsin, College of Agriculture, Experiment Station 27 (Madison: Experiment Station, College of Agriculture, University of Wisconsin, 1967).

64. William L. Wilkie and Elizabeth S. Moore, "Scholarly Research in Marketing: Exploring the '4 Eras' of Thought Development," *Journal of Public Policy and Marketing* 22, no. 2 (October 1, 2003): 116–46; Hartmut Berghoff, Uwe Spiekermann, and Philip Scranton, eds., *The Rise of Marketing and Market Research* (New York: Palgrave Macmillan, 2012).

65. Roland Marchand, *Advertising the American Dream: Making Way for Modernity, 1920–1940* (Berkeley: University of California Press, 1985); Jean M. Converse, *Survey Research in the United States: Roots and Emergence, 1890–1960* (Berkeley: University of California Press, 1987); Kenneth Lipartito, "Subliminal Seduction: The Politics of Consumer Research in Post-World War II America," in Berghoff, Spiekermann, and Scranton, *Rise of Marketing*, 215–36.

66. Peggy J. Kreshel, "John B. Watson at J. Walter Thompson: The Legitimation of 'Science' in Advertising," *Journal of Advertising* 19, no. 2 (1990): 49–60; Forrest Clements and Trienah Meyers, "How They Tell What We Want," in *Marketing: The Yearbook of Agriculture* (Washington, DC: USDA, 1954), 208.

67. Charles Winick, "Anthropology's Contributions to Marketing," *Journal of Marketing* 25, no. 5 (July 1, 1961): 53–60; Dorothy Ross, *The Origins of American Social Science* (Cambridge: Cambridge University Press, 1991).

68. Vance Packard, *Hidden Persuaders* (New York: D. McKay, 1957), 4; Lipartito, "Subliminal Seduction," 228.

69. National Association of Retail Grocers of the United States, "Canned Tuna"; "Marketing and Selling: Tuna Back in Favor."

70. Lizabeth Cohen, *A Consumers' Republic: The Politics of Mass Consumption in Postwar America* (New York: Vintage Books, 2004), 7. Alan Brinkley, in *The End of Reform: New Deal Liberalism in Recession and War* (New York: Alfred A. Knopf, 1995), also describes the emergence of a focus on mass consumption as a result of business growth and policy in the postwar years.

71. Historian Lawrence Glickman has recently questioned the idea that consumer activism disappeared during the 1940s and 1950s, instead claiming that it shows more continuity. Still, even he acknowledges that a "consumer movement" as a self-labeled entity was less forceful during these years. See chap. 8 of Lawrence B. Glickman, *Buying Power: A History of Consumer Activism in America* (Chicago: University of Chicago Press, 2009).

72. As cited in Gary S. Cross, *An All-Consuming Century: Why Commercialism Won in Modern America* (New York: Columbia University Press, 2000), 147.

73. John F. Kennedy, "Special Message to the Congress on Protecting the Consumer Interest," March 15, 1962, www.presidency.ucsb.edu/ws/?pid=9108; Glickman, *Buying Power.*

74. El Stark, "Let's Not Allow a "Consumers Department' to Be Set Up," *Canner/Packer* 130, no. 12 (November 1961): 52.

75. Dennis H. Murphy, "Sometimes It Is Better to Stay Home . . .," *Canner/Packer* 132, no. 3 (March 1963): 66.

76. Industry criticism of Food Additive Amendment from Dennis Murphy, "We've Never Solved the Problem of the Dirty Plant," *Canner/Packer* 134, no. 2 (February 1965): 64. Warren J. Belasco, *Appetite for Change: How the*

Counterculture Took On the Food Industry, 2nd ed. (Ithaca, NY: Cornell University Press, 2006), 136.

77. There had been previous concerns about pesticides, culminating in the passage of the 1954 Miller Act, which historians have argued reinforced the chemical industry and did not protect public health. Thomas R. Dunlap, *DDT: Scientists, Citizens, and Public Policy* (Princeton, NJ: Princeton University Press, 1981); Pete Daniel, *Toxic Drift: Pesticides and Health in the Post-World War II South* (Baton Rouge: Louisiana State University Press, 2005).

78. Mark H. Lytle, *The Gentle Subversive: Rachel Carson, Silent Spring, and the Rise of the Environmental Movement* (New York: Oxford University Press, 2007); Lisa H. Sideris and Kathleen Dean Moore, eds., *Rachel Carson: Legacy and Challenge* (Albany: State University of New York Press, 2008).

79. Roy G. Lucks, "Industrial Research—A Teamwork Operation," NCA press release, May 21, 1963, 4, GMA Library.

80. Charles S. Mayer, "Requiem for the Truth-in-Packaging Bill?," *Journal of Marketing* 30, no. 2 (April 1, 1966): 1–5.

81. "Export Trade, Tariffs, Labeling Controls, Processing and Packaging Innovations Challenge Canners," *Canner/Packer* 132, no. 2 (March 1963): 38.

82. Robert Sidney Dickens, "Prepare for Food Packaging Mediocrity under the Hart Bill Now—It May Pass," *Canner/Packer* 132, no. 10, Yearbook Number (September 25, 1963): 3.6.

83. Mayer, "Requiem?"; Cross, *All-Consuming Century*; Eric Wall, "A Comprehensive Look at the Fair Packaging and Labeling Act of 1966 and the FDA Regulation of Deceptive Labeling and Packaging Practices: 1906 to Today," May 2002, http://dash.harvard.edu/bitstream/handle/1/8846774/Wall.html?sequence=2; Glickman, *Buying Power*.

84. Wall, "Comprehensive Look."

85. NCA Information Division, "Canner Lucks and FDA Head Larrick Stress Teamwork in Research at Golden Anniversary of N.C.A. Laboratories," press release, May 21, 1963, 1, GMA Library; Lucks, "Industrial Research," 6; NCA Information Division, "Fifty Years"; NCA Information Division, "Ask the National Canners Association," 3.

86. Thomas J. Serb, "Credibility vs. Opportunity," *Canner/Packer* 139, no. 5 (May 1970): 56.

87. "Distinguished Contributors to 20th Century Food Processing," *Canner/Packer* 139, no. 6 (June 1970): 31.

88. Belasco, *Appetite for Change*; Michael Egan, *Barry Commoner and the Science of Survival: The Remaking of American Environmentalism* (Boston: MIT Press, 2007); Christopher Sellers, *Crabgrass Crucible: Suburban Nature and the Rise of Environmentalism in Twentieth-Century America* (Chapel Hill: University of North Carolina Press, 2012).

89. "IFT Explores New Directions," *Canner Packer* 146, no. 5 (May 1977): 50.

90. Ralph Nader, *Unsafe at Any Speed: The Designed-in Dangers of the American Automobile* (New York: Grossman, 1965); James S. Turner and Ralph Nader, *The Chemical Feast: The Ralph Nader Study Group Report on Food Protection and the Food and Drug Administration* (New York: Penguin Books,

1970); Michael F. Jacobson and Catherine Lerza, *Food for People, Not for Profit: A Source Book on the Food Crisis* (New York: Ballantine Books, 1975).

91. Frances Moore Lappé, *Diet for a Small Planet,* 20th anniversary ed. (New York: Ballantine Books, 1991), 8, 217; John McMillian and Paul Merlyn Buhle, *The New Left Revisited* (Philadelphia: Temple University Press, 2003); Levenstein, *Paradox of Plenty;* Belasco, *Appetite for Change.*

92. Just some of this legislation included the 1963 Clean Air Act, the 1964 Wilderness Act, the 1969 National Environmental Policy Act, the 1970 US Environmental Protection Agency, the 1972 Clean Water Act, and the 1974 Safe Drinking Water Act. James Morton Turner, *The Promise of Wilderness: American Environmental Politics since 1964* (Seattle: University of Washington Press, 2012).

93. Co-op Handbook Collective, *The Food Co-op Handbook: How to Bypass Supermarkets to Control the Quality and Price of Your Food* (Boston: Houghton Mifflin, 1975); Belasco, *Appetite for Change,* 87–94; Andrew N. Case, "Looking for Organic America: J.I. Rodale, the Rodale Press, and the Popular Culture of Environmentalism in the Postwar United States" (PhD diss., University of Wisconsin-Madison, 2012).

94. Michael F. Jacobson, Bonnie F. Liebman, and Greg Moyer, *Salt: The Brand Name Guide to Sodium Content,* Center for Science in the Public Interest (New York: Workman, 1983).

95. Jacobson and Lerza, *Food for People,* 8.

96. J.S. Turner and Nader, *Chemical Feast;* Jacobson and Lerza, *Food for People,* 21.

97. Michael Jacobson, Benjamin Rosenthal, and Marcy Boehm, "Professors on the Take," *Progressive* 40, no. 11 (1976).

98. Charles E. Neu, ed., *After Vietnam: Legacies of a Lost War* (Baltimore: Johns Hopkins University Press, 2000).

99. A.S. Clausi, "Modifying Foods—A Typical Attitude," *Canner Packer* 142, no. 2 (February 1973): 20.

100. Richard D. McCormick, "Product and Process Responses to a Moving Nutritional Target," *Canner/Packer* 145, no. 6 (June 1976): 50.

101. Jacobson and Lerza, *Food for People,* 19.

102. Tom Donnelly, "The New Way of Cooking," in Jacobson and Lerza, *Food for People,* 138–40.

103. "Communicating Scientific Information to the Consumer," *Canner/Packer* 142, no. 10 (October 1973): 8; Theodore P. Labuza, "Regulation of Nutrition or the Nutrition of Regulation," *Canner/Packer* 145, no. 6 (June 1976): 46.

104. Fritz C. Friday, "Regulation, Reason, Responsibility, Respect," in *Industry Speaks: A Presentation at the Annual Convention of the National Canners Association, San Francisco,* ed. NCA (Washington, DC: NCA, 1976), 19, GMA Library.

105. "A Rose by Any Other . . .," *Canner/Packer* 143, no. 7 (August 1974): 14.

106. James J. Albrecht, "Industry Platform: You'd Think They Were Dropping Like Flies," *Canner/Packer* 143, no. 7 (August 1974): 16.

107. "IFT Report, Part I: Ralph Nader, Magnus Pyke, Ethics and Research," *Canner Packer* 139, no. 7 (July 1970): 21.

108. Albrecht, "Industry Platform," 16.

109. Andrew McMeekin, Sally Randles, and Alan Warde, *History of Market Research: Intermediating Production and Consumption* (New York: Routledge, 2009).

110. Wilkie and Moore, "Scholarly Research in Marketing," 124–26; Dick R. Wittink, "Market Measurement and Analysis: The First 'Marketing Science' Conference," *Marketing Science* 20, no. 4 (October 1, 2001): 349–56.

111. "Consumers Change Eating and Food Buying Habits: Some Reasons Why and How," *Canner/Packer* 143, no. 7 (August 1974): 18–19; Paul A. Lachance, "Future Nutrition Regulations in Perspective," *Canner/Packer* 145, no. 6 (June 1976): 56; "What the Public Thinks about the Environment," *Canner Packer* 146, no. 4 (April 1977): 67; "Pro-consumer Action Stressed at 70th Annual NCA Conevntion [*sic*]," *Canner Packer* 146, no. 4 (April 1977): 55.

112. Laurie Johnston, "Notes on People: Nader Quits Consumers Union," *New York Times*, August 23, 1975; Landon R. Y. Storrs, *Civilizing Capitalism: The National Consumers' League, Women's Activism, and Labor Standards in the New Deal Era* (Chapel Hill: University of North Carolina Press, 2000); Carolyn M. Goldstein, *Creating Consumers: Home Economists in Tw entieth-Century America* (Chapel Hill: University of North Carolina Press, 2012); Angie M. Boyce, "'When Does It Stop Being Peanut Butter?': FDA Food Standards of Identity, Ruth Desmond, and the Shifting Politics of Consumer Activism, 1960s–1970s," *Technology and Culture* 57, no. 1 (2016): 54–79.

113. Friday, "Regulation, Reason," 12.

114. Richard L. McKee, "How Much Regulation Is Enough?," *Canner Packer* 142, no. 5 (May 1973): 6. These agencies are the USDA, the Food and Drug Administration (FDA), the Environmental Protection Agency (EPA), the Federal Trade Commission (FTC), and the Occupational Safety and Health Administration (OSHA).

115. Friday, "Regulation, Reason," 19.

116. Ibid., 15; Robert L. Gibson, "Closing Remarks," in NCA, *Industry Speaks*, 29.

117. The Arab members of OPEC were retaliating against the United States for its support of Israel in the October 1973 Yom Kippur War. Michael B. Oren, *Six Days of War: June 1967 and the Making of the Modern Middle East* (Novato, CA: Presidio Press, 2003); Michael J. Graetz, *The End of Energy: The Unmaking of America's Environment, Security, and Independence* (Cambridge, MA: MIT Press, 2011).

118. Richard L. McKee, "In a Crisis, Ya Gotta Cope," *Canner Packer World* 143, no. 1 (January 1974): 4.

119. William F. Allewelt Jr., "Energy Requirements and the Canning Industry," in NCA, *Industry Speaks*, 9; Gibson, "Closing Remarks," 30.

120. "Consuming the Processors' Environment—A Convention Report," *Canner/Packer* 139, no. 3 (March 1970): 26; Richard L. McKee, "Energy Crisis—Opportunity?," *Canner Packer* 142, no. 12 (December 1973): 4.

121. Marion Nestle, *Food Politics: How the Food Industry Influences Nutrition and Health* (Berkeley: University of California Press, 2002), 103.

122. The acronyms stand for National Canners Association (NCA), Grocery Manufacturers Association (GMA), Super Market Institute (SMI), National

Association of Food Chains (NAFC), and National-American Wholesale Grocers' Association (NAWGA). R. Burt Gookin, "Business Capital Requirements," in NCA, *Industry Speaks,* 27.

123. Nestle, *Food Politics,* 99.

124. Harry Stagnito, "Formerly Canner Packer: Processed Prepared Food," *Processed Prepared Food* 146, no. 11 (November 1977): 1. This followed on the heels of the merger of the National Association of Food Chains with Super Market Institute to form Food Marketing Institute in 1977. Elliott Zwiebach, "Alphabet Soup," July 22, 2002, *Supermarket News,* http://supermarketnews .com/archive/alphabet-soup#ixzz2P49sK8fJ.

125. Lachance, "Future Nutrition Regulations," 55.

126. "Pro-consumer Action Stressed."

127. Jacobson and Lerza, *Food for People,* 22; Glickman, *Buying Power,* 277.

128. Cross, *All-Consuming Century,* 163.

129. Stagnito, "Formerly Canner Packer."

6. BPA IN CAMPBELL'S SOUP

1. Healthy Child Healthy World, "Petition to Campbell's: Stop Endangering Kids' Health!," Change.org, 2011, https://www.change.org/p/campbell-s-stop-endangering-kids-health.

2. Katie Moisse, "BPA in Canned Foods: Should You Worry?," ABC News, September 21, 2011, http://abcnews.go.com/Health/w_ParentingResource/bpa-canned-foods-worry/story?id=14563600.

3. Amy Westervelt, "Responding to Consumer Concern, Campbell's Goes BPA-Free," *Forbes,* March 5, 2012, www.forbes.com/sites/amywestervelt /2012/03/05/under-pressure-from-parents-advocacy-groups-campbells-goes-bpa-free/.

4. "Campbell to Remove BPA from Packaging by Mid-2017," *Business Wire,* March 28, 2016, www.businesswire.com/news/home/20160328005722 /en/.

5. Jon Entine, "Campbell's Big Fat Green BPA Lie—and the Sustainability Activists Who Enabled It," *Forbes,* September 18, 2012, www.forbes.com/sites /jonentine/2012/09/18/campbells-big-fat-green-bpa-lie-and-the-sustainability-activists-that-enabled-it/#251e6d711e78.

6. Bruce J. Schulman and Julian E. Zelizer, eds., *Rightward Bound: Making America Conservative in the 1970s* (Cambridge, MA: Harvard University Press, 2008).

7. Michael Pollan, *The Omnivore's Dilemma: A Natural History of Four Meals* (New York: Penguin Press, 2006); Michael Pollan, "When a Crop Becomes King," *New York Times,* July 19, 2002, http://michaelpollan.com /articles-archive/when-a-crop-becomes-king/.

8. Shira Ovide, "The Long, Strange History of Kraft Foods," *Wall Street Journal,* August 4, 2011, http://blogs.wsj.com/deals/2011/08/04/the-long-strange-history-of-kraft-foods/; Kenneth M. Davidson, *Megamergers: Corporate America's Billion-Dollar Takeovers* (Washington, DC: Beard Books, 2003).

9. Anna Kramer, "10 Everyday Food Brands—and the Few Giant Companies That Own Them," *Oxfam's First Person Blog,* March 1, 2013, http://firstperson.oxfamamerica.org/2013/03/10-everyday-food-brands-and-the-few-giant-companies-that-own-them/; Wenonah Hauter, *Foodopoly: The Battle over the Future of Food and Farming in America* (New York: New Press, 2012).

10. Andrew F. Smith, *Eating History: 30 Turning Points in the Making of American Cuisine* (New York: Columbia University Press, 2009), 292; Marion Nestle, *Food Politics: How the Food Industry Influences Nutrition and Health* (Berkeley: University of California Press, 2002).

11. Grocery Manufacturers Association, "History: A Century of Leadership," n.d., accessed June 28, 2016, www.gmaonline.org/about/history/.

12. To read about these concerns, see writings by Michael Pollan, Mark Bittman, Marion Nestle, and Eric Schlosser.

13. Michele Simon, *Appetite for Profit: How the Food Industry Undermines Our Health and How to Fight Back* (New York: Nation Books, 2006), 172, 176.

14. Warren J. Belasco, *Appetite for Change: How the Counterculture Took On the Food Industry,* 2nd ed. (Ithaca, NY: Cornell University Press, 2006); Bonnie F. Liebman, Michael Jacobson, and Greg Moyer, *Salt: The Brand Name Guide to Sodium Content,* Center for Science in the Public Interest (New York: Workman, 1983).

15. Many in the local food movement use the term *food miles* to indicate how far food travels between sites of production and consumption. The focus on a small ingredient list is touted in Michael Pollan's *In Defense of Food: An Eater's Manifesto* (New York: Penguin Press, 2008) and *Food Rules: An Eater's Manual* (New York: Penguin, 2009).

16. Simon, *Appetite for Profit;* Nestle, *Food Politics.*

17. Jean C. Buzby et al., "Canned Fruit and Vegetable Consumption in the United States: An Updated Report to Congress," US Department of Agriculture, November 2010, www.ers.usda.gov/publications/ap-administrative-publication/ap-050.aspx.

18. Kevin B. Comerford, "Frequent Canned Food Use Is Positively Associated with Nutrient-Dense Food Group Consumption and Higher Nutrient Intakes in US Children and Adults," *Nutrients* 7, no. 7 (July 9, 2015): 5586–5600.

19. Canned Food Alliance, "Telephone Survey (Landline and Mobile Numbers) of 1007 American Adults by Caravan(®) Survey, April 4–7, 2013, Margin of Error +/– 3.1%," 2013, cited in Canned Food Alliance, "Consumer Confusion about Canned Food Persists, According to New Survey," PR Newswire, June 11, 2013, www.prnewswire.com/news-releases/consumer-confusion-about-canned-food-persists-according-to-new-survey-210981151.html.

20. Buzby et al., "Canned Fruit," 15.

21. Robert Klara, "Legend in a Can," *Adweek,* September 15, 2014.

22. Matthew Sedacca, "How 'Foodie' Culture Survived the Recession," *Eater,* May 19, 2016, www.eater.com/2016/5/19/11705966/foodie-millennials-recession.

23. Josee Johnston and Shyon Baumann, *Foodies: Democracy and Distinction in the Gourmet Foodscape* (New York: Routledge, 2009).

24. Alice Z. Cuneo, "Del Monte Aims for Revival by Touting Virtues of Canned Food," *Advertising Age,* August 2, 1999.

25. "Campbell's Prize Harvest," *Brandweek,* March 22, 2010.

26. Comerford, "Frequent Canned Food Use"; Steven R. Miller and William A. Knudson, "Nutrition and Cost Comparisons of Select Canned, Frozen, and Fresh Fruits and Vegetables," *American Journal of Lifestyle Medicine,* 8, no. 6 (February 27, 2014): 430–37.

27. Robert Klara, "Perspective: Bowl Game," *Adweek,* February 10, 2013.

28. Pollan, *Food Rules.*

29. "Campbell's Prize Harvest."

30. Neil Howe and William Strauss, *Millennials Rising: The Next Great Generation* (New York: Vintage, 2000). The term *millennials* refers to the generation born roughly between 1982 and 2000.

31. Sedacca, "How 'Foodie' Culture Survived."

32. S. Samuel Babu and Thalluri Prasanth Vidyasagar, "Neuromarketing: Is Campbell in Soup?," *IUP Journal of Marketing Management* 11, no. 2 (May 2012): 76–100.

33. Rosland Briggs-Gammon, "Campbell Unveils Soup Label du Jour," *Philadelphia Inquirer,* August 26, 1999, http://articles.philly.com/1999–08–26 /business/25482625_1_red-and-white-label-condensed-soups-campbell-soup.

34. Babu and Vidyasagar, "Neuromarketing."

35. Ibid., 90.

36. Gary Ruskin, "Neuromarketers Search for 'Buy Button' in the Brain: Commercial Alert Asks Emory University to Halt Neuromarketing Experiments," Commercial Alert press release, December 1, 2003, www.rense.com /general45/neur.htm.

37. Robert Klara, "Selling Soup as a Main-Dish Food Isn't Easy—and Never Was," *AdWeek,* February 7, 2013, www.adweek.com/news/advertising-branding /perspective-bowl-game-146993.

38. Candice Choi, "Campbell Soup Tries to Reinvent Itself," *Huffington Post,* September 7, 2012, www.huffingtonpost.com/2012/09/07/campbell-soup-reinvents_n_1864170.html.

39. "Campbell's Soup's New Direction Inspired by Food Trucks," *Huffington Post,* August 23, 2012, www.huffingtonpost.com/2012/08/23/campbells-soup-food-trucks_n_1825833.html; Choi, "Campbell Soup Tries."

40. Campbell Soup Company, "CEO Denise Morrison Unveils Products Developed by Campbell's Breakthrough Innovation Teams," press release, February 22, 2012, http://investor.campbellsoupcompany.com/phoenix.zhtml? c=88650&p=irol-newsarticle_pf&id=1663883.

41. The full line also included Chicken & Quinoa with Poblano Chilies, Golden Lentil with Madras Curry, Moroccan Style Chicken with Chickpeas, and Spicy Chorizo & Pulled Chicken with Black Beans. See www.campbellsgo .com/ (accessed May 2013).

42. Laura Northrup, "Campbell's Opens Pop-Up Hipster Soup Kitchens to Promote Soulless $3 Soup Pouches," *Consumerist,* November 14, 2012, https:// consumerist.com/2012/11/14/campbells-opens-pop-up-hipster-soup-kitchens-to-promote-soulless-3-soup-pouches/.

43. Choi, "Campbell Soup Tries."

44. Jenna Goudreau, "Kicking the Can: Campbell's CEO Bets on Soup-In-a-Bag for 20-Somethings," *Forbes,* December 6, 2012, www.forbes.com/sites /jennagoudreau/2012/12/06/kicking-the-can-campbells-ceo-bets-on-soup-in-a-bag-for-20-somethings/#5b6fe1ff33a5.

45. Northrup, "Campbell's."

46. Hamilton Nolan, "Campbell's New Millennial Soups Embody Entire Millennial Generation in Soup Form," *Gawker,* November 14, 2012, http:// gawker.com/5960482/campbells-new-millennial-soups-embody-entire-millennial-generation-in-soup-form.

47. See chapter 1.

48. Jeffrey L. Meikle, *American Plastic: A Cultural History* (New Brunswick, NJ: Rutgers University Press, 1995), 176.

49. Breast Cancer Prevention Partners, "Buyer Beware: Toxic BPA and Regrettable Substitutes Found in the Linings of Canned Food" (partnership of Breast Cancer Fund, Campaign for Healthier Solutions, Clean Production Action, Ecology Center, Mind the Store Campaign), March 30, 2016, www .breastcancerfund.org/assets/pdfs/publications/buyer-beware-report.pdf; Jonathan Waldman, *Rust: The Longest War* (New York: Simon and Schuster, 2015), 120.

50. Heather Caliendo, "History of BPA," *Packaging Digest,* June 28, 2012, www.packagingdigest.com/shipping-containers/history-bpa; U.S. Food and Drug Administration (hereafter FDA), "Generally Recognized as Safe (GRAS)—FDA's Approach to the GRAS Provision: A History of Processes," accessed June 29, 2016, www.fda.gov/Food/IngredientsPackagingLabeling/GRAS/ucm094040 .htm.

51. Thomas McGarity et al., "Opening the Industry Playbook: Myths and Truths in the Debate over BPA Regulation," white paper, Center for Progressive Reform, May 2011, 1, www.progressivereform.org/articles/BPA_Myths_ 1107.pdf. Health concerns about BPA also extend to laborers in the canning industry. James T. Brophy et al., "Breast Cancer Risk in Relation to Occupations with Exposure to Carcinogens and Endocrine Disruptors: A Canadian Case-Control Study," *Environmental Health* 11, no. 87 (2012): 1–17.

52. Howard A. Bern et al., "Statement from the Work Session on Chemically-Induced Alterations in Sexual Development: The Wildlife/Human Connection," in *Chemically-Induced Alterations in Sexual and Functional Development: The Wildlife/Human Connection,* ed. Theo Colborn and Coralie Clement (Princeton, NJ: Princeton Scientific Publishing, 1992), 1–8, www.ourstolenfuture .org/consensus/wingspread1.htm.

53. For a selection of the studies, see Theo Colborn, Dianne Dumanoski, and John Peterson Myers, *Our Stolen Future: Are We Threatening Our Fertility, Intelligence, and Survival? A Scientific Detective Story* (New York: Dutton, 1996); Hanako Nishizawa et al., "Effects of in Utero Exposure to Bisphenol A on mRNA Expression of Arylhydrocarbon and Retinoid Receptors in Murine Embryos," *Journal of Reproduction and Development* 51, no. 3 (2005): 315–24; Catherine A. Richter et al., "Estradiol and Bisphenol A Stimulate Androgen Receptor and Estrogen Receptor Gene Expression in Fetal Mouse Prostate

Mesenchyme Cells," *Environmental Health Perspectives* 115, no. 6 (2007): 902–8.

54. Sarah A. Vogel, "From 'The Dose Makes the Poison' to 'The Timing Makes the Poison': Conceptualizing Risk in the Synthetic Age," *Environmental History* 13, no. 4 (October 2008): 667–73.

55. Breast Cancer Prevention Partners, "Buyer Beware," 41.

56. Some other nonprofits engaged in this activism include the Breast Cancer Fund, Campaign for Healthier Solutions, Clean Production Action, Ecology Center, and Mind the Store Campaign.

57. McGarity et al., "Opening the Industry Playbook," 12–13.

58. FDA, "Update on Bisphenol A for Use in Food Contact Applications," January 2010, 6, www.fda.gov/downloads/NewsEvents/PublicHealthFocus /UCM197778.pdf.

59. Thomas G. Neltner et al., "Conflicts of Interest in Approvals of Additives to Food Determined to Be Generally Recognized as Safe: Out of Balance," *JAMA Internal Medicine* 173, no. 22 (December 9, 2013): 2032–36.

60. Breast Cancer Prevention Partners, "Buyer Beware," 14–15.

61. Environment and Human Health, Inc., "Plastics That May Be Harmful to Children and Reproductive Health," 2008, www.ehhi.org/reports/plastics /ehhi_plastics_report_2008.pdf.

62. John Peterson Myers et al., "Why Public Health Agencies Cannot Depend on Good Laboratory Practices as a Criterion for Selecting Data: The Case of Bisphenol A," *Environmental Health Perspectives* 117, no. 3 (March 2009): 309–15.

63. FDA, "Update on Bisphenol A."

64. Breast Cancer Prevention Partners, "Buyer Beware," 47.

65. Many historians of science have written on the contested question of expertise and trust in the scientific landscape. See, for example, Wiebe E. Bijker, Roland Bal, and Ruud Hendriks, *The Paradox of Scientific Authority: The Role of Scientific Advice in Democracies* (Cambridge, MA: MIT Press, 2009); Steven Shapin, *Never Pure: Historical Studies of Science as If It Was Produced by People with Bodies, Situated in Time, Space, Culture, and Society, and Struggling for Credibility and Authority* (Baltimore: Johns Hopkins University Press, 2010).

66. See the investigative articles by the *Milwaukee Journal Sentinel* that are listed on its website under the heading "Chemical Fallout," under "Watchdog Online," accessed June 29, 2016, www.jsonline.com/watchdog/34405049 .html.

67. Myers et al., "Why Public Health Agencies."

68. Dexter S. Goldman, "Chemical Aspects of Compliance with Good Laboratory Practices," in *Good Laboratory Practices: An Agrochemical Perspective,* ed. Willa Y. Garner and Maureen S. Barge (Washington, DC: American Chemical Society, 1988), 13–23.

69. Myers et al., "Why Public Health Agencies," 309.

70. Blake writes, "By the late 1990s, when tobacco companies agreed to drop deceptive marketing practices under a settlement agreement with forty-six states, many of the scientists and consultants on the industry's payroll transitioned seamlessly into defending BPA." Mariah Blake, "The Scary New Evidence on

BPA-Free Plastics and the Big Tobacco-Style Campaign to Bury It," *Mother Jones,* April 2014, www.motherjones.com/environment/2014/03/tritan-certichem-eastman-bpa-free-plastic-safe. Oreskes and Conway, among many other historians, have written persuasively about the tobacco industry's efforts to subvert the scientific and regulatory process. Naomi Oreskes and Erik Conway, *Merchants of Doubt: How a Handful of Scientists Obscured the Truth on Issues from Tobacco Smoke to Global Warming* (London: Bloomsbury Press, 2011).

71. Lila Guterman, "Scientists Accuse Toxicology Journal of Industry Ties, Urge Disclosure of Conflicts of Interest," *Chronicle of Higher Education,* November 20, 2002, http://chronicle.com/article/Scientists-Accuse-Toxicology/115196/.

72. Blake, "Scary New Evidence."

73. McGarity et al., "Opening the Industry Playbook," 11. McGarity et al. point to the historical example of automakers similarly suggesting that it would be too expensive to introduce air pollution control technologies; when regulation was imposed, the automakers were incentivized to introduce catalytic converters to efficiently address the problem.

74. Waldman, *Rust,* 100.

75. Breast Cancer Prevention Partners, "Buyer Beware," 20; "Eden Foods Bisphenol-A (BPA) Free Pioneer," *Eden Foods,* accessed June 29, 2016, www.edenfoods.com/articles/view.php?articles_id=178.

76. "NAMPA Responds to Bangor Daily News: 'The Consumer Game of Whack-a-Mole with Chemical Dangers'," April 18, 2016, *Bangor Daily News* editorial with comments by NAMPA, www.metal-pack.org/docs/pdf/BDN%20Editorial%20Remarks%20NAMPA.pdf.

77. NAMPA, "Minutes from BPA Joint Trade Association Meeting on Communications Strategy," May 28, 2009, www.jsonline.com/blogs/news/46630742.html.

78. Blake, "Scary New Evidence."

79. Breast Cancer Prevention Partners, "Buyer Beware."

80. "Campbell's: What's In My Food?," accessed June 28, 2016, www.whatsinmyfood.com/.

81. Campbell Team, "Why We Support Mandatory National GMO Labeling," Campbell Soup Company, January 7, 2016, www.campbellsoupcompany.com/newsroom/news/2016/01/07/labeling/.

82. For just one example, see Ben Forer, "Study: Eating Fresh Food Reduces Exposure to BPA," *ABC News,* March 30, 2011, http://abcnews.go.com/Health/study-reduce-bpa-exposure-cutting-consumption-packaged-foods/story?id=13256098.

83. Judy S. Lakind and Daniel Q. Naiman, "Daily Intake of Bisphenol A and Potential Sources of Exposure: 2005–2006 National Health and Nutrition Examination Survey," *Journal of Exposure Science and Environmental Epidemiology* 21, no. 3 (June 2011): 272–79.

84. Sheela Sathyanarayana et al., "Unexpected Results in a Randomized Dietary Trial to Reduce Phthalate and Bisphenol A Exposures," *Journal of Exposure Science and Environmental Epidemiology* 23, no. 4 (July 2013): 378–84; Lakind and Naiman, "Daily Intake."

85. Tom Philpott, "Buying Local and Organic? You're Still Eating Plastic Chemicals," *Mother Jones,* March 4, 2013, www.motherjones.com/tom-philpott/2013/03/study-eating-fresh-local-and-organic-wont-protect-you-nasty-chemicals.

86. McGarity et al., "Opening the Industry Playbook," 14.

CONCLUSION

1. I'm borrowing the term *edible foodlike substances* from Michael Pollan, *In Defense of Food: An Eater's Manifesto* (New York: Penguin Press, 2008).

2. Michael Pollan, "Voting With Your Fork," *New York Times,* May 7, 2006, http://pollan.blogs.nytimes.com/2006/05/07/voting-with-your-fork/.

3. For a recent take on this argument, see Phoebe Maltz Bovy, "Food Snobs Like Mark Bittman Aren't Even Hiding Their Elitism Anymore," *New Republic,* March 25, 2015, https://newrepublic.com/article/121374/foodie-elitism-are-mark-bittman-and-michael-pollan-elitist.

4. US Department of Agriculture Economic Research Service, "Definition of a Food Desert," June 29, 2016, www.ers.usda.gov/datafiles/Food_Access_Research_Atlas/Download_the_Data/Archived_Version/archived_documentation.pdf.

5. In other parts of the world, like China and India, cans continue to be a status symbol. Christophe Jaffrelot and Peter van der Veer, eds., *Patterns of Middle Class Consumption in India and China* (New Delhi: SAGE Publications India, 2008).

6. Bee Wilson, *First Bite: How We Learn to Eat* (New York: Basic Books, 2015).

Selected Bibliography

ARCHIVAL SOURCES

California State Archives, Sacramento, CA.

College of Agriculture and Life Sciences, Record Group 9. University of Wisconsin-Madison Archives. Madison, WI.

Ernest Charles Dickson Papers, 1881–1939, Acc. # MSS 21. Lane Medical Archives, Stanford University Medical Center, Palo Alto, CA.

Grocery Manufacturers Association Library. National Canners Association Archives. Washington, DC.

National Archives and Records Administration, National Archives at College Park, College Park, MD.

Wisconsin Historical Society Archives, University of Wisconsin-Madison.

PERIODICALS

American Food Journal
Canner, Canner/Packer, Processed Prepared Food
Canning Age
Chicago Tribune
Journal of Marketing
Los Angeles Times
Market Growers Journal
New York Times
Western Canner Packer
Wisconsin Canners Bulletin
Wisconsin Farmer

PRINT SOURCES

Appert, Nicolas. *The Art of Preserving All Kinds of Animal and Vegetable Substances for Several Years: A Work Published by Order of the French Minister of the Interior, on the Report of the Board of Arts and Manufactures.* 2nd ed. London: Black, Perry and Kingsbury, 1812.

Armstrong, Chas, R. V. Story, and Ernest Scott. "Botulism from Eating Canned Ripe Olives." *Public Health Reports* 34, no. 51 (December 19, 1919): 2877–2905.

Baba, S. Samuel, and Thalluri Prasanth Vidyasagar. "Neuromarketing: Is Campbell in Soup?" *IUP Journal of Marketing Management* 11, no. 2 (May 2012): 76–100.

Backer, Kellen. "World War II and the Triumph of Industrialized Food." PhD diss., University of Wisconsin-Madison, 2012.

Belasco, Warren J. *Appetite for Change: How the Counterculture Took On the Food Industry.* 2nd ed. Ithaca, NY: Cornell University Press, 2006.

Belasco, Warren J., and Roger Horowitz, eds. *Food Chains: From Farmyard to Shopping Cart.* Philadelphia: University of Pennsylvania Press, 2008.

Bentley, Amy. *Eating for Victory: Food Rationing and the Politics of Domesticity.* Urbana: University of Illinois Press, 1998.

———. *Inventing Baby Food: Taste, Health, and the Industrialization of the American Diet.* Berkeley: University of California Press, 2014.

Berghoff, Hartmut, Uwe Spiekermann, and Philip Scranton, eds. *The Rise of Marketing and Market Research.* New York: Palgrave Macmillan, 2012.

Berle, Adolf A., and Gardiner C. Means. *The Modern Corporation and Private Property.* New York: Commerce Clearing House, 1932.

Blake, Mariah. "The Scary New Evidence on BPA-Free Plastics and the Big Tobacco-Style Campaign to Bury It." *Mother Jones,* April 2014. www .motherjones.com/environment/2014/03/tritan-certichem-eastman-bpa-free-plastic-safe.

Blanke, David. "Consumer Choice, Agency, and New Directions in Rural History." *Agricultural History* 81, no. 2 (April 1, 2007): 182–203.

Blaszczyk, Regina Lee. *Imagining Consumers: Design and Innovation from Wedgwood to Corning.* Baltimore, MD: Johns Hopkins University Press, 2002.

Bobrow-Strain, Aaron. *White Bread: A Social History of the Store-Bought Loaf.* Boston: Beacon Press, 2012.

Boyce, Angie M. " 'When Does It Stop Being Peanut Butter?': FDA Food Standards of Identity, Ruth Desmond, and the Shifting Politics of Consumer Activism, 1960s–1970s." *Technology and Culture* 57, no. 1 (2016): 54–79.

Brophy, James T., et al. "Breast Cancer Risk in Relation to Occupations with Exposure to Carcinogens and Endocrine Disruptors: A Canadian Case-Control Study." *Environmental Health* 11, no. 87 (2012): 1–17.

Brown, Martin, and Peter Philips. "Craft Labor and Mechanization in Nineteenth-Century American Canning." *Journal of Economic History* 46, no. 3 (1986): 743–56.

———. "The Evolution of Labor Market Structure: The California Canning Industry." *Industrial and Labor Relations Review* 38, no. 3 (1985): 392–407.

Bruegel, Martin. "How the French Learned to Eat Canned Food, 1809–1930s." In *Food Nations: Selling Taste in Consumer Societies,* edited by Warren James Belasco and Philip Scranton, 113–30. New York: Routledge, 2002.

Burke, Georgina S. "Spoiled Canned Foods and Botulism." *Journal of the American Medical Association* 73, no. 14 (October 4, 1919): 1078–79.

Campbell, Persia. *Consumer Representation in the New Deal.* New York: Columbia University Press, 1940.

Campbell Soup Company. "Grower-Canner Agreements: An Abuse of Mass Standardized Contracts." *Yale Law Journal* 58, no. 7 (June 1, 1949): 1161–71.

Chandler, Alfred D. *The Visible Hand: The Managerial Revolution in American Business.* Cambridge, MA: Belknap Press, 1977.

Cohen, Benjamin R. "Analysis as Border Patrol: Chemists along the Boundary between Pure Food and Real Adulteration." *Endeavour* 35, nos. 2–3 (June 2011): 66–73.

Cohen, Lizabeth. *A Consumers' Republic: The Politics of Mass Consumption in Postwar America.* New York: Vintage Books, 2004.

———. *Making a New Deal: Industrial Workers in Chicago, 1919–1939.* Cambridge: Cambridge University Press, 1990.

Colborn, Theo, Dianne Dumanoski, and John Peterson Myers. *Our Stolen Future: Are We Threatening Our Fertility, Intelligence, and Survival? A Scientific Detective Story.* New York: Dutton, 1996.

Coles, Jessie V. "Compulsory Grade Labeling." In *Marketing: The Yearbook of Agriculture.* Washington, DC: Government Printing Office, US Department of Agriculture, 1954.

Cooke, Kathy J. "Expertise, Book Farming, and Government Agriculture: The Origins of Agricultural Seed Certification in the United States." *Agricultural History* 76, no. 3 (2002): 524–45.

Coppin, Clayton A., and Jack C. High. *The Politics of Purity: Harvey Washington Wiley and the Origins of Federal Food Policy.* Ann Arbor: University of Michigan Press, 1999.

Cowan, Ruth Schwartz. *More Work for Mother: The Ironies of Household Technology from the Open Hearth to the Microwave.* New York: Basic Books, 1983.

———. *A Social History of American Technology.* New York: Oxford University Press, 1997.

Cronon, William. *Nature's Metropolis: Chicago and the Great West.* New York: W. W. Norton, 1991.

Crosby, Alfred W. *America's Forgotten Pandemic: The Influenza of 1918.* New York: Cambridge University Press, 1989.

Cross, Gary S. *An All-Consuming Century: Why Commercialism Won in Modern America.* New York: Columbia University Press, 2000.

Cross, Gary S., and Robert N. Proctor. *Packaged Pleasures: How Technology and Marketing Revolutionized Desire.* Chicago: University of Chicago Press, 2014.

Danbom, David B. "The Agricultural Experiment Station and Professionalization: Scientists' Goals for Agriculture." *Agricultural History* 60, no. 2 (Spring 1986): 246–55.

de la Peña, Carolyn. *Empty Pleasures: The Story of Artificial Sweeteners from Saccharin to Splenda*. Chapel Hill: University of North Carolina Press, 2010.

Delwiche, E. J., and E. J. Renard. *Breeding New Varieties of Canning Peas*. Research Bulletin 70. Madison: Agricultural Experiment Station of the University of Wisconsin, 1926.

Deutsch, Tracey. *Building a Housewife's Paradise: Gender, Politics, and American Grocery Stores in the Twentieth Century*. Chapel Hill: University of North Carolina Press, 2012.

Dicke, Tom. "Red Gold of the Ozarks: The Rise and Decline of Tomato Canning, 1885–1955." *Agricultural History* 79, no. 1 (Winter 2005): 1–26.

Dickson, Ernest C. "Botulism, an Experimental Study: A Preliminary Report." *Journal of the American Medical Association* 65, no. 6 (August 7, 1915): 492–96.

Dodd, Walter L. "Botulism." *American Food Journal* 15, no. 2 (February 1920): 12–14.

Donohue, Kathleen G. "What Gender Is the Consumer? The Role of Gender Connotations in Defining the Political." *Journal of American Studies* 33, no. 1 (April 1, 1999): 19–43.

Dupree, A. Hunter. *Science in the Federal Government: A History of Policies and Activities to 1940*. Cambridge, MA: Harvard University Press, 1957.

DuPuis, E. Melanie. *Nature's Perfect Food: How Milk Became America's Drink*. New York: New York University Press, 2002.

Edgerton, David. *The Shock of the Old: Technology and Global History since 1900*. Oxford: Oxford University Press, 2007.

Entine, Jon. "Campbell's Big Fat Green BPA Lie—and the Sustainability Activists Who Enabled It." *Forbes*, September 18, 2012.

Fitzgerald, Deborah Kay. *The Business of Breeding: Hybrid Corn in Illinois, 1890–1940*. Ithaca, NY: Cornell University Press, 1990.

———. *Every Farm a Factory: The Industrial Ideal in American Agriculture*. New Haven, CT: Yale University Press, 2003.

Frank, Dana. "Housewives, Socialists, and the Politics of Food: The 1917 New York Cost-of-Living Protests." *Feminist Studies* 11, no. 2 (July 1, 1985): 255–85.

Freidberg, Susanne. *Fresh: A Perishable History*. Cambridge, MA: Harvard University Press, 2009.

Geiger, J. C., E. C. Dickson, and K. F. Meyer. *The Epidemiology of Botulism*. Public Health Bulletin No. 127. Washington, DC: Government Printing Office, 1922.

Glickman, Lawrence B. *Buying Power: A History of Consumer Activism in America*. Chicago: University of Chicago Press, 2009.

Goldstein, Carolyn M. *Creating Consumers: Home Economists in Twentieth-Century America*. Chapel Hill: University of North Carolina Press, 2012.

Goodwin, Lorine Swainston. *The Pure Food, Drink, and Drug Crusaders, 1879–1914*. Jefferson, NC: McFarland, 1999.

Hagemann, J. A., and W. E. Nicholoy, "University Service to the Pea Canning Industry." *Wisconsin Alumni Magazine* 26, no. 7 (May 1925): 255–57.

Hall, Greg. "The Fruits of Her Labor: Women, Children, and Progressive Era Reformers in the Pacific Northwest Canning Industry." *Oregon Historical Quarterly* 109, no. 2 (July 1, 2008): 226–51.

Hamilton, Shane. "The Economies and Conveniences of Modern-Day Living: Frozen Foods and Mass Marketing, 1945–1965." *Business History Review* 77, no. 1 (April 1, 2003): 33–60.

Hampe, Edward C., and Merle Wittenberg. *The Lifeline of America: Development of the Food Industry*. New York: McGraw-Hill, 1964.

Horowitz, B. Zane. "Polar Poisons: Did Botulism Doom the Franklin Expedition?" *Journal of Toxicology—Clinical Toxicology* 41, no. 6 (2003): 841–47.

Horowitz, Roger. *Putting Meat on the American Table: Taste, Technology, Transformation*. Baltimore: Johns Hopkins University Press, 2006.

Hurt, R. Douglas. *American Agriculture: A Brief History*. Rev. ed. West Lafayette, IN: Purdue University Press, 2002.

Inness, Sherrie A., ed. *Kitchen Culture in America: Popular Representations of Food, Gender, and Race*. Philadelphia: University of Pennsylvania Press, 2001.

Jacobs, Meg. "'Democracy's Third Estate': New Deal Politics and the Construction of a 'Consuming Public.'" *International Labor and Working-Class History* 55 (Spring 1999): 27–51.

———. *Pocketbook Politics: Economic Citizenship in Twentieth-Century America*. Politics and Society in Twentieth-Century America. Princeton, NJ: Princeton University Press, 2005.

Jacobson, Michael F., and Catherine Lerza. *Food for People, Not for Profit: A Source Book on the Food Crisis*. New York: Ballantine Books, 1975.

Johnston, Ralph W., John Feldman, and Rosemary Sullivan. "Botulism from Canned Tuna Fish." *Public Health Reports* 78, no. 7 (July 1963): 561–64.

Judge, Arthur I., ed. *A History of the Canning Industry*. Baltimore: Canning Trade, 1914.

Judge, Edward S. "American Canning Interests." In *1795–1895: One Hundred Years of American Commerce*, edited by Chauncey M. Depew. New York: D. O. Haynes, 1895.

Kallet, Arthur. *100,000,000 Guinea Pigs: Dangers in Everyday Foods, Drugs, and Cosmetics*. New York: Grosset and Dunlap, 1933.

Keezer, Dexter M. "The Consumer under the National Recovery Administration." *Annals of the American Academy of Political and Social Science* 172 (March 1, 1934): 97.

Kennedy, David M. *Freedom from Fear: The American People in Depression and War, 1929–1945*. New York: Oxford University Press, 2004.

Keuchel, Edward F. "The Development of the Canning Industry in New York State to 1960." PhD diss., Cornell University, 1970.

Kline, Ronald R. *Consumers in the Country: Technology and Social Change in Rural America*. Baltimore: Johns Hopkins University Press, 2000.

Koehn, Nancy F. "Henry Heinz and Brand Creation in the Late Nineteenth Century: Making Markets for Processed Food." *Business History Review* 73, no. 3 (1999): 349–93.

Laird, Pamela Walker. *Advertising Progress: American Business and the Rise of Consumer Marketing*. Baltimore: Johns Hopkins University Press, 2001.

Lappé, Frances Moore. *Diet for a Small Planet.* Twentieth anniversary ed. New York: Ballantine Books, 1991.

Leach, William. *Land of Desire: Merchants, Power, and the Rise of a New American Culture.* New York: Basic Books, 1993.

Lears, Jackson. *Fables of Abundance: A Cultural History of Advertising in America.* New York: Basic Books, 1994.

Leavitt, Judith Walzer. *Typhoid Mary: Captive to the Public's Health.* Boston: Beacon Press, 1996.

Levenstein, Harvey A. *Paradox of Plenty: A Social History of Eating in Modern America.* New York: Oxford University Press, 1993.

Marchand, Roland. *Advertising the American Dream: Making Way for Modernity, 1920–1940.* Berkeley: University of California Press, 1985.

Markowitz, Gerald, and David Rosner. *Deceit and Denial: The Deadly Politics of Industrial Pollution.* Berkeley: University of California Press, 2002.

Max Ams Machine Company. *The Seal of Safety: Year Book of the Max Ams Machine Co.* Mount Vernon, NY: Max Ams Machine Company, 1914.

May, Earl Chapin. *The Canning Clan: A Pageant of Pioneering Americans.* New York: Macmillan, 1938.

McGovern, Charles. *Sold American: Consumption and Citizenship, 1890–1945.* Chapel Hill: University of North Carolina Press, 2006.

Mintz, Sidney W. *Sweetness and Power: The Place of Sugar in Modern History.* New York: Penguin Books, 1986.

Myers, John Peterson, et al. "Why Public Health Agencies Cannot Depend on Good Laboratory Practices as a Criterion for Selecting Data: The Case of Bisphenol A." *Environmental Health Perspectives* 117, no. 3 (March 2009): 309–15.

National Canners Association. *The Canning Industry: A Series of Articles Furnishing Information on the History, Organization, Methods and Products of the Industry, with Selected List of References.* Washington, DC: National Canners Association, 1939.

———. *The Canning Industry: Its History, Importance, Organization, Methods, and the Public Service Values of Its Products.* Washington, DC: National Canners Association, 1952, 1963, and 1971 editions.

Nestle, Marion. *Food Politics: How the Food Industry Influences Nutrition and Health.* Berkeley: University of California Press, 2002.

Oden, Derek. "From Cob to Can: The Development of Iowa's Canning Industry in the Late Nineteenth and Early Twentieth Centuries." *Annals of Iowa* 63 (Fall 2004): 390–418.

Olmstead, Alan L., and Paul Rhode. *Creating Abundance: Biological Innovation and American Agricultural Development.* New York: Cambridge University Press, 2008.

Orem, Hugh S. "Address at the Joint Meeting Growers and Canners." In *Report of the Maryland Agricultural Society.* College Park: Maryland Agricultural Society, 1917.

Oreskes, Naomi, and Erik Conway. *Merchants of Doubt: How a Handful of Scientists Obscured the Truth on Issues from Tobacco Smoke to Global Warming.* London: Bloomsbury Press, 2011.

Parkin, Katherine. *Food Is Love: Food Advertising and Gender Roles in Modern America* Philadelphia: University of Pennsylvania Press, 2006.

Pearson, Gregg. "The Democratization of Food: Tin Cans and the Growth of the American Food Processing Industry, 1810–1940." PhD diss., Lehigh University, 2016.

Petrick, Gabriella. "An Ambivalent Diet: The Industrialization of Canning." *OAH Magazine of History* 24, no. 3 (July 2010): 35–38.

———. "The Arbiters of Taste: Producers, Consumers, and the Industrialization of Taste in America, 1900–1960." PhD diss., University of Delaware, 2006.

———. "Industrial Food." In *The Oxford Handbook of Food History,* edited by Jeffrey M. Pilcher, 258–78. New York: Oxford University Press, 2012.

———. "'Purity as Life': H. J. Heinz, Religious Sentiment, and the Beginning of the Industrial Diet." *History and Technology* 271, no. 1 (2011): 37–64.

Phillips, M. C., and F. J. Schlink. *Discovering Consumers.* New York: John Day, 1934.

Phillips-Fein, Kim. *Invisible Hands: The Businessmen's Crusade against the New Deal.* New York: W. W. Norton, 2009.

Pollan, Michael. *In Defense of Food: An Eater's Manifesto.* New York: Penguin Press, 2008.

———. *The Omnivore's Dilemma: A Natural History of Four Meals.* New York: Penguin Press, 2006.

Prescott, S. L., and W. L. Underwood. "Microorganisms and Sterilizing Processes in the Canning Industry." *Technology Quarterly* 10 (March 1897): 183–99.

Proctor, Robert. *Golden Holocaust: Origins of the Cigarette Catastrophe and the Case for Abolition.* Berkeley: University of California Press, 2011.

Rees, Jonathan. *Refrigeration Nation: A History of Ice, Appliances, and Enterprise in America.* Baltimore: Johns Hopkins University Press, 2013.

Reich, Leonard S. *The Making of American Industrial Research: Science and Business at GE and Bell, 1876–1926.* New York: Cambridge University Press, 1985.

Rome, Adam. "'Give Earth a Chance': The Environmental Movement and the Sixties." *Journal of American History* 90, no. 2 (September 2003): 525–54.

Root, Waverly, and Richard De Rochemont. *Eating in America.* New York: Morrow, 1976.

Rosenberg, Charles E. *The Cholera Years: The United States in 1832, 1849, and 1866.* Chicago: University of Chicago Press, 1987.

Ruiz, Vicki L. *Cannery Women, Cannery Lives: Mexican Women, Unionization, and the California Food Processing Industry, 1930–1950.* Albuquerque: University of New Mexico Press, 1987.

Russell, H. L. "Gaseous Fermentation in the Canning Industry." *Annual Reports of the Wisconsin Agricultural Experiment Station* 12 (1895): 227–31.

Sackman, Doug. *Orange Empire: California and the Fruits of Eden.* Berkeley: University of California Press, 2005.

Sathyanarayana, Sheela, et al. "Unexpected Results in a Randomized Dietary Trial to Reduce Phthalate and Bisphenol A Exposures." *Journal of Exposure Science and Environmental Epidemiology* 23, no. 4 (July 2013): 378–84.

Schafer, Joseph. *A History of Agriculture in Wisconsin*. Madison: State Historical Society of Wisconsin, 1922.

Schlosser, Eric. *Fast Food Nation: The Dark Side of the All-American Meal*. Boston: Houghton Mifflin, 2001.

Scott, Roy Vernon. *The Reluctant Farmer: The Rise of Agricultural Extension to 1914*. Urbana: University of Illinois Press, 1971.

Sevey, Glenn Cyrus. *Peas and Pea Culture*. New York: Orange Judd, 1911.

Shapiro, Laura. *Something from the Oven: Reinventing Dinner in 1950s America*. New York: Viking Press, 2004.

Shepard, Sue. *Pickled, Potted, and Canned: How the Art and Science of Food Preserving Changed the World*. New York: Simon and Schuster, 2006.

Shields, Clyde Morse. *The Pea Growing Areas and the Pea Canning Industry in Wisconsin in Their Relation to Natural Environment*. Madison: University of Wisconsin, 1928.

Simon, Michele. *Appetite for Profit: How the Food Industry Undermines Our Health and How to Fight Back*. New York: Nation Books, 2006.

Sinclair, Upton. *The Jungle*. New York: Doubleday, 1906.

Smith, Andrew F. *American Tuna: The Rise and Fall of an Improbable Food*. Berkeley: University of California Press, 2012.

———. *Eating History: 30 Turning Points in the Making of American Cuisine*. New York: Columbia University Press, 2009.

Smith-Howard, Kendra. *Pure and Modern Milk: An Environmental History since 1900*. New York: Oxford University Press, 2013.

Stare, Frederick Arthur. *The Story of Wisconsin's Great Canning Industry*. Baltimore: Canning Trade, 1949.

Statz, Stephanie Fuglaar. "California's Fruit Cocktail: The Industrial Food Supply, the State, and the Environment of Northern California." PhD diss., University of Houston, 2012.

Steinberg, Theodore. *Down to Earth: Nature's Role in American History*. Oxford: Oxford University Press, 2002.

Stine, Jeffrey K., and Joel A. Tarr. "At the Intersection of Histories: Technology and the Environment." *Technology and Culture* 39, no. 4 (1998): 601–40.

Stoll, Steven. *The Fruits of Natural Advantage: Making the Industrial Countryside in California*. Berkeley: University of California Press, 1998.

Storrs, Landon R. Y. *Civilizing Capitalism: The National Consumers' League, Women's Activism, and Labor Standards in the New Deal Era*. Chapel Hill: University of North Carolina Press, 2000.

Strasser, Susan. *Satisfaction Guaranteed: The Making of the American Mass Market*. Washington, DC: Smithsonian Institution Press, 1995.

Thom, Charles. "Botulism from the Regulatory Viewpoint." *American Journal of Public Health* 12, no. 1 (January 1922): 50.

Thomas, Courtney I. P. *In Food We Trust: The Politics of Purity in American Food Regulation*. Lincoln: University of Nebraska Press, 2014.

Thompson, George E. "Temperature-Time Relations in Canned Foods during Sterilization." *Journal of Industrial and Engineering Chemistry* 11 (July 1919): 657–64.

Tomes, Nancy. *The Gospel of Germs: Men, Women, and the Microbe in American Life*. Cambridge, MA: Harvard University Press, 1998.

Tracey, Minnie B. "The Present Status of Frozen Food Marketing." *Journal of Marketing* 13, no. 4 (April 1, 1949): 470–80.

Turner, Katherine Leonard. *How the Other Half Ate: A History of Working-Class Meals at the Turn of the Century*. Berkeley: University of California Press, 2014.

Veit, Helen Zoe. *Modern Food, Moral Food: Self-Control, Science, and the Rise of Modern American Eating in the Early Twentieth Century*. Chapel Hill: University of North Carolina Press, 2015.

Vileisis, Ann. *Kitchen Literacy: How We Lost Knowledge of Where Food Comes From and Why We Need to Get It Back*. Washington, DC: Island Press/Shearwater Books, 2008.

Vogel, Sarah A. "From 'The Dose Makes the Poison' to 'The Timing Makes the Poison': Conceptualizing Risk in the Synthetic Age." *Environmental History* 13, no. 4 (October 2008): 667–73.

Weinzirl, John. "The Bacteriology of Canned Foods." *Journal of Medical Research* 39, no. 3 (January 1919): 411.

Wilde, Mark W. "Industrialization of Food Processing in the United States, 1860–1960." PhD diss., University of Delaware, 1988.

Wiley, Harvey W. "Don't Be Afraid of Canned Goods." *Good Housekeeping*, April 1913, 539.

Williams, B. E. W. "Frozen Foods 2000 A.D.: A Fantasy of the Future." *Quick Frozen Foods*, February 1954, 108.

Williams, Faith M., and Ethel D. Hoover, "Measuring Price and Quality of Consumers' Goods." *Journal of Marketing* 10, no. 4 (April 1946): 354–69.

Young, James Harvey. "Botulism and the Ripe Olive Scare of 1919–1920." *Bulletin of the History of Medicine* 50 (1976): 372–91.

———. *Pure Food: Securing the Federal Food and Drugs Act of 1906*. Princeton, NJ: Princeton University Press, 1989.

Zeide, Anna. "Building Taste and Trust: The Civil War's Influence on the U.S. Canning Industry." *Repast* 29, no. 1, Civil War Sesquicentennial Series, pt. 4 (Winter 2013): 4–7.

Ziegelman, Jane, and Andrew Coe. *A Square Meal: A Culinary History of the Great Depression*. New York: Harper, 2016.

Index

accessibility: GMA and, 6, 168; non-ordinary public and, 12; socio-economic factors and, 183, 192, 193, 250n5; Union army and, 18, 19; urbanization and, 27

advertising: advertising agencies, 3, 120, 188, 189; advertising specialists, 189; consolidation and, 167; consumer activism and, 108, 153, 162; consumer confidence, 133; consumer confidence and, 103, 105, 129; costs of, 63, 113, 136; influence of, 130, 169; investment in, 102, 122; media outlets and, 139, 222n32; NCA funding of, 6, 33, 35; rise of, 130, 134, 137, 190, 222n32; scientists and, 95; target audiences, 131; use of, 3, 4. *See also* advertising campaigns; branding

advertising campaigns: Campbell Soup Company, 130–32; consumer confidence and, 76, 190; costs of, 131; frozen-food industry and, 141; NCA and, 6; olive packers and, 100, 102; tuna and, 137, 143–45, 148

Agricultural Adjustment Administration, 107, 124, 125

agricultural experiment stations: agricultural problems and, 8; archival research, 5; Bureau of Raw Products Research and, 67; corporations and, 45–48; farmers and, 46–47, 59, 218n116;

funding of, 45–48, 48, 67–68, 72, 189, 211n14; grading, 114; Hatch Act and, 46–47; initiative projects and, 68; production and, 70; relationships with, 43, 45, 47–48, 188; USDA and, 215n59; value of, 46, 47–48; in Wisconsin, 44, 47, 48, 50–53, 56, 58, 59, 68, 70, 71, 210n6, 211n14. *See also* agricultural scientists

agricultural improvements: consumer confidence and, 189, 191; consumer taste and, 55–56, 72; Delwiche and, 211n10; environmental contamination and, 189; food processors and, 43–45; labor systems and, 188; Mendelism and, 211n10; production and, 63, 72–73; of raw crops, 8, 43, 45, 136, 214n57; seed improvement, 70–71, 213n31, 218n123; wilt resistance, 215n59

agricultural pests: combating, 8, 44, 54–55, 64, 67, 188, 189; pea aphids, 44, 55, 68; plant resistance to, 54–55. *See also* pesticides

agricultural production: agricultural depressions, 62; agricultural policies and, 56–57, 62, 212n21, 212n26; agro-industrial complex, 59, 190; decisions of, 186; external experts and, 134; Golden Age of Agriculture, 46, 211n13, 212n21; problems of, 67, 72, 129, 162; shifts in, 48,

agricultural production *(continued)*
58–59, 62. *See also* agricultural
experiment stations; agricultural
improvements; agricultural pests;
agricultural scientists; breeders;
diseases

agricultural scientists: Bureau of Raw
Products Research and, 67; consumer
taste and, 52; farmer skepticism and, 47;
pea development and, 52; product grade
and, 104; relationships with, 8, 42, 46,
48, 61, 62, 67–68, 189; seed-breeding
programs, 68. *See also* agricultural
experiment stations; agricultural
improvements

Alsberg, C. L., 38

American Can Company, 119, 120

American Council on Fitness and Nutrition,
168

American Farm Bureau, 66

Appert, Nicolas, 13, 18, 20, 26, 38, 145, 190

Appetite for Profit (Simon), 6

*The Art of Preserving All Kinds of Animal
and Vegetable Substances for Several
Years* (Appert), 13, 18

Atlantic States Packers' Association, 27

Babcock, Stephen M., 48

bacteriology, 74–102; bacterial contamination, 2, 14, 26–27, 50, 80, 187, 189;
canners' concerns for, 7; germ theory
and, 77, 95, 189, 207n67, 220n11;
Koch, Robert, 26, 27, 207n67; mold,
50, 115; Pasteur, Louis, 26, 38, 95,
207n67; research techniques, 20;
scientific expertise and, 27, 188; value
of, 26–27. *See also* botulism; spoilage

Bailey, Brent, 171

Baltimore, 18, 20, 22, 24

Baumann, Shyon, 171

Belasco, Warren, 151, 154

Bentley, C. H., 83–84

Bentley, R. I., 91, 92

Berle, Adolph, 129

Bigelow, W. D., 36, 37, 90, 101

Big Food: Coca-Cola, 6, 216n78; key
players in, 6; Kraft Foods, 6, 137, 167;
McDonald's, 4, 6, 140. *See also* Grocery
Manufacturers Association (GMA);
trade associations

biological research: on botulism, 238n44;
consumer confidence and, 137; on
diseases, 45; funding of, 45; peas and,
214n57; reliance on, 8

Bisphenol-A (BPA). *See* BPA (Bisphenol-A)

Blanke, David, 129

blight: contracting system and, 51, 58;
research on, 44, 51, 59, 68, 214n43;
resistance development, 51–52, 54–55,
72, 73

Board of Food and Drug Inspection, 36

Bonaparte, Napoleon, 13

Borden, Gail, 17

Borden's Condensed Milk Company, 10,
11, 17, 19, 38, 146

botulism: bacteria and toxin, 78, 220n16;
Botulism Commission, 77, 90–94, 101,
102; consumer confusion over, 85–90;
Curtis Corporation of California, 99; in
fish, 238n44; marketing research and,
143–48; media outlets on, 79–85;
outbreaks, 75–76, 188; public health
reform and, 96–100; scientific research
and, 90–95, 96; Young on, 224n79. *See
also* olive scare

BPA (Bisphenol-A), 163–85; BPA-free
containers, 186; Campbell Soup
Company, 163–66, 172–75, 179–80,
184–85, 192; customer responses,
182–83, 186; dangers of, 176–79;
defense of, 248n70; food industry and,
9, 179; regulation of, 177–78, 190; use
of, 175. *See also* endocrine system
disruptors

branding: advertising costs and, 113; brand
names and labels, 189; brand recognition, 131–32, 132 fig.9; Pure Food and
Drug Act of 1906, 31–32; reputation
shaping and, 190; scientific expertise as,
189

Brown, Martin, 24

Bureau of Agricultural Economics, 125

Bureau of Chemistry, US, 35–38, 88, 96–97,
219n2, 223n58, 224n74. *See also* FDA
(Food and Drug Administration)

Bureau of Publicity, 35

Bureau of Raw Products Research, 66–67,
67

Burke, Georgina, 91–92

CAB (Consumers' Advisory Board): canning
codes, 113–16; Committee on Standard,
107; grade labeling, 104, 109–13;
labeling debate, 116–28

calcium chloride system, 18, 22, 206n52

California Agricultural Experiment Station,
215n59

California Olive Association, 102

California Packing Corporation, 42, 83, 92, 219n7. *See also Pick of the Pod* (1939 film)

California Pure Foods Act, 93

California State Board of Public Health, 96–100

California State Department of Health, 8, 90

Campbell, Persia, 124, 130

Campbell Soup Company, 163–85; advertising campaigns, 130–32; BPA and, 163–66, 172, 175, 179–80, 184–85; emotional resonance, 192; Gowen, P. L., 117; grade labeling, 122; market research, 130–31; popularity of, 143, 173; research funding from, 45

Can Manufacturers Institute (CMI), 171

canned food: awareness of, 1; consumer relationship with, 191, 192–93; early market slowness, 3; growth of, 39 fig. 3; revolutionary aspects of, 2, 193; sensory deprivation of, 2; as tough sell, 3

canneries: in Baltimore, 20; feeding operations of, 216n81; geographical distribution of, 20, 21 fig. 1; in Wisconsin, 49

Canners League of California (CLC), 76, 84, 91, 99, 227n102

Canners Seed Corporation (CSC), 70–71, 218n126

canning crops: breeding of, 2, 188; contractual obligations and, 215n74; disease and, 64; grower cooperation, 217n110; peas as, 48–49; research, 50, 59; research funding, 68. *See also* pea varieties

canning process: battling opacity of, 190; calcium chloride system, 18, 22; cold-pack method, 78; invention of, 13; technology perfecting of, 2. *See also* mechanization

Cannon, Poppy, 142

can openers, 18, 142, 174

Center for Science in the Public Interest. *See* Jacobson, Michael.

Chemical Manufacturing Industry, 122

Chippewa Falls Canning Company, 216n81

Civil War: canned food and, 15, 16–17; canners' contracts with Union Army, 188; condensed milk contract, 17–18, 19

CMI (Can Manufacturers Institute), 171

Cohen, Lizabeth, 149

Colborn, Theo, 176

Columbus Canning Company, 59–60, 68, 70, 138, 214nn43–44, 215n74, 216n78, 238n51

Commercial Alert, 173

Community Supported Agriculture (CSA), 191

Conant, Doug, 173

condensed milk. *See* Borden's Condensed Milk Company

consolidation: competition decrease, 7, 141, 159, 190; NCA and, 34, 159–60; political lobbying and, 167–68; political power and, 159, 184

consumer activism: advertising and, 108; BPA and, 177; canners concerns for, 7; consumer advocates, 186; environmental issues, 153–56; food activists, 235n3; industry priorities, reshaping of, 187; limitations of the individual, 191; market research and, 149; New Deal era and, 104–5, 106–9; opacity demands, 9; purity of food debates, 28–33

consumer choice: advertising and, 130–31; deep history and, 5; driving move to processed food, 3; emotional resonance and, 192–93; foodies and, 169–72; food industry development and, 3; income and, 192; infrastructure and, 5, 186; market research and, 130, 189; "uncanned" approach, 172–75

consumer confidence: 19th century consumers, 4, 188; 21st century consumers, 4; 1960/1970s, 189; abandonment of canned foods, 186; advertising and, 76, 103, 105, 129, 133, 136; advertising campaigns and, 190; botulism scare and, 85–90; building, 2; in canned food, 191; early 20th century consumers, 188; foodborne illnesses and, 3; food processors response to, 193; initial earning of, 3; laboratory science and, 188; olive scare, 74–102; powerlessness and, 186; product development and, 42–43, 191; public relations and, 189; scientific research and, 72, 90–95; shifting of, 192

consumer education: informative labeling and, 112; NRA and, 109–13; on production costs, 63

consumer movements: 1930s, 188–89; incremental changes, 191; New Deal policies, 149; Progressive Era reform, 149; third wave, 149, 153

consumers: consumer surveys, 189; direct access to, 190; early awe and suspicion, 2; eatting habits of, 3; farmer relationships, 191; during New Deal, 103–34; stereotype images of, 190; trade associations and, 6; trust relationships, 2; visibility of, 190
Consumers' Advisory Board (CAB). *See* CAB (Consumers' Advisory Board)
Consumers' Counsel, 107, 124, 125
Consumers' Division, 107
Consumers' Republic, 149
Consumers' Research, 108
containers: aluminum, 235n7; early, 13; glass, 14, 19, 74, 75, 166, 183, 192, 200n8, 224n74; tin cans, 13, 22–23; visual display fixtures, 122, 123 fig. 8, 124
Continental Can Company, 146
contract systems, 58–59, 62, 188, 215n74
Cowan, Ruth Schwartz, 11
Cross, Gary, 161
Cruess, W. V., 83, 85, 89
CSA (Community Supported Agriculture), farm shares, 191
CSC (Canners Seed Corporation), 70–71, 218n126
Curtis Corporation of California, 99

dairy industry: business principles and, 59, 216n77; endocrine system disruptors and, 183, 192; rise of, 59; scientific research, 48; swill milk trade scandal, 17
Danbom, David, 48
Delwiche, Ernest J., 44, 52–56, 68; breeding research, 58, 68; Mendelism and, 45, 211n10; pea varieties, 71; Renard and, 70
Department of Agriculture, U.S. (USDA), 51, 215n59, 218n130; Bureau of Raw Products Research and, 67; Canners Short Course, 68; cold-pack method, 78; grading system, 114–15; research funding from, 68; Wiley, Harvey W., 29–31, 35–36, 38, 85–86, 89
Deutsch, Tracey, 109
Dickson, Ernest C., 78, 82–83, 88–95
diseases: biological research and, 45, 51; crop-producing interests and, 64; fungal pea blight, 44; germ theory and, 77; 1918 influenza, 81; marketing-related diseases, 173; panic and, 80; peas susceptibility to, 50; public health

reform and, 96; resistance, 66. *See also* blight; botulism
Doolittle, R. E., 97

edible foodlike substances, 187, 250n1
endocrine system disruptors, 163–85, 186; dangers of, 176–78; food industry and, 9; in milk, 183, 192. *See also* BPA (Bisphenol-A)
environmental issues: advertising campaigns and, 190; consumer activism and, 153–56; federal government attentions to, 187; industrial food system and, 191; industry attentions to, 187
Environmental Protection Agency (EPA), BPA and, 178
Ermengem, Emile van, 78
expert collaboration, 74–102
external experts: 1930s-1940s decline of, 188; advertising specialists, 189; expert collaboration, 188, 189; push back against, 190; shifting of, 189. *See also* advertising agencies; agricultural experiment stations; government bodies; government regulators; media outlets; scientists; universities

farmers: business principles and, 59, 216m77; consumer relationship with, 191; contract systems, 43–44, 62; cooperative organizations, 46, 62, 65–66; relationships with, 43
Farmers' Alliance, 46, 65
farmers' markets, 191, 192
Federal Meat Inspection Act of 1906, 31
Fitzgerald, Deborah, 68, 218n116
Food, Drug and Cosmetic Act of 1938, 127
Food and Drug Administration (FDA): regulatory systems and, 135, 177–78, 223n58
Food and Drugs Act of 1906: food purity and, 190. *See also* McNary-Mapes Amendment
food industry systems: consumer choice and, 3; foundation of, 191; machinations beyond view and move to, 187; regulation resistance, 187; relationship networks, 3; transparency in, 191; transparency lack in, 187
Food Inspection Decision No. 126, 36–37. *See also* salts of tin issue
Food Products Association (FPA). *See* FPA (Food Products Association)
FPA (Food Products Association), 168

Franklin, John, 14–15
Fraser, A. C., 28
frozen-food industry, 141
funding, of agricultural experiment stations, 51, 58, 72, 188, 189
Funk Brothers Seed Company, 218n116
Fusarium wilt fungus, 53, 55, 56, 68, 69 fig. 5, 70, 71, 215n59

Gaylord, Fay C., 114–15
Geiger, J. C., 90, 93
General Foods Corporation: consolidation and, 167; in-house laboratories, 146, 155; research funding from, 45, 67
genetically modified organisms (GMOs), 182, 184
George W. Cobb Preserving Company. *See* Sanitary Can Company
germ theory, 26–27, 77, 95, 189, 207n67, 220n11
glass jars, 13, 19, 74, 75, 126, 166, 183, 200n8, 224n74
GMA (Grocery Manufacturers Association), 6; BPA and, 181; branding, 132 fig.9; FPA and, 168; history of 201n15; membership, 6; Nutrition Foundation and, 146; opposition to Hart Bill, 151; research funding from, 67–68; role of in Tuna Emergency Committee, 145
GMOs (genetically modified organisms), 182, 184
Golden Age of Agriculture, 46, 211n13, 212n21
Golden Age of Processed Food, 137, 146
Gorrell, Frank, 33, 36
government regulations, 3, 5, 188; decisions of, 186; legislation and, 188; lobbying for, 189; push back against, 190; under-regulations, 191–92; relationships with, 188
government research, WWII improvements and, 138, 141
Gowen, P. L., 117
grade labeling, 103–34, 109–16, 117 fig. 7, 148, 189
grain processing, 3
GRAS (generally regarded as safe) additives, BPA as, 177–78
Greene, Gael, 170
Grocery Manufacturers Association (GMA). *See* GMA (Grocery Manufacturers Association)
grower cooperation, canning crops and, 217n110

Hambrecht, George P., 50
Hatch Act, 46–47, 211n14
health ideas, 5
health issues: federal government attentions to, 187; industrial food system and, 191; industry attentions to, 187; ptomaine poisoning, 26
Hehner, Otto, 36
Henry Romeike, Inc., 82
H. J. Heinz, 214n44
home canning, 19, 78, 126, 166, 191, 200n8
home cooking, 191
Hooper Research Foundation, 90
Humphreys, Margaret, 80

incremental changes, 191, 215n74
Industrial Fellowships Finding Aid, 218n116
industrial food system: environmental issues, 191; faith in, 4; food flavor and, 191; health issues, 191; infrastructure of, 5, 186, 187; labor systems and, 191; opacity of, 4, 190; transparency and, 9
industrialization: canning industry growth and, 20, 23–24; farmers and, 59; Industrial Revolution, 11; trade associations and, 6. *See also* processed food
inspection programs, NCA promotion of, 6, 76
investments: in advertising, 63, 102; in collaboration, 62–68, 70–71; in market research, 128; in mechanization, 24

Jackson, Jeff, 172
Jacobs, Meg, 112
Jacobson, Michael, 153, 155, 169
Jaffray, Julia K., 124
Johns Hopkins University, 34
Johnston, Joseé, 171
Jones, L. R., 214n43
The Jungle (Sinclair), 31

Keezer, Dexter M., 110–11, 118
Koch, Robert, 26, 27, 207n67
Kraft Foods, 6, 137, 167

labor systems: can production mechanization and, 23–24, 40; food industry and, 5; grade labeling and, 126; industrial food system and, 191; pea-canning plants and, 216n90; reshaping of, 188; WWI and, 57–58
Landreth, Albert, 27, 49, 50

Lappé, Frances Moore, 153–54
Leitsch, William C., 59
Levenstein, Harvey, 67, 137
Lister, Joseph, 38, 210n112
lobbying, 32, 189
Logan, Thomas M., 96
Lynd, Robert, 108
Lynd, Robert S., 112

Macklin, Theodore, 63
marketing: food industry and, 5, 187;
    marketing-related diseases, 173; opacity
    of, 5
market research: botulism scare and, 148;
    consumer choice and, 148, 149, 189;
    consumer surveys, 189; early attempts
    at, 119, 130; focus groups, 189;
    investment in, 128, 148; NCA and, 128;
    neuromarketing, 172–73; product
    development and, 191; quality standards
    and, 112. See also advertising
Mason, John Landis, 19
Max Ams Machine Company, 26
May, Earl C., 32–33
McDonald's, 4, 6, 140
McDuffie, Bruce, 135, 137
McNary-Mapes Amendment, 115–16, 190
Means, Gardiner, 129
meat industry, 3, 31
mechanization: labor systems and, 23–24;
    new inventions and, 24, 25 fig. 2;
    pressure cookers, 22; standardization
    and, 23–24; of tin can production,
    22–23
media outlets: advertising, 139; advertising
    and, 222n32; botulism scare and,
    79–85; internet sites, 175; reputation
    shaping and, 190
Meikle, Jeffrey, 176
Mendel, Gregor, 53, 54. See also Mendelism
Mendelism: Delwiche and, 45, 53–54,
    211n10; limited value of, 211n10; plant
    varieties and, 71, 72; seed-breeding
    programs and, 68
Meyer, Karl F., 90, 92, 95, 98
Middletown Studies (Lynd), 108
milk: endocrine system disruptors in, 183,
    192; swill milk trade scandal, 17. See
    also Borden's Condensed Milk
    Company; dairy industry
money, GMA and, 6
Moore, R. A., 50
Morrill Act, 212n15
Morrison, Denise, 174, 182

motivational research: hidden from
    public, 189; opacity and, 137, 189;
    opacity of, 148; use of, 136, 148

NAMPA (North American Metal Packaging
    Alliance), 180–81
National Association of Canned Food
    Packers, 29, 30, 32
National Association of Packers of Pure
    Canned Goods, 33
National Canners Association (NCA). See
    NCA (National Canners Association)
National Canners' Laboratory, 34–35, 38, 39
National Consumers' League, 31, 158
National Emergency Council, 107
National Food Manufacturers' Association
    (NFMA), 30
National Food Processors Association
    (NFPA), 166, 168
National Grange, 46, 65
national marketing, understanding of, 4
National Recovery Administration (NRA).
    See NRA (National Recovery
    Administration)
NCA (National Canners Association), 8,
    30, 224n74; advertising and, 33, 35;
    advertising campaign funding, 6;
    advertising campaigns, 6; beginnings of,
    6; Bureau of Raw Products Research,
    66–67; decisions of, 186; formation of,
    32, 33, 74; industry representation
    before federal government, 6; inspection
    program promotion, 6; journals of, 6;
    labeling debate, 104; National Canners'
    Laboratory, 34–35, 38; national
    conferences of, 6; NFMA and, 30;
    political process intervention, 6; purity
    of food debates, 6; research initiatives,
    6; scientific research and, 34; Sears,
    Walter J., 60; tin safety and, 37; tuna
    recall and, 135. See also GMA (Grocery
    Manufacturers Association); National
    Food Processors Association (NFPA)
negotiations, 5, 187
neuromarketing, 172–73; marketing-related
    diseases and, 173
New Deal policies, 104–5, 225n86;
    consumer activism and, 104–5, 106–9;
    National Recovery Administration, 8
NFMA (National Food Manufacturers'
    Association), 30
Nichols, Nell B., 119–20
1960/1970s: consumer confidence, 189;
    federal regulation in, 190

1930s: consumption rates, 188; McNary-Mapes Amendment, 190

1920s: agricultural experiment stations, 188; agricultural improvements, 41–73; agricultural improvements of, 189; state public health officials, 190

North American Metal Packaging Alliance (NAMPA), 180–81

Norton Brothers Company, 23

NRA (National Recovery Administration), 8, 104; consumer activism and, 109–13; disbanding of, 134; establishment of, 107; grade labeling, 116–18, 122

nutrition: advertising campaigns and, 190; research on, 140, 193; Stare and, 216n78

obesity, 167; processed food link, 3

olive scare, 74–102; media outlets on, 79–85; safety advertising campaigns, 100, 102; as symbolic, narrative device, 7. *See also* botulism

opacity: battling, 190; of canned food, 3–4, 187; food origins and, 190; of food production, 4–5; increase of, 191; labeling debate and, 189; metaphorical, 200n8; motivational research and, 189; public mistrust of, 191; visual display fixtures, 122, 123 fig. 8, 124

Orem, Hugh S., 16, 38

organic labeling, 191

Orr, Howard A., 121

outsourcing, of pea cultivation, 51

overcooking, 2, 93

oversight: funding of, 188; lobbying to minimize, 190

oysters, 20

packaging, understanding of, 4

packers, incremental changes, 215n74

Palladino, Paolo, 53

Parkin, Katherine, 131

Pasteur, Louis, 26, 38, 95, 207n67

pea aphids, 44, 55, 68

pea-canning industry, canning-crop research, 50, 59

peas, 41–73, 216n90, 218n116; as canned food, 41–43; as canning crop, 48–49; canning plants, 214n47; pea varieties, 68–71, 69 fig. 5; study of, 214n57; as symbolic, narrative device, 7

pesticides: consumer activism and, 146, 150–51, 154, 189; consumer confidence and, 137; dependency on, 136, 139–40;

legislation and, 152; Miller Act of 1954, 241n77; NCA and, 146; production and, 63; regulatory system and, 147

pests. *See* agricultural pests

Phelps, H. W., 119

Philips, Peter, 24

Phillips, Lena M., 108, 125, 126–27

Philpott, Tom, 183

Pick of the Pod (1939 film), 41–42, 71

politics: food industry and, 5; GMA and, 6; NCA intervention in, 6; opacity of institutions, 5; political lobbying, 189, 190; political process intervention, 187; product development and, 191

Pollan, Michael, 4, 171, 191, 235n3, 250n1

Powell, Ola, 87

Prescott, Samuel C., 27

pressure cookers, 22

processed food: growth of, 188; machinations beyond view and move to, 3; obesity and, 3; origin of, 3; postwar challenges, 135–62; precursors of, 3; promotion of, 216n78

product development: consumer confidence and, 2, 191; marketing strategies and, 191; political influence and, 191; scientific expertise and, 191

profitability, 67, 218n126

Progressive Era reform, 9, 77, 91, 149, 207n64

public health reform, 77, 89, 96, 96–100, 99, 188, 225n84

public relations: botulism and, 147–48; consumer confidence and, 189

pure food advocates, 6, 32, 188

Pure Food and Drug Act of 1906, 31–32, 33, 39, 74, 85, 97, 115, 225n86

purity of food, 31; Food and Drugs Act of 1906, 190; marketing and, 17; NCA and, 6

Randolph Canning Company, 216n81

raw crop improvements: agricultural research and, 43; Bureau of Raw Products Research and, 67

regulatory systems: BPA and, 177–78; canners' attitudes toward, 190; canners concerns for, 7; conformity to, 8; decisions of, 186; failures of, 186; resistance to, 187; understanding of, 4

Renard, Earl J., 70

Roper, Elmo, 119, 128, 131

Rosenau, Milton J., 78, 227n106

Rosenberg, Charles, 47–48

Rumsey, Mary Harriman, 110, 113
Ruskin, Gary, 173
Russell, Harry Luman, 27, 47, 50

salts of tin issue, 36–37, 39, 175, 188,
    223n60
Sanitary Can Company, 24, 26, 28
Sanitary Commission, U.S., 18
Sanzio, Anthony, 163
Sathyanarayana, Sheela, 183
Schmidt, C. T., 124
scientific expertise, 7; advertising and, 95;
    consumer confidence, 189; consumer
    confidence and, 190; decline of, 189;
    marketing research, 189; product
    development, 191; spoilage and, 27;
    understanding of, 4
scientific research: botulism and, 75, 78,
    101–2; BPA and, 9; Bureau of Raw
    Products Research and, 67; collaboration
    and, 47–48, 56–57, 77; consumer
    confidence and, 38–40, 42, 55–56, 67,
    90–95; consumer demand for, 32, 45;
    dairy industry and, 48; early forms of,
    50; food processors and, 27; food
    production and, 5; funding of, 45–48;
    in-house laboratories, 146; industrializa-
    tion and, 20; internalization of, 146–47;
    media outlets and, 79–85; NCA and, 6,
    34–38, 39, 101; profitability and, 67;
    raw crop improvements, 43, 67; reliance
    on, 8. See also agricultural production;
    bacteriology; botulism; Delwiche, Ernest
    J.; universities
scurvy, 14
Sears, Walter J., 35, 61, 64, 65
Sherman, Wells A., 125
Shriver, Andrew Keyser, 22
Simon, Michele, 6
Sinclair, Upton, 31
Solomon, Isaac, 18
spoilage: bacterial contamination, 2, 14,
    26–27, 50, 80, 188, 189; in canned
    olives, 94; in canned peas, 26–27, 50;
    detection of, 87–88; germ theory and,
    26–27, 77, 95, 189, 207n67, 220n11;
    health effects of, 26; mold, 50; as
    production issue, 187; ptomaine
    poisoning, 26; purity and, 32; reduction
    of, 136; scientific expertise and, 27, 188.
    See also bacteriology; botulism
standardization: grade labeling, 109–16;
    mechanization and, 23–24; rise of, 8
Stangis, David, 164

Stare, Fred A., 59, 60, 216n78
Stare, Frederick J., 216n78
steam retort. See pressure cookers

Thom, Charles, 88–89, 97
tin cans, 13, 22–23, 188
tomatoes, 7, 33, 101, 103–104, 114-115,
    117, 153
Tomes, Nancy, 86
toxicity: advertising campaigns and, 190;
    food contact materials and, 192; lead
    toxicity, 14–15, 26; mercury levels, 135;
    metal toxicity, 14–15, 135–62; Miller
    Act of 1954, 241n77; salts of tin issue,
    36–37, 39, 175, 188, 223n60; Tritan,
    181–82. See also BPA (Bisphenol-A);
    tuna safety issue
trade associations: Atlantic States Packers'
    Association, 27; botulism outbreak and,
    76; Bureau of Raw Products Research,
    67; decisions of, 186; power of, 5–6;
    Western Packers' Canned Goods
    Association, 28; Wisconsin Pea Packers
    Association, 45–46. See also Grocery
    Manufacturers Association (GMA);
    NCA (National Canners Association)
trade organizations, 7; archival research, 5;
    state and local organizations, 32. See
    also NCA (National Canners
    Association)
transparency, food industry and, 4, 5, 9, 34,
    71, 101, 165, 172, 182, 187, 190–91
Tuna Foundation, 135
tuna safety issue, 135–62; advertising
    campaigns and, 137, 143–45,
    148; botulism, 238n44; consumer
    activism and, 153–56; consumer
    confidence and, 137–43; consumer
    movements and, 149–53; government
    regulation and, 156–61; industry
    strategies and, 161–62; labels as
    response to, 143–48; overview, 135–37;
    popularity of tuna, 137, 235n3; as
    symbolic, narrative device, 7
Turow, Eve, 172
Tyndall, John, 38, 210n112

Underwood, W. Lyman, 27
Union Army: canned food and, 17–18;
    canners' contracts with, 188; condensed
    milk contract, 17–18, 19; sutlers, 18
universities, 3, 188; archival research, 5;
    canning-crop research, 50–52; disease
    resistance and, 66; funding of, 8, 34,

45–48, 68, 72; NCA and, 34; relationships with, 39, 45, 59–60, 67, 212n27
urbanization, 17, 27, 211n11
USDA (United States Department of Agriculture), 51, 67, 215n59; Bureau of Raw Products Research and, 67; Canners Short Course, 68; cold-pack method, 78; grading system, 114–15; research funding from, 68; Wiley, Harvey W., 29–31, 35–36, 38, 85–86, 89
US Warehouse Act of 1916, 104

Vileisis, Ann, 2
Vogel, Sarah, 177

Waldman, Jonathan, 180
Ware, Caroline, 105
Warehouse Act of 1916, 114, 125–26

Waterloo Canning Company, 216n81
Webb, Walter Prescott, 16
Weinzirl, John, 91
Western Packers' Canned Goods Association, 28
Wiley, Harvey W., 29–31, 35–36, 38, 85–86, 89
Williams, Paul M., 118
wilt resistance, 53, 55, 56, 68, 69 fig. 5, 70, 71, 215n59, 218n126
Wingspread Statement, 176
Wisconsin Canning Crop Growers' Association, 66
Wisconsin College of Agriculture, 45, 45–46, 47, 50–51, 60, 68, 212n27
Wisconsin Experiment Growers Association, 70
Wisconsin Pea Packers Association, 44–46, 48, 50, 70

CALIFORNIA STUDIES IN FOOD AND CULTURE

Darra Goldstein, Editor

1. *Dangerous Tastes: The Story of Spices,* by Andrew Dalby

2. *Eating Right in the Renaissance,* by Ken Albala

3. *Food Politics: How the Food Industry Influences Nutrition and Health,* by Marion Nestle

4. *Camembert: A National Myth,* by Pierre Boisard

5. *Safe Food: The Politics of Food Safety,* by Marion Nestle

6. *Eating Apes,* by Dale Peterson

7. *Revolution at the Table: The Transformation of the American Diet,* by Harvey Levenstein

8. *Paradox of Plenty: A Social History of Eating in Modern America,* by Harvey Levenstein

9. *Encarnación's Kitchen: Mexican Recipes from Nineteenth-Century California: Selections from Encarnación Pinedo's* El cocinero español, by Encarnación Pinedo, edited and translated by Dan Strehl, with an essay by Victor Valle

10. *Zinfandel: A History of a Grape and Its Wine,* by Charles L. Sullivan, with a foreword by Paul Draper

11. *Tsukiji: The Fish Market at the Center of the World,* by Theodore C. Bestor

12. *Born Again Bodies: Flesh and Spirit in American Christianity,* by R. Marie Griffith

13. *Our Overweight Children: What Parents, Schools, and Communities Can Do to Control the Fatness Epidemic,* by Sharron Dalton

14. *The Art of Cooking: The First Modern Cookery Book,* by the Eminent Maestro Martino of Como, edited and with an introduction by Luigi Ballerini, translated and annotated by Jeremy Parzen, and with fifty modernized recipes by Stefania Barzini

15. *The Queen of Fats: Why Omega-3s Were Removed from the Western Diet and What We Can Do to Replace Them,* by Susan Allport

16. *Meals to Come: A History of the Future of Food,* by Warren Belasco

17. *The Spice Route: A History,* by John Keay

18. *Medieval Cuisine of the Islamic World: A Concise History with 174 Recipes,* by Lilia Zaouali, translated by M. B. DeBevoise, with a foreword by Charles Perry

19. *Arranging the Meal: A History of Table Service in France,* by Jean-Louis Flandrin, translated by Julie E. Johnson, with Sylvie and Antonio Roder; with a foreword to the English-language edition by Beatrice Fink

20. *The Taste of Place: A Cultural Journey into Terroir,* by Amy B. Trubek

21. *Food: The History of Taste,* edited by Paul Freedman

22. *M. F. K. Fisher among the Pots and Pans: Celebrating Her Kitchens,* by Joan Reardon, with a foreword by Amanda Hesser

23. *Cooking: The Quintessential Art,* by Hervé This and Pierre Gagnaire, translated by M. B. DeBevoise

24. *Perfection Salad: Women and Cooking at the Turn of the Century,* by Laura Shapiro

25. *Of Sugar and Snow: A History of Ice Cream Making,* by Jeri Quinzio

26. *Encyclopedia of Pasta,* by Oretta Zanini De Vita, translated by Maureen B. Fant, with a foreword by Carol Field

27. *Tastes and Temptations: Food and Art in Renaissance Italy,* by John Varriano

28. *Free for All: Fixing School Food in America,* by Janet Poppendieck

29. *Breaking Bread: Recipes and Stories from Immigrant Kitchens,* by Lynne Christy Anderson, with a foreword by Corby Kummer

30. *Culinary Ephemera: An Illustrated History,* by William Woys Weaver

31. *Eating Mud Crabs in Kandahar: Stories of Food during Wartime by the World's Leading Correspondents,* edited by Matt McAllester

32. *Weighing In: Obesity, Food Justice, and the Limits of Capitalism,* by Julie Guthman

33. *Why Calories Count: From Science to Politics,* by Marion Nestle and Malden Nesheim

34. *Curried Cultures: Globalization, Food, and South Asia,* edited by Krishnendu Ray and Tulasi Srinivas

35. *The Cookbook Library: Four Centuries of the Cooks, Writers, and Recipes That Made the Modern Cookbook,* by Anne Willan, with Mark Cherniavsky and Kyri Claflin

36. *Coffee Life in Japan,* by Merry White

37. *American Tuna: The Rise and Fall of an Improbable Food,* by Andrew F. Smith

38. *A Feast of Weeds: A Literary Guide to Foraging and Cooking Wild Edible Plants,* by Luigi Ballerini, translated by Gianpiero W. Doebler, with recipes by Ada De Santis and illustrations by Giuliano Della Casa

39. *The Philosophy of Food,* by David M. Kaplan

40. *Beyond Hummus and Falafel: Social and Political Aspects of Palestinian Food in Israel,* by Liora Gvion, translated by David Wesley and Elana Wesley

41. *The Life of Cheese: Crafting Food and Value in America,* by Heather Paxson

42. *Popes, Peasants, and Shepherds: Recipes and Lore from Rome and Lazio,* by Oretta Zanini De Vita, translated by Maureen B. Fant, foreword by Ernesto Di Renzo

43. *Cuisine and Empire: Cooking in World History,* by Rachel Laudan

44. *Inside the California Food Revolution: Thirty Years That Changed Our Culinary Consciousness,* by Joyce Goldstein, with Dore Brown

45. *Cumin, Camels, and Caravans: A Spice Odyssey,* by Gary Paul Nabhan

46. *Balancing on a Planet: The Future of Food and Agriculture,* by David A. Cleveland

47. *The Darjeeling Distinction: Labor and Justice on Fair-Trade Tea Plantations in India,* by Sarah Besky

48. *How the Other Half Ate: A History of Working-Class Meals at the Turn of the Century,* by Katherine Leonard Turner

49. *The Untold History of Ramen: How Political Crisis in Japan Spawned a Global Food Craze,* by George Solt

50. *Word of Mouth: What We Talk About When We Talk About Food,* by Priscilla Parkhurst Ferguson

51. *Inventing Baby Food: Taste, Health, and the Industrialization of the American Diet*, by Amy Bentley

52. *Secrets from the Greek Kitchen: Cooking, Skill, and Everyday Life on an Aegean Island*, by David E. Sutton

53. *Breadlines Knee-Deep in Wheat: Food Assistance in the Great Depression*, by Janet Poppendieck

54. *Tasting French Terroir: The History of an Idea*, by Thomas Parker

55. *Becoming Salmon: Aquaculture and the Domestication of a Fish*, by Marianne Elisabeth Lien

56. *Divided Spirits: Tequila, Mezcal, and the Politics of Production*, by Sarah Bowen

57. *The Weight of Obesity: Hunger and Global Health in Postwar Guatemala*, by Emily Yates-Doerr

58. *Dangerous Digestion: The Politics of American Dietary Advice*, by E. Melanie duPuis

59. *A Taste of Power: Food and American Identities*, by Katharina Vester

60. *More Than Just Food: Food Justice and Community Change*, by Garrett M. Broad

61. *Hoptopia: A World of Agriculture and Beer in Oregon's Willamette Valley*, by Peter A. Kopp

62. *A Geography of Digestion: Biotechnology and the Kellogg Cereal Enterprise*, by Nicholas Bauch

63. *Bitter and Sweet: Food, Meaning, and Modernity in Rural China*, by Ellen Oxfeld

64. *A History of Cookbooks: From Kitchen to Page over Seven Centuries*, by Henry Notaker

65. *Reinventing the Wheel: Milk, Microbes, and the Fight for Real Cheese*, by Bronwen Percival and Francis Percival

66. *Making Modern Meals: How Americans Cook Today*, by Amy B. Trubek

67. *Food and Power: A Culinary Ethnography of Israel*, by Nir Avieli

68. *Canned: The Rise and Fall of Consumer Confidence in the American Food Industry*, by Anna Zeide